D1121302

Dangerously Divided

As the United States has become more racially diverse and economic inequality has increased, American politics has also become more clearly divided by race and less clearly divided by class. In this landmark book, Zoltan L. Hajnal draws on sweeping data to assess the political impact of the two most significant demographic trends of the last fifty years. Examining federal and local elections over many decades, as well as policy, Hajnal shows that race – more than class or any other demographic factor – shapes not only how Americans vote but also who wins and who loses when the votes are counted and policies are enacted. America has become a racial democracy, with non-Whites and especially African Americans regularly on the losing side. A close look at trends over time shows that these divisions are worsening, yet also reveals that electing Democrats to office can make democracy more even and ultimately reduce inequality in well-being.

Zoltan L. Hajnal is Professor of Political Science at the University of California, San Diego. He is the author of the award-winning books *White Backlash* (with Marisa Abrajano), *Why Americans Don't Join the Party* (with Taeku Lee), and *America's Uneven Democracy* and has published op-eds in the *New York Times*, the *Washington Post*, and the *Wall Street Journal*. He is actively involved in voting rights litigation and local election law reform.

Dangerously Divided

How Race and Class Shape Winning and Losing in American Politics

Zoltan L. Hajnal

University of California, San Diego

CAMBRIDGE UNIVERSITY PRESS

CAMBRIDGE
UNIVERSITY PRESS

University Printing House, Cambridge CB2 8BS, United Kingdom

One Liberty Plaza, 20th Floor, New York, NY 10006, USA

477 Williamstown Road, Port Melbourne, VIC 3207, Australia

314–321, 3rd Floor, Plot 3, Splendor Forum, Jasola District Centre, New Delhi – 110025, India

79 Anson Road, #06–04/06, Singapore 079906

Cambridge University Press is part of the University of Cambridge.

It furthers the University's mission by disseminating knowledge in the pursuit of education, learning, and research at the highest international levels of excellence.

www.cambridge.org
Information on this title: www.cambridge.org/9781108487009
DOI: 10.1017/9781108765039

© Cambridge University Press 2020

First published 2020

Printed in the United Kingdom by TJ International Ltd. Padstow Cornwall

A catalogue record for this publication is available from the British Library.

ISBN 978-1-108-48700-9 Hardback
ISBN 978-1-108-71972-8 Paperback

To Mom

For everything.

CONTENTS

ILLUSTRATIONS

TABLES

ACKNOWLEDGMENTS

Most books are collaborative affairs. This one is absolutely no exception. My name is on the cover but so many have contributed in so many different ways. There would be no book without that wide-ranging support.

Over the years it took to write this book – and I do mean years – I benefited widely from thoughtful and impactful exchanges with scholars across the country. In particular, Matt Barreto, Shaun Bowler, James Gimpel, Bernie Grofman, Rodney Hero, Jennifer Hochschild, Tomás Jiménez, Martin Johnson, Morgan Kousser, David Leal, Jeff Lewis, David Nickerson, Justin Phillips, David Sears, Gary Segura, Michael Tesler, and Nick Valentino all gave generously of their time and offered their keen insights while asking for nothing in return. I am also deeply indebted to anonymous reviewers at Cambridge University Press and the University of Chicago Press whose careful and perceptive comments helped shape the book in profound ways.

I have had the good fortune to be able to present parts of this project to audiences at many of the nation's top research universities. Feedback from participants at the University of California, Berkeley, the University of California, Davis, the University of California, Irvine, the University of California, Merced, Harvard University, the University of Michigan, Northwestern University, Princeton University, and Stanford University was instrumental at every stage of this project. All kindly listened to my story and then helped me tell it better. I also benefited from wide-ranging comments and critiques from audience members and fellow panelists at several annual meetings of the American Political

Science Association, the Midwest Political Science Association, and the Politics of Race, Immigration, and Ethnicity Consortium. I greatly appreciate Spencer Overton and the Joint Center for Political and Economic Studies for their financial support at a critical time when this project was just getting off of the ground.

I want to thank Michael Dawson, William J. Wilson, Don Green, Doug Massey, and Paul Sniderman. None actually worked on this book, but all helped to get me here. Their early mentoring and their long-term support have been instrumental to the progression of my career. They helped when I needed it most. If this group of radically different thinkers and scholars can all work with me, there is, I think, hope for real dialogue and a better future on race.

Then there are a few people who very much straddle the line between friend and colleague. Taeku Lee, Chris Parker, and Paul Frymer are my closest friends in the business. They give me advice on the most difficult career matters, they provide deep insight into the most difficult academic questions, and they help me to realize time and time again that none of that matters as much as friendship.

The University of California, San Diego, has given me an amazing intellectual home for my work on this project. Colleagues at UCSD – Claire Adida, Amy Bridges, Dan Butler, Scott Desposato, Karen Ferree, LaGina Gause, Clark Gibson, Seth Hill, Gary Jacobson, Sam Kernell, Thad Kousser, Isaac Martin, Molly Roberts, Phil Roeder, John Skrentny, and Tom Wong – all offered wise counsel and wide-ranging support. I will always be grateful to UCSD not only for hiring me but for shepherding me through tenure and beyond. I am also grateful for the significant nurturing role that the Center for Comparative Immigration Studies, the Yankelovich Center for Social Science Research, and the Race, Ethnicity, and Identity workshop played in this book and in my broader development as a scholar. All not only provided challenging intellectual environments but – even more critically – all were filled with like-minded scholars who inspired me with their passion for understanding and helping society's most disadvantaged.

Many of my students worked long hours doing the mundane work that this project required and that I desperately tried to avoid. Their tireless efforts were only barely rewarded with graduate student wages. To Lucas de Abreu Maia, Nhat-Dang Do, Hans Hassell, John Kuk, Nazita Lajevardi, Elizabeth Meeker, Kristy Pathakis, and Neil Visalvanich, I offer my thanks for all you contributed.

This book has one name on the title page. It could have many more. It is, in no small part, a culmination of a number of different projects, many of which were co-authored and previously published. I owe my co-authors in each of those projects a deep debt of gratitude. John Griffin, Brian Newman, and David Searle were amazing partners on a project that sought to uncover the underlying determinants of winning and losing on policy. They were everything that one could hope for in co-authors – creative, thoughtful, entertaining, and hard-working. Mike Rivera and Jeremy Horowitz both began as research assistants and both became much more. Mike was crucial in jumpstart-ing the New Democratic Defection project by framing the original question for our article. Jeremy did all of the hard lifting on the data side for our article on Black well-being. Even though both were subject to often incomprehensible and always incomplete directives, neither complained and both ultimately became well-deserved co-authors. Marisa Abrajano was my partner in crime on White Backlash. We both knew that immigration mattered but we both, unfortunately, had no idea how much that backlash would ultimately come to drive our nation's politics. Jessica Trounstine has been a long-time friend and co-conspirator on all things urban. Her imprint is all over all of the parts of this book that touch on local democracy. To all of my co-authors: I truly appreciate your willingness to let me use your research, your words, and your insights here.

I am especially thankful that I got to work with Karen Brandon on this book. She has played almost every role in this endeavor – from part-time co-author, to editor extraordinaire, to amazing cheerleader. She helped me not only to conceive of the project in the first place but also to really understand what it is I was trying to say. If the book is "readable," it is in large part because of her helping hands.

Cambridge University Press has been a great partner in this project. Sara Doskow was the book's first and foremost champion. She knew all along what it could be and she worked skillfully and unstintingly to get it there. Her expert and efficient guidance ultimately made this a much better book than it would otherwise have been. As production editor, Sarah Payne helped expertly and efficiently move the project through the last of its many hurdles.

My final words and biggest thank-you's go to the most impor-tant people in my life – my family. Everyone thinks their parents are great. My parents are truly exceptional. Their never-ending love made me comfortable in my own skin and their expert guidance gave me the confidence and the skills to charge forward in life. In fifty-plus years of raising a son, they have done everything right. I really miss you, mom. To my sister, Catherine – going through life's travails with you has been an unexpected joy. It hasn't always been easy but whatever life has sent our way, we have overcome together as a team and as friends. I could not have asked for a better big sister (except of course when you were mean to me as a kid even though I was always one hundred percent innocent). Lina – it is hard to overstate how impressed I am with you. You are, of course, super-smart and incredibly talented. But what really makes you special is how kind you are. I love that you always want to help others. I love that you always have my back. I love that you want to give before you receive. I hope your life brings you as much joy as you have given me. To my wife and soulmate – I love you very much. I can't believe how lucky I am to have found you. I can't imagine life without you. I can't wait to spend the rest of my life with you.

INTRODUCTION

Case study

This book is the story of Beau and Malik and American democracy. I do not actually know Beau and Malik. In fact, I do not even know their real names. But I do know a lot about Beau and Malik. In 2016, they both provided wide-ranging details about matters such as their race, their economic status, their demographic characteristics, and their politics to the American National Election Survey, a prominent political science survey.

Beau and Malik are similar in many ways. The first and perhaps most important is class. Neither Beau nor Malik has progressed very far along the pathway to economic success. Beau made it only as far as high school graduation. He did not attend college. Malik made it only a little further. He managed to obtain an associate degree. Both earn very little. In fact, they are both poor, reporting household income of less than $5,000 annually. Both are very much part of America's disadvantaged working class.

Beau and Malik are similar in other potentially relevant ways. Both are male – as their names suggest. Both were born in the United States. Both are middle-aged and both are now single. Both live in the South, as residents of the state of Georgia.

Beau and Malik are, however, very different in other ways. Beau and Malik are very different politically. One is a conservative who opposes Obamacare, more restrictions on gun ownership, and allowing more refugees into the country. He likes Trump's border wall. The other is a liberal who favors Obamacare, greater gun control, and a higher minimum wage. One is a Republican. The other is a Democrat.

Beau and Malik are different in one other potentially, critically important way. Beau is White, as his made-up name is supposed to signal. Malik is Black, as his assigned name is designed to tell you. In this book I contend that race – the fact that one is White and the other is Black – is critical for understanding Beau and Malik and their place in American democracy, and, more broadly, for understanding the nature of contemporary American democracy.

Dangerously Divided

Despite their strikingly similar economic circumstances, Beau and Malik have sharply divergent political preferences. The implication is clear. Race, not class, is the issue that divides voters. That premise is a central theme of this book. Yes, of course, class matters. One cannot have followed the 2016 presidential election without knowing that one of the keys to Trump's victory was a shift in working-class White votes (Casselman 2017, Cohn 2016, McGillis 2016, Porter 2016). Accounts of 2016 and 2018 also rightly noted the significance of other demographic characteristics such as religion, gender, age, and urbanicity (Chalabi 2018, Gamio 2016, Scott 2018, Velencia 2018). There is no denying that many demographic factors help to explain the vote. But the reality, as I show in these pages, is that race matters far more.

In some respects, this is not a terribly novel story. Racial divisions in American politics are relatively well known (Carmines and Stimson 1989, Kinder and Sanders 1996, King and Smith 2011, Valentino and Sears 2005). Yet because of what this book says about the depth and degree of the racial divide in the vote, the analysis presented here will reveal much that is new. Even those who are well aware of America's racial divide may be shocked by the degree to which it is a force in virtually all US elections. It is simply not enough to say that race matters. Race certainly does matter – but it matters to such a degree that it overshadows all other important dividing lines in American society. Race is central in contexts where political parties are the principal players, and when parties are peripheral. Race is central when candidates from different racial and ethnic groups face off against each other. Race is even central when all of the candidates are White. Race is so central it eclipses the economic conditions that many consider the key factor driving our politics. When the vote so closely resembles a racial census, tyranny of the White majority and racial conflict may not be that far behind. We are, in short, a nation and a society deeply – and dangerously – divided.

America's Uneven Democracy

The division documented in this book represents just the beginning of a broader story. The central focus of this book concerns what happens *after* the vote. This focus on the *outcomes* of democracy is relatively new. The bulk of political science research targets the *inputs* of democracy. Political scientists generally examine question such as: What are the public's preferences? Who votes? And how are those votes counted?

These inputs are important. But, ultimately, the outcomes of that process matter most. Democracy is not a game played for the fun of it. The outcomes carry immense consequences. A majoritarian democracy, by definition, creates winners and losers. After the campaign ends and the votes are tallied, winners control the levers of power. They control vast economic resources. And they make policy decisions that deeply affect the well-being of every citizen in the nation. On the other side of the contest, losers are left on the outside looking in. Their interests and wishes may be ignored. Their pocketbooks may or may not be filled. Their well-being may be completely disregarded.

This is a normal and perhaps even a healthy aspect of democracy. But what if some win consistently and others lose consistently? What if those from a particular social class or a specific racial group are losers over and over again? What if the advantaged class or the advantaged race tramples the rights and interests of the disadvantaged class or the disadvantaged race?

In short, with democracy comes the possibility of tyranny of the majority. This is not a new concern. Anxiety about the fate of minorities in this nation extends back to the Founders. James Madison famously declared that, with majority rule, policy can "too often be decided, not according to the rule of justice and the rights of the minor party but by the superior force of an interested and overbearing majority" (Hamilton et al. 1961:77). America's electoral system does little to allay these fears. The fact that almost every election in the United States follows "winner-take-all" majoritarian rules – as opposed to the proportional allocation of seats and power used in many other democracies – only serves to heighten concerns about the welfare of losers in American democracy.[1] At least in theory, a slim majority of voters could elect candidates and pass laws that a large minority strongly opposes. Tyranny of the majority is a very real prospect.

As old as democracy itself, these concerns are especially relevant today. Concerns about conflict between the haves and the have-nots have only grown with America's increasing economic inequality. Moreover, with almost unimaginable quantities of money being funneled into the political process, the political advantages of the economically advantaged may grow, too. This leads to the fear that the rich can now dictate outcomes, while the poor have little say. Do the rich effectively rule America?

Such questions have also grown in importance as America has become more racially diverse. America is poised at a demographic tipping point. America's White majority is likely to lose its majority status. A more racially diverse population could encourage greater collaboration and engender greater compromise. But racial diversity could also spark greater conflict and greater upheaval. Racial changes – the possibility of White Americans losing their majority status, the calls by African Americans to address age-old racial inequities once and for all, and the efforts of America's new immigrants to become full-fledged Americans with equal rights and equal access – raise the stakes for our democracy.

With all of this in mind, the bulk of this book examines people, processes, and outcomes. It starts by looking at candidates for office. Which kinds of candidates tend to win, and which tend to lose? Does the leadership of the nation mirror the public? The book then moves from candidates to the voters themselves. Which voters wind up on the winning side of elections? Which voters wind up on the losing side? How do these winners and losers differ? What factors – class, race, or other basic demographic characteristics – determine who is most apt to win and who is most apt to lose?

Moving further along the pathway of democracy, the book analyzes winners and losers in the policy process. Whose opinions matter? Whose views are largely ignored? Do our nation's policies reflect the views and interests of a broad array of the public, including Blacks and other disadvantaged groups? Or is government operating largely for Whites and the privileged few? Next, the book seeks to understand how all of this impacts the economic well-being of individual Americans. Are outcomes for different groups on basic measures such as income, poverty, and employment impacted by who is in office?

The aim of this book is to provide a better understanding of whether the outcomes of American democracy are fair and open, with diverse winners and losers, or whether its outcomes are decidedly lopsided, with winners restricted to one group, one race, or one class, and losers in another.

With this aim in mind, I return to Beau and Malik again, and examine how their experiences exemplify the trends borne out in this book. Despite many similarities between Beau and Malik, the two men diverge sharply in terms of how they fare in American democracy. Despite a common working-class background, Beau, a White man, and Malik, a Black man, are radically different in terms of how much of a "say" they appear to have in the political arena. By almost all obvious measures, Beau has been a winner in the democratic process. When he voted in the 2016 presidential election, he favored Donald Trump, the winner. In fact, when he voted in the 2016 election, Beau ended up a winner in every context addressed in the survey. His favored candidate for Congress, Republican Tom Graves, won. His favored candidate for US Senate, Republican Johnny Isakson, won. Given that Beau calls himself a strong Republican, and given that he voted consistently for Republicans in 2016, one can assume that he is happy that both his governor and other US senator are Republicans. Moreover, Beau is not just a winner in the voting booth. He is, by most available measures, a winner on policy as well. Georgia's gun-control laws are among the least restrictive in the nation; Beau supports this. Georgia favors the death penalty. It executed nine people in 2016, and has an execution rate higher than almost any other state; Beau supports this. Georgia has among the highest uninsured rates in the nation; Beau, one can assume, is not troubled by this. He opposes Obamacare. (Why should his tax money pay to insure people who ought to work hard enough to pay for it themselves or to find jobs that carry insurance?)

By contrast, by almost every measure, Malik is a loser in American democracy. He lost in every election that the survey assessed. He voted for Hillary Clinton. He voted for Jim Barksdale, the losing Democratic candidate in the state's senatorial contest. He voted Democratic in a House district that was won by Republican Bob

Woodward. His straight-line Democratic vote in 2016 suggests that he likely voted Democratic and thus lost again in the state's last gubernatorial and Senate elections. Malik's losses extend beyond the candidates themselves. The policies that he favors have not been enacted. He favors increasing the minimum wage, yet Georgia has a minimum wage of $5.15, tied for lowest in the nation. He wants more gun control, yet Georgia allows almost everyone to own a gun, and allows all types of guns; almost everything but a sawed-off shotgun, a machine gun, or a rocket launcher is legal. There is no waiting period. He supports Obamacare. Georgia has done relatively little to support Obamacare or to expand the ranks of the insured in the state.

In short, Beau, the White man, generally ends up on democracy's winning side, no matter how it is defined, while Malik, the Black man, generally ends up on the losing side. Beau and Malik and their political views are not fully representative of the nation as a whole, but, as the evidence in this book amply demonstrates, their political views and the degree to which Beau and Malik win and lose in the political arena mirror the uneven nature of American democracy. Of course, democracy, by its very definition, means that some people and some ideas win, and others lose. Nevertheless, as the political successes and failures of Beau and Malik suggest, America's democracy is racially uneven. Whites are likely to end up on the top as winners, and racial and ethnic minorities are likely to end up near the bottom as losers. This discrepancy – between the democracy as experienced by Whites and by minorities – is the main theme of this book. Time and time again, as the data here reveal, American democracy gives more weight to the views and votes of White Americans than to the views and votes of racial and ethnic minorities. Race – more than class, and more than any other demographic characteristic – determines who wins and who loses in American democracy. This is a deeply troubling feature of American democracy – a democracy that was founded on the principle that all men are created equal, and that often thinks of itself as color-blind. I am writing this book because this racial pattern is one that every citizen should be aware of, and because it is a pattern Americans can, and should, address.

What Can Drive Change?

Can American democracy be made more equitable? Identifying problems is one thing. Coming up with solutions – let alone solutions that are feasible – is almost always much harder. Fortunately, hidden beneath the overall pattern of inequality in American democracy is considerable variation in the size of the racial imbalance. There are times when racial and ethnic minorities are deeply disadvantaged, and when their opinions are largely ignored. But there are other times when racial and ethnic minorities win more regularly and their views hold just as much sway as those of White Americans. That variation holds the key to understanding and perhaps even eliminating American democracy's racial inequities.

As I will show, one factor consistently and powerfully predicts when minorities win and when they lose. That factor is who controls the levers of power. When Democrats control the White House and Congress, all or almost all of the racial imbalance in policy responsiveness fades away. And these results extend beyond policy. I show that Democratic Party control matters for a deeper, more fundamental outcome – the economic well-being of racial and ethnic minorities. When the nation is governed by Democrats, racial and ethnic minority well-being improves dramatically. By contrast, under Republican administrations, Blacks, Latinos, and Asian Americans generally suffer losses. Remarkably, if Democrats had been in power over the last five decades, the data show that most of America's racial inequality in economic well-being could very well have been erased. It is also worth underscoring the following: *a political agenda that advances the well-being of minorities does not lead to a decline in the well-being of Whites.* In fact, to the contrary. I find that under Democrats, *White well-being improves* – perhaps even more than under Republicans. The only difference? White gains are not as large as those of racial and ethnic minorities. One could argue that Democratic control actually leads to win-win policies for the electorate as a whole – even though some partisans are unlikely to see it this way.

To many, the greater effectiveness of the Democratic Party will be unsurprising. After all, over the last few decades racial and ethnic minority voters have supported the Democratic Party – usually in over-whelming numbers. They must be doing so for a reason. But many others have been skeptical about how hard the Democratic Party has been working for minorities (Fraga 1992, Frymer 1999, Kim 2006). There are also some who would argue that the Republican Party's more conservative, race-blind approach does more for racial and ethnic minorities than the Democratic Party's liberal, race-conscious agenda (Thernstrom and Thernstrom 1997). And still others doubt the power of either political party or the government as a whole to sway fundamental outcomes such as income and employment (Blinder and Watson 2016, Caughey and Warshaw 2017, Hayek and Hamowy 2011). Unfortunately, despite the obvious importance of the question, researchers have to this point been unable to systematically assess the impact of either party's control on policy responsiveness to minorities, or its effects on racial and ethnic minority well-being.

Thus, the patterns I uncover are quite novel. Moreover, they could be consequential. Electing more Democrats to office will not be easy. Republicans currently control the presidency, the Senate, and most state legislatures. They will not give up power without a fight. Indeed, just showing that Democratic Party control benefits minorities could galvanize ever larger shares of White America in opposition to the Democratic Party. Electing Democrats also will not be a cure-all. Skepticism about just how much the Democratic Party is currently concerned with the welfare of racial and ethnic minorities, and uncertainty about the future direction of Democratic leadership are both warranted.[2] But for those who care about the fairness of American democracy, and for those who care about the well-being of racial and ethnic minorities, these findings do point clearly to a path forward. If Democrats take power and continue to pursue policies that champion minority interests, American democracy can become more equitable, and this nation can begin to eliminate the racial inequality that continues to plague it.

That is the story of this book.

The Case for Class

Even those who are well informed about political matters may be surprised at the premise of this book: that America's racial divide is more profound that its economic divide. Most of the public and most of those who study American politics believe that economic concerns always have been and likely always will be the core dividing line in American politics. America is, after all, a highly unequal society. The top 1 percent of the nation's households earn almost a quarter of the nation's income (Piketty 2014). The average employee needs to work more than a month to earn what the typical CEO earns in an hour (Blodget 2013). Disparities in wealth are even greater. The wealthiest 1 percent possesses 40 percent of the nation's wealth (Stiglitz 2012). Given these sharp economic inequalities, class *must* be the defining feature of our politics.

Moreover, there is every reason to believe that the importance of class is growing. The nation is in the midst of a period of prolonged, large, and perhaps unprecedented growth in income inequality. Since 1970, the share of income going to the top 1 percent has more than doubled. Since the end of the latest recession, the overwhelming majority of the gains in income have accrued to the top 1 percent (Reich 2012). For many, this decades-long increase in income inequality is *the* defining development of the century, the reason why Barack Obama, the nation's first Black president called income inequality "the defining issue of our time" (Borosage 2016).

What do such great and growing economic disparities mean for the political sphere? The single most common narrative stemming from America's growing inequality is that class has become increasingly central to the nation's politics. Many scholars and political observers argue that the United States of America has always been a nation divided by economic interests. Those divisions have only been heightened by expanding income inequality (Abramowitz and Teixeira 2009, McCall 2013, McCarty et al. 2007, Reich 2012, Stonecash 2000). The result, according to this view, is that we are now "a society sharply divided by class" (Rhodes et al. 2017).

With the Supreme Court allowing almost unfettered financial influence over campaigns and politics, the fear is that the privileged few run American politics according to their interests, leaving the broader concerns of the masses largely excluded. Those fears, according to an array of recent works in political science, are close to becoming reality (American Political Science Association 2004, Carnes 2013, Gilens and Page 2014, Hacker and Pierson 2011, Jacobs and Page 2005). Gilens (2012) and Bartels (2008), in particular, both convincingly demonstrate that government policy now closely follows the preferences of those in the top one-third of the income scale, while largely ignoring the views of those in the bottom third. Put succinctly by Larry Bartels, one of the central figures in this research agenda, "Rich People Rule" (Bartels 2014).[3] From all of this, one might well conclude that class dominates race in the political system.

Why Race Should Not Matter

My claim that race dominates class may also seem startling in light of a range of developments on the racial front. Over the last half-century America has become much more diverse. Not long ago, Whites dominated numerically, socially, politically, and in just about every other way. As late as 1950, non-Hispanic Whites represented 88 percent of the population. Today, the nation stands at a demographic precipice. Half of all babies born in this country are non-White. Racial diversity also has a very different, more complex meaning than it once had. The nation used to be defined by a relatively simple Black-White dichotomy. Now, Latinos outnumber Blacks, Asian Americans are the fastest growing racial or pan-ethnic group, and multiracial Americans have emerged as a vocal entity.

What do radical shifts in the racial diversity of the nation mean for American politics? Some believe that greater diversity is bringing people closer together. This argument suggests that increasing diversity means increasingly blurred and fluid racial and ethnic lines. Increasing diversity from this perspective has led to dramatic increases in inter-racial marriage (Bean and Stevens 2003), improved racial attitudes (Schuman et al. 1997, Sniderman and Carmines 1997), and more malleable racial dividing lines (Hochschild et al. 2012). "Progress," Abigail and Stephan Thernstrom claim, "is the largely suppressed story of race and race relations over the past half-century" (Thernstrom and Thernstrom 1997).

Within the political sphere itself, evidence suggests that as the nation has become more diverse, barriers against minority participation are falling, and White Americans are becoming more and more willing to support racial minority candidates (Hajnal 2001, Highton 2004, Thernstrom and Thernstrom 1997). All of this, the argument goes, has led to a less-defining role for race in the politics of the nation. The election of Barack Obama was just the last and most recent sign of this increasingly post-racial society. As the Cleveland Plain Dealer put it, "This nation [has] unburdened itself of the albatross of race" (Cleveland Plain Dealer 2008). From all of this one might conclude that race is largely irrelevant.

Why Race Matters

My claim that race dominates, however, is not all that surprising in light of much of what has been learned from those who closely study racial politics in the United States. Most experts in this field offer a more pessimistic account of the nation's recent trajectory on race.

These scholars contend that as America has become more racially diverse, it has also become more racially divided. The election of Barack Obama may have raised hopes, but the reality is that it also heightened racial tensions (Kinder and Dale-Riddle 2011, King and Smith 2011, Tesler 2016a, Tesler and Sears 2010). Donald Trump's campaign and presidency have further amplified racial discord (Drutman 2016, Gimpel 2017, Mutz 2018, Schaffner et al. 2018, Sides et al. 2018). And this tension is likely to grow as America becomes more and more diverse.

Looking more broadly, across the long arc of American history, scholars who express this pessimistic view do not deny that real progress has been made, but they maintain that progress has been uneven, and that the goal of full equality has yet to be reached (Klinkner and Smith 1999). At the end of the day, discrimination continues to be a potent force in American society (Bertrand and Mullainathan 2004, Edelman et al. 2017).

Within the political arena itself, barriers to full participation, although less severe than they once were, remain very real (Butler and Broockman 2011, Hajnal et al. 2017, Lerman and Weaver 2014, Terkildsen 1993). And despite shifts in racial views, racial prejudice continues to undergird many of our political choices (Kinder and Kam 2012, Kinder and Sanders 1996). America has been and continues to be divided between racially conservative forces that seek to limit the advancement of racial and ethnic minorities, and racially progressive forces that challenge the nation to live up to its ideals of equality for all (Anderson 2016, Carmines and Stimson 1989, Gottschalk 2015, Hutchings and Valentino 2004, Key 1949, Murakawa 2014, Myrdal 1944). The battle between these "two utterly dissimilar publics" forms the backbone of our politics (Kinder and Sanders 1996:27).

An Outline of the Book

By engaging in a series of rigorous, wide-ranging empirical assessments of American democracy, the rest of this book seeks to test these different perspectives, and to tell us how much race and class do or do not impact our politics. More precisely, I ask and answer three questions:

- What politically divides America?
- How do those divisions determine who wins and who loses?
- Can anything make American democracy more equitable?

Each chapter assesses a different stage in the democratic process, and highlights different elements of the overarching stories of race and class in American politics. I briefly highlight key chapters and points here, as follows:

Race Dominates the Vote

This book begins at the heart of the democratic process: the voting booth. Elections can be said to hold up a mirror to a society. The decisions made privately on ballots reflect who we are and provide indications of whether the nation is what it aspires to be.

In Chapter 1, I explore many questions about the dividing lines revealed in the voting booth. What is the current role of race in American elections? How has this changed over the last half-century? Is race receding as younger Americans grow up and become more comfortable with the nation's increasingly diverse populace? Or, are things deteriorating – as suggested by the racial conflicts, such as those that emerged in 2014 in Ferguson, Mo., following the shooting of an 18-year-old Black man by a White police officer? And beyond race, how much is the sustained widening of economic inequality reshaping our politics? Is class likely to replace race as the main dividing line? Or is some other dimension, such as religion, gender, or age, increasingly driving the vote?

Some of these questions have already received significant attention. For example, political science research has looked extensively at racial divides in the vote (Abrajano and Hajnal 2015, King and Smith 2011, Valentino and Sears 2005). Similarly, extensive knowledge exists about how class divides us in the voting booth (Abramowitz and Teixeira 2009, Giedo et al. 2013, Kenworthy et al. 2007, Stonecash 2000). The data are clear that both racial and class divides are large enough to be viewed as significant. But less is known about the *relative* roles of race and class in shaping our political choices. And even less is understood about how the impact of these two factors compares to that of other demographic factors such as age, gender, urbanicity, and religion. Thus, one of the keys to the analysis in Chapter 1 is to incorporate race and class and other demographic characteristics simultaneously, and to explicitly compare the relative impact of each. What really lies at the root of America's fault lines?

To examine these questions, I analyze an immense amount of data on the vote and party identification in many election contexts and over many periods of time. I look at our choices in Donald Trump's remarkable presidential contest; I examine votes in local elections for mayor, city council, and the like; and I assess preferences at most levels in between. I focus on patterns in the nation's most recent elections, and I examine dividing lines in contests up to five decades ago. And in each case, I analyze each contest through the different lenses of race, class, age, gender, religion, and other demographic characteristics.

The data reveal findings that are surprising, disturbing, and insistent. Race is a powerful demographic force dividing Americans. The candidate that the majority of White America chooses is generally the candidate that non-White America opposes. Race is central, from the highest to the lowest office. Race is central, whether or not political parties are on the ballot. Race is central, whether or not the candidates are from different racial and ethnic groups.

A key aspect of this story is not just that race matters but also that it eclipses the other important dividing lines in American society. We may be experiencing unprecedented economic tumult – with jobs, homes, and economic prospects for the next generation at risk, and those on the top further from those on the bottom than they have ever been – but little of that economic divide seems to be affecting our political choices. When compared to race, class plays a peripheral role in the electorate's choices. When it comes to political positions, one's race is more revealing than is one's gender, age, region, or sexuality. Race dwarfs all of these other individual characteristics when it comes to explaining who people vote for.

Moreover, this trend is becoming more pronounced over time. A little over a half-century ago, before the onset of the civil rights movement, neither party was closely associated with a racial group – an irony, certainly, given the overt discrimination and segregation in the public sphere of that day. Today, shockingly, the racial gap among voters has effectively grown to become a racial chasm, even though laws prevent racial discrimination, and, on some levels, American society seems more tolerant and racially mixed. Over the same time period, Whites have become more Republican, and minorities have become more Democratic. The end result is a national party system increasingly and sharply divided by race. The party that is dominant among Whites is overwhelmingly opposed by minorities.

It is also important to note that the role of race is not simply a function of partisan politics. Even when I take into account an individual's partisan identity, race still shapes the vote. Even in local nonpartisan elections where parties play much less of a role, race dominates. Race, in many ways, seems more fundamental than party in driving our politics.

By contrast, the level of influence of class on the political choices of individual Americans has experienced little growth. Despite decades-long growth in income inequality, the role of class in American politics has not expanded in any evident way. Some shifting has occurred: more working-class Whites joined the Republican Party, and more well-educated Whites joined the Democratic Party. Nevertheless, the average Trump voter was still marginally better off than the average Clinton supporter. Perhaps surprisingly, given the contemporary economic backdrop, today's political battles are rarely a contest between the working class on the left and the wealthy on the right.

Explaining the Racial Divide

These patterns seem to defy belief. How can a nation that long ago triumphed over slavery now find itself so deeply divided by race? How can a nation that outlawed racial discrimination and segregation a half-century ago find that political choices are to a greater degree determined by the color of one's skin than by anything else? Broadly, how can America have overcome and achieved so very much, and, yet, still, be so riven by race? Likewise, how can the politics of a nation in which the lifestyles and largesse of the top few are so remarkably dissimilar to the toil and troubles of the working class *not* be wholeheartedly focused on class? How can a nation in which people's life chances are increasingly shaped by their economic status at birth and rich and poor stand further and further apart *not* be increasingly defined by those gaps?

One part of the answer to these questions is that race and racism are, unfortunately, simply part of who we are. As humans, we instinctively form groups (Tajfel 1981). Those groups then almost naturally define who is more or less deserving and who is more or less threatening (Blalock 1967). With race as one of the most visible dividing lines, it almost inevitably becomes a central focus of our societal divisions. The result is that one racial and ethnic group views members of other racial and ethnic groups as a threat (Key 1949). In some cases that threat is decidedly material – focusing on real political, social, and/or economic challenges to one's well-being (Bobo 1983, Bobo and Hutchings 1996). In other instances, the threat is primarily symbolic or cultural (Parker and Barreto 2013, forthcoming, Kinder and Sanders 1996, Sears and Kinder 1985).

According to this view, America has always been and continues to be susceptible to this racial division. From the nation's founding, through the Civil War, continuing through the civil rights movement, and on to the present, the argument is that America has been deeply divided between its egalitarian and liberal tendencies on one side and, on the other, an equally core belief that some Americans are more deserving than others (Du Bois 1949, Myrdal 1944, Smith 1993). The battle between these two institutional orders – a White supremacist order and an egalitarian transformative order – defines and explains the checkered pattern of progress on race over the course of the nation's history (King and Smith 2005, 2011, Klinkner and Smith 1999).

As part of this process, those who claim privileged membership in the White category have developed narratives that justify their power and dominance. These narratives have been modified over time – from viewing minorities as inherently inferior, to seeing them today as less deserving or demanding of special treatment – but the impact of race has endured. In short, since the earliest development of American politics, race has played a fundamental role in shaping the priorities and loyalties of White and non-White Americans.

But why would the impact of race grow in recent decades? One part of the answer is that as the size of the racial and ethnic minority population has grown, it has become more of a threat to the existing White majority (Key 1949). But another critical element of the answer is explicitly political and partisan. Race has become more consequential in American politics in recent decades because leaders of the two major political parties, the Democrats and the Republicans, have each offered increasingly divergent positions on matters of race (Carmines and Stimson 1989).[4] Prior to the 1960s, neither Democrats nor Republicans were particularly vocal champions of minority rights. But since that time the two parties have diverged. Out of a desire to garner more votes from racial and ethnic minorities, the Democratic Party has increasingly situated itself as the defender of minority interests (Dawson 1994). By contrast, the Republican Party has used opposition to a civil rights agenda to try to attract more White support (Carmines and Stimson 1989, Edsall and Edsall 1991). Both strategies have been highly effective. The stark choice between the two parties' positions on race-related policies has propelled more and more racial and ethnic minorities into the Democratic Party and, conversely, more and more White Americans into the Republican Party (Carmines and Stimson 1989, Dawson 1994). The end result is a tight relationship between how we think about race and how we think about politics, including everything from our partisan identities to our electoral choices and policy preferences (Abramowitz 2018, Hutchings 2009, Kinder and Sanders 1996, Parker and Barreto 2013, Schaffner et al. 2018)

For much of American history, African Americans have been the most common and visible object of White fear and antagonism. But recent developments, including, most importantly, demographic change wrought by new waves of Latino and Asian immigration, have begun to alter the target of White fear and backlash. I argue (see chapters 5 and 6) that immigrants (and by extension all Latinos) have joined African Americans in being viewed by many Whites as threatening and undeserving. These growing fissures could become even more pronounced and even more problematic as White America faces the prospect of losing its majority status.

But why would working-class Whites buy into this racial narrative when they potentially have much to gain by aligning with other disadvantaged segments of the population? And why wouldn't increasingly severe economic inequality heighten class conflict, and mitigate racial and ethnic tensions? The answer offered first by Du Bois (1949) and many others since is that White identity provides lower-class Whites with a "psychological wage." Their membership in the White category sets them apart from racial and ethnic minorities, and it gives them a certain privilege that would not exist if racial lines were blurred. Moreover, this desire for a psychological wage is surely exacerbated by economic anxiety. As they fall further and further behind economically, lower-class Whites have more incentive to act in defense of their limited privilege, and to pursue an agenda that disadvantages others on the basis of race (Gest 2016, Kuk 2019, Mutz 2018, Wetts and Willer 2018). In that sense economic stress and racial attitudes interact to shape the nation's partisan politics (Kuk 2019).

I am firmly convinced that racial considerations stand at the core of America's racial divide. The existing evidence offered in the literature and in the data is too compelling to conclude otherwise. But, at the same time, it is important to note that I offer no direct tests of this explanation in this book. A direct and decisive test of the source of America's growing racial divide has proven to be elusive to this point. Part of the problem is complexity, both of the issues and of human beings. Different segments of the electorate almost certainly have different motivations and different ways of reaching conclusions about the political world. Even the same person can have different motivations at different times or even contrasting emotions in the same political instant. The other problem is methodological. The methodological tools at our disposal are imperfect and often unable to effectively and definitively distinguish the effect of one motivation from another. Once we cross the threshold from dealing in demographic characteristics to focusing on attitudes and perceptions, firm statements about what is driving what are much harder to make.

There are, of course, many other readily available explanations for patterns in American partisanship. For many, the primary motivation for partisan choice is and perhaps always has been economic considerations (Abramowitz 1994). According to this second account, views about the government's role in the economy and, in particular, its responsibility to redistribute economic resources have become increasingly correlated with partisanship and have ultimately spurred Whites into the Republican fold. Yet others insist that the primary driver of White partisan defections is a suite of cultural or moral issues that includes abortion and gay rights (Adams 1997, Carsey and Layman 2006, Frank 2004). The argument is that the increasingly tight relationship between leaders of Evangelical churches and the Republican Party convinced religiously conservative White Americans that their home was in the Republican Party. Still others point to larger ideological divisions between liberals and conservatives over the proper role of government in the economy and society as the fundamental dividing line in American politics (Abramowitz and Sanders 1998, Layman and Carsey 2002). From this perspective, conservatism stands at the heart of Whites' opposition to the Democratic Party and its activist agenda on civil rights (Sniderman and Carmines 1997). Given the increasingly close correlations between partisanship and each of these different factors, it seems likely that each has contributed at least somewhat to America's growing racial divide. As such, whenever possible, I incorporate measures of each of these alternative explanations into the analysis. The results show that while these other factors matter, race remains central both in determining the candidates we vote for, and in shaping who wins, and who loses, in American democracy overall.

The Consequences of America's Racial Divide

Regardless of its causes, a growing racial divide raises real concerns for the well-being of racial and ethnic minorities in American democracy. The potential consequences are not difficult to imagine. Indeed, the logic and math are quite simple. Although America is much more diverse than it once was, the nation remains a majority-White nation and, even more importantly, a nation with a majority-White electorate. Even in 2018, Whites represented 72 percent of all voters. With most Whites now opposing the candidates favored by most racial and ethnic minorities, the odds that minorities will lose are high. If the White majority wants to elect leaders and pass policies that serve its own interests, there is little within the American electoral system to stop it. The opportunity for tyranny of the White majority is very real.

But what is the reality in the United States today? Does a growing racial divide also signal increasingly unequal political representation? Part II of this book seeks to answer these questions by examining the degree to which racial and ethnic minorities are disadvantaged in different stages of the democratic process. Each chapter in this section assesses a different form of minority representation. I examine whether racial and ethnic minority voters are more likely than White voters to end up on the losing side of the vote, whether racial and ethnic elected officials are under-represented in the halls of power, and whether government policy is less responsive to the interests and preferences of racial and ethnic minority citizens. As a whole, this section shows that race, more than class or any other demographic factor, determines who wins and who loses in American democracy.

Race Shapes Who Wins Office

When scholars and others seek to understand how well a group is represented in a democracy or how much influence they have in a political system, the first measure they typically turn to is descriptive representation.[5] Do elected officials look like the voters they represent? That choice is a reasonable one. Holding the levers of power and having a voice in the deliberations that determine policy are critical. If a group is shut out of the governing process, it is likely to be at a severe disadvantage.

In Chapter 2, I begin the process of gauging winners and losers in American democracy by examining trends in the number of racial and ethnic minorities elected to public office across the country. Here I expand on the already extensive research on descriptive representation by providing a slightly broader and longer-term picture of minorities in office.

A troubled portrait of descriptive representation emerges. Although racial and ethnic minorities have made enormous gains in winning office, they remain greatly under-represented. Moreover, signs suggest that White voters are responsible for much of this under-representation. An analysis of the vote reveals that White voters tend to favor White candidates over minority candidates. Additional analysis of geographic patterns in minority representation shows that the gains that minorities have made have occurred disproportionately in areas where Whites are the minority. In places where Whites constitute the majority and can essentially elect whomever they want, they almost always choose to elect White representatives. As a result, the nation's halls of power remaining overwhelmingly White.

Race Shapes Which Voters Win Elections

An assessment of descriptive representation is an important first step in gauging the fate of minorities in American democracy, but it provides a far-from-complete picture. In counting minority office-holders, the underlying assumption is that elected officials who are racial and ethnic minorities themselves represent the interests of racial and ethnic minority voters. But that is a naïve assumption. Would Latinos be well represented if Ted Cruz, the Republican senator from Texas, or Marco Rubio, the Republican senator from Florida, had won the last presidential election, even though few Latinos voted for them? Likewise, would African-American interests have been better served if Ben Carson, the Black neurosurgeon who sought the Republican presidential nomination, had won in 2016 even though he received almost no Black support? By using minority office-holders as our measure of minority representation, we also assume that White politicians cannot represent minority interests. By this metric, a Hillary Clinton win over Donald Trump would not have meant stronger representation for racial and ethnic minorities. But given that the overwhelming majority of racial and ethnic minority voters favored Clinton over Trump, wouldn't the minority population have been better represented with a Clinton victory? And, given that the overwhelming majority of elected officials are White, is a count of minority office-holders ignoring most of the representation that minorities receive?

To help provide a more complete picture of minority representation, I introduce a novel measure of representation that focuses squarely on the voters themselves. For any given voter in any given election, I simply ask, "Does your favored candidate ultimately win the election or lose the election?" For each election, I can then count how many voters from different racial or demographic groups end up voting for a candidate who eventually wins, and how many voters from different demographic groups end up voting for a candidate who eventually loses.

Counting winners and losers this way has several advantages over existing measures of representation. It requires no subjective evaluation of minority interests. Minorities themselves choose which side they are on. It also incorporates the preferences of all members of a given group – regardless of whether they vote with or against the group's majority-preferred candidate. And it is intuitive. Winners and losers are simply determined by the outcome of the vote.

Despite the intuitive logic of the measure, scholars of American politics have rarely used it to try to provide an overall accounting of the rate at which minority voters win or lose across American democracy. The success or failure of minority voters in particular elections in particular cities and districts is evident, but political science has yet to understand whether race, class, or some combination of these and other factors predicts winning and losing in American elections more broadly.

In Chapter 3, I count up winners and losers for an array of national, state, and local elections over the last two decades. No group of voters loses all of the time. Nevertheless, a clear hierarchy emerges in the vote results, with Whites on the top and African Americans on the bottom. African Americans, more than any other racial or demographic group, are consistently more likely to end up as political losers. Blacks are the only group that loses more than half of the time across most of the contests I examine. This racial disadvantage holds even after controlling for an array of other demographic characteristics such as education, income, age, and gender. Race, more than class or any other demographic factor, determines who loses in the vast array of elections in American democracy. Moreover, the analysis shows that Blacks are not losing simply because they identify overwhelmingly as Democrats in a period when the Republican Party has been ascendant. Blacks are uniquely disadvantaged even after taking into account the political views and party identification of each voter. Variation in outcomes across different contexts does, however, suggest that there are some settings in which Black voters are more successful. I examine these contexts toward the end of the chapter.

Race Shapes Who Loses on Policy

The ultimate standard by which a democracy should be judged is the policies it passes. Do the policies that a government enacts favor the preferences of one group over another? In Chapter 4, I assess policy outcomes over the last four decades to see who is more likely to get what they want from government. Innovative studies have already shown that the rich get more of what they want on policy than do the poor (Bartels 2008, Druckman and Jacobs 2011, Gilens 2012, but see Soroka and Wlezien 2008, Ura and Ellis 2008). Other studies have found that Whites get more of what they want than racial and ethnic minorities do (Griffin and Newman 2007). Unfortunately, existing methods do not allow scholars to determine whether race or class underpins these patterns or, more broadly, what the relative contributions of race, class, and other demographic and political factors are in shaping government responsiveness.

To assess the relative contributions of all of these factors, I employ a novel but relatively straightforward research design. I gauge the congruence between *individual-level* policy preferences and policy outcomes. That is, I compile spending preferences for almost half a million Americans over almost four decades on eleven core policy areas and then look to see if subsequent federal government spending matches those preferences. The main advantage of looking at individual policy preferences – rather than at group-level preferences, as others have done in the past – is that one can simultaneously assess several characteristics of each individual to determine the degree to which each characteristic drives responsiveness. Also, by focusing on the individual level, one can incorporate the preferences of all individuals regardless of whether they agree with their group's majority position; one need not simply assume that all of the members of a group have the same preferences.

This analysis of policy "winners" and "losers" demonstrates the uniquely powerful role of race in shaping political responsiveness. Class does matter as past studies have indicated. Lower-class Americans are slightly less likely than the upper class to win on policy. But these class-based inequities, as well as gaps by age, gender, urbanicity, and religion, are all small compared to racial inequalities. Blacks stand out among all of the examined groups. Blacks lose more on policy, they lose more consistently across all policy areas, and they lose more consistently over time. Blacks, the group that by many metrics needs the most, gets the least.

Critically, this differential responsiveness by race cannot be easily explained away by some other cause. African Americans are not losing in the policy arena because they are poorer or less educated than others. They are not losing because they favor more spending increases, or because they oppose the public's favored position more than others. Even more surprisingly, they are not losing because they are more liberal or more Democratic than others. The disadvantage Blacks face in the American policy world seems to be unique and profound. This raises real questions about equity in American democracy.

Part II shows that America has become a racial democracy with Whites disproportionately on the winning side of that democracy, and non-Whites much more likely to be on the losing side.

A New Dimension to America's Racial Conflict: The Return of Anti-Immigrant Nativism

The contours of that racial divide are changing over time. Throughout most of American history, the main dividing line has been between White and Black America (Du Bois 1949, Myrdal 1944, Smith 1993). Although there have been periods of nativism and sharp anti-immigrant resentment, Blacks, as the largest racial and ethnic minority group, have represented the largest threat, and, as a result, they have generally been the primary target of a White backlash.[6] That explains why I find that Blacks are the biggest losers in American democracy.

But it is also becoming increasingly apparent that this may be changing. Large-scale immigration has radically altered the racial demographics of the country. Many believe that immigration is also radically altering the politics of the nation. In Part III, I examine this critical new development – the arrival of 60 million migrants – and assess its political consequences. Specifically, in Chapter 5, I argue that an influx of millions of Americans has sparked widespread anxiety among many native-born Whites who see these immigrants as different and threatening. In turn, the Republican Party has seized on and sometimes helped to heighten those concerns with an increasingly anti-immigrant narrative. This strategy was epitomized by the grainy footage of immigrant hordes crossing the border, a feature of Republican Pete Wilson's successful bid to be re-elected governor of California in 1994.[7] This strategy has perhaps reached its apex with Donald Trump's 2018 comments about Mexican immigrants: "These aren't people. These are animals" (Korte and Gomez 2018). Either unwittingly, or by design, the Democratic Party has played into this new Republican strategy by welcoming immigrants into the Democratic fold, and by campaigning on a more balanced approach to immigration. The net result is a stark partisan choice. I argue that for Americans who are anxious about immigration, that stark choice creates a powerful motivation to defect to the Republican Party.

American anxiety about immigration is well documented (Citrin et al. 1997, Gimpel 2017). How much impact these immigration-related concerns have had on partisan defections is less clear. Are fear and anxiety about immigration really strong enough to be responsible for the movement of so many White Americans to the Republican Party in the twenty-first century? On this question political scientists have had remarkably little to say. Until Trump's election, few had attempted to link views on immigration to the partisan choices of White Americans. To date, no research has demonstrated those ties in a robust, causal way.

Thus, much of Chapter 5 provides clear and compelling data that illustrate just how immigration is changing the balance of partisan power in American politics. Using an array of survey data, I demonstrate that concerns about immigration are now strongly correlated with White Americans' policy preferences, their partisan identities, and their electoral choices. Americans who believe immigrants are a burden overwhelmingly favor Republican candidates and the Republican Party. Likewise, those who believe immigrants add to the American mosaic and benefit the nation overwhelmingly support Democratic candidates and the Democratic cause. More critically, from a methodological viewpoint, I also demonstrate that views on immigration predict future partisan defections. White Democrats who fear immigration are much more likely than those who are not worried about immigration to defect to the Republican Party. In short, concerns about immigration have been instrumental in growing the racial divide in recent years. The dramatic rise of Donald Trump in 2016 with a platform that consistently highlighted the negative consequences of immigration is only the culmination of a two-decades-long Republican campaign to use immigration to win White votes.

Immigration vs. Race

This "immigrant-threat" strategy is, I contend, similar to but distinct from the Republicans' earlier Southern Strategy – a campaign strategy that used a racially conservative agenda to try to appeal to White voters who were resentful of the gains made by Blacks during the era of the civil rights movement (Carmines and Stimson 1989, Edsall and Edsall 1991, Kinder and Sanders 1996). My analysis shows that attitudes on immigration are correlated with attitudes to African Americans. Those who resent African Americans are also likely to feel that immigrants are a burden. Moreover, some evidence suggests that attitudes on immigration and race have similar psychological sources. Whether called ethnocentrism, intolerance, social dominance, author-itarianism, or any of the other terms employed by social psychologists to explain attitudes about "in-groups" and "out-groups," attitudes on race and immigration often have the same basic roots (Adorno et al. 1950, Allport 1954, Kinder and Kam 2012, Sidanius and Pratto 1999).

But my analysis also shows that immigration represents a new and emerging dimension of conflict. How Americans think about immi-grants matters – even after taking into account their views on Blacks and the civil rights agenda. The Black-White divide continues to be a dominant factor shaping American politics, but immigration is becom-ing ever more important.

Moreover, concerns about immigration are not really driven by the entire immigrant population or, conversely, by immigrants alone. Concerns about immigration essentially reflect concerns about the lar-ger Latino population. Most White Americans rightly believe that the immigrant population is largely Hispanic. They also wrongly believe that the immigrant population is largely undocumented (Citrin and

Sides 2008, Kaiser Family Foundation 2004). As a result, when individual Americans think of an immigrant or when they think of a Latino, the image in their heads is typically one of an undocumented Latino (Brader et al. 2008, Pérez 2016, Valentino et al. 2013). The net effect is that an immigrant backlash in the United States is now largely a backlash against Latinos. Importantly, the backlash is decidedly not a backlash against Asian Americans – even though most of the nation's newest immigrants are Asian Americans. The public distinction between the two immigrant groups has many sources. Asian Americans are, on average, wealthier and more educated than Latinos (Pew 2017a, b). Stereotypes of Asian Americans differ markedly from stereotypes of Latinos (Bowler and Segura 2011, Lee 2000), and Asian immigrants are less likely to be undocumented than Latino immigrants (Pew 2018a). And even today, Asian Americans represent a much smaller share of the US population than do Latinos. In other words, Asian Americans hold a very different place in America's racial hierarchy. As such, how individual White Americans think about Asian Americans typically reveals little about how they think about immigrants. There is resentment against Asian Americans, too, but that resentment does not drive the larger backlash against immigration.

In Chapter 6, I examine some consequences of the White backlash against immigrants. Although much of the discussion about immigration is at the federal level, policy backlash often takes place at the state level. Across the states, legislatures are passing a range of policies that directly and *explicitly* target the immigrant community (Monogan 2013, Rivera 2015). Perhaps the best-known example of these anti-immigrant laws is Arizona's 2010 passage of SB 1070, which allowed police officers to target individuals suspected of being undocumented, prohibited unauthorized immigrants from applying for work, required individuals to carry their alien registration cards, and permitted warrantless arrest in cases involving probable cause of a deportable offense.

But these laws may only be the tip of the iceberg. I contend that the backlash against the immigrant or Latino community extends much more broadly to a range of policy areas – such as education, welfare, crime, health, and taxes – that are only *implicitly* tied to immigration. Policies that defund schools or that criminalize certain behaviors may not explicitly focus on immigrants but may nonetheless be created and passed with immigrants in mind – especially where immigrants make up a large proportion of the individuals who could be impacted by the policies. Just as health care under Obama was racialized, a range of core policy areas in immigrant-heavy states could be shaped by anxiety about immigration (Tesler 2012).

I find a clear and compelling pattern in spending and taxation across states. All else equal, as a state's Latino population increases, it invests less in public services such as education and health care; it spends more for prisons and punishment; and it enacts more regressive tax systems that favor the wealthy and that target the relatively poorer immigrant population. In short, when the policy is more apt to impact Latinos, benefits decline and punishments increase. All this indicates that America's increasingly diverse population is generating a real, wide-ranging policy backlash.

There is, however, more encouraging news. Latinos, despite all of the barriers they face, also have some agency, and they are able to shift policy in a pro-Latino direction once their numbers are large enough. Once the Latino population passes a certain threshold, a greater concentration of Latinos is associated with more liberal policy outcomes on education and corrections. That policy shift is exemplified by California's sharp reversal from an anti-immigrant state in the 1990s to a progressive, immigrant-embracing state in the 2010s.

Again, none of this is to say that immigration is replacing race as the primary driver of America's racial divide, but immigration is reshaping American politics and policy at ever deeper levels.

Searching for Greater Equality

America's democracy is uneven. Whites and White interests tend to prevail. Racial and ethnic minorities and their interests are more apt to lose out. That is the current reality of American democracy. But it does not have to be the future.

Finding effective and achievable solutions to the problem of minority under-representation in American democracy is not easy. Nevertheless, in Part IV, I contemplate and examine potential changes designed to alter the balance of power in American politics. Fortunately, there may be a pathway forward. Hidden beneath the aggregate patterns is wide variation in the impact of race. Despite generally poor outcomes for minorities in American democracy, deeper analysis reveals cases in which minorities win more regularly. These exceptions suggest changes that could potentially lead to greater inclusion.

Democratic Party Control and Equality in Policy Representation

Are there ways to limit or even eliminate racial inequalities in the democratic process? In Chapter 7, I dive deeper into the data on policy responsiveness. Those data reveal substantial variation in the degree to which Black voices are heard in American democracy. Blacks are more apt than Whites to lose on policy, but the gap is smaller in some years than others; in a select few years, Black voices have as much influence as White voices.

What is behind that variation? One obvious suspect is partisan control of government. Many believe that the Democratic Party is more responsive to minority interests. The Democratic Party makes that claim, and racial and ethnic minorities appear to believe it. The overwhelming majority of racial and ethnic minority voters would be unlikely to consistently support the Democratic Party if they did not think it served their interests.

But surprisingly, researchers have not systematically assessed the impact of Democratic Party control on the degree to which policy outcomes follow African-American interests.[8] In Chapter 7, I assess the effects of partisan control of the two most powerful institutions in American democracy: Congress and the presidency. All else equal, I find that responsiveness to minority preferences changes dramatically when partisan control of the presidency or Congress shifts. In fact, all or almost all of the racial imbalance in responsiveness fades away when Democrats control both institutions. If current patterns continue into the future, electing Democrats into office could eliminate deep patterns of inequality.

Democratic Party Control and Minority Well-Being

In Chapter 8, I assess the impact of Democratic control on an even deeper, more fundamental outcome: the economic well-being of racial and ethnic minorities. Can Democratic control ultimately lift the economic fate of minorities, and reduce some of the racial inequality that exists in American society?

The empirical test is simple and straightforward. I trace the well-being of racial and ethnic minorities over the last half-century using objective, empirical measures of income, poverty, and unemployment. I then compare the relative annual progress of each racial and ethnic group under different partisan regimes. The patterns are stark.

When the nation is governed by Democrats, racial and ethnic minority well-being improves dramatically. By contrast, under Republican administrations, Blacks, Latinos, and Asian Americans generally suffer losses. These partisan differences persist even after controlling for a range of economic and social factors. Even more telling is the fact that partisan differences are more pronounced in second-term presidencies. Democrats are not just getting lucky and inheriting robust economies. Critically, *these minority gains do not come at the expense of Whites*. I find that, on average, White incomes have also grown, and White joblessness and poverty have also declined under Democratic administrations.

The cumulative effects of these partisan differences are enormous. If Democrats had been in power over the entire period I examine, much of America's racial inequality might well have been erased.

Although there are real barriers to minority representation in American politics, there are also potential pathways to greater inclusion. Electing Democrats into more offices will not be easy. Republicans have been successful in winning office at almost all levels, and they will try to hold onto and even expand control over those offices well into the future. But for those interested in a more even democracy, there is a clear pathway forward.

Where Will America Go from Here?

What path is the nation likely to take in the future? Demographic projections suggest that racial and ethnic minorities will eventually win out over a shrinking White population, but likely only after prolonged racial conflict. That will almost certainly mean more racial strife as the diminishing White majority struggles against the rising minority tide. That scenario will also eventually bring about the demise of the Republican Party. That outcome is also one that most pundits and prognosticators predict.

In this last chapter, I agree that this particular path is possible. But I also argue that demography is not the only factor that drives our destiny. I contend that the future pathway for race, partisanship, and democracy is far from certain. I show that there is great partisan ambivalence among minorities – most Latinos and Asian Americans profess no allegiance to either political party. Likewise, surveys often reveal equally deep ambivalence among Whites on both race and immigration. Many more Whites could shift to the Republican Party because of racial concerns or immigration anxieties. But some Whites who feel more comfortable with the nation's diversity could also shift the other way. New developments such as the current ebb in immigration, a sharp rise in the share of the population who claim multiracial identities, or elevation of Muslim Americans as the main target for exclusionary policies could also radically alter America's fault lines and shape its democratic outcomes.

The situation raises both challenges and opportunities for the nation's two major parties, and it generates considerable uncertainty about the nation's future. The outcome is, as of yet, unclear. What is clear is that demographic change will have enormous implications not only for the long-term balance of power in American partisan politics but also for the state of race relations and the well-being of minorities in the nation.

Evaluating American Democracy

This book answers three questions:

• What divides the nation politically?
• How do those divisions determine who wins and who loses?
• How can American democracy become more equitable?

These questions are not new, but they are central and important. Thus, it should not be surprising that political scientists and others have long been interested in addressing them. As such, we already have answers to key pieces of the puzzle. There is, for example, great work analyzing divides in the vote by race and by class (Abramowitz and Teixeira 2009, Stanley et al. 1986). There are compelling studies focusing on descriptive representation by race and by class (Brown-Dean et al. 2015, Carnes 2013). Nicholas Carnes is able to weave together different data sets to show that the share of all state legislators with blue-collar backgrounds has actually fallen from 5 percent to 3 percent since 1976 (Carnes 2013). There are also impressive studies assessing policy responsiveness by class and to a lesser extent by race (Bartels 2008, Gilens 2012, Griffin and Newman 2008). Larry Bartels, for example, is able to artfully combine senators' voting patterns and constituent policy views to find that "the views of constituents in the bottom third of the income distribution received no weight at all in the voting decisions of their senators" (2008:254) I rely on these studies, and I outline their findings, where relevant, throughout the book.

But the existing research is also far from complete. This book attempts to expand on existing efforts in three ways. The first is a focus on *outcomes* in American democracy. Most of what political scientists study consists of *inputs* into the political process. Political scientists examine the public's preferences, who votes, and how those votes are compiled. Understanding these inputs is critical. But it is just the first step. A fuller understanding of a democracy requires more knowledge about outcomes. At the end of the day, who wins and who loses? Are the voices of individual Americans influential or are they being ignored? Do policy outcomes favor some voices more than others? In short, is the government a government of all of the people or of just a small subset of the people? These questions about winners and losers are at the heart of this book and its contributions.

Another element that makes this book unique is the *broad* scope of the analysis. The book not only examines who wins and who loses in a single election or a small set of elections, as has often been done in the past, but also examines more broadly the outcomes across the entire arc of elections. It analyzes not only who wins in one policy area in one part of the country, as many studies have done in the past, but also who wins across an array of policy decisions for the nation as whole.

The final way this book differs from the existing literature is its explicit and rigorous comparison of race and class. Those who write about class tend to live and write in their own world. They have shown, often convincingly, that class is highly relevant. But their analysis tends to ignore race entirely. Those who study and write about race also tend to live in their own parallel, isolated world. The two sides rarely communicate or engage with each other. This book engages both race and class. It compares the impact of one while incorporating the effects of the other to determine which is primary. For good measure, it also engages a host of other potentially important dividing lines, such as age, gender, and religion. This is critical if we want to know the individual contribution of each of these different factors. Because race, class, and other factors are often correlated and interrelated, understanding the independent effect of each issue can only be achieved by incorporating all of them.

In doing all of this, I hope to provide an honest and complete picture of what drives choices and outcomes in American democracy. The object is to better understand our politics and our democracy: to know what matters the most, what matters less, and what does not matter at all.

New Findings

This unique approach leads to some novel findings that are worth highlighting:

- An Extensive Racial Divide
  o Racial division in American politics is a well-known phenomenon; here we learn that *racial divisions are more pronounced than divisions of class, age, gender, and any other demographic factors* that we think shape our politics.

- Outcomes in American Democracy Are Skewed
  o The fact that racial and ethnic minorities have lost at particular times and in specific places has been well documented; here we learn that there is a clear racial imbalance to *almost all outcomes in American democracy.*
  o Using a new measure that counts up winners and losers in the vote across a wide array of elections, I find that *Blacks lose the vote more than any other group.*
  o Using a new method that combines the policy preferences of individual Americans with government actions on those policies, I find that *Blacks lose on policy more than any other group.*

- The Backlash Against Immigration Has Broad Consequences
  o The fact that many Americans are anxious about immigration is evident; here we learn that *fears about immigration are greatly reshaping our politics.*
  o A systematic analysis shows that *concerns about immigration are moving large numbers of Whites to the Republican Party and impacting the partisan balance of power.*
  o An examination of state-level policy *reveals that anxiety about the growing Latino population is leading to substantial disinvestment in public services, more regressive taxes, and a greater focus on crime.*

- Democratic Party Control Reduces Racial Inequality
  - o Looking at how outcomes change over time, I find that *Democratic Party control at the presidential and congressional levels eliminates much, if not all, of the racial bias in policy responsiveness.*
  - o Applying an old method to a new problem, I find that *Democratic Party control leads to major increases in racial and ethnic minority well-being on basic measures such as income, poverty, and employment.*
  - o I also find that *Democratic Party control does not reduce White well-being and, in fact, may lead to greater gains in White well-being than Republican control.*

Being Balanced

The findings in this book can be viewed as alarming. All told, they indicate that American democracy is divided and flawed. As America has become more diverse, it has become more divided racially. In turn, that growing racial division has led to unequal outcomes by race. There is a clear racial tint to America's democracy.

At the same time, some measure of balance is warranted. American democracy is skewed but the data also clearly show that no single group is totally excluded. There is no overwhelming tyranny of the majority in which members of one group always win and members of another group always lose. Racial and ethnic minorities lose disproportionately on the vote and in policy, but they do not all lose all of the time. America may be a flawed democracy, but it is still very much a democracy.

Those interested in balance might also want to know why I raise an alarm about a minority group losing a little more than the majority. After all, shouldn't democracy represent the majority? In fact, the problem is not that minorities lose. The issue, rather, is how consistently they lose and why they lose. If Blacks did well for some outcomes and did poorly on others, then there would likely be little cause for alarm. But if Blacks lose disproportionately on every outcome, as this book demonstrates is the case, the cause for concern is greater. Consistently losing is not only likely to be undemocratic, it is likely to breed alienation, resentment, and conflict. Even more concerning is the reason why racial and ethnic minorities lose. As subsequent chapters show, none of the usual factors can explain the racial imbalance in democracy. Blacks do not lose on policy, for example, because they are more liberal than others, because they favor the Democrats more than others, or even because their spending preferences go against the norm. Blacks with the same policy preferences as Whites simply have less influence than Whites. When the color of one's skin is the only available explanation for a group's lack of success, concerns about discrimination and the fairness of American democracy rightly emerge.

Those interested in balance may also be put off by my findings in support of one political party. Some may find my potential solution – essentially, electing Democrats – simplistic in light of the tremendous complexity of these issues. Of course, what I advocate does not guarantee that all racial problems will be solved. Political parties, like the human beings that operate them, are complex, evolving, and flawed. Both Democratic and Republican positions may change. Nevertheless, I can only go where the data lead, and the data are unequivocal. These data powerfully show that just one of the two main political parties enacts policies that address Black policy concerns and improve the well-being of minority citizens. In the highly polarized atmosphere that increasingly characterizes the American political theater, politics itself is frequently characterized as a zero-sum game; benefits that go to one group (such as minorities) are often perceived as coming at the expense of another group (such as Whites). Crucially, the data show that policies that benefit minorities do not necessarily harm Whites. Yes, voting, by its nature, is a contest in which certain people and certain ideas win and others lose. But good policies themselves can make winners of almost everyone – of most Americans, from every racial background.

Limitations

Finally, it is worth highlighting a few limitations of this book. One is that it is primarily about demographics and much less about attitudes. I examine race, class, age, gender, religion, and the like. I often ignore racial attitudes, economic concerns, and cultural or moral perspectives. There are plenty of excellent studies of attitudes and the role that attitudes play in helping to determine our political choices. For example, research has already provided extensive insight about the depth of racial resentment in this country and its influence on almost every possible political decision (Kinder and Kam 2012, Kinder and

Sanders 1996, Sides et al. 2018, Tesler 2016a). Likewise, many studies have documented close ties between economic anxiety, cultural considerations, and other concerns and political preferences (Abramowitz 1994, Adams 1997, Carsey and Layman 2006). These illuminating attitudinal studies help us to understand why Americans do the things they do in politics. That is why the overwhelming majority of scholars who write about race and class and American politics focus their research on attitudes.

But attitudes are also messy. One set of attitudes is often correlated with another. How individual Americans think about economic inequality and economic policy is often deeply intertwined with and impacted by how they think about race (Gilens 1999, Tesler 2012a, b, Winter 2006). And the reverse is just as true (Sniderman and Carmines 1997). In the parlance of academia, attitudes are often endogenous – that is, one attitude is correlated with the other, and one affects the other. As a result, it is almost impossible to know what drives what, and what the relative impact of different attitudes is on human decision-making. We know all of these problems all too well.

Demographics are not so messy. They are, to use the same academic parlance, largely exogenous. That is to say that we do not change our age, our gender, our education, our income, or (except for the rarest of cases) our race or religion to reflect our politics. If there is a causal arrow, it runs from our demographic characteristics to our political choices, not the other way around. Thus, by focusing on demographics, I can provide a relatively clear picture of what divides Americans, and of what shapes victory and defeat in the democratic arena.

A second limitation of this book is a tendency to pay less attention to smaller racial and ethnic minority populations. It is not an exaggeration to say that the racial and ethnic minority population in America is now extremely diverse. America's minority population – a category that includes everyone but non-Hispanic Whites – encompasses African Americans, Latinos, Asian Americans, Native Americans, multiracial Americans, and Arab or Muslim Americans. Some of these racial and ethnic minority groups receive extensive attention in this book. Others do not.

African Americans, until recently the largest racial and ethnic minority group, receive extensive attention in part because the Black-White divide has been at the center of racial conflict in this nation almost from its inception. From slavery to Jim Crow, America's focus has often been on the Black population and its role in American society (Klinkner and Smith 1999). Blacks are also a primary concern because the African-American population is, by many core measures of well-being, one of the most disadvantaged racial and ethnic groups in the nation. In terms of income, poverty, wealth, education, incarceration, and health, African Americans fall near the bottom of America's racial hierarchy (Pew 2016). They deserve our help. But the main reason Blacks are a primary focus for the chapters in this book is because of the story the data reveal: African Americans are often the most disadvantaged group in American democracy. They, more than any other racial and ethnic minority population, are rendered losers in the democratic processes in contemporary America. They deserve attention.

Latinos, currently the largest racial and ethnic minority group, are also a regular focus of this book. This is in part because of their disadvantaged status in American society. On many of the same metrics, such as income, education, and poverty, Latinos (as a group) fare almost as poorly or even more poorly than African Americans (Pew 2016). They, too, deserve attention. But the larger reason to focus on Latinos is a concern that the attention of White America has begun to shift to the Latino population. Latinos are being targeted in different ways and in different contexts than African Americans, but the data also show that Latinos are often major losers in American democracy. Latinos are not replacing Blacks at the core of America's racial conflict, but they are making the story of racial politics in America much more complex. For this reason, they, too, deserve help.

Asian Americans, by some metrics the fastest-growing racial and ethnic minority population, also receive considerable attention. The Asian-American population is not, as many assume, always advantaged. Despite having high average outcomes for income and education and other markers of well-being, the Asian-American population includes many people who are suffering (Pew 2017b). Asian Americans, in short, fall both near the top and near the bottom of America's racial hierarchy. In addition, what might be construed as a positive stereotype – the sense that Asian Americans are the model minority – can sometimes create resentment and can be used as a tool to target members of the Asian-American population. Because White Americans believe Asian Americans are doing so well, Whites often can and do feel that Asian Americans do not need or deserve help (Lee

2000). Evidence also suggests that many Whites have grown resentful of Asian Americans' successes (Lee 2000). Thus, Asian Americans constitute yet another group deserving of attention.

But Asian Americans are less of a focus in this book simply because their place in American democracy is less clear. On many of the core outcomes in American democracy examined in this book, Asian Americans end up somewhere closer to the middle – not especially advantaged, but not nearly as disadvantaged as the African-American or Latino populations. Put simply, Asian Americans hold a unique place both in the American psyche and in its political processes.

Other groups – multiracial Americans, Native Americans and Arab or Muslim Americans – receive almost no attention here. This is not because they do not suffer disadvantages in American democracy. Native Americans suffer from extremely difficult economic circumstances (Pew 2014). They are greatly under-represented in the halls of power (Bowler and Segura 2011). Multiracial Americans also fall well below Whites on basic indicators of well-being, and they have unique political views (Davenport 2018). Growing evidence suggests that discrimination against Arab and Muslim Americans is increasing both within and outside the political arena (Lajevardi 2018, Lajevardi and Abrajano 2019). One need look no further than Trump's Muslim travel ban and his verbal assaults on refugees to believe that this is the case. These groups receive almost no attention in these pages not because they do not deserve attention but because information about them is lacking. These groups are often too small to effectively analyze using available surveys and existing data sets. These groups deserve attention, but I must leave that task to the next generation of scholars.

Part I
Fault Lines

Part I assesses the roles of race and class and other demographic characteristics in electoral choice. What are the basic fault lines in American politics? Which groups favor which candidates and parties? How have these patterns changed over time? How do they differ from the national to local levels? And what happens when political parties are not on the ballot?

In Chapter 1, I show that race clearly dominates other demographic factors in shaping the vote. Regardless of the context, the office, or the year, race trumps class in predicting which candidates and which parties Americans support. Most of the time most of White America ends up on one side of democracy opposing the vast majority of racial and ethnic minority voters. Over time that racial divide is becoming a racial chasm. A party system that was largely unrelated to race has become a party system that is now at its heart structured around race. The chapter closes by offering an explanation of why Americans are increasingly divided by race.

1 WHAT DIVIDES US? RACE, CLASS, AND POLITICAL CHOICE

Donald J. Trump put his hand on Lincoln's Bible on a cold, gray, and damp day in January 2017, and swore to faithfully execute his presidential duties. This was a moment that few had predicted.[1] Less than a year before, Donald Trump had been widely viewed as certain to lose. He had none of the credentials typically required for elevation to the nation's highest office. In all of his years, he had done no public service. He had no experience with national security issues. His greatest claim to fame was as a self-aggrandizing celebrity. Past actions and events seemed to jeopardize his candidacy, and, perhaps, to disqualify him from the office. He had been caught on tape boasting about grabbing women "by the pussy" (Victor 2017). In an exciting but checkered career in business he had filed for Chapter 11 bankruptcy six times. In multiple years, he had paid no income taxes despite garnering earnings that were unimaginable to most Americans. Moreover, Donald Trump faced a deep bench of seemingly attractive and qualified opponents. In the Republican primary, he started at the very bottom of a field that included candidates with sterling résumés, dynastic family names, solid conservative records, and appealing moderate positions. In the general election, he faced perhaps the most qualified presidential nominee in the nation's history. And to top it all off, polls on the eve of the election were clear: Hillary Clinton was going to win.

Yet the polls were wrong. All of the early predictions were off. Donald Trump ultimately won the election and assumed the presidency. Why, against all of the odds, did Donald Trump become president?

Since that January day in 2017, two narratives have come to dominate our understanding of Trump's electoral victory. One is about class and the other is about race. The class-based story argues that economic decline in working-class communities was the main factor driving support for Trump (Altik et al. 2018, Casselman 2017, Cohn 2016, McGillis 2016, Porter 2016). Globalization, free trade, and the demise of manufacturing had left behind whole communities of poor and working-class Americans who were ripe targets for Donald Trump's populist economic message. The oft-repeated story puts economics at the heart of the Trump victory. Trump's guarantees to bring back manufacturing, to end unfair trade deals, and to do everything possible to help upend decades of growing income inequality to benefit American workers led to a decisive shift in working-class support (Porter 2016). As National Public Radio put it, "There's no question that one of the key issues in this election year has been the frustration of workers over wages, debt, and a sense of economic stagnation in too many households" (NPR 2016). Echoing that sentiment, Diana Mutz writes, "To date, the dominant narrative explaining the outcome of the 2016 presidential election has been that working-class voters rose up in opposition to being left behind economically" (2018:1).

Powerful anecdotal accounts support this compelling storyline and these conclusions. In southeast Ohio, a young White woman who had graduated from a program to fight heroin addiction said that she was voting for Trump to save her boyfriend's job at a General Electric lightbulb plant, suggesting that economic considerations were central in the minds of White voters (McGillis 2016). Others like Sharla Baker, a two-time Obama supporter from Stark County who had worked a series of poorly paid jobs since graduating from high school in 2007, said she liked how Trump talked about jobs and wages and the people being left behind (Tavernise and Gebeloff 2018).

This story is not just driven by anecdotes. Data back up elements of this argument, too. Whites without a college degree disproportionately supported Trump. Some 67 percent of non-college-educated Whites voted for Trump, while only 49 percent of college-educated Whites did so.[2] More critically, class seemed to clearly shape defection from the Democratic Party. Data analysis shows that 22 percent of White non-college-educated voters who had supported Obama in both 2008 and 2012 shifted to Trump in 2016 (Sides 2017). Others have also shown that White counties with slower job growth were the counties most likely to shift votes to the Republican side in 2016 (Casselman 2017).[3] Similarly, voters swung toward Trump to a greater degree in counties with a larger presence of subprime mortgages, and with a larger proportion of residents receiving disability payments (Casselman 2017). In short, Trump did well among Whites in the parts of America where economic prospects were on their steepest decline.

The other narrative focuses squarely on race. In this version of reality, Trump won over White voters, not because of his economic agenda, but rather because of his racial agenda (Griffin and Teixeira 2017, Klinkner 2016, Schaffner et al. 2018, Sides 2017, Tesler 2016a, b, d). White Americans may have been worried about change, but the change that concerned them most was not fundamentally an economic issue. Instead, the issue was racial. Under this interpretation of events, Whites who had once been at the center of power felt that the growing diversity of the nation was threatening their grasp on power and privilege. Increasing immigration – especially from Mexico – and the government's willingness to offer African Americans a seemingly endless expansion of rights and services was breeding more and more resentment among White Americans. Trump, the story goes, appealed to these anxious White Americans by attacking Barack Obama for being an illegitimate, un-American president, by promising to reverse decades of minority giveaways, and by offering a hard-line anti-immigrant message.

Although few White Americans were willing to admit that race and immigration were the main motivating factors behind their Trump vote, emerging studies show a close correlation between the vote in 2016 and attitudes about race and immigration (Abramowitz 2018, Gimpel 2017, Griffin and Teixeira 2017, Mutz 2018, Schaffner et al. 2018, Tesler 2016a). Even after taking into account partisanship, racial views had an oversized impact on the vote. According to one analysis, Republicans who scored high on racial resentment – one of the most widely accepted measures of modern-day racial attitudes – were about 30 percentage points more likely to support Trump than their more racially liberal Republican counterparts (Tesler 2016d). Racial attitudes also very clearly predicted electorally critical shifts in the vote from Obama in 2012 to Trump in 2016 (Sides 2017). The consensus, at least among these studies, is that measures of racial prejudice predicted the vote better than measures of economic dissatisfaction (Klinkner 2016, Schaffner et al. 2018). American politics may have once conformed to the old adage – "It's the economy, stupid" – but in 2016 political commentators were more likely to argue, "It's race, stupid."[4]

This debate about the lessons from the results of the 2016 election and the larger debate about the roles of race and class in American politics have reached somewhat of a stalemate, with each of the two sides largely ignoring the findings and conclusions of the other. Some still maintain that economic concerns and class divisions are the fundamental driving forces in American politics (Abramowitz 1994, Bartels 2014, Cramer 2016, Edsall 2012, Hacker and Pierson 2011, McCarty et al. 2007, Stonecash 2017). Others are adamant that race is of central importance in understanding American democracy (Carmines and Stimson 1989, Hutchings and Valentino 2004, Klinkner and Smith 2002, Valentino and Sears 2005). That stalemate is perhaps best reflected in the ongoing debate within the Democratic Party over whether to wage the 2020 campaign on an economically progressive agenda that targets the White working class and deliberately ignores issues of race, or to instead advocate for a racially inclusive policy agenda that seeks to create a large multiracial coalition. With few clear answers, the debate rages on.

In this chapter, I offer an alternate perspective, using a different set of data. This chapter differs from many of the analyses to date in two respects. First, unlike most others, I do not focus on the relatively small slice of the population that shifted votes from Obama to Trump – under 5 percent of the electorate by one estimate (Sides 2017). These voters are interesting, but they are an anomaly. If 5 percent of Americans shifted, that means that 95 percent of voters did not. Thus, I focus on the entire electorate in the hopes of providing a broader picture of what shapes the electorate as a whole.

Second, rather than analyze attitudes on the economy or race, I concentrate on demographic patterns underlying the vote. It is certainly helpful to know whether attitudes about economic considerations or opinions about race are most correlated with vote choice. Indeed, a deep bench of informative articles already has addressed that issue. But there are real problems with an exclusive focus on attitudes. One is that it is often far from clear how honest individual Americans are about their views on race (Pérez 2016). If accurately assessing those racial views is impossible, then knowing the extent to which race matters is impossible as well. Another issue is that attitudes on race and attitudes on economic considerations are often highly interrelated. Studies clearly show that how individual Americans view welfare and income is in no small part linked to their perceptions about Blacks (Gilens 1999, Wetts and Willer 2018). More broadly, ample evidence shows that views on a wide range of ostensibly non-racial policy areas, including everything from health to social security, are intricately intertwined with views on race (Tesler 2012, Winter 2006). If a focus on attitudes makes it impossible or nearly impossible to disentangle race from class, then an alternate method is needed. Analysis of underlying demographic patterns provides that alternate method. By objectively measuring race and class, one can analyze which of the two most closely shapes the American public's political views.

Which version of reality best describes the larger patterns of the election? Judged simply by who voted for whom, the answer is clear. Race – much more than class – dominated the vote. It is possible to know a lot about the likely actions of people in the voting booth simply by looking at the race of each and every voter. In sharp contrast, ascertaining only the income and education of each voter tells us relatively little about his or her electoral decisions.

Trump is a fascinating character, and the story underlying Trump's victory in 2016 is an interesting one; nevertheless, the 2016 presidential election is, after all, only one election in a nation that annually conducts thousands of elections across a dizzyingly diverse set of states and localities for positions as varied as senator and city council member. The 2016 election was important, but to identify larger patterns in the vote and in partisanship, this larger array of contests is more important. Thus, this chapter examines the 2016 election, and it then offers an analysis of this entire range of elections to try to identify the core elements of America's political divide.

One conventional story of the 2016 presidential election is that it was exceptional (Cohn 2016, Edsall 2016). It was different. It was unique. It was extraordinary. But the reality, as this chapter demonstrates, is that the patterns we saw in 2016 in the presidential contest were far from an aberration. Indeed, 2016 is much more accurately seen as a continuation of previous elections. Trump's tactics were a little more extreme, his rhetoric a little coarser, and his language on race and immigration a little more explicit. However, the patterns behind the vote in 2016 were almost identical to patterns in the vote in 2012, remarkably similar to patterns in the vote in previous presidential contests, and comparable to patterns in the vote for other offices from the national to the local.

Across a broader set of elections over the last two decades, the data show that race remains the most powerful force dividing voters. The data are surprising, disturbing, and insistent. It is an irony of contemporary times that as America has become more diverse, it has become a more racially divided polity. Race – more than any other characteristic – defines which party Americans favor and which candidates they support. By contrast, class has lost much of its influence on the political choices individual Americans make. In spite of the nation's sharp and growing economic inequality, income does little to affect people's voting decisions.

Assessing Demographic Divides in Partisanship and the Vote

The path to uncovering the demographic factors underlying America's political divide is relatively straightforward. I use an array of exit polls and other surveys to count up the number of Americans of different stripes and types on each side of the partisan competition. Who do people vote for? Which party do people identify with? And how consistent are people's votes and attachments over time and across different types of contests?

I focus primarily on race and class. That focus is warranted not only by the fact that growing racial diversity and growing income inequality represent the two most significant demographic challenges that the nation has faced in the last half-century, but also by the fact that race and class are the two factors most commonly seen as dividing America. When possible, I also incorporate other demographic characteristics that are included in the typical survey or poll. In most cases, that means that I can also ascertain the vote or party attachments by religion, gender, age, marital status, family status, and region.

Though there is important variation across the different surveys, across the different years, and across different types of offices, the story that emerges is a fairly consistent one. Regardless of which surveys I use, which types of contests I focus on, or which years I examine, the story is strikingly similar. I turn to that story now.

The Vote Today

I begin with a look into the most recent presidential election – the 2016 contest.[5] Looking first at race, the exit polls reveal a nation deeply divided by race and ethnicity. The contest between Hillary Clinton and Donald Trump pitted the clear majority of Whites on one side against the overwhelming majority of racial and ethnic minorities on the other. Whites opposed Clinton in large numbers. All told, only 37 percent of White voters favored Clinton. By contrast, the non-White vote was largely a Democratic one. Overwhelming majorities of each racial and ethnic minority group chose Clinton. Among Blacks, 89 percent favored Clinton. For Asian Americans, the figure was 75 percent.[6] And among Latinos, some 79 percent went for the Democratic candidate.[7] This, by any estimate, is a dramatic racial divide. Without a doubt, race is a central factor in the vote today.

But what about class? Given growing inequality and the increasing attention to issues of class by the media and other political observers, one would think that class is just as sharply or perhaps even more sharply dividing the electorate. The truth is that class played a relatively minor role in shaping the vote in 2016. The preferences of middle-class Americans were often not all that different from the preferences of working-class Americans. Those near the top end of the income scale (earning more than $200,000) were about evenly divided between Clinton and Trump. Some 48 percent of these wealthy Americans chose Clinton. An almost identical share (49 percent) favored Trump. Poorer Americans were not more likely to favor the Republican candidate, despite media accounts suggesting otherwise. Clinton actually did relatively well among Americans at the bottom end of the income ladder. Some 53 percent of Americans earning less than $30,000 voted for Clinton.[8]

Differences across education were just as muted. In 2016, a very slight majority – 51 percent – of those without a high school education favored the Republican candidate. Trump lost the vote of college graduates but also by a similarly slight difference (49 percent for Clinton vs. 44 for Trump).[9] And differences across other markers of class (profession, employment status, union membership, home ownership) were not appreciably larger. These all helped to shape the vote, but much less so than race.

Of course, race and class were not the only narratives present during and after the 2016 election. Gender, too, received extensive media attention. With the first female major party nominee running in 2016, gender was expected to be a major factor in the vote. At least judging by the exit poll, it was not. Female voters did favor Clinton, and male voters did prefer Trump, but neither won an overwhelming margin. Only 54 percent of women voted for Clinton. Likewise, only 52 percent of male voters supported Trump.

Despite the attention journalists have paid to age, generation played a relatively small role, as well. Younger Americans (those aged 18–24) were more likely to favor the Democratic nominee – 56 percent did so. And older Americans were more likely to favor the Republican on the ballot – 52 percent did so. But those numbers hardly represent a dramatic generational gap.

The exit poll does, however, reveal substantial gaps by religion. Protestants were particularly likely to favor Trump – 59 percent did so. Likewise, Catholics were slightly likely to vote for Trump – 50 percent did so. By contrast, the other religious groups identified in the national exit poll strongly favored Clinton. All told 71 percent of Jewish voters and 58 percent of voters with no religious attachments favored Clinton. And in some ways, these figures understate the importance of religion. When religion and race are combined, religious gaps grow. Fully 81 percent of those White voters who said they were born again or Evangelical favored Trump. The increasingly central role of morality and culture is also underlined by what appear to be increasingly large divisions by sexual preference. In 2016, LGBT voters overwhelmingly supported Clinton. Some 77 percent did so. By contrast straight voters were evenly split between Clinton and Trump (47 percent vs. 47 percent).

The overall demographic story of the 2016 election is illustrated in Figure 1.1. It provides a snapshot of the roles of race, class, religion, and other factors in American democracy. Specifically, it shows the gap between different groups in the likelihood of voting for the Democratic candidate, Hillary Clinton. The gap between Whites, who gave only 37 percent of their votes to the Democratic candidate, and African Americans, who gave 89 percent of their votes to the same candidate, was a whopping 52 points. That is more like a racial chasm than a racial gap. The gap between Whites and Asian Americans was also a robust 42 points, and between Whites and Latinos it was a substantial 38 points.

Those racial gaps far outweighed any of the class divides that the exit polls recorded in 2016. The gaps by income (7 points), education (4 points), and union membership (5 points) all fall far short of the

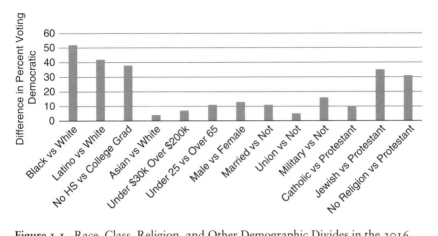

Figure 1.1. Race, Class, Religion, and Other Demographic Divides in the 2016
Presidential Contest
Source: National Election Pool Exit Polls, Latino Decisions Election Eve Poll,
Asian Decisions Election Eve Poll

racial divides. Critically, it is important to note that the effects of
different measures of class work in different directions in 2016.
Wealthier Americans are more likely than poorer Americans to vote
Republican – a pattern that aligns with traditional class-based theories
of American politics. But Americans with postgraduate degrees are
actually less likely than Americans with a high school diploma to
favor the Republican candidate. In other words, increased class status
is sometimes associated with the political left, and sometimes associated
with the political right – a pattern repeated across elections and time,
not just in 2016. If I try to add all of the effects of class together by
comparing the votes of wealthy, well-educated, full-time workers to the
votes of lower-income, unemployed, high school dropouts, I find that
class plays almost no net role in the vote.[10] Because some class-based
factors pushed toward Trump, and others led toward Clinton, the net
effect of being high class was only 4 points. Not only does race have
a larger impact than class when it comes to Americans' political diversity, it also has a much clearer and more consistent impact.

The 2016 racial divides also dwarf divisions by gender (13
points), age (11 points), marital status (11 points), or military status
(16 points). The only factor that begins to rival race is religion. The gaps
between Protestants and atheists (31 points) and between Protestants
and Jews (25) are both quite substantial but fall somewhat below all of
the White/non-White divides.

The electoral story in 2016 is one in which race is central. Judging by this one election, American politics today pits the White majority against the bulk of the racial and ethnic minority population. Politics is bound to create division, but when those divisions so closely mirror racial and ethnic identity, the situation is troubling. With race and party so closely matching each other, it is perhaps not surprising that hostility between Democrats and Republicans is increasing (Haidt and Hetherington 2012, Iyengar et al. 2012, Mason 2018). Today, Americans tend to view fellow partisans as patriotic, well informed, and altruistic, while they tend to attribute almost the opposite characteristics to members of the opposite party (Iyengar et al. 2012). Experiments reveal that partisan division has become so heated that Democrats and Republicans now regularly and openly discriminate against each other (Iyengar and Westwood 2015). Division today could become conflict tomorrow.

The 2014 Congressional Vote

Understanding patterns in the presidential vote in 2016 is important. The president does, after all, hold the highest office in the land. Moreover, the 2016 campaign represented one of the most interesting contests with one of the most surprising outcomes in recent history. However, for both of these reasons – and for many more – the 2016 presidential contest might be unique. Perhaps race mattered more in 2016 because Trump ran a campaign that was focused more explicitly on race and immigration than ever before. Perhaps class divisions were muted by a Republican candidate directly appealing to working-class Americans with an economic message they had not heard before.

Before I can offer a broader statement about race and class in American politics, I must look beyond the presidency and beyond 2016.[11] I start that investigation with the 2014 midterm congressional elections. The data from votes across the 435 House contests that year are equally unequivocal. Race dominated. Class did not. In fact, the 2014 exit polls once again reveal dramatic racial divides in the vote. Across the range of elections for the US House of Representatives, Whites favored Republicans – and decidedly so. Fully 60 percent of all White voters across the nation sided with Republican candidates. By contrast, the racial and ethnic minority vote was a decidedly Democratic one. Overwhelming majorities of each racial and ethnic minority favored Democratic candidates. Fully 89 percent of African Americans favored

Democrats. Among Asian Americans the figure was 66 percent.[12] Some 62 percent of Latino voters went Democratic. In other words, most Whites favored candidates that most non-Whites opposed.[13]

And what about class? With the growing gap between the wealthiest and poorest Americans making class a key issue in the media, one would predict sharp class divides. In defiance of this expectation, however, class played a relatively minor role in shaping voters' choices in 2016. This is not to say that class was irrelevant. The preferences of middle-class Americans did diverge from the preferences of working-class Americans. Americans earning more than $200,000 were more likely to favor Republican candidates, as one might expect. Overall, 57 percent of wealthy Americans voted for Republicans. By contrast, poorer Americans (those earning less than $30,000) were more likely to favor Democrats. Across all of the contests, only 39 percent of poorer Americans supported Republican candidates. Differences were not so sharp among voters with varying levels of education. In 2016, a slight majority – 53 percent of those without a high school education favored Democrats. But so, too, did a slight majority of Americans with postgraduate degrees.[14] Other markers of class did not reveal appreciably larger gaps. Employment status, profession, being a member of a union, and being a home owner all helped to shape the way people vote, but none so dramatically as one might expect in a time of profound economic class differences. In the end none of these economic divides rivaled racial gaps in the election.

Figure 1.2 illustrates this. It provides the same snapshot of the roles of race and class in 2014 that we saw earlier for 2016. Specifically, it shows how much more likely was one group of voters to support Democratic House candidates than another group of voters. The gap between Whites, who gave 60 percent of their votes to Republican candidates, and African Americans, who gave only 10 percent of their votes to Republicans, was a massive 50 points. Remarkably, that 50-point gap is almost identical to the 52-point Black-White divide in 2016. The White-Latino and White-Asian American divides in 2014 were smaller than in 2016 but were still sizable. Whites were 28 percent more likely than Latinos to vote Democratic. Between Whites and Asian Americans, the figure was 24 points.

Once again, class did not match race in shaping the vote. The gap by income (18 points), the gap by education (1 point), work status

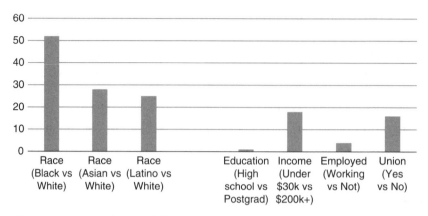

Figure 1.2. Race, Class, and the 2014 House Vote
Source: National Exit Polls

(4 points), and union membership (16 points) all fall far short of the racial divides. At least over the last two election cycles, the data are unequivocal. Race dominates class.[15]

The Vote More Broadly

Moreover, if one looks more broadly across the range of national and state elections and assesses a longer time frame, one sees essentially the same pattern. In every type of contest, from presidential elections all the way down to state legislative elections, and in every election year between 2006 and 2012, race typically outweighs class. To look at these elections I use data from the 2006–12 Cooperative Congressional Election Study, which includes more than 200,000 self-reported votes across these contests.

As Figure 1.3 shows, the average Black-White gap hovers between 40 and 50 points for almost all of the different types of elections. At every level, Whites and Blacks generally want different outcomes. But it is not just the Black-White divide that stands out. The gap between White voters and Latino voters is typically a little less or a little more than 20 points across the different types of contests. Asian Americans and Whites differ by almost the same average margin across these elections. In almost every type of office over this recent period, the majority of Whites typically favor the candidate that the majority of Latinos, Asian Americans, and Blacks oppose.

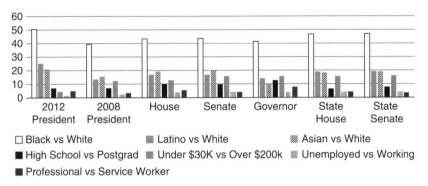

Figure 1.3. Race and Class in American Elections
Source: Cooperative Congressional Elections Surveys (2006–14)

What makes these racial divides so remarkable is not just their magnitude but also their consistency. One might not be surprised by massive racial division in Obama's two presidential contests. Racial division is understandable in a historic election that pitted an African American against a White opponent. Blacks were, unsurprisingly, excited by the prospect of a Black president. Some Whites, perhaps also unsurprisingly, might have been fearful about the historic transition to Black leadership. But what is notable about Figure 1.3 is this: *the 2012 and 2008 presidential contests do not stand out.* The racial gaps in both presidential elections were large, yet they are not unusual for American politics today. Across every type of contest that I could examine, the average Black-White, Latino-White, and Asian American-White divides were similar. Blacks were as divided from Whites in gubernatorial contests as they were in Senate elections. Likewise, Latinos and Whites disagreed about as often in state attorney general elections as they did in House elections.

To be sure, there was variation between one individual contest and another. Mississippi's 2014 senatorial contest, for example, was particularly racially divided (16 percent of Whites voted for Democrat Travis Childers, while 92 percent of Blacks did so), while California's gubernatorial election that year was less divided (54 percent of Whites, 73 percent of Latinos, and 89 percent of Blacks voted for Jerry Brown, the Democratic incumbent). But elections for the House of Representatives, the Senate, state governors, state houses, and state senates all divide American citizens racially to a roughly equal extent.

Moreover, as Figure 1.3 illustrates, those racial divides generally dwarf divisions by class. The best-educated Americans – those with postgraduate degrees – only differ from the least-educated Americans – those who did not complete high school – by an average of about 9 points in the typical contest. Income has a slightly larger but more variable impact on the vote. The preferences of poorer Americans (those earning less than $30,000) differ from the preferences of wealthier Americans (those earning more than $200,000) by an average of anywhere from 4 to 16 points across the different types of elections. Moreover, regardless of how I try to measure class, it does not seem to divide America as much as race. Differences by occupational category (professionals and managers vs. service workers and laborers), union membership, home ownership, and every breakdown of income and education that I could access in the surveys all tended to pale in comparison to racial divides. Class and growing income inequality have been receiving a tremendous amount of attention from scholars and the media, but it seems that race has replaced class as the primary dividing line in American politics.

Race is certainly not the only dividing line. A range of other demographic factors have small but consistent effects across all of these different types of elections. The partisan gap between young (under 25) and old (over 65) Americans typically hovers around 10 points in these contests. The gender gap is roughly the same – about 12 points. Marriage plays a slightly larger role. Typically, there is a little less than a 20-point partisan gap between single and married Americans across these different offices.

And once again the main rival for race is religion. Americans who describe themselves as born again are about 25 points more likely to end up on the Republican side of these contests than are other Americans. Likewise, Americans who say that religion is "very important" are roughly 40 points more likely to favor Republican candidates for the House, the Senate, a governor's office, and state legislative positions. Religious denomination can matter even more. Non-believers are about 40 points more likely to vote Democratic across the array of elections than are Catholics, and almost 50 points more likely than Protestants to do so.

We are a polity primarily divided not by class or gender or age, but much more so by race and religion.

Party Identification

So far, this analysis has examined the vote. However, shifting the focus to party identification allows for an even deeper look at divisions in American politics. Many consider party identification as the bedrock upon which American politics rests. One's attachment to a political party has enormous consequences not only for the vote but also for almost any other politically motivated decision we make. Moreover, for most Americans, party identification provides a longer-lasting and more fundamental political identity (Campbell et al. 1960, Green et al. 2002). Many, if not most, people have deep psychological attachments to a party, and they generally maintain these attachments throughout their lives. If Americans are divided by partisan attachments, then the nation's citizens are truly divided.

The data on party identification are equally unequivocal.[16] Once again, race strongly determines where Americans stand in the political arena. All minority groups tilt sharply toward the Democratic Party. African Americans are the best-documented supporters of the Democratic Party, but the strength of those Democratic ties is, nevertheless, striking. In 2014, fully 82 percent of African Americans identified as Democrats. Only 6 percent aligned with the Republican Party.[17] Latinos and Asian Americans greatly favor the Democratic Party, as well. Latino Democratic identifiers outnumber Latino Republican identifiers by almost three to one (60 percent Democratic vs. 22 percent Republican). Likewise, the number of Asian-American Democratic identifiers is now more than double the number of Asian-American Republicans (56 percent Democratic vs. 24 percent Republican). Whites, by contrast, are ever so slightly more likely to identify as Republican than they are to favor the Democratic Party (43 percent vs. 42 percent).

As can be seen in Figure 1.4, all of this leads to racial gaps in party identification that mirror the racial gap in the vote. To calculate an overall racial gap in partisanship, I subtract the share of Blacks that identifies with the Republican Party from the share of Blacks that identifies with the Democratic Party; I then compare that figure with the partisan leaning of Whites. This calculation shows an overall racial gap in partisanship of 77 points, with Blacks 76 percent *more* likely to identify as Democrats than Republicans, and Whites 1 percent *less* likely to identify as Democrats than Republicans. Between Latinos and Whites, the partisan gap declines, but it is still a substantial 39 points, and between Asian Americans and Whites, it is a sizable 33 points.

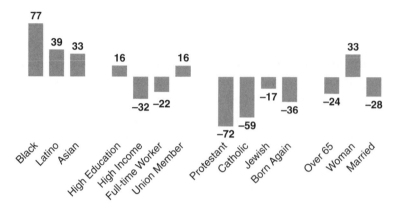

Figure 1.4. Racial, Class, Religion, and Other Demographic Divides in Party Identification
Source: Cooperative Congressional Elections Surveys (2006–14). Each column shows the divide between the group and a comparison group. For race, the comparison group is Whites. For class it is low education, low income, unemployed, and non-union member. For religion it is atheist and not born again. For age it is under 25. For gender it is men, and for marital status it is single

What does change a little from an analysis of the vote to one of party identification is the relative size of racial and non-racial gaps. Race is still a dominant factor but, as can be seen in Figure 1.4, it is now very much rivaled by religion. With Protestants leaning slightly Republican and atheists identifying overwhelmingly as Democrats, the gap between the two religious groups is a whopping 72 points. The partisan gap between Catholics and atheists is not much smaller – a still dramatic 59 points. If one instead compares Americans who say they are born again with others, the gap is 36 points. When Americans choose which party to favor, that decision is very much colored by religion.

There are also sizable class gaps to partisanship. Richer Americans are disproportionately Republican (32 points more likely to be Republican than poorer Americans). The gap between the well- and less-educated groups is 16 points but in the opposite direction. Once again, income and education work in opposite directions.

Age and gender also tend to have bigger impacts with party identification than with the vote. With women being disproportionately Democratic and men being disproportionately Republican, the male-female partisan gap grows to 33 points. Likewise, the divide between older and younger Americans increases to 24 points.

All told, across all of the different assessments of the vote and party identification, a clear story emerges. Race is generally the most central dividing line. Whites and racial and ethnic minorities tend to want different candidates and to favor different parties. That racial divide is often followed reasonably closely by a religious divide. White Evangelicals, Protestants, and Catholics tend to side with the Republican Party and its candidates, while atheists, agnostics, Jews, and others tend to end up on the left. What does not seem to matter nearly as much is class or economic position. America's partisan politics are anything but a contest between the working class on the left and the upper class on the right. Education and income now work in opposite directions, and the overall impact of class appears to be relatively marginal.

Is the Issue Really Race?

This sharp racial divide within the political arena is alarming. When the political preferences of Whites and non-Whites so sharply diverge, it seems almost inevitable that racial conflict of one form or another will ensue. When a Black man like Barack Obama is opposed by most White voters but wins election with overwhelming racial and ethnic minority support, is it surprising to see a surge in white racial resentment and a flood of interest in hate groups such as the Ku Klux Klan and the Council of Conservative Citizens (Bigg 2008)? Similarly, with the polity divided, individual incidents – another White officer shooting another Black man – have the potential to ignite a firestorm of protest and violent riots, creating the "powder keg" that the US Justice Department report concluded Ferguson had become years before the fatal meeting of Darren Wilson and Michael Brown in 2014 (Apuzzo and Eligon 2015). Racial gaps in the political arena are thus a potential warning sign of heightened racial tensions outside of politics. All of this is troubling.

But is it also misleading? Maybe very little of what is taking place across these elections actually has to do with race. Race in America is bound up with many other factors that we know can and do influence voters. Race is highly correlated with class. Whites tend to be well off, minorities less so. Perhaps some of the racial effect is actually driven by class but manifests itself through race. Indeed, if we think back to the 2016 election, much of the media's attention was to the role of class *within* the White population. As one *New York Times* reporter notes, "The role of economic anxiety becomes even clearer in the data once you control for race" (Casselman 2017).

Moreover, class is not the only demographic factor that could explain racial gaps. Religious congregations are some of the most highly racially segregated places in America. Age may also be structuring a lot of what we have seen here. Due in part to immigration, minorities tend to be younger, while Whites tend to be older. A younger generation that has grown up in a much more diverse, technologically sophisticated, and globalized world may have radically different cultural and political mores than older generations (Hochschild et al. 2012). That cultural gap between young and old could be behind some of the divisions we have identified. Where people live could also shape their politics (Gelman 2009). Americans, it can be argued, are increasingly divided between red states and blue states, between urban and rural settings, between liberal and cosmopolitan locations on the one hand and conservative and traditionalist enclaves on the other. All of that could help to shape or explain the racial gap among voters. To this laundry list of potential influences, we might thus add urban-rural, sexuality, marital status, and labor union ties.

Without incorporating each of these varied and important elements of America's demography, one cannot offer firm conclusions about the place of race. Fortunately, I can examine these forces, along with race, by integrating each of these different elements into a single regression model that seeks to explain electoral choice. That model can reveal how much of the partisan divide is directly related to race and how much of the "race" effect is actually driven by other demographic factors. With this more inclusive test, I can also directly assess how much religion, region, age, and gender matter on their own, and how all of this compares to race. Is the American vote fundamentally driven by race, by other factors linked with race, or by a complex array of these?

As an illustration of this test, I first turn to the vote in the 2012 presidential election. Nevertheless, I underscore that the overall patterns that emerge in the 2012 election are strikingly similar if I look at other recent elections. In Figure 1.5, I assess and illustrate the relative and independent effects of race, class, and other factors on the vote. Each bar in the figure shows the net impact of a given characteristic on the

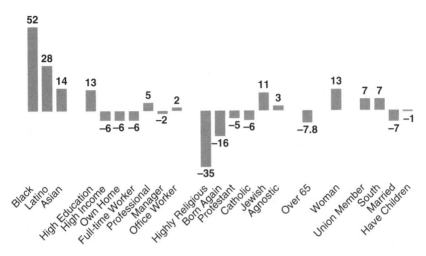

Figure 1.5. Explaining the Vote in the 2012 Presidential Election
Source: Cooperative Congressional Elections Surveys (2012)

likelihood of voting for Barack Obama, the Democratic candidate, after controlling for all of the other factors in the figure. So, for example, one can read the first bar in the figure and see that Blacks are, all else equal, 52 percent more likely than Whites (the comparison group) to vote Democratic.

The sizes of the bars clearly show that race has become the most important driving force in American electoral democracy. Even after controlling for class, religion, age, gender, region, and other individual characteristics, race very much divides us. The 52-point Black-White divide overshadows every other demographic divide that I look at. But race is not just about Black and White. Latinos are, all else equal, 28 percent more likely than Whites to vote Democratic and Asian Americans are 14 percent more likely to favor Democrats. Both are, relatively speaking, sizable gaps.

The next biggest influence on the vote is not, in fact, class. Instead, religion – and in particular the degree to which religion is important in one's life – greatly shapes the vote. Americans who describe themselves as deeply religious are 35 percent less likely to vote Democratic than Americans who indicate that religion is not at all important to their lives. Being born again also has a sizable impact. Americans who describe themselves as born again are 16 percent less likely than others to vote for Obama. Religious denomination also matters, although generally not as much. The most distinct religion is Jewish. Jews are

11 percent more likely to vote Democratic than are atheists, the omitted category. All of this suggests that religion has become a central feature of American politics. Whether Americans support the left or the right in no small degree comes down to their religious ties.

Relatively speaking, class plays little role in the vote. All of the different measures of class had smaller effects on the vote. As Figure 1.5 illustrates, the largest class factor, education, only shifted the vote by 13 points after considering other factors. More importantly, different measures of class worked in different directions. Income worked in the direction one would typically expect. Americans with the highest incomes (over $200,000) were 6 percent more likely than those with the lowest incomes (under $30,000) to vote for the Republican candidate. By contrast, education and occupation worked in the opposite direction. Professionals and Americans with more education were more likely than laborers and high school dropouts to favor Obama.

The net effect is that higher-class status leads to a marginal boost for Democrats. Americans who scored in the highest category on all measures of class were 12.2 percent more likely to vote for Obama than were lower-status Americans. *Once I control for race, the traditional story of American class politics, with those on the top favoring Republicans and those on the bottom favoring Democrats, ceases to exist.* Once I account for the effects of race, one finds that lower-class Americans are no longer tied to the Democratic Party. They are, in fact, more closely linked to the Republican Party. Class no longer matters in the way it once did.

This more rigorous and more inclusive analysis also reveals that age and gender have a relatively limited impact on the vote. All else equal, women were 13 points more likely than men to favor Obama. Likewise, the youngest voters were only 8 points more likely to vote for Obama than were the oldest Americans. Despite all of the discussion of gender and age and America's cultural wars, age and gender are secondary factors when it comes to the vote (Hochschild et al. 2012, Norris 2017, Taylor 2014, Teixeira 2009).[18]

Different Elections, Same Pattern

Some might question whether a historic election involving a first-time African-American incumbent offers the best case to assess the relative effects of race, class, and other factors. Barack Obama was, by some measures, one of the most divisive presidents in American history. The racially charged nature of his presidency must surely have exaggerated the effects of race, and reduced the impact of class.

This is a legitimate question. Nevertheless, the reality is that it does not much matter which elections I examine. The overall conclusions about race, class, religion, and other factors are almost identical whether I focus on the presidency in 2012, or if I focus on other recent presidential elections, or a decade of House elections, senatorial elections, gubernatorial elections, or even state legislative elections. No matter what the context or the contest, racial effects outweigh all other factors including class. Religion is generally the second biggest influence on the vote across these elections. Finally, class matters, but its effects are generally small and always in the non-traditional direction. Across each of the six different types of offices, higher status is always slightly associated with a left-leaning Democratic vote.

What Drives Party Identification?

Perhaps more importantly, little change surfaces in the relative impact of race, class, religion, and other factors when I shift from the vote to an examination of party identification. Americans' attachment to the Republican or Democratic party is very much a function of their racial identity and their religious ties, and less so a matter of class, age, or gender.[19]

Figure 1.6 illustrates the independent effect of race, class, religion, gender, age, and other demographic factors on the likelihood that any individual will identify as a Democrat. The figure shows just how important race is in structuring our partisan politics.[20] An African American is 47 percent more likely to choose to identify as Democratic than is a White American with essentially the same class position, gender, age, religion, and regional location. Latinos are roughly 16 percent more likely to identify as Democratic than Whites who are similar in many respects. And, all else equal, Asian Americans are 8 percent more likely to identify as a Democrat.

Class matters, as well, but its effects are once again varied and they push in different directions. Those who are well educated are about 10 points more likely than those who are less educated to identify as Democratic – all else equal. But higher-income Americans are less likely than lower-income Americans to choose a Democratic identity – a difference of 4 percent. If I add up all of the different measures of

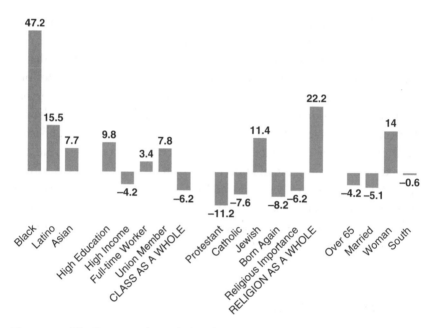

Figure 1.6. The Demographics of Identifying as a Democrat
Source: Cooperative Congressional Elections Surveys (2014)

class and compare an individual who is on the top in all measures (postgraduate degree, more than $250,000 income, employed full-time, non-union member) to one who is on the bottom on all of the same measures, the difference is slight. The most privileged Americans are only 6 percent less likely to identify as Democratic than the least privileged, all else equal.

Although certainly relevant, other demographic factors such as age, gender, and region tend to play a limited role. Living in the South – often touted as a central variable in American political culture – is of limited import here. After considering race and class and other individual characteristics, those living in the South are only 1 percent less likely to identify as a Democrat than similar individuals living elsewhere. Age, likewise, has a limited effect. Older Americans are 4.2 points less likely to identify as Democratic. Here, gender has a slightly larger effect, with women 14 percent more likely to feel an attachment to the Democratic Party.

The one factor that begins to rival race is once again religion. Born-again Americans and those who state that religion is very important to their lives are, all else equal, significantly less likely to identify as Democrats (8 percent and 6 percent, respectively) than those who are not born again or those for whom religion is not important. Moreover, Catholics and Protestants are also less likely than atheists – the comparison category – to choose the Democratic Party (11 percent and 8 percent, respectively). Adding up all of the effects of religion, those at one end of the religious spectrum (religion unimportant, not born again, atheist) are 22 percent more likely than extremely religious Evangelicals to identify as Democratic. That outweighs the difference between Whites and Latinos, and between Whites and Asian Americans, but falls well below the gap between Whites and Blacks.

The Deep Roots of Race

All of the individual choices I have examined so far are tightly bound up with political parties. That is certainly reasonable given that most American elections are structured around political parties. But it does raise an important question. Is all of the racial division in these elections driven by political parties? Could it be that Whites and non-Whites are divided electorally simply because historical quirks have aligned them with different parties? If true, these results might be overstating the importance of the racial divide.

Would different, less racialized patterns emerge if one could minimize or even eliminate the role of parties? I can begin to answer this question, and to assess just how deep racial divisions run, through two kinds of analysis. First, I can look at the effect of race (and other variables) on the vote after controlling for party identification. In other words, does race still matter after I take party into account? Second, I can look at local elections, most of which are at least officially nonpartisan. In essence, does race matter when parties are less central?

The Impact of Race Beyond Partisanship

To dig further into the relationship between race and party, I return briefly to the national and state elections that we examined earlier in the chapter. Here I look at vote choice in these elections *after* controlling for both partisan ties and political ideology. I want to know if racial divisions in national and state elections persist. If so, then race would not only shape partisan attachments, it would go beyond them – and racial divisions would seem to be more fundamental, more difficult to address, and thus more troubling.

The simple answer is that racial effects do persist. Even after controlling for party identification and liberal-conservative ideology, race helps to predict which candidates individual Americans favor. Moreover, race still matters more than other issues. In the 2012 presidential election, even after incorporating partisanship and ideology, Blacks were estimated to be 43 percent more likely than Whites to vote for Obama. That dwarfed the class, age, and gender divides in the contest, and it exceeded the effect of religiosity and being born again. Moreover, the relatively strong impact of race persisted in other elections I examined. For every election, from the presidency to the state house, the impact of race matched or exceeded every other demographic divide. Race very much matters beyond partisanship in these national contests.[21]

Race in Local (Non-partisan) Politics

I can also see how deep racial divisions run in America by looking more closely at local politics. In local elections parties often play a less direct role. Across the nation, 80 percent of all municipalities hold non-partisan elections in which neither party's name is permitted on the ballot (Hajnal 2010). The question then becomes: What matters when there is no formal role for parties? Or, put another way, when parties matter less, does the impact of race decline? To provide an answer I looked at an array of local elections in large American cities over the past two and a half decades. Specifically, to ensure as broad a sample as possible, I collected data on voting patterns for every available city-level exit poll over a twenty-five-year period. That led to a data set that includes the vote choice of 56,000 respondents across sixty-three elections for a range of different local offices in five cities (New York, Los Angeles, Chicago, Houston, and Detroit).[22] Figure 1.7 illustrates average divides in the vote in those elections by race and class.

Despite all of the differences between local and national politics, similar patterns emerge in the urban vote. Again, even when parties are not featured in the electoral process, race overshadows class. The issues at the local level may be different – more contests over the location and quality of city services, and fewer ideological policy divides – but the large racial divide persists. The average gap between Black and White voters was 32 points. Assessed another way, across the entire set of local elections, the Black vote was significantly and negatively correlated with the White vote. Black and White voters generally did not support the same

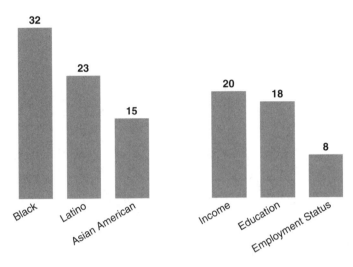

Figure 1.7. Race and Class in the Urban Vote
Source: Urban Elections Exit Poll Data Set

candidates. The gap between Latinos and Whites was 23 points. And the gap between Asian Americans and Whites was 15 points. It appears that, regardless of the context, race sharply divides the American electorate.

The one difference between national and local politics is that class politics appears to play a slightly larger role in local contests. Race is still the primary dividing line but, as Figure 1.7 illustrates, class is only marginally less divisive in these elections for mayor, council, and other local offices. Income, in particular, separates voters more in local elections than in the national contests. The gap between higher- and lower-income voters averages 20 points across the different urban contests. At the local level, both race and class matter.[23]

Assessing Relative Contributions to the Urban Vote

As was the case with the national data, at the local level analysis cannot simply examine each demographic factor in isolation; rigorous regression analysis is required to assess the relative contribution of all of the different demographic characteristics that could drive the vote.[24] Once I control for religion, gender, age, and other core dividing lines, does race still dominate? Figure 1.8 displays the results of that analysis. It shows the average estimated impact of each factor across all of the city elections in the data set.

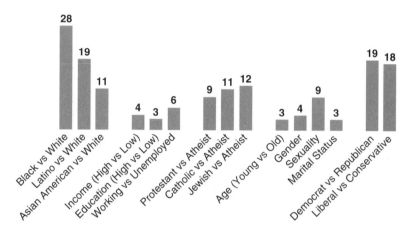

Figure 1.8. Explaining the Urban Vote
Source: Urban Elections Exit Poll Data Set

Perhaps the most striking feature of the figure is the degree to which the racial divide overshadows other demographic divides. Even after controlling for a range of demographic characteristics and key political markers, race still greatly shapes the urban vote. The average predicted gap between the Black vote and the White vote is 27.6 points.

That dwarfs the estimated impact of class, age, gender, sexuality, and even religion.[25] As we saw before with the simpler, bivariate results, there is a substantial but smaller divide between Latino and White voters. The predicted gap between Latino and White voters is 19 points. All else equal, Asian-American and White voters also differ in their preferences by 11 points on average. Black voters stand out, but all racial divides are relatively speaking substantial.

The results for the rest of the demographic characteristics largely mirror what we saw in national and state contests. Class is once again a secondary factor. Income and education sometimes shape the urban vote, but the effects of class are, on average, about one-fifth of the size of the racial effects. Factors such as gender and age play an even smaller and less consistent role. As with national contests, religion is the second most important demographic factor in local elections. Even though the data do not allow me to assess religiosity or Evangelical ties directly, religion still strongly predicts the vote. There are substantial predicted divides between Jews, Catholics, Protestants, and atheists. And, once again, we see that sexuality also matters, with a 15-point predicted average gap between gay and straight voters.

A striking feature of the role of race in the urban vote is its dominance over political variables such as party and ideology. The predicted Black-White gap (28 points) significantly exceeded the predicted partisan gap (19 points) as well as the liberal-conservative gap (17 points). Party and ideology do shape the mayoral vote, but race is the more dominant factor. This is perhaps the starkest evidence yet that race is a central driving force in American politics.

Remarkably, even if I focus on contests involving two candidates of the same race, race still emerges as the most important factor shaping the urban vote. Even when voters cannot choose on the basis of the race of the candidates, the average effect of race remains far more important than other demographic characteristics, and continues to be on a par with or more influential than party and ideology.[26]

Are We Becoming More or Less Divided? Trends over Time

Race clearly trumps class and most other demographic factors when it comes to recent elections and our partisan attachments. But what about trends over time? As more and more racial and ethnic minorities have entered the country and the polity, are Whites and non-Whites increasingly squaring off against each other? Similarly, given the dramatic growth in income inequality over the last few decades, have those on the top moved further politically from those on the bottom?

To answer these questions, I turn to the best long-term sample of American electoral preferences – the American National Election Survey (ANES).[27] The ANES has polled large numbers of Americans on their votes and partisan proclivities for more than half a century. Using these surveys, I present data on the rate at which each racial and ethnic group has supported the Democratic Party over the last 50 years. Figure 1.9 shows these data.

Trends for Race

Looking back over the last half-century shows that the politics of the nation have become more and more divided by race. Beginning in the 1960s and continuing to the present day, a slow and uneven but inexorable shift of racial and ethnic minorities to the Democratic Party has

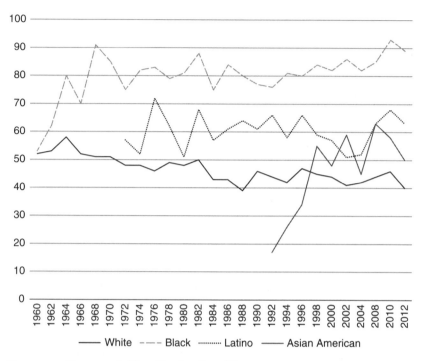

Figure 1.9. Democratic Identification Over Time
Source: American National Election Study Cumulative File

occurred. That shift is most apparent among African Americans. African Americans, once evenly divided between the two parties, are now firmly and almost unanimously on the side of the Democratic Party. In 1960, African Americans were already pro-Democratic, but the partisan gap was not nearly as large as we see today. In that year, 54 percent of Blacks identified as Democratic but a full 38 percent identified as Republican. Today, as I have already noted, Blacks are overwhelmingly Democratic – just over 90 percent identify with the Democratic Party according to the ANES. That shift to the Democratic Party has been well documented and generally well explained (Carmines and Stimson 1989, Dawson 1994). African Americans switched to the Democratic Party just as the Democratic and Republican parties diverged on racial policy. When the Democratic Party chose to favor a more racially liberal policy agenda, and the Republican Party a more conservative racial platform, African Americans responded with a slow but pronounced shift to the Democratic Party. As can been seen in Figure 1.9, that shift accelerated with the election of Barack Obama as the Democratic Party nominee.

But African Americans are not the only minority group to shift allegiances toward the Democratic Party. We have less data on Asian-American partisan preferences in early parts of this period but since 1990, when more reliable data do become available, there is an obvious and dramatic swing toward the Democratic Party. In the early 1990s the Republican Party held a slight edge among Asian Americans, but by 2010, Democratic identifiers outnumbered Republican identifiers by almost three to one. Asian Americans now appear to be firmly in the Democratic fold. Latinos, too, have moved toward the Democratic Party. The Latino shift is less pronounced, but given the growth in the Latino population, no less important for the dynamics of racial politics in this nation. In the early 1970s, only about half of Latinos identified with the Democrats. By 2010, over 65 percent of Latinos in the ANES claimed allegiance to the Democratic Party. There have been ups and downs in the Democratic Party's relationship with Latino voters, but it is clear that Latinos, as a group, are now firmly aligned with the Democratic Party.[28] Over the last few decades, as more and more racial and ethnic minorities have entered the country and become engaged in the political arena, they have spoken with an increasingly clear partisan voice.

The last five decades have also witnessed a substantial shift in White partisanship (see also Zingher 2018 on this trend). Whites are, however, moving in the opposite direction: toward the Republican Party. In the 1950s Democrats dominated the White electorate. In 1952, for example, White Democrats outnumbered White Republicans by a two-to-one margin (46 percent Democratic vs. 27 percent Republican). But that Democratic advantage has slowly and surely eroded to the point where White Republicans now outnumber White Democrats.

The same story emerges if I focus on the vote rather than on party identification. Since 1960 Latinos, Asian Americans, and African Americans have increasingly sided with Democratic candidates while White Americans have increasingly favored Republican candidates.[29] Voting patterns are more variable from one contest to another than are partisan attachments but at every level, from presidential to congressional and state-level elections, the data show an increasing divergence between White and non-White voters over time.

The end result is a nation sharply divided by race. The party that is dominant among Whites is overwhelmingly opposed by minorities.

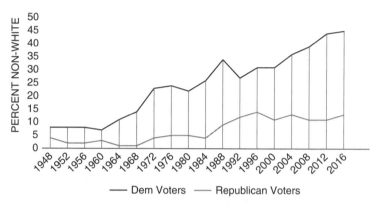

Figure 1.10. The Changing Racial Composition of the Democratic and Republican Parties: Non-White Share of the Presidential Vote by Party and Year
Source: ANES Cumulative File and 2016 National Exit Poll.

The candidates who are favored by the vast majority of Blacks, Latinos, and Asian Americans compete against candidates who are favored by a clear majority of the White population. Today, almost all of the votes that Republican candidates receive come from White voters. Roughly 90 percent of the vote that McCain won in 2008, that Romney won in 2012, and that Trump garnered in 2016 came from White Americans. The Republican Party is for almost all intents and purposes a White party. By contrast, as Figure 1.10 illustrates, the share of Democratic Party votes coming from Whites has declined sharply since the 1960s. As the population has become more diverse, and more and more minorities have shifted to the Democratic Party, the Democratic base has become more and more diverse. Today, a little fewer than half of Democratic voters are non-White. Politics in America is not perfectly correlated with race, but it seems to be deeply and increasingly intertwined with race.

Trends for Class

By contrast, little clear change is evident in the overall magnitude of the impact of class on American politics over time.[30] As best I can measure, class appears to be no more or less important over time. One way to see this is to look at the correlation between class and partisanship over time to see whether members of different classes are increasingly sorting into one or the other parties. Judging from Figure 1.11, which shows the size of the correlation between income and

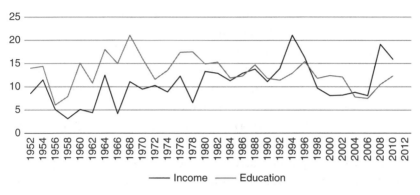

Figure 1.11. The Correlation Between Class and Party Identification Over Time
Source: American National Election Study Cumulative File.

education and party identification for each year of the ANES survey, no obvious trend has taken place. The relationship between class and the partisan attachments varies from year to year, but it does not grow noticeably stronger or weaker over time. Despite growing inequality and the increasing attention of scholars on the unequal representation of America's rich and poor, little evidence suggests that class is increasingly central to the political decisions voters make.

How Can This Be?

These conclusions about class seem to defy belief. We are in the midst of a half-century of expanding economic inequality. And yet the impact of class on the vote has not increased. Those on the top may be further removed from those on the bottom than they have ever been. And yet the preferences of the rich and poor hardly diverge. How can this be?

What's more, many in the media seem certain that class is the defining feature of our current political environment. So much of the media's attention in recent years and recent elections has focused on class and the growing disillusionment of the White working class – what *American Prospect* calls "The Democrats' Working Class Problem" (Greenberg 2017). "If the party cares about winning," *The Atlantic* intoned, "it needs to learn how to appeal to the White working class" (Foer 2017). Famed *New York Times* columnist, Thomas Edsall, chimed in with a like-minded headline, "The Democrats' Gentrification Problem" (Edsall 2018).

And the media are not alone. Scholars, too, have focused on class voting as *the* way to understand the rise of Trump and the patterns underlying modern-day partisan politics. One academic study boldly stated, "We conclude that material issues were a more important cause of the decline in Democratic identification than social/cultural ones" (Kenworthy et al. 2007). Another noted that "The US is a world leader in class conflict" (Bartels 2014). Study after study has highlighted the economic inequities of the American political system, the economic anxieties of working-class voters, and the resulting impact on political choice (Abramowitz 1994, Abramowitz and Teixeira 2009, Autor et al. 2017, Bartels 2008, Carnes 2015, Cramer 2016, Gilens 2012, Hacker and Pierson 2011, McCarty et al. 2007, Stonecash 2017).

This political narrative has not been lost on the Democratic Party, which finds itself in a deep, soul-searching debate about how to move forward, and whether to focus primarily on appealing to the White working class to win elective offices. In fact, the main issue heading into the 2020 campaign appears to be how the party can attract more White working-class voters. As the *New York Times* noted, the Democratic Party "stung by their eroding support from working-class voters" is involved in deep reflection about how to best win them back (Tankersley 2018).

How does one square the circle? How does class garner so much attention when the numbers so clearly demonstrate that class plays a marginal role in the vote? The answer is that almost all of those who highlight class tend to be focused on a very narrow slice of the electorate. In the most recent presidential election, the focus was on Whites who shifted their votes from Barack Obama to Donald Trump. Prior to that, the focus was White Democrats who failed to vote for Obama. These voters are important in helping to explain close elections. In an extremely tight contest, any marginal voting bloc can serve as the margin between victory and defeat.

However, the overall reality is different from the tightly focused narrative. These switchers make up a tiny segment of the population. Only one county in the entire nation voted in a landslide for both Obama and Trump (Wasserman 2017). Overall, less than 5 percent of the electorate switched from Obama to Trump (Sides 2017). If the focus remains exclusively on them, the other 95 percent of the electorate are ignored. If the focus remains on switchers and highlights the fact that most of them are working-class Whites, the millions of lower-income voters who favored Clinton – roughly 53 percent of all lower-income voters – are also ignored.

Any credible analysis can and should admit that a significant number of White working-class voters have shifted to the Democratic Party. Indeed, this is something that I seek to explain in Chapter 5 when I address the role of immigration. But the first essential point is to recognize that a larger share of the White working class has not shifted. By focusing on the few, we ignore the pattern of the many.[31]

None of this is to say that economic concerns are not important. Americans should be very concerned about increasing inequality and declining social mobility, and the implications of this trend. Americans are suffering. They are anxious about the future. American society and its political system should care about this trend, and should take steps to address it. But at the same time, the American public should recognize that economic anxiety is not the sole purview of White America. Racial and ethnic minorities in this country are much more likely than Whites to be poor or economically insecure. They suffer, too. In fact, they suffer disproportionately. Yet, they are not shifting toward the Republican Party. If anything, the opposite is true. The *same* economic circumstances are leading to the *opposite* partisan choices. That, again, reveals something about the racial nature of American politics. The numbers tell a different story than the received narrative. The numbers unequivocally show that class plays a minor role in the overall vote. Few changes took place in the role of economic class over time, but the role of race grew markedly. The main dividing line in American politics is now race.

Other Trends

The American National Election Study, unfortunately, does not consistently include the religious measures necessary to do a thorough analysis of the changing role of religion. Nevertheless, strong signs suggest that religion is becoming more important to the partisan identities of individual Americans over time. Specifically, the data show that the gap between those who attend church once a week or more and those who never attend has grown measurably over time. Much of the increasing tie between religiosity and the Republican Party is driven by the movement of White Evangelicals to the Republican Party but the defection of some White Catholics away from the Democratic Party and the increasing attachment of atheists to the Democratic Party have also contributed to the growing impact of religion in American partisan politics.

A partisan gender gap has also emerged over time. In the early 1960s, women were a little *less* likely than men to identify with the Democratic Party. In 2014, women were 12 percent *more* likely than men to feel an attachment to the Democratic Party. There have, by contrast, been few clear or consistent changes over the last half century in the effect of age on partisanship.

Summary and Concerns

On almost every imaginable metric Donald J. Trump and Barack Hussein Obama, America's last two presidents, could not be more different. Perhaps the most obvious distinction is this: One is White; the other is Black.[32] Perhaps the most important difference is this: One is a Republican; the other is a Democrat. One seeks a largely conservative agenda; the other pursued a largely liberal agenda. Their upbringings contrast sharply, too. One is the privileged son of a multi-millionaire businessman; the other was raised by a single, teenage mother. Their styles are polar opposites. Trump tweets using brash, often profane, language; Obama was known for his eloquent and extended speeches. Trump campaigned, by many accounts, on the politics of fear; Obama, by many accounts, campaigned on a politics of hope. Trump's victory was seen by many as a sign of deep racial discord in the nation; Obama's victory, by contrast, was seen by many as a sign of burgeoning racial unity.

Yet the reality is that Donald Trump's and Barack Obama's electoral victories tell essentially the same story about the politics of this nation. Despite all of the personal differences between Donald Trump and Barack Obama, despite all of the differences in the tone and content of their campaigns, and despite the radically different signals that a Trump victory and an Obama victory supposedly delivered, the three previous presidential contests all tell the same story.

That story is a racial one. When America has voted for president, it has voted largely along racial lines. The vast majority of African Americans, Latinos, and Asian Americans have chosen one side. The clear majority of Whites have chosen the other. And despite the fact that much of the media's attention to these contests centered on economic concerns and the growing disillusionment of the White working class, class divisions have been consistently dwarfed by racial divides. Judging by these three contests, race, more than anything else, tells us who we are politically.

Moreover, as we have seen in this chapter, that racial divide is not limited to the three recent presidential elections. Race is central from the highest to the lowest office. It is central when parties are principal and when parties are peripheral. It is central when the candidates are all White and when they are not. America's growing racial and ethnic diversity has not been accompanied by greater racial harmony – at least in the political sphere. Instead, Blacks, Latinos, Asian Americans, and Whites each tend to vote as blocs and, often, as competing blocs.

Moreover, this divisive trend is becoming more pronounced over time. A half-century ago, racial divisions were relatively muted; neither party was closely associated with a racial group – an irony given the institutionally sanctioned discrimination and segregation of that day. Today the racial gap has effectively grown to a racial chasm; the Republican Party is very clearly the White party, while the Democratic Party has become closely linked with the minority vote.

A key aspect of this story is not just that race matters, but that it tends to overshadow all of the other important dividing lines in American society. The nation may be experiencing an unprecedented increase in income inequality, and those at the top may be more economically and socially distant from those on the bottom, but little of that economic divide seems to be affecting political choices. At least when compared to race, class plays a peripheral role in the electorate's choices. One's race is also more telling about one's politics than is one's gender, age, region, or sexuality. Race dwarfs all of these other individual characteristics when it comes to explaining who Americans vote for.

Perhaps even more remarkable is the fact that race can rival the core political affiliations of Americans when it comes to predicting their votes. At least at the urban level, race is just as important and sometimes more important than party identification and ideology in shaping electoral choice. The decisions Americans make when they cast their ballots seem intricately intertwined with racial identities.

Why Race?

In many ways the patterns I have identified raise more questions than they answer. The first and most obvious question is: why? Why is the nation so divided by race? Why do a majority of Whites generally favor one party and one set of candidates, while most non-Whites oppose that party and those candidates? And why are Americans becoming more divided over time?

Scholars have offered a number of different answers, and an active debate has ensued. But for many observers of American politics, including me, an explanation focused on race itself is the most compelling. From this perspective, racial diversity is a key force driving White political behavior. Those who are different racially will generally represent a threat, a threat that grows as the diversity of a society increases (Key 1949). The underlying logic is that as humans we are naturally inclined to form groups and to identify with those groups (Tajfel 1981). In-group formation then leads almost inevitably to out-group denigration (Blalock 1967). As a result, readily identifiable out-groups such as racial and ethnic minorities are apt to represent a threat to the in-group.

That racial threat can take many forms, ranging from highly symbolic to more concrete. Symbolic threats often center on things such as language, culture, or a cherished way of life (Kinder and Sanders 1996, Parker and Barreto 2013, forthcoming, Sears and Kinder 1985). These symbolic concerns can be incredibly powerful motivators. Scholars have, for example, demonstrated close ties between feelings of symbolic racism and a vote choice across a range of contests and contexts (Parker and Barreto 2013, Schaffner et al. 2018, Sides et al. 2018). Ample evidence suggests that even on ostensibly non-racial policy preferences – such as social security, health care, welfare, and crime – these kinds of symbolic concerns often drive White Americans' views (Kinder and Sanders 1996, Tesler 2012, Winter 2006).

More material threats to concrete matters such as economic resources or political power can also spur opposition to the racial and ethnic minority population (Bobo 1983, Bobo and Hutchings 1996). Whites, for example, tend to be more opposed to racial and ethnic minority interests when the local racial and ethnic minority population is larger, and thus represents a more significant threat to the well-being of the White community (Key 1949). Studies have shown that proximity to higher concentrations of African Americans is associated with more negative White racial attitudes, more regressive policy preferences, greater Republican Party registration, more support for racist candidates and campaigns, and heightened violence against Blacks (Black and Black 1973, Dixon and Rosenbaum 2004, Giles and Evans 1986, Giles and Hertz 1994, Glaser 1996, Soss et al. 2006, Taylor 1998). White support for Obama also closely fits with this pattern. States with the highest share of Blacks were also the states in which Whites were most opposed to an Obama presidency (Donovan 2010).

All of this explains not only the racial patterns of today but also why race has been so deeply entrenched in the nation's psyche and its politics throughout its history. Although the nation was founded on the principle of equality and the notion that every person is created equal, the reality is that from the very beginning that principle has clashed with an equally elemental belief that some Americans are more deserving than others (Du Bois 1949, Myrdal 1944, Smith 1993). The ebb and flow of the struggle between a progressive, racially egalitarian order and a more conservative, racially ascriptive order helps not only to demarcate the core division that has shaped much of our politics but also explains the checkered pattern of progress on race over the course of the nation's history (King and Smith 2005, 2011, Klinkner and Smith 1999).

Of course, race has not always been front and center in American partisan politics. Racial considerations have surged and receded from the political sphere as different developments – political and otherwise – have highlighted or deflected from the topic of race. The current period's fixation with race and racial issues began a half-century ago with the onset of the civil rights movement, and has since been accentuated by the two major parties' sharply divergent stances on race.

Before the 1960s racial issues were largely ignored and race hardly divided Americans politically. The racial and ethnic minority population did not have a clear partisan home. Nor did White America. White Democrats did outnumber White Republicans by an almost two-to-one margin, but Whites effectively dominated both major parties. All of that began to change in the 1960s. Seeing an opportunity to secure a national majority by garnering Black votes, elites in the Democratic Party began to publicly embrace the basic goals of the civil rights movement (Carmines and Stimson 1989, Edsall and Edsall 1991).[33] That strategy was, as we have seen, extremely effective. Blacks, in ever larger numbers, shifted to the Democratic Party, where they have remained to this day. The data show very clearly that the movement of African Americans to the Democratic Party was driven by racial considerations and the belief that the Democratic Party had become the party of Black interests (Dawson 1994).

While an extremely effective strategy for attracting Black votes, the Democratic Party's support of civil rights legislation turned off many White Americans (Black and Black 2002, Carmines and Stimson 1989, Edsall and Edsall 1991). President Lyndon Johnson himself, though euphoric at the signing of the Civil Rights Act of 1964, then grew melancholy, privately confessing to press secretary Bill Moyers, "I think we just delivered the South to the Republican Party for a long time to come" (Moyers 2011:167). Leaders of the Republican Party countered with what came to be known as the Southern Strategy – a plan to spur the defection of racially conservative Southern Whites (Black and Black 2002, Carmines and Stimson 1989, Edsall and Edsall 1991).[34] The campaign strategy tended to depict Blacks as lazy, demanding, and undeserving, and called for an end to special privileges for African Americans; this strategy was designed to appeal to a broad swath of Whites who felt threatened or were resentful of Black gains. These tactics ultimately helped pushed millions of White Americans into the eager arms of the Republican Party (Carmines and Stimson 1989).

The end result is a polity in which race is central and racial division remains paramount. The evidence marshaled in support of this race-based account is impressive. Researchers have repeatedly shown that racial concerns strongly predict both the vote and partisan attachments (Valentino and Sears 2005, Carmines and Stimson 1989). Those who express concern about Blacks or anxiety about the demands of the minority community, generally vote Republican, while those who express support tend to favor the Democratic Party. Critically, these studies show that racial attitudes matter even after taking into account economic considerations, social leanings, and opinions on a host of other issues and subjects. Perhaps most convincing of all are studies that show that how one thinks about race at any one point in time strongly predicts subsequent defections between the parties (Kuziemko and Washington 2018, McVeigh et al. 2014). Those who are racially resentful today are especially likely to become Republican tomorrow.[35]

The election of a Black man to the Oval Office in a majority-White nation has done little to repudiate this racial story. Despite or perhaps because of the historic election of the nation's first African-American president, racial considerations have only grown in importance. Recent studies show very clearly that racial concerns were especially prominent in Obama's two elections (Hutchings 2009, Kinder and Kam 2012, Parker 2016, Pasek et al. 2009, 2014, Piston 2010, Schaffner 2011, Tesler 2016a, Tesler and Sears 2010). Trump's arrival on the political scene has almost certainly exacerbated such concerns. Trump's racially explicit campaign appears to have inflated the effects of race. According to several new studies, the impact of racial considerations on the vote became even more pronounced in 2016 (Abramowitz 2018, Sides 2017, Sides et al. 2017, Tesler 2016a). Almost everyone who scored highest on a racial resentment scale voted for Trump, while almost everyone at the opposite end of the scale supported Clinton (Enders and Small 2016). Little appears to have changed in 2018 (Bacon 2018, Hooghe and Dassonneville 2018, Yglesias 2018). Even after controlling for an array of different election-relevant factors, one recent study found that racially resentful White Americans were 35 percent more likely to vote for Trump than were less racially resentful Whites (Schaffner et al. 2018).

But why align along racial lines instead of class lines? After all, working-class Whites have much in common with the relatively poor racial and ethnic minority population. Why would working-class Whites who could potentially gain by aligning with racial and ethnic minorities choose to buy into this racial narrative? And why would recent growth in income inequality heighten racial divisions when increased economic inequality could instead create an incentive for all disadvantaged groups to work together to bring about a redistribution of economic resources? Here again, the literature offers a clear answer. As Du Bois (1949) so long ago and so insightfully argued, lower-class Whites stand to gain both psychologically and at times materially from their membership of the White race. An end to racial lines would mark an end to White privilege – one of the few advantages that lower-class Whites retain. Moreover, as lower-class Whites' economic status becomes increasingly precarious, the fear of losing that privilege increases, and the incentive to defend that privilege by disparaging racial and ethnic minorities also increases (Gest 2016, Mutz 2018, Wetts and Willer 2018). For working-class Whites, falling further behind can actually spark more attacks against minorities, and can provide greater motivation to align with other Whites.

Studies also show that the importance of race in shaping electoral choices is not confined to White America. Researchers have found that racial considerations also matter for Blacks, Latinos, and Asian Americans (Barreto and Collingwood 2015, Dawson 1994, Hajnal and Lee 2011, Kuo et al. 2017, Lien et al. 2004, Nicholson and Segura 2005, Ramakrishnan et al. 2009). For many minority voters, feeling a sense of linked fate with their own racial group can dramatically increase the odds of a Democratic vote. All told, there is ample reason to believe that the story behind America's racial divide is a deeply racial one.

Ultimately, while the evidence behind this race-based explanation seems especially compelling to me, I admit that I do not rigorously test it in this book.[36] I also willingly admit that race is not the only possible explanation of the racial divide in the vote. Many argue that economic concerns and the role of government in shaping the economy continue to be the fundamental factors behind partisan divisions (Abramowitz 1994, Brewer and Stonecash 2001, Lublin 2004, Shafer and Johnston 2005). According to this account, while race and party may be correlated, the true driving force shaping White partisan attachments is economic attitudes (Abramowitz 1994, but see Abramowitz 2018). Others single out the increasingly prominent role of a host of social morality issues such as abortion, gay rights, and women's rights as primary drivers of recent partisan change (Adams 1997, Carsey and Layman 2006). Still others point to the increasing importance of liberal-conservative ideology in shaping partisan identity (Abramowitz and Saunders 1998, Sniderman and Carmines 1997).[37] To this list of conventional explanations I will seek to add one more: immigration. In chapters 5 and 6, I examine the issues surrounding the influx of immigrants over the last few decades, and I argue that feelings about immigration have in recent years also been instrumental in growing the racial divide.

The Consequences?

Regardless of the sources of the nation's growing racial divide, the fact that White America tends to oppose non-White America in the voting booth raises serious questions about consequences. This is the core subject of this book.[38] Does a growing racial divide also signal increasingly unequal political representation and increasingly unequal economic outcomes? The underlying logic of a majoritarian, winner-take-all electoral system like the United States is clear. The group that wins 50+1 percent of the vote can control 100 percent of the power. With growing racial polarization defining the party system and with Whites still numerically dominant, a White majority could control the political arena, elect candidates, and pass policies over the strong and consistent objections of the minority population. In short, the patterns documented in these pages raise real concerns about who is winning and who is losing in democracy and in life. Given these concerns, considerably more information is needed about the consequences of America's growing racial divide – a subject that both scholars and other observers have not been able to tackle. As such, a key aspect of the remainder of this book examines whether and how minorities are disadvantaged in different stages of the democratic process: from the vote itself, to who wins office, and ultimately to what policies are passed. Put simply, do minorities have less of a say than Whites?

But for now, it is important to admit that stark racial divides are increasingly defining the American electorate.

Part II

The Consequences – Racial Inequality in Representation

In part II I assess the consequences of the growing racial divide for the representation of minorities in American democracy. With Whites largely favoring the political right, and minorities overwhelmingly supporting the political left, there is a very real possibility of majority-White tyranny and large-scale losses for the minority population. Each chapter in this section assesses a different form of minority representation. Collectively, this section demonstrates that race, more than class or any other demographic factor, shapes who wins and who loses in American democracy.

2 WHO WINS OFFICE?

Racial divisions in the vote raise concerns. In American democracy most White Americans end up on one side of the vote, while the overwhelming majority of racial and ethnic minorities end up on the other. This racial divide is growing, now rivaling or surpassing all other demographic divisions in the vote. Division may be a normal and healthy part of democracy, but when the main political divide in a society so closely mirrors the racial identities of its public, larger issues emerge.

The potentially negative consequences of this large and growing racial divide are not hard to imagine. Indeed, the math is quite simple. Although America is becoming more and more racially diverse, it is still a nation dominated by Whites. Whites still represent 61 percent of the population. And more critically, they still account for over 70 percent of the active voters in the country. Given that most Whites oppose candidates favored by most racial and ethnic minorities, the odds that minorities will lose out in American democracy are high. The White majority could effectively shut out racial and ethnic minorities from most aspects of the democratic process. There is a very real opportunity for tyranny of the White majority.

A fear of majority tyranny is, of course, far from new. Anxiety about the fate of minorities in this nation goes back to the Founders and James Madison's concerns about the potentially overwhelming power of majorities. An electoral system in which almost every election is conducted under rules that offer a slim majority the power to dominate outcomes only heightens those concerns. Comparative, cross-national data add fuel to that anxious fire. Research suggests that majoritarian systems such as those used in the United States tend to be less friendly to minority interests than proportional representation systems, used in countries such as Germany or Sweden, that distribute electoral offices and political power roughly in proportion to the vote.[1] Thus, if "tyranny of the majority" is a concern in any democracy, a majoritarian system like the United States is a likely candidate.

Moreover, America's historic record on race is obviously less than stellar. No one would deny that instances have surfaced in the nation's past in which the White majority trampled the rights of African Americans, Latinos, Asian Americans, and native Americans (Almaguer 1994, Kousser 1999, Takaki 1989). Slavery in the early decades of the Republic, Indian removal in the early nineteenth century, the maltreatment of Mexican landholders in the mid-nineteenth century, the widespread abuse of Chinese immigrants at the end of the nineteenth century, and the internment of Japanese Americans during World War II offer egregious examples.

But what is the reality in the United States today? Does a tyranny of the White majority exist? Are Whites using their numerical dominance to trample racial minorities in the electoral arena? In this chapter I begin to assess racial and ethnic minority influence in the electoral arena. There are several different ways of assessing minority influence and access. In subsequent chapters I look at a range of the standard measures as well as at some new ways of gauging minority representation. But in this chapter I begin by focusing on the most common measure – a count of the number of racial and ethnic minorities in office.

When scholars and others seek to understand how well a group is incorporated into a democracy or how much influence they have, the first measure they almost always turn to is descriptive representation.[2] Do elected officials look like the voters they represent? That makes sense. Winning office is a critical sign of the openness of a democracy. If minorities are shut out of the governing process, they are at a severe disadvantage. Holding the levers of power and having a voice in the deliberations that determine policy are critical. Black, Latino, and Asian-American leaders almost certainly need to be in office for meaningful policy change to occur. In fact, studies have shown that under the right circumstances having minorities in office can and does lead to noticeable shifts in government policy.[3] Many of the cities that have elected Black mayors have, for example, seen meaningful shifts in hiring that lead to police forces that begin to reflect the true diversity of their cities (Saltzstein 1989). Would events in Ferguson, Missouri, have been different if that city had had a Black mayor? If Ferguson had elected a Black mayor, would a city that is roughly 70 percent African American have only three Black police officers out of a total force of fifty-three? And with a Black mayor would the city have made a practice of routinely arresting and issuing traffic citations to Blacks to generate revenue? Would the city have become, as a US Justice Department investigation concluded, a place in which "African Americans experience disparate impact in nearly every aspect" of the law enforcement system (Berman and Lowery 2015)? Would a White police officer have been less likely to shoot a Black teenager in the back? Would race riots have been less likely to erupt in the city and to spread? As the situation in Ferguson powerfully illustrates, ample evidence leads one to believe that descriptive representation can make a difference.

The election of minorities to office is also important to minority communities for other, less concrete reasons.[4] Having minorities in office can be a powerful signal about the openness and legitimacy of a political system. Studies show that when minorities win office, racial and ethnic minority political participation grows, and minorities express more confidence in the political process (Barreto 2007, 2011, Bobo and Gilliam 1990, Gay 2001, Tate 2003, but also see Fraga 2016 and Gay 2002). Descriptive representation can also change White attitudes. I have shown in previous research that living under Black mayors can change how White residents think about Blacks and Black leadership (Hajnal 2006). Whites tended to display decreasing racial prejudice the longer they lived under a Black mayor. In these cities, descriptive representation helps to demonstrate the competence of minority leaders and the compatibility of minority interests with those of the majority-White community.[5] Finally, it is clear from a wide range of studies that minority voters tend to overwhelmingly favor minority candidates (Hero 1989, McCrary 1990). As I will also show going forward, the minority community generally wants descriptive representation.

For all of these reasons, few would deny that the election of minorities to office is a major marker of minority empowerment. A singular focus on descriptive representation will not give us a complete picture of minority representation but it does serve as a critical first step in assessing the fate of racial and ethnic minorities in American democracy.[6]

Minorities in Office

Are fears of a majority tyranny in the United States founded? Are racial and ethnic minorities shut out of the governing process? At first glance, the pattern seems to be one of inclusion rather than exclusion. Minorities seem to be well represented in the ranks of America's elected officials. The nation's highest office was until recently occupied by an African American. Moreover, Barack Obama not only won office, he also won his only re-election bid. Obama's success is far from the only case of minority triumph. Just as there is no doubt that racial and ethnic minorities were almost totally shut out of office before the 1960s, there is also no doubt that the list of minority success stories in the last half-century has been long and notable.[7] Over that time, African Americans have won office at every conceivable level. Carl Stokes became the first Black mayor of a major city in 1967. His victory in Cleveland was eventually followed by Black mayoral victories in almost every major American city. African Americans have served as mayor in New York City, Los Angeles, Chicago, Houston, Philadelphia, Dallas, San Francisco, and many other places. A similar pattern is evident in Congress. In the early 1960s, there were only four African-American members of Congress. Today there are fifty-seven.[8] African Americans have also won office as governors, state legislators, and city council members, and been elected to every other elected office imaginable. And the number of Black victories may be continuing to expand. Even today African Americans continue to achieve elective "firsts." St. Paul, Minnesota, elected its first Black mayor in 2017. California elected Kamala Harris, the state's first African-American senator, in 2016.

The importance of these historic firsts is underlined by the intense fear that they often generated within the White community.[9] Early Black challengers faced White opponents who repeatedly highlighted the potentially disastrous consequences of a Black victory. For example, in Los Angeles when Tom Bradley, an African-American challenger, ran against Sam Yorty, the White incumbent, in 1973, Yorty asked: "You know what kind of city we've got. We do not know what we might get. So we'd be taking quite a chance with this particular kind of candidate ... Will your city be safe with this man?"[10] Yorty even suggested that much of the police force would leave the city if Tom Bradley – a member of the Los Angeles police for twenty-one years – were elected. Similarly, in 1987, Chicago mayoral candidate

Eddie Vrdolyak highlighted White concerns about Harold Washington, a Black man, running the city: "It's a racial thing. Don't kid yourself. I am calling on you to save your city, to save your precinct. We're fighting to keep the city the way it is."[11] In Newark, the White police chief was even more dramatic, "Whether we survive or cease to exist depends on what you do on [election day]."[12] In Atlanta, when Maynard Jackson ran in 1973, the slogan was, "Atlanta is too young to die." Jackson's White opponent, Sam Massell, stated that a Black victory would mean, "an end to progress, an end to opportunity, an end to faith."[13]

When African Americans did win, victory typically came only after a period of prolonged electoral struggle. The first Black candidates to win office faced almost insurmountable White opposition. Early Black challengers who won the mayoralty for the first time in their cities often had to overcome record White turnout and near-unanimous opposition by White voters.[14] For example, when Willie Herenton became the first Black mayor of Memphis in 1991, he overcame the opposition of 97 percent of White voters and record White turnout. Successful Black challengers were often only able to win by turning out African-American voters in equally high numbers, and by forging an equally unified Black vote (Hajnal 2006). Herenton won – where a dozen other Black candidates had failed before him – because African Americans had grown to become the majority of the population in Memphis, because Blacks turned out in historically high numbers, and because Blacks gave him 98 percent of their votes (Hajnal 2006, Wright 1996).

These Black electoral victories have often been seen as a major achievement by the African-American community. In the 1960s, 1970s, and 1980s, as Blacks began to displace White incumbents in office, many members of the African-American community were understandably euphoric. In the words of one voter who witnessed the transition, "It was almost like the feeling you have when you see your first-born – a sense of accomplishment, of utter elation."[15] When Birmingham elected its first Black mayor in 1981, "jubilation swept much of the city," according to the *New York Times* (Stuart 1981). The tears of thousands of African Americans who celebrated Barack Obama's presidential victory continue to attest to the importance of these electoral achievements. All of this suggests that Black electoral victories have not only been numerous but also important markers of the growing power of the Black community.

Of course, such experiences are not limited to African-American candidates. Latino and Asian-American elected officials have had a growing impact on American politics, as well. Latino electoral victories often started later than those of African Americans. The first Latino mayor in one of the nation's twenty-five largest cities – Henry Cisneros in San Antonio – was not elected until 1981. But since that time the number of Latinos has grown rapidly at almost all levels. Latinos have since garnered the governor's office in three states; they have won an increasing number of seats in the House and Senate; and they have held office at every state and local level. Likewise, Asian Americans lacked substantial representation until well into the 1970s. But the last four decades have seen a rapid rise in the number and stature of Asian-American leaders. The first Asian-American governor – George Ariyoshi – took office in Hawaii in 1974, and was followed by increasing numbers of Asian Americans elected to the Senate, House, and state legislatures. The nation has never elected an Asian-American or Latino president, but the 2016 crop of presidential hopefuls contained a number of Latino and Asian-American contenders including Marco Rubio, Ted Cruz, Bobby Jindal, and Nikki Haley.

A more systematic look at the numbers in Figure 2.1 confirms the enormous gains each racial and ethnic minority group has made.[16] As illustrated by the figure, a steady and dramatic increase in empowerment has taken place for all three groups. Each of these groups has gone from having almost no representation in elected office to holding a large number and wide array of offices. Over this time period African Americans have gone from holding fewer than 1,000 offices nationwide to presiding over 10,000 positions across the country. Likewise, Latinos have grown from a small number of offices to more than 6,000 elected officials nationwide. And Asian-American representation grew from under 100 documented cases to almost 1,000 offices. Racial and ethnic minorities are an increasingly large presence in the nation's halls of power.

Importantly, for each group, substantial gains have been made at almost every level of office from Congress to state legislators and on down to local offices. The number of Latinos in Congress, for example, has grown from just five in 1973 to forty today. The Black presence in state legislators has ballooned from only 169 in 1970 to 628 in 2015. Likewise, Asian-American officeholding at the local level expanded from just 52 in 1978 to more than 450 today. Judging by the enormous

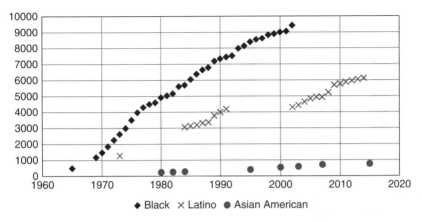

Figure 2.1. Increasing Minority Representation
Source: JCPS, NALEO, APALC, ICMA

growth in minority office-holders, it is hard not to conclude that minorities have made it in American democracy. These numbers and all of the
faces and stories behind the numbers may be why so many – including
perhaps the Supreme Court – believe that there is little ongoing racial
discrimination and that minorities are well represented in American
democracy.

A Fair Share of Offices?

The fact that enormous change has occurred is incontrovertible.
Rapid growth in the number of minority candidates who have been
elected as officials across the country over the last 50 years is
a development that should be applauded. Each of these electoral victories is meaningful. But viewed through a different lens, the gains that
minorities have made can be seen as much less significant. Ultimately,
the *number* of minority officeholders may be less consequential than the
share of all offices that minorities hold. There are, after all, hundreds of
thousands of elected offices across the nation – roughly 511,000,
according to the US Census. Thus, the more critical question becomes:
Do minorities hold their fair share of offices? Or, put another way: Do
elected officials mirror their constituents?

On that question the data are clear. Comparing the number of
racial and ethnic minorities in office to the number of Whites in office
shows that the political leadership of the nation remains overwhelmingly

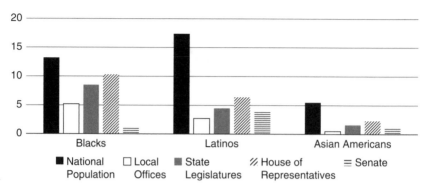

Figure 2.2. Minority Under-representation in Office
Source: JCPS, NALEO, APALC, ICMA

White, and that racial and ethnic minorities are greatly under-represented at almost every level of government. Figure 2.2 provides a telling picture of minority under-representation in American politics. It shows both the share of minorities in the national population and the share of minorities in various offices from the Senate to city councils.[17]

Despite all of the gains, racial and ethnic minorities remain grossly under-represented at every level of American democracy.[18] According to the latest census figures Latinos represent 17.4 percent of the population, yet they hold only 2.7 percent of city council positions, 4.5 percent of all state legislative offices, 4 percent of the Senate and 6.4 percent of the seats in the House. Asian Americans fare no better. Only about one-half of 1 percent of all city council members are Asian American, despite the fact that 5.4 percent of the urban population is Asian American. The Asian-American share of the population also greatly eclipses the share of Asian Americans in state legislatures (1.6 percent), in the Senate (1 percent), and in the House (2.3 percent). Finally, African Americans, as the group who has had the longest and most sustained presence in American politics, are somewhat closer to parity in office but still greatly under-represented at almost every level. Blacks represent roughly 13 percent of the population nationwide, but they only hold 5.2 percent of all city council seats, 8.5 percent of all state legislative districts, 1 percent of the Senate, and 10.3 of House seats. In no case does a minority group's representation match its population size.[19]

The under-representation of racial minorities is reflected in the over-representation of Whites, who make up 62 percent of the population and yet hold 90 percent of all council seats, 85 percent of state legislative seats, 94 percent of the Senate, and 81 percent of Congress. A recent study also found similar imbalances in the criminal justice system. Across the nation, as of 2015, 95 percent of the 2,437 elected state and local prosecutors were White. Fully 66 percent of the states that elect prosecutors have no Blacks in those offices (Women Donors Network 2015). Political decisions at every level continue to be made overwhelmingly by Whites.

All of this suggests that Ferguson, although an extreme case, is hardly an anomaly. When violence erupted in the city, journalists bemoaned the lack of minority representation in Ferguson, and cited that under-representation as one of the primary causes of the unrest. At the time of the incident, the mayor, five of six city council members, and six of seven school board members were all White even though Blacks represented two-thirds of the city's population. If that severe minority under-representation explains the situation that erupted in Ferguson, then the numbers bode poorly for much of the rest of the country where Blacks, Latinos, and Asian Americans are often grossly under-represented. Violence, conflict, and protest could emerge almost anywhere.

And even if no violence occurs, these patterns of under-representation likely have far-reaching consequences for the well-being of minority communities. Would Arizona's state legislature have passed SB 1070 – a strict anti-illegal immigration measure that many felt was designed to target the larger Latino community – if the Latino share of the state legislature had not been its present 14 percent, but instead mirrored the state's 30 percent Latino population? Would the legislatures of so many states across the South have supported the Confederate flag for so many decades if Blacks had served in proportion to their numbers in the population? How sharply would the politics of Texas move to the left if the Latino share of that state's leadership matched Latinos' 38 percent share of the state population?

Are White Voters Responsible?

Who is responsible for this dismal state of affairs? Answering that question is not easy. As with any complex, real-world problem, many different factors likely contribute to the under-representation of minorities. I will not profess to offer any definitive answers.

At the same time, I want to examine more closely the role played by White voters. The racialized patterns in the vote that have emerged in this book suggest that White voters could play a role in this phenomenon. In almost every type of election, a majority of White Americans favored one side while a clear majority of non-Whites favored the other. Logic suggests that if Whites are the majority – and even today Whites represent almost three-quarters of all active voters – White voters could be the main barrier to minority under-representation. Put simply, Black, Latino, and Asian-American candidates could be losing because so many White Americans are not voting for them.

Of course, getting a good sense of how much White voters object to African-American, Latino, and Asian-American candidates is a difficult task. Racist White voters are not likely to be honest about their views or their intentions in the voting booth.[20] That problem is clearly illustrated if one simply asks individual Americans about their own willingness to vote for minority candidates. The last time Gallup surveyed the population, 92 percent of Americans indicated that they would vote for "a generally well-qualified person ... who happened to be Black."[21] But when asked about the behavior of *other* Americans, individual Americans are much less sanguine about the color-blind nature of the vote. In fact, in another poll just over half (54 percent) of Americans admitted that in a biracial election "most White voters will tend to vote for the White candidate regardless of qualifications." Only about a third of Americans felt that White Americans would vote for the most qualified candidate regardless of race. Based on these two very different responses, it is hard to know where the truth lies.

Researchers have tried through an array of ingenious research designs to get a little closer to the truth. Some of the earliest studies asked indirectly about the stereotypes that White voters have about Black candidates. One of the best studies asked Whites to rate a typical Black candidate on a variety of traits (Williams 1990). But rather than accept these evaluations at face value, the study also asked Whites to rate a typical White candidate on the same traits. Here the results were alarming. Without knowing anything about a candidate other than his or her race, large shares of those surveyed rated Black candidates as worse than White candidates across a range of key attributes. Some 42 percent of Whites thought that a White politician would be more likely than a Black politician to increase economic growth. Only 4 percent expected the Black politician to create more growth. The only area in which the Black candidate fared better than the White candidate was in "helping the poor." Even more troubling, Whites rated Black candidates as worse on most individual traits. On average, Whites rated the typical Black candidate as less intelligent, less likely to have good judgment in a crisis, less likely to be a strong leader, less hard-working, less trustworthy, and less fair.[22] Again, without knowing anything about the candidate except race, Blacks were placed below Whites.

That study certainly suggests that Americans have deep-seated stereotypes about minority candidates. But even with that knowledge, it is hard to know how those views translate into the vote.[23] What if a Black candidate, someone like Barack Obama, or a Latino candidate, someone like Marco Rubio, displayed characteristics that defied negative stereotypes?

One way to more definitely identify the causal link between attitudes on race and the vote is to run experiments. In these experiments, adults read about fictitious candidates and are randomly assigned to assess candidates of different races or skin colors who are otherwise identical. In recent years political scientists have relied increasingly on this method to see how much the race of the candidate affects vote choice. There is some variation in the results across different experiments, but the bottom line here is once again that race matters – although the effects are typically not that large.[24] White and light-skinned candidates typically do a few percentage points better than identical Black, Latino, or dark-skinned candidates.

But again, what happens in a real-world context when candidates are actual people with different personalities, story lines, and policy positions? When voters have a lot more information than simply the race of the candidates, do these racial effects endure? Or do they fade away?

Ultimately, to know how much race matters in the real world, we need to examine real-world elections. But the real world is quite complicated. When one researcher examined whether being Black, Latino, or Asian American hurts a candidate's chances of being elected, he found that after controlling for a range of variables like political party, experience, fund-raising, and endorsements, race had no effect (Highton 2004).[25] Black candidates for Congress did just as well among White voters as equally qualified White candidates. That suggests that race is irrelevant in the real world and that White voters are not the problem.

The issue with all of these studies – in experimental or real-world settings – is that they may be asking the wrong question. Each of these studies is essentially testing to see if Whites are racists. Do they vote against minority candidates *because* of their race? But for minority candidates and for the well-being of minority communities, this question is likely to be of secondary importance. The first and most important question is whether White voters vote for minority candidates at all. Regardless of their reasons, will White Americans support candidates put forward by the minority community?

The simplest and most direct way to answer this question is to look at the White vote in biracial contests. When White voters have a choice between a White candidate and a non-White candidate, whom do they choose? The answer to this question is clear. Given a choice, a majority of White voters favor the White candidate most of the time. At the local level the results are particularly stark. When I tracked the White vote in mayoral elections in the nation's thirty largest cities over a twenty-year period (between 1989 and 2009), I found that Whites tended to strongly oppose Black, Latino, and Asian-American candidates. On average, across the forty-one Black-White contests for which I could acquire the vote by race, fully 80 percent of all White voters opposed the Black mayoral candidate. In only one of these forty-one elections did a majority of Whites favor a Black candidate. In Detroit in 2005, 56 percent of Whites voted for Freman Hendrix, an African American who was one of four candidates in the contest. But even this one exception actually shows that Whites were trying to limit Black control in the city. In that election, most Whites opposed Kwame Kilpatrick, the African-American candidate favored by the majority of the Black community.[26]

White voters were almost as likely to oppose Latino candidates for mayor. Across the twenty-six Latino-White contests in the data set, on average 75 percent of White voters voted White. There were many fewer Asian American-vs.-White mayoral contests but in the three elections for which I have data, 81 percent of Whites voted against the Asian-American candidate.[27]

I have systematic data on the vote by race at one other level: Congress.[28] Although the congressional-level patterns are not nearly as extreme as those at the mayoral level, once again I find that most Whites opposed most minority candidates. Between 2010 and 2012, ninety African-American candidates ran for Congress against White opponents.

In the typical contest, 59 percent of White voters voted for the White candidate. That figure is the same in Latino-White contests – 59 percent – and only drops slightly to 56 percent in Asian American-White contests. There are times when the majority of Whites support racial and ethnic minority candidates for Congress, but these exceptions usually occur when that minority candidate is a Republican who garners little support from racial and ethnic minority voters. For example, when Tim Scott was elected as the first Black senator of South Carolina in 2014, he won with 88 percent of the White vote but only 10 percent of the Black vote.

Ultimately, White opposition to minority candidates can perhaps best be illustrated by looking at where minority candidates do and do not win office. Across the nation at almost every level of office, minority candidates generally win office in majority-minority localities, political districts where Whites represent a minority of the population. At the congressional level, 89 percent of Black representatives, 91 percent of Latino representatives, and 70 percent of Asian-American representatives in office today are elected in majority-minority districts. At the local level, the figures are equally remarkable. In the data set, 81 percent of Black mayors and 77 percent of Latino mayors win office in cities where Whites are the minority.[29] When minorities win, they tend to win largely or exclusively in majority-minority places.[30]

Equally illuminating are the patterns in areas where Whites are the majority. When Whites constitute the majority of voters and can essentially control the outcome of the vote, whom do they choose? Here, the data are equally unequivocal. In Congress today, 96 percent of all of the majority-White districts are led by White legislators. That figure is worth pondering more closely. When Whites have the power to elect whomever they want, 96 percent of the time they choose White. The number at the mayoral level is not nearly as severe. Eighty percent of the majority-White cities in the data set elect White mayors. That means that Whites favor White politicians the vast majority of the time, but it also means that White-majority cities appear to be slightly more open to minority leadership and, in certain cases, they help to elect a minority mayor, such as was the case with the elections of Norm Rice in Seattle, Wellington Webb in Denver, and Michael Coleman in Columbus.

Other factors – such as the gerrymandering of district lines, a limited supply of minority candidates, meager financial resources for campaigns in minority communities, and the relatively low turnout rate of minority voters – contribute to the under-representation of minorities in American democracy. But the distribution of minorities who have been elected to public office tells us emphatically that Whites generally oppose non-White candidates. Certainly, partisanship drives lots of this opposition. How much of a role the race of a candidate plays is far from clear. But the reality is that most White Americans are not helping the minority cause.

Brighter Days

The overall patterns are not very encouraging. America's political leadership remains persistently and alarmingly White. Moreover, most White voters appear to like this outcome. But amid these dark clouds are reasons for hope. As stark as the patterns are today, a similar analysis three or four decades ago would have revealed even more minority under-representation and even more White opposition. As I have briefly mentioned, early studies of the White vote in biracial elections revealed active and almost unanimous White opposition to minority candidacies (Hajnal 2006). Black mayors were, at one point, a scary proposition to much of the White community. Whites mobilized in record numbers to prevent them from winning. Today the prospect of electing a Black mayor or even a Black president does not appear to provoke nearly as much fear or counter-mobilization as it once did. Minority candidates today typically lose most White votes, but they tend to get more White support than they received in the past. One can recognize that most White Americans still do not support most minority candidates, but one can also appreciate that in recent years larger and larger shares of the White public have voted for minority candidates – including Barack Obama. Things are improving. There is no denying that.

And across the country today, plenty of bright spots are evident. Minority under-representation exists at every level for every racial and ethnic minority group. Blacks have almost achieved proportional representation in the House of Representatives in Washington, DC, although Blacks and Latinos continue to be largely shut out of the Senate and city councils across the nation. In some cities and states, minority outcomes are markedly better than the averages I have presented in this chapter. New Jersey, a state that is 73 percent White, has elected Bob Menendez, a Latino, and Cory Booker, an African American, as the state's two senators. At the congressional level, Missouri's 5th District, a predominantly White district, elected Emanuel Cleaver, an African American, to office in 2004, and has re-elected him every cycle since then. Likewise, majority-White districts in California elected Asian-American congressmen Ami Bera and Ted Lieu in 2014. Even at the city-council level, minority success stories have emerged in White-dominated cities. Blacks have represented about two-thirds of the councils in Hillsborough, North Carolina; North Chicago, Illinois; and Bluffton, South Carolina – all cities in which Blacks constitute only about a third of the population. Latinos are under 10 percent of the population in Roy, Utah, and West Hollywood, California, yet both cities elected city councils that were 40 percent Latino in 2001. Asian Americans are similarly over-represented on the city council in places such as West Sacramento, California, and New Philadelphia, Ohio.

All of these patterns merit further exploration. They may, in fact, be a key in helping to identify reforms that may ultimately help to make the nation's leaders more representative of its people. This is a subject I tackle in later chapters.

A Few Words on the Representation of Other Disadvantaged Groups

Throughout this book I endeavor to compare outcomes on race to outcomes on other potentially important demographic dimensions such as class, gender, age, and religion. The data on descriptive representation are, unfortunately, not systematic enough to offer a direct test of the relative contributions of race, class, and other factors. However, I can provide some simple descriptive data to give the reader a sense of how under-representation varies across the different dimensions.

A simple tally shows that racial and ethnic minorities are not the only population that is disadvantaged in terms of descriptive representation. Working-class Americans are also starkly under-represented in office. The working class – those employed in manual labor, service industries, clerical, or informal sector jobs – make up over half of the labor force but occupy less than 2 percent of the seats in Congress (Carnes 2013). By contrast, more than 75 percent of Congress is comprised of former lawyers and business people, even though only about 10 percent of the overall population fits into those categories. And this skewed composition is true well beyond the halls of Congress. Comparable figures are not available for every level of office, but data at the city-council level indicate that about a third of all council members in the country have backgrounds as lawyers or as business professionals.[31] The people making the nation's laws are much more privileged than the nation as a whole. The skew by gender is similarly severe. Despite accounting for half of the population – 51 percent to be precise – women hold a small fraction of all the elected offices in the country. Men hold 79 percent of the seats in Congress, they occupy the governor's mansion in 44 of 50 states, they run the city in 77 of the 100 largest cities, and account for 75 percent of the state legislative positions in the nation (Center for American Women in Politics 2019). Figures for religion and age are less readily available, but evidence shows that in Congress, Catholics and Protestants are over-represented while Buddhists, Muslims, and the non-religious are under-represented. One in five Americans is atheist, agnostic, or not religious, but only one of 533 members of the Senate and House is not identified with a particular religion (Pew 2013). We also know that elected officials skew older. All of this is to say that gender, class, religion, and age may even rival race in shaping who does and who does not win office. This does not in any way limit concern for the plight of racial and ethnic minorities in American democracy. But it does reveal that American democracy tilts along all sorts of dimensions.

3 WHICH VOTERS WIN ELECTIONS?

As the world knows, Donald Trump, a White male, won the presidency in 2016. But entertaining the hypothetical, one wonders, what if he had lost?[1] What if one of the other twenty or so serious contenders for the presidency had emerged victorious? And what if the winner had not been a White male?

The unprecedented diversity of the presidential candidates in 2016 – two Hispanics, one African American, one Asian American, and two women – gives us the chance to think more deeply about race and representation. In the previous chapter, to gauge minority representation, I simply tallied how many racial and ethnic minorities won office. The 2016 presidential election tells us why this calculus is insufficient to understand the complexity of race in the American political context.

What if Ben Carson, the African-American former neurosurgeon and author, had gone on to win the Republican nomination and, ultimately, the presidency? A second African American would then have occupied the highest office in the land. But would his presidency really have signaled a shift toward greater Black representation? Given that the overwhelming majority of African-American voters are not Republican and did not vote for him in the primary, and given that the policies Carson has espoused often align poorly with the stated views of African Americans in national surveys, a Carson presidency would have been unlikely to be seen as a strong sign of minority incorporation and influence. Much the same argument could be made for Texas senator Ted Cruz and Florida senator Marco Rubio, the two Hispanic candidates for the Republican nomination. As Cuban Americans, both men are Latino and would count as Hispanic in any measure of descriptive representation. But would a Cruz or Rubio presidency mark a historic watershed in Latino representation? Neither appears to match all that well with the bulk of Latino voters, either in terms of partisanship – Latino Democrats outnumber Latino Republicans two to one – or in terms of policy. Likewise, a victory for Bobby Jindal, the Indian-American former governor of Louisiana who campaigned for the Republican nomination, would have led to an Asian-American presidency; nevertheless, a Jindal win would hardly represent a large victory for Asian-American voters, most of whom voted on the Democratic side. In each case, victory by a racial and ethnic minority candidate would meet the definition of minority advancement under simple measures of descriptive representation; however, such a victory would not necessarily mean that minority citizens were better represented. In short, racial and ethnic minorities who are elected to public office do not always represent the interests of racial and ethnic minority voters.

The other problem with using the race of the candidate as *the* marker of representation is that it implicitly assumes that members of the White majority cannot represent minority interests.[2] This is a critically important assumption in a nation where roughly 90 percent of all elected officials are White. Is it possible that, of the thousands and thousands of White elected officials across the country, none seeks to represent minority constituents?[3] Or is it possible, as some recent research suggests, that White leaders can and often do act in alignment with the wishes of their racial and ethnic minority constituents?[4]

Returning to 2016, what if Hillary Clinton had won? She garnered the support of the overwhelming majority of African-American, Latino, and Asian-American voters. By many accounts, her policy priorities and issue platform accorded well with the preferences of large shares of the racial and ethnic minority population. Her victory as a White woman would not count toward minority representation in the descriptive sense, but one could reasonably argue that her victory would have signaled a substantial rise in the representation of minority interests in American democracy.

Thus, a clearer picture of the nature of race in American politics requires more complex measures that shift attention to the voters themselves, and examine what they want and which candidates they favor. A more complete metric of minority representation could take into account the preferences of voters, and assess whether election outcomes match those preferences. Under this rubric, the question is no longer whether minority *candidates* win. The question, instead, is: Do minority *voters* win?

Counting Winners and Losers

In this chapter, I use this voter-oriented measure of winning and losing to gauge the fate of minorities (and other groups) in American democracy. I develop a simple measure of success and failure in the electoral arena. For any given voter in any given election, I simply ask, does your favored candidate ultimately win the election or lose the election? For each election, I compare voters from different demographic groups to see which types of voters are more likely to win and which types are more likely to lose. I repeat this for a wide range of elections and different demographic groups to attain a more global assessment of how well members of different groups fare in democracy. After the tabulations are complete, I compare the proportion of winners and losers across a range of key demographic characteristics that regularly divide the electorate. I examine two questions: Are racial minorities regularly and repeatedly on the losing side of democracy? And are outcomes skewed more by race than by other dimensions?

Why Counting Winners and Losers Makes Sense

In a democratic system, winners and losers are defined by the outcome of the vote. If your side gets more votes, you win. If your side gets fewer votes, you lose. Counting winners and losers in the vote thus gets at the heart of democracy. How often the members of a group win or lose, therefore, seems to provide a direct and telling overall account of democratic outcomes.

A count of winners and losers also gets at basic notions of fairness and equity. If members of different groups all end up on the winning side of the vote a roughly equal amount of the time, then outcomes do not appear to be particularly biased against any group. If, on the other hand, members from one group consistently end up on the losing side of democracy, then it seems likely that their interests are not being well represented by the system in which they live.[5]

A key aspect of this measure is that it requires no subjective evaluation of minority interests. Minorities themselves choose which side they are on. If they favor a White candidate and that candidate wins, they win. Likewise, if they oppose a minority candidate and that minority candidate loses, the voter wins again.

Another advantage of counting winners and losers in this way is that it incorporates the preferences of every member of a given group, regardless of whether they vote with or against the group's majority-preferred candidate. That contrasts with descriptive representation, which essentially assumes that minority voters are all of one mind, and all favor one racial and ethnic minority candidate. The reality, however, is that support within the minority population in any given election is typically far from unanimous. How can analysis take into account the outcomes for those minority voters who opt for a candidate of a different race? Is it fair to count those minority voters who opposed minority leadership as being well represented when their preferred candidate loses? If, instead, I include every member of the group and simply record whether he or she won or lost, all of their preferences are incorporated into the overall count. If a group is evenly divided, that is reflected in the fact that half end up winners and half end up losers. If a group is almost unanimous in its preferences – as, say, African Americans are in the typical national contest – that will also be reflected in the measure.

Looking at voters and their electoral outcomes also has the added benefit of coming closer to standards that are often used in court cases involving minority voting rights. The Voting Rights Act itself and legal rulings based on the act have in recent decades made it clear that racial and ethnic minorities should have the same right as others "to elect a representative of their choice" (Section II of the Voting Rights Act). If your choice consistently loses, you almost by definition have less opportunity to elect representatives of your choice. Thus, counting votes and adding up winners and losers by race and ethnicity offers an assessment that closely approaches the core legal metric of "minority vote dilution," the rate at which minority voters lose elections, which courts view as a critical standard (Grofman and Davidson 1994). As a result, we have data on the fate of minority voters in some particular cities and districts.[6]

Unfortunately, while an assessment of winners and losers has regularly been undertaken at the local level in Voting Rights Act cases, it has not been used more broadly to assess the nation as a whole. Despite the intuitive logic of the measure, scholars have yet to provide an overall accounting of the rate at which minority voters win or lose in American elections.

Concerns with Counting Winners and Losers

It is important to recognize that counting winners and losers is by no means a perfect test. If minority voters have no good option among the available candidates, then the outcome does not matter. Most African-American voters, for example, are likely to have no real choice in a Republican Party primary in the south featuring two candidates who support the Confederate flag, monuments to the Civil War's Confederate leaders, the repeal of Obamacare, retrenchment on education and welfare spending, and other policies that are strongly opposed by the clear majority of African-American voters. In this case, regardless of who wins, Black voters lose. Of course, African Americans rarely vote in Republican primaries in the South. But other similarly limited choices can and do occur at different electoral levels for public office in different parts of the county. This means that even if minorities win at the same rate as Whites, outcomes may not be equal. Winning and losing should offer a rough sense of the balance of power in American democracy, but it will not reveal exactly how well represented each group is.

Another limitation warrants mention. A count of voters' wins and losses tells us little about what happens *after* the election. Government policies will likely follow voters' choices, at least partially. But that will not always be the case. Thus, studying the ensuing policymaking period is also important. This is the only way to evaluate whether minorities are substantively represented in the aftermath of elections. (Chapter 4 examines post-election policy outcomes.) Nevertheless, counting winners is an important element of a much broader evaluation of minority interests in democracy.

Finally, a focus on individual voting behavior also implicitly assumes that voters are informed enough to make reasonable decisions about candidates. Given that scholars have argued that many Americans simply do not have enough information about politics to make reasoned, rational decisions, this may be a difficult assumption for some to accept (Converse 1964, Delli Carpini and Keeter 1996). However, more recent scholarship seems to suggest that the average American can use a range of shortcuts to make reasonable decisions in the political arena (Lupia 1994, Popkin 1991). Scholars find that the vast majority of voters end up choosing the candidate whose positions are closest to the voter's positions (Bartels 1996, Lau and Redlawsk 1997).[7] In other words, most voters vote correctly.

At the end of the day, a count of winners and losers, while imperfect, says a great deal about how well different groups are faring in democracy.

Adding Up Elections

The outcomes of one or two elections cannot reveal much about the broader contours of representation in American politics. A true understanding of who wins and who loses in American politics requires an examination of an array of the voting experience that has emerged nationwide in elections over many years for different types of offices, and at different levels of government. In essence, I need a global assessment of electoral outcomes in the United States. Thus, I gathered election results and data on individual voting preferences for a wide number of presidential, congressional, state-level, and local elections in the United States over the course of two decades. Specifically, I compiled winners and losers for all elections represented in the *Voter News Service* data series from 1994 to 2006 – a period that includes three presidential, 139 gubernatorial, 198 senatorial, and 919 congressional contests. The data set includes 298,000 individual votes, a volume of opinions that exceeds most other survey resources.[8] Additionally, for the mayoral votes, I collected all available data by race/ethnicity for any contested primary or general election that occurred in the nation's twenty largest cities between 1989 and 2009.[9] All told I collected data for ninety-one mayoral elections.

These elections do not offer a complete picture of democracy in America. The data set does not include state legislative contests, direct democracy ballot initiatives, or local offices below the mayoralty.[10] But these data represent a broad enough set of cases that the patterns they expose cannot be dismissed as mere anomalies.

Who Loses?

When the vote is counted, who tends to lose in American elections? I provide one of the first comprehensive answers to that question in Table 3.1. The table shows the proportion of different demographic voter groups that supported losing candidates in presidential, senatorial, gubernatorial, congressional, and mayoral elections. The last

Table 3.1 Who Loses in American Democracy?

	Percent of Voters on the Losing Side – Elections for .... Percent					
	President	Senate	House	Governor	Mayor	Super Losers
RACE						
African Americans	59%	55%	29%	52%	53%	41%
Whites	50	42	43	44	47	9
Latinos	54	55	32	52	52	4
Asian Americans	59	34	31	42	53	14
INCOME						
Low	53	46	46	47	–	17
Middle	51	43	43	46	–	12
High	50	41	40	44	–	9
EDUCATION						
High school or less	51	46	47	45	–	13
Some college	50	46	45	45	–	17
College Grad	54	43	47	45	–	14
GENDER						
Men	51	44	44	45	–	11
Women	52	43	38	45	–	12
AGE						
18–29	52	44	40	47	–	15
30–49	51	43	41	45	–	11
50+	51	43	39	45	–	10
RELIGION						
Catholic	51	42	45	43	–	9
Protestant	46	42	47	45	–	7
Jewish	62	37	47	49	–	0
No Affiliation	65	47	37	48	–	17
URBANICITY						
City	65	48	42	47	–	–
Suburb	52	43	46	48	–	–
Rural	47	42	49	42	–	–
ORIENTATION						
Gay/Lesbian	–	48	–	43	–	–
Heterosexual	–	41	–	45	–	–

Source: Voter News Service Exit Polls (1994–2006), Mayoral Elections Data Set

column also shows the proportion of voters from each demographic group that voted for the loser in the presidential, senatorial, and gubernatorial election in the same year – a group which I refer to as "Super Losers."

I look not just at the race and ethnicity of the voters but also at an array of other demographic dividing lines that shape the American public. The issue is to understand not just whether racial minorities lose regularly, but also, crucially, whether racial minorities lose more or less often than other potentially disadvantaged groups. Do members of the lower classes also tend to be on the outside looking in? Are particular religious groups, distinct age groups, or certain sexual orientations also associated with losing?

The first and probably the most obvious conclusion is that no one group is totally shut out from the winning side of electoral democracy. Across all of the demographic groups and all of the types of elections, the worst outcome for any single group is to end up on the losing side of the vote 65 percent of the time. In most cases, the majority of voters from each group end up on the winning side of the vote. America's democracy may be divided, but it is not the case that an overwhelming majority consistently wins out against a united minority voting bloc.

This does not mean that all groups win equally often. The top of the table reveals a clear racial hierarchy, with Whites on the top and African Americans on the bottom. During this period, Blacks are the least successful group in American elections. Blacks are the only group that loses more than half the time in most contests. A majority of all Black voters ends up on the losing side in presidential elections (59 percent), senatorial elections (55 percent), gubernatorial elections (52 percent), and mayoral elections (53 percent). The one important exception for Black voters is House elections, where some 74 percent of Black voters end up getting their favored candidate into office. (I discuss the distinctiveness of House elections in more depth later in this chapter.) African Americans stood out compared to almost all groups – be it racial, political, or demographic. No group, aside from Latinos, loses more than half the time in more than one type of contest.

The limited success of African Americans in mayoral elections is especially striking. These elections occur in cities where Blacks make up a much larger share of the electorate (28 percent) than at the national level, and where the electorate tends to be significantly more Democratic than the national population.[11] If Black voters were going to be on the winning side anywhere, one would expect it to be in these disproportionately Black and liberal cities. The mayoral results are illuminating for one other reason: The vast majority of these contests are non-partisan, which suggests that Black losses are not entirely a function of partisan contests leading to Republican winners.

At the other end of the racial spectrum, White voters stand out for their consistent success. In particular, for four of the five different kinds of contests, White voters are substantially more likely than Black and Latino voters to win. Whites win half or more of the time in every contest, and, in most cases, close to 60 percent of White voters wind up as winners. This leads to a fairly substantial racial gap. The difference between White and Black success is 13 points for the Senate, 12 points in gubernatorial contests, 9 points in presidential contests, and 6 points for the mayoralty.

Latino voters fare almost as poorly as Blacks. In four of the five types of contests, a slim majority of Latino voters ends up on the losing side and in two sets of these elections, Latinos lose just as often as Blacks. Latinos fare substantially better than Blacks in only one type of contest. In presidential elections Latino voters are 5 percent more likely to end up winners than African-American voters. Asian Americans are the most difficult racial group to characterize because they have the most mixed outcomes – sometimes surpassing Whites and sometimes losing more than any other racial group.[12]

Super Losers

In some ways, these figures understate the depth of America's racial hierarchy. Looking at each type of election in isolation cannot tell us how often *individual* voters lose across multiple elections. If, however, one looks simultaneously at an individual's vote in three elections (president, Senate, and governor), as I do in the last column of the table, the consistency with which African Americans lose is even more apparent.[13] Overall, 41 percent of all Black voters can be characterized as "super losers," meaning that they choose the loser in all three contests. By contrast, only 9 percent of Whites, 4 percent of Latinos, and 14 percent of Asian Americans can be categorized as super losers. By this measure, Blacks stand out from every other demographic group in the United States. Blacks also stand out in terms of how often they win. Across the three contests, the average Black voter wins only 0.76 times, a rate that is far below the figure for Whites (1.67 wins on average), Latinos (1.87 wins), and Asian Americans (1.14 wins).[14]

Class and Other Demographics

Importantly, none of the other demographic factors seems to have a consistent impact on winning and losing in American elections. Looking more closely at class, one sees little indication that lower-class Americans are particularly disadvantaged in these electoral contests. Members of the lower class – as measured by income and education – win more than half of the time in at least three of the four types of contests.[15] Class may be an important factor in other aspects of American democracy, but it appears to play little role here.

Indeed, I could find no group other than racial minorities that tended to lose more often than win. Members of every non-racial group in the table win more than half of the time in most types of elections. In terms of losing, no consistent pattern emerges for age, gender, religion, urbanicity, or sexual orientation. City residents, for example, may have fared worse than any other group in the three presidential contests, but they wound up as regular winners in the other three types of contests. Rural voters were, however, reasonably successful in most types of contests. When I dug deeper, I could find no connection between region and electoral victory.

Is Race Really the Cause?

Racial and ethnic minorities, and in particular African-American voters, appear to be especially disadvantaged in American electoral politics. Across this broad range of contests, Blacks are consistently more likely than all others to find themselves losing. But is race really driving these results? Perhaps race is just a proxy for political affiliation. The two biggest losers here, Blacks and Latinos, are more likely than most other groups to support Democrats. It could be that party and politics, rather than race, drive these patterns. Are Black and Latino voters losing simply because they happen to be liberal and Democratic at a time when conservatives and Republicans are more frequently coming out on top?[16]

To assess this possibility, and, more broadly, to isolate the independent effect of each demographic characteristic, I estimated the effect of race on losing after controlling for each individual's political preferences (party identification and ideology) and all other demographic characteristics. Figure 3.1 presents the results of this individual-

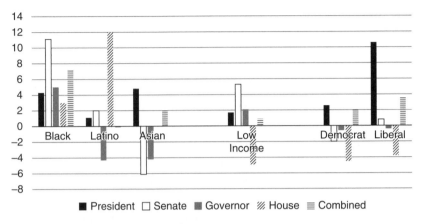

Figure 3.1. Relative Probability of Losing
Source: Voter News Service exit polls. The analysis includes controls for age, gender, religion, region, the margin of victory, and voter turnout in each contest

level analysis. It shows the estimated effect of race, class, and political leaning on the probability of being a loser for each type of election.[17] Outcomes for each racial group are compared to Whites; low-income Americans are compared to high-income Americans; and those on the political left are compared to individuals on the right.

The figure is telling. Even after considering political views and party identification, African-American voters are substantially more likely than Whites to be on the losing side of democracy for every type of election. As can be seen in the figure, Blacks are 11 percent more likely than Whites to lose in senatorial contests, 5 percent more likely to lose in gubernatorial elections, 3 percent more likely to lose in congressional contests, and 4 percent more likely to lose in presidential elections.[18] The figure also indicates that Blacks are 7.2 percent more likely than Whites to become super losers, all else equal. This does not mean that all Blacks lose. But many do lose, and lose consistently across all types of contests.[19] At the end of the day Blacks are distinctively disadvantaged in American democracy, and that disadvantage is not simply due to their liberal or Democratic tendencies. There is something unique about their role in American society or American politics that singles them out as the biggest losers.

No other political or demographic group ends up as losers as consistently across the four types of elections. In terms of race and ethnicity, the results for Asian Americans and Latinos are both mixed but tend to suggest that Latinos are somewhat disadvantaged, while

Asian Americans may be slightly privileged in American democracy. In two cases (Senate and House elections), Latinos are substantially more likely than Whites to end up losers (2 percent and 12 percent more likely, respectively) and in another (presidential elections) they win slightly less often than Whites. For Asian Americans, the pattern is one of sometimes winning disproportionately (Senate and governor) and sometime losing disproportionately (president and combined).

These findings suggest that there is a racial hierarchy to American elections. Whites appear to be the most privileged voters in American democracy. When election results have been posted, their preferences are more likely to triumph than to be defeated. The story changes as one moves down the racial hierarchy. Asian Americans, the other racial group that maintains a relatively privileged economic status, tend to fall somewhere near the middle of the spectrum. Latinos are not consistent losers, but they are clearly more likely than Whites and Asian Americans to lose in most American elections. Then there are African-American voters. They reside at the bottom of the spectrum. In every type of contest I examined, African Americans – and African Americans only – always lose disproportionately.

Returning to the figure, I find once again that class has little clear impact on winning or losing the vote. The effects of having a low income are both small and inconsistent – sometimes leading to slightly higher rates of losing, but sometimes leading to slightly lower rates of losing. Likewise, I find that having a low level of education (e.g. less than a high school degree) had no consistent effect on losing.

How is this possible? Income inequality is growing. The rich and the poor lead lives that are so different from each other. And study after study has found that the rich dominate American politics (Bartels 2008, Gilens 2012). All of this may be true but the reality is – as we saw in Chapter 1 – that rich and poor tend to agree more than they disagree. Rich and poor tend to favor the same candidates. The votes of those with higher levels of education are not that different from the votes of those with lower levels of education. Because class does not really divide us politically, class does not have a big impact on determining winners and losers. These results stand in sharp contrast to the results for race, a source of true political division. Once race is taken into account, class becomes peripheral.

This is not to say that class never matters in American democracy. As Chapter 2 demonstrates, the halls of power include relatively few working-class Americans (see also Carnes 2013). And there seems little doubt that wealthy interest groups are sometime able to effectively lobby to shift policy outcomes in their direction (Gilens and Page 2014). But by the standard of who wins and loses the vote, class makes little difference in American elections.

Critically, politics also plays no clear role. Democrats are more likely than Republicans to end up on the losing side of presidential contests. But the effects are not particularly large (3 percent more likely to lose). Moreover, Democrats fare marginally better than Republicans (5 percent less likely to lose) in one case (House elections), all else equal. In the other two types of elections, Democrats are no more or less likely to lose than Republicans. Similarly, liberals are disproportionate losers in one case (presidential elections), disproportionate winners in another case (House elections), and on a par with conservatives in the other two types of contests. It is African Americans – and only African Americans – who are consistently less likely to win.[20]

Do Some Whites Lose More?

Another way to assess whether race is the central factor driving outcomes is to look at different sub-types of White voters. Are outcomes for lower-class Whites, for example, different from outcomes for middle-class Whites? And, more generally, is there a "type" of White voter who loses as consistently as Black voters?

The short answer is no. I examined outcomes for different subsets of White voters that combined different characteristics of education, income, religion, and political orientation. Although there were marginal differences, and some groups such as White liberals were somewhat less successful than the median White voter, no combination of characteristics led to losing on a par with Black voters. Once again, I find that Black voters are uniquely disadvantaged in American elections.

When Do Blacks Lose?

Though these results are discouraging for those interested in the representation of African Americans, they provide only a general overview of Black success rates. These aggregate patterns hide considerable variation across time and context. A better understanding of where and when Black voters are successful might help to identify reforms that could lead to greater balance in American democracy.

For example, Blacks experience greater success in House elections. House elections are, of course, the only elections in the data in which electoral boundaries are regularly manipulated. The fact that Blacks (and Latinos) appear to do much better in the one area of democracy in which district lines are repeatedly reshaped (as opposed to the established borders of a given state or city) reinforces the view that gerrymandering can strongly benefit minority voters.[21] The larger implication is that minority interests may be more fully incorporated in democracy if district lines can be drawn so that minority voters are paired with other minority voters or like-minded members of the majority group.[22] Of course, none of this means that redistricting cannot be used to try to reduce minority influence, a pattern that may be occurring in several states around the country (Newkirk II 2017).

There are also important variations in Black success across time and context. In additional analysis, I attempted to determine how different contexts affect the success of Black voters in senatorial and gubernatorial elections – two of the cases in which Blacks fare the worst.[23] In two separate regressions, I examined the role of a series of state-level factors that have in the past been linked to Black representation (Grofman and Davidson 1992, Huckfeldt and Kohfeld 1989, Key 1949, Manza 2006).[24] In particular, I assessed: the role of state politics and partisanship (percentage Democrats, percentage Republicans, and mean citizen ideology); key state demographics (percentage Black, and percentage with only a high school degree); and measures of institutional barriers to voting (whether a state is under the jurisdiction of Section 5 of the Voting Rights Act, level of felon disenfranchisement, how long before the election voters must register, and eligible voter turnout).[25] To gauge how electoral outcomes vary for Blacks over time, I also included the year of the election. Finally, to determine if Black failure is restricted to certain types of Black voters, I incorporated typical measures of individual socioeconomic status and individual political orientation. The dependent variable is the same – whether or not the respondent ended up on the losing side of the election.[26]

The results (displayed in the appendix) tell a largely familiar story. Black voters are more successful when they live in states that are more Democratic, more liberal, and less Republican. The effects are dramatic. All else equal, Black voters in more liberal, Democratic states are 74 percent less likely to lose in Senate elections (38 percent more likely to lose in gubernatorial contests) than Black voters in more conservative, Republican states. Black success in American democracy rests substantially on the willingness of their neighbors to support a liberal, Democratic agenda.

Also, as expected, the size of the Black population matters. The relationship is, however, a complex one. Mirroring other studies of Black-White relations, there is an inverse U-shaped relationship between the proportion of the state's population that is Black and electoral outcomes (Blalock 1967). Black voters in Senate elections are quite successful when the Black population is small (only 44 percent lose in states that are 7 percent Black), but as the Black population grows White resistance to Black interests grows. Black failure peaks in about the median state (15 percent Black), where the likelihood of losing grows to 65 percent. Then, as Blacks become a more numerous and decisive voting bloc, the likelihood of ending up on the losing side of the vote declines to 58 percent (in states with a 29 percent Black population). In gubernatorial elections, the benefits of living in a state with a large Black population are even more pronounced. The likelihood of losing drops from 58 percent in the median state to 32 percent in states with a large Black population. It is not just the racial make-up of the population that matters. In line with research showing that less-educated Americans are more intolerant and less prone to support pro-Black policy, the analysis here indicates that Black voters in Senate elections are 8 percent more likely to end up winners in more educated states (Schuman et al. 1997).

The last critical factor for Black voters is whether they reside in a state that is covered under Section 5 of the Voting Rights Act (Black and Black 1987, Menifield 2001).[27] States with a history of disenfranchising African Americans continue to have reduced Black representation today. Blacks in Voting Rights Act states are 15 percent more likely to be defeated in Senate elections – even after controlling for the partisan leaning, racial make-up, and educational attainment of the population in a given state. In gubernatorial elections, this gap (between Voting Rights Act states and other states) grows to 26 percent. This is an important finding in light of the Supreme Court's decision in Shelby v. Holder. In that landmark 2013 case, the Supreme Court effectively gutted core elements of the Voting Rights Act; the five-to-four vote contended that there was little recent evidence of covered jurisdictions limiting minority representation. The data from voter outcomes, however, suggest that minority representation continues to be especially limited in states covered by the Voting Rights Act.

A number of frequently mentioned institutional levers appear to be much less consequential for African-American representation than might have been thought.[28] Contrary to concerns about the anti-Black implications of felon disenfranchisement laws (Manza 2006), these laws have no consistent effects on Black outcomes. The effect of registration deadlines on outcomes for Blacks is also mixed. Alternate tests further indicate that a range of reforms that attempt to make voting easier and more open (e.g. allowing early voting, mailing sample ballot, and vote-by-mail) have no clear effect on Black representation. This parallels results demonstrating that these reforms have at best a marginal impact on turnout (Blais 2006, Gronke et al. 2007). It may be, as some have argued, that reforms in recent decades have so reduced the ability of states to set their own registration procedures, and to alter their electoral institutions that state laws today are of little consequence to democratic outcomes (Highton 2004).

Half Full or Half Empty?

A count of winners and losers in American elections reveals a mixed story about outcomes in American democracy. From one perspective, the patterns tell a relatively positive story. There is nothing close to a pattern of total tyranny of the majority. Most racial, demographic, and political groups win more often than they lose in most types of electoral contests. There are winners and losers across all groups – White or Black, privileged or not. Put simply, the results are not all that bad.

But from a second perspective the data raise alarms. Clearly, certain groups end up as winners far more regularly, and certain groups routinely end up as losers. Critically, race, more than anything else, helps define the winners and losers. White voters, as many would have predicted, are the most privileged. Election results show that their preferences win much more often than those of other groups. And African Americans, perhaps too predictably, are the most disadvantaged. Blacks are substantially more likely than Whites to lose across every type of contest. Fully 41 percent of Black voters lost in every contest I could examine. Latinos are not too far behind in the losing column. These patterns raise legitimate questions. Do groups that lose so regularly have enough of a say in the political arena? Are these patterns so imbalanced that they cast doubt on the inherent fairness of American democracy?

Such concerns about minority interests only grow when the consequences of losing the vote are taken into account. One of those consequences is feeling isolated and ignored. The surveys examined here do not ask voters how they feel about the outcomes of the elections, but others have looked closely at what winning and losing does to a voter. These studies indicate that voting for a losing candidate has real consequences. Supporters of losing candidates have substantially lower levels of trust in government, less political efficacy, and greater feelings of powerlessness (Anderson and LoTempio 2002, Craig et al. 2006). These studies also find that losers are less satisfied with government performance, and are more apt to believe that the electoral system is unfair (Anderson and Guillory 1997, Craig et al. 2006, Nadeau and Blais 1993). Finally, losers are more likely to want to reform electoral institutions (Bowler and Donovan 2006).

It should, therefore, come as no surprise that nationally African Americans and to a lesser extent Latinos feel substantially more dissatisfied with American democracy. Wide gaps emerge in the degree to which members of different racial groups believe they are represented, as evidenced in surveys that put the question to voters in a wide range of circumstances. Study after study has shown that minorities – and most emphatically African Americans – are much less satisfied than White Americans with government (Hajnal and Trounstine 2013, Rahn and Rudolph 2005). Blacks and other minorities are also less trusting of the political process and feel they have less of a say than others (Marschall and Shah 2007). A high share of the Black population expresses little hope for the future of American democracy. Almost half of Blacks believe equality will never be achieved (Pew 2017c). Of course, a range of factors beyond winning and losing elections is driving these sentiments among minorities. But if Blacks and to a lesser extent Latinos feel dissatisfied, disengaged, and powerless because they believe their votes do not count, then American democracy has a real problem.

What, if anything, can address these issues? The very preliminary analysis presented here points to gerrymandering as one potential solution. African-American voters fare better when they are placed in districts with other racial and ethnic minorities and like-minded

Whites.[29] State-level results echo the advantages of living in proximity to more Blacks and more liberal, Democratic Whites.[30] In addition, many other reforms beyond the scope of the research presented here offer potential. Advocates of proportional representation, cumulative voting, and a number of other alternatives have offered some evidence of the merits of these alternate institutions (Bowler et al. 2003, Guinier 1994). At the same time, before advocating for any of these reforms, a better understanding of variations in minority representation across different contexts is required.

Perhaps the best way to assess the implications of a losing vote is to see if losing has broader consequences for other more downstream outcomes in democracy. Logically, one would expect losses in the vote to translate into losses on policy. Presumably, people support candidates who promise policies that serve their own interests. They oppose candidates who favor policies that could harm their own interests. If your candidate loses, then your policy preferences likely lose, too. Losing the vote on election day could mean losing throughout the democratic process. Thus, in the next chapter, I assess these broader consequences for policymaking in American democracy.

4 WHO WINS ON POLICY?

When President Donald Trump signed the Tax Cuts and Jobs Act of 2017, his signature put into effect one of the biggest tax cuts in the history of American democracy.[1] The act that Trump and the Republican majority in the House and Senate implemented was remarkable for another reason: the overwhelming majority of Americans did not favor it. Only 26 percent of Americans polled before the bill's passage approved of the bill. And it is not as if the American public was not watching or did not care. Nearly half of all Americans – 43 percent – said they would be less likely to vote for a senator or congressperson who supported the tax plan.[2] Yet, despite such opposition, Trump and the Republican Party not only passed the law, but they triumphally fêted its passage. As Trump proclaimed at a ceremony on the White House lawn to celebrate the passing of the sweeping tax bill, "It's always a lot of fun when you win" (Walsh et al. 2017). Republican leaders who joined him on the lawn were equally ebullient. This was, after all, the signature policy initiative of the first years of the Trump presidency.

The passage of a law that runs counter to public preferences seems strange in a democracy. Shouldn't elected officials who owe their position to voters govern according to the preferences of their constituents? Shouldn't citizens vote out elected officials who go against their wishes? How does all of this work in the American context?

In this chapter, I ask whether government does, in fact, do what the public wants. Or, more precisely, does government do what the broader public wants, or does it, instead, act on the wishes of a relatively small and relatively advantaged segment of the public? These questions lie at the very heart of the democratic process. If a government's actions generally reflect the public's preferences, then we tend to think of that government as responsive and, therefore, as reasonably democratic.[3] If, however, a ruling regime does not follow the public's preferences at all, then it can hardly be deemed a democracy. The question of policy responsiveness also lies at the core of my efforts in this book. We care deeply about who wins the vote, and who wins election, but what matters more is what government does after an election. Who wins then? Does American government follow the preferences of some groups? Does it ignore some groups? Do our nation's policies reflect the views and interests of a broad array of the public, including Blacks and other disadvantaged groups? Or is government operating largely for Whites and the privileged few?

Existing Views on Government Responsiveness

I am not the first to try to gauge winners and losers in the policy world. Indeed, research into policy responsiveness in American democracy has a long history. Early studies provided relatively reassuring findings. In a landmark study, Warren Miller and Donald Stokes showed that the voting records of members of Congress often closely tracked constituent opinions in their districts (Miller and Stokes 1963). Two decades later, Ben Page and Robert Shapiro showed that large shifts in national public opinion on a particular issue were often followed by a similar shift in federal government policy. They found, for example, that the Civil Rights Act was passed shortly after public opinion shifted, revealing that a clear majority of the public was, for the first time, in favor of a law giving Blacks "the right to be served in public places." Likewise, the Supreme Court's Roe v. Wade decision making abortion legal came only after the share of Americans who thought abortions should be legal had grown dramatically (Page and Shapiro 1983).[4] These findings seem to suggest that government closely follows the interests of the masses, and that American democracy functions relatively well.[5]

But spurred in part by growing inequality and the increasing role of money in politics, scholars have recently revisited the issue of government responsiveness, and they have uncovered glaring inequalities in that responsiveness. This new generation of research examines whether the actions of government correlate more with the opinions of some classes of Americans than of others.[6] The findings are alarming.[7] After perhaps the most encompassing study of public preferences and policy change, Martin Gilens offers this bleak conclusion about American democracy: "What I find is hard to reconcile with the notion of political equality ... responsiveness is strongly tilted toward the most affluent citizens. Indeed, under most circumstances, the preferences of the vast majority of Americans appear to have essentially no impact on which policies the government does or does not adopt" (Gilens 2012:1).[8] Larry Bartels' seminal study of class and the voting patterns of senators likewise finds that "the views of constituents in the bottom third of the income distribution received no weight at all in the voting decisions of their senators" (Bartels 2008:254). Perhaps the most egregious example was one failed 1989 attempt to raise the minimum wage, in which the voices of the poor were essentially ignored even though they were the ones most directly impacted by the proposed measure. These are eye-opening and deeply troubling findings. They have not gone unnoticed. Anger over inequality in government responsiveness drove many Americans to unite under the Occupy Wall Street movement. The chanting of "We are the 99 percent," and the request for "A government accountable to the people, freed up from corporate influence," underscores that participants were drawn to the movement by outrage over inequality in government responsiveness.[9]

Although the lion's share of recent attention has focused on income-based inequalities, at least one study has looked at race and the question of whether the policy actions of government are more closely aligned with the preferences of Whites than they are with those of racial and ethnic minorities.[10] The results here are equally disturbing and compelling. John Griffin and Brian Newman have shown quite convincingly that government policymakers weigh the opinions of Whites much more than the views of Blacks and Latinos. One need only point to the Tax Cuts and Jobs Act of 2017 as a prime illustration of this racial imbalance. Although Americans as a whole opposed the measure, that opposition was racially uneven. Polls showed that 80 percent of Blacks and 72 percent of Latinos opposed the Republican tax cuts. By contrast, less than half of Whites (48 percent) opposed the measure. Many Americans lost when the bill passed, but racial and ethnic minorities lost more. Race, it appears, is also driving who wins and who loses in the policy world.

The sense that both race and class are helping to shape political inequality is emerging from research and from the American experience. Nonetheless deep questions remain about the relationship between the two. Studies of class-based inequalities in representation almost never account for race; studies of race-based inequalities almost never account for income. Thus, the question of whether income or race is the chief driver of political inequality remains unanswered. The lack of research that simultaneously explores both is especially problematic given that race and class are so deeply intertwined in the United States. Two figures underscore the connection: 66 percent of the poor in this country are non-White; 9 percent of the wealthy are non-White (Keister 2014).[11] Is the lack of responsiveness largely a function of class or largely a function of race? No one knows.

Also lacking is an understanding of how much other core divisions in American politics help shape responsiveness. As Chapter 2 underscores, religion – perhaps even more so than class – structures our political choices. Liberal scholars and activists have repeatedly lamented what they view as the oversize influence of the religious right on our politics (Skocpol and Williamson 2013). Could religion trump race and class in determining whose voices are heard? How about gender? It would not be surprising to find that the interests of men dominate policy decisions, given that the vast majority of elected officials are men, and that women still earn only 79 percent of what men earn (Blau and Kahn 2017). Significant differences of opinion surface among people of different ages and of different sexual orientations. Other demographic dividing lines could shape the policy world.

None of these other demographic factors has been incorporated into previous analyses of policy responsiveness. Yet all could clearly be important. A study that brings together all of these different factors could distinguish the sets of voices that hold sway in the policymaking arena from those that do not. That is the task to which I now turn.

Trying to Assess Race, Class, and Everything Else: A New Method

To assess the relative roles of race, class, and other factors in policy responsiveness I employ a novel but relatively straightforward research design. I gauge the congruence between individual-level policy preferences and policy outcomes. That is, I examine whether government spending matches preferences expressed by Americans in response to surveys about their spending preferences across eleven core policy areas. For example, if you favor more military spending, does the federal government respond by substantially increasing military spending? Or does it ignore your preference and choose instead to spend at the same or lower levels? In this way, I can see whose preferences end up mirroring policy outcomes and whose do not in eleven spending areas: welfare, national defense, education, foreign aid, parks and recreation, law enforcement, improving and protecting the nation's health, solving the problems of big cities, improving and protecting the environment, the space exploration program, and highways and bridges. These eleven areas do not cover all issues of concern to the public or even all major government spending areas, but they do address many of the most important spending decisions the government makes, and, collectively, they cover half of the federal budget. They should provide a relatively broad window into policy responsiveness in American democracy.

This method is unlike most existing studies in that I gauge congruence between *individual-level* policy preferences and policy outcomes rather than *group-level* policy preferences. For example, I do not look at average Black preferences. I instead focus on the preferences of each individual African American.

This focus on the individual level has several key advantages over an examination of group-level preferences. One advantage is that I do not assume that all members of a group have the same preferences. To assess policy representation, existing studies have generally had to assume that there is one preferred outcome for the group as a whole. This essentially ignores the interests and preferences of any group members who oppose the group's majority-preferred outcome. In any group, a mix of views will surface on almost every imaginable policy choice. White Americans, for example, tend to be fairly divided over spending on cities. In the data set, 38 percent favor a spending increase, 37 percent would prefer no change, and 24 percent opt for a decrease. Are Whites well represented when spending on cities increases? And even when there is a clear majority – as there is on foreign aid, where 73 percent of Whites favor a spending decrease – the preferences of the group are far from unanimous.[12] An accurate measure of representation thus requires the incorporation of each individual's preferences into the analysis.

What makes matters worse is that cohesion – as we have already seen – varies greatly from group to group. Blacks, for example, tend to be more cohesive politically then Latinos, Asian Americans, or Whites. And racial groups, in general, are often more cohesive than members of a given economic class. Because some groups are much more cohesive than others, existing studies that focus only on mean group opinion will understate or overstate the influence of members of these different groups. By contrast, with this new method one can incorporate the preferences of all individuals regardless of whether or not they agree with their group's majority position. Every individual and every opinion counts.

Critically, by focusing on individual preferences one can also look at several different demographic factors at once. In a larger model, one can simultaneously incorporate race, class, and a range of other individual demographic and political characteristics. Race, class, and many other factors are all closely related, and any or some combination of all of them could be the sources of unequal responsiveness. The kind of analysis I undertake here lets us disentangle each strand from this knot of information. When I have done this, I am able to see which issue – class, race, or some other force – is the primary cause of political inequality.

Finally, by using the individual rather than the group as the unit of analysis, this method essentially controls for the size of each group. Comparing the influence of average White opinion to average Black opinion, as others have done in the past, makes it nearly impossible to tell if the greater influence of White opinion on policy is due to the much larger size of the White population. If one believes that democracy should generally weigh the opinion of the majority more than that of the minority, then interpreting the results of group-level analysis is problematic.[13] In the individual-level approach, because the opinions of each person are counted once, the size of each group is essentially factored in, allowing for a more definitive determination of who wins and who loses in American democracy.

I focus on spending because it is arguably one of the most important indicators of a government's priorities. Where governments spend money (and where they do not) says a lot about how much each policy area is valued. With a federal budget of more than $3 trillion, the government has enormous power to shift resources toward or away from certain groups and certain interests.

At the same time, I recognize that spending is not the only aspect of policy that individual Americans might care about. In criminal justice, for example, individual citizens may care as much or more about the severity of criminal sentencing policy than they do about the amount spent on criminal justice. Likewise, the amount of money spent may be less important than how that money is spent. The choice in criminal justice might, for example, be between money for prisons or money for rehabilitation. Thus, the analysis represents an important but far-from-complete picture of policy responsiveness in the American context.

The data on spending preferences come from the General Social Survey (GSS), which has asked a wide swath of Americans about their opinions on spending for almost fifty years.[14] All told, I have been able to compile more than 400,000 individual spending preferences across eleven core policy areas between 1972 and 2010.[15] The sample of opinion is both representative and large. This suggests the final advantage of the data set: its scope. By looking over an extensive time period – spanning almost four decades – and by incorporating an array of issues from welfare and health care at one end of the spectrum to the military, foreign aid, and space exploration at the other, I can examine not only the overall pattern of who wins and who loses in American policy contests but also the variation in responsiveness over time, across issue areas, and across potentially critical economic and political contexts. I can assess who wins overall – as well as who wins at particular times and on particular issues.

In the surveys, individual Americans are asked whether they think the government should increase spending in a particular area, decrease spending, or keep spending at about the same level.[16] To see if they get what they want, I match those individual preferences with actual federal government spending outcomes in each area. Fortunately, the eleven policy areas in the surveys match up nicely with "functions" defined in the federal budget.[17] Combining individual preferences and governmental spending patterns, I can observe whose policy preferences are enacted by government and whose are not. If, for example, a particular individual favored a decline in federal welfare spending, and the federal government chose to significantly decrease welfare spending in the following year, that individual is a policy "winner."[18]

In each case I match individual spending preferences on a given issue in a given year with changes in government spending on that same issue in the *following* fiscal year. That one-year time difference is important to know if public opinion actually leads to policy change.[19] By focusing on changes in government spending in the year after the public expresses its preferences, this approach comes much closer to testing whether or not government is responsive.

Another issue that one has to consider is how to define what constitutes a change in government spending. Because no single cut-off point is obvious or compelling, I use a range of different cut-offs in the analysis. For the main analysis, I measure change as any spending increase/decrease that is greater than a one standard deviation shift in annual spending change in that policy area. This measure highlights spending changes that are larger than normal, and it might be what citizens are actually thinking about when they indicate a preference for spending increases/decreases. But to ensure that the results are not dependent on this particular cut-off, I re-analyze the data with several other cut-offs.[20]

Another issue involves whether individual Americans actually hold meaningful opinions on these spending measures. Individual Americans may not have thought much about these spending questions, and they may not know what government is doing. If true, they may not be able to express coherent or meaningful views in surveys. I readily admit that survey opinions often represent ill-informed, top-of-the-head responses.[21] All survey analyses should, therefore, be undertaken with a real dose of caution. Null findings are likely to be prevalent. If, however, I find significant patterns, despite this noise, I can be more confident in those relationships.

There is reason to believe that opinions in this particular case are, in general, coherent. First, existing research suggests that opinions on federal government spending are often quite reasoned. As Wlezien and Soroka's (2009) thermostatic model has demonstrated, shifts in public opinion on these spending questions follow logically and predictably from shifts in government spending.

Second, patterns within and across groups are predictable and coherent. A brief examination of the GSS public opinion data reveals that a clear majority of Blacks in the surveys favors spending increases on education (79 percent), health care (79 percent), welfare (61 percent), and cities (58 percent), while a clear majority of Blacks opposes increases on space (96 percent), defense (81 percent), and foreign aid (89 percent). Compared to Whites, Blacks are much more likely to favor increased spending on cities (58 percent vs. 38 percent) and education

(79 percent vs. 65 percent), and much less likely to favor cuts on welfare (16 percent vs. 38 percent). All of this fits with our existing knowledge of the politics of Black and White Americans.

Nevertheless, there is still little doubt that some individual survey respondents will have little interest in and little knowledge of some spending areas. To address this concern, I repeated the analysis by singling out and analyzing only the better educated and more politically engaged respondents. When I do this, I get the same overall pattern of results.[22] In a different test, I repeated the analysis by analyzing the spending areas that tend to get the most attention, as well as those areas that represent the largest share of the federal budget. Both sets of analyses led to conclusions that are essentially identical to those I present here.

Who Wins in the Policy Process?

To capture a global picture of policy responsiveness I simply counted how often members of different demographic groups got what they wanted and how often they did not. Again, if a citizen favored a spending increase (or decrease or no change) in a given policy area and government increased spending (or decreased it or undertook no change) in that policy area in the next year, he or she is viewed as a policy winner. Figure 4.1 presents the overall picture of policy responsiveness that emerged. It shows the percentage of cases in which individuals in various demographic categories were policy winners across the four-decade span of the data.[23]

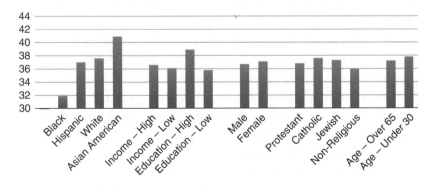

Figure 4.1. Policy Winners
Source: General Social Survey (1972–2000), Historical Tables (US Govt Printing Office)

Looking across the entire figure, a perceptive reader might notice that responsiveness to all groups is relatively low. For every group in the figure, less than half end up policy winners. This may at first be somewhat surprising. But it is more understandable when one considers that there are three different possible spending preferences (increase, decrease, no change) and three different spending outcomes (increase, decrease, no change) so it is unlikely that the two will be perfectly aligned. Also, the fact that governments have limited funds while citizens can effectively favor government spending increases unencumbered by these budget constraints suggests that there will often be mismatches between preferences and spending.[24] In other words, it is not entirely clear what the threshold for high overall representation would be.[25]

The other overall picture that emerges from Figure 4.1 is one of relatively even responsiveness. Most of the group-level differences are relatively small – often less than 1 percentage point. Women, for example, win in the policy realm 37.1 percent of the time – a figure that differs only very marginally from the 36.7 percent success rate for men. The biggest group-level difference (discussed in greater detail later in this chapter) is only 5.7 percentage points. All of this confirms that there is no overwhelming tyranny of the majority. No group is getting what it wants all the time. No group is losing every time. American democracy may not be perfect – a claim I make time and again – but it is not completely shutting out the voices of its minorities.

There are, however, real differences in responsiveness, and the pattern to those differences is a familiar one. Mirroring Chapter 3, race, more than any other factor, once again shapes who wins and who loses in American democracy. Blacks are the least advantaged group, and by a considerable margin. Blacks are winners in only 31.9 percent of cases. The group that comes closest to suffering political losses on a par with Blacks is Americans without a high school education, who win 35.8 percent of the time. Blacks stand out as policy losers, and they very much stand out compared to Whites who, overall, see their favored policy enacted 37.6 percent of the time.

The Black-White gap may not be large – an important point to underscore – but it does dwarf every other group factor that I could examine. Race clearly trumps class. The 5.7-point difference between Blacks and Whites is almost twice as large as the 3.1-point difference between college graduates and high school dropouts, and roughly 10 times larger than the 0.5-point difference between high- and low-income earners. Class may work in the way we would expect it to. Well-educated voters get what they want more than poorly educated voters, and the rich do better than the poor. Nevertheless, gaps in responsiveness are much smaller for class than for race.

Even when I look at more extreme categories, such as the top 10 percent of earners, or the top 1 percent of earners, class still fails to drive policy responsiveness to any great degree. The top 10 percent of earners win on policy 37.9 percent of the time, while the top 1 percent win 36.8 percent of the time. This is a better success rate than among the poor, but surprisingly it is not much better. Alternate analysis of other potential markers of class, such as being unemployed (35.4 percent winners), also fails to reveal major differences in responsiveness.

I can also compare the importance of race and class by looking at how responsiveness varies by class within each racial group. This reveals that income makes essentially no difference among Blacks. Blacks in the top income quartile actually win at about the same rate (32.0 percent) as Blacks in the bottom income quartile (32.1 percent). In other words, Blacks lose more regularly than Whites regardless of their class status. Among Whites, the income gap is in the expected direction but still small (38.8 percent winners for wealthier Whites vs. 36.9 percent for poorer Whites). Whites win more often at all class levels. By contrast, there are relatively large differences in success rate between wealthy Whites and wealthy Blacks (38.8 percent winners versus 31.1 percent winners) or between poor Whites and poor Blacks (36.9 percent winners versus 32.1 percent winners). Race again trumps class.

I also find that race additionally trumps religion – although it is important to note that the measures of religion I have available are limited.[26] The biggest gap for religious groups, between the non-religious and Catholics, is just 1.6 points (37.6 percent for Catholics, and 36.0 percent for non-religious). Differences across other religious groups are even less pronounced. Jews and Protestants win at almost the same rates as Catholics. Even smaller gaps emerge when I focus on age and gender. Those over 65 win only slightly more often than those under 30 (37.8 percent compared to 37.2 percent). The gender gap, as I have already mentioned, is only 0.4 points. The urban-rural divide – which is not pictured in Figure 4.1 – is also tiny (0.7 points). All told, by far the largest differences between groups are in the race category.

I have not mentioned Latinos and Asian Americans yet because the data on Latinos and Asian Americans are unfortunately quite limited. The GSS survey that I use only started including the Latino and Asian-American racial categories in 2000. As such, it is hard to compare their success rates to other demographic groups that are analyzed over a much longer period of time. Also, the GSS sample of Latinos and Asian Americans is far from perfect.[27] At best, I can offer some preliminary conclusions about these two groups. Over the ten-year period for which I have data for all four racial groups, Latinos won in 37.0 percent of cases, just slightly below the figure for Whites for the same period (38.1 percent), suggesting that Latinos could have less influence than Whites over policy. By contrast, Asian Americans won at higher rates than Whites (40.9 percent), and might therefore be viewed as privileged in the political system.

Is Race Really the Cause?

The results to this point suggest that Black voices are not equal to others when it comes to policy. But is race really driving the effects? The patterns are eye-opening, but they by no means prove that race is actually driving inequities in policy responsiveness. It is important to acknowledge that Blacks could be losing in the policy arena for reasons that have little to do with race. Indeed, I think, there are two possible *non*-racial explanations for the racial patterns we see here. The first relates to politics. It may be that Blacks win less often because of their extreme political preferences. The second relates to the intertwined nature of race and many of the other demographic characteristics examined here. It could be that the racial effects seen in Figure 4.1 are actually driven by class, religion, and other demographic divides. I assess these possibilities in the next section.

I have so far presumed that demographics shape the policy responsiveness observed here, but it is also possible that the relationships are spurious. Politics and political orientation could be at the root of these inequalities. For any number of reasons politicians may be more apt to be responsive to members of their own political party or to people ideologically similar to them. And, as this book has shown, Blacks are unique in their political orientation. They are far more Democratic than any other demographic group. They also tend be more liberal than other groups. It may be that Blacks win less often than others, not because of their race, but rather because of this left-leaning political orientation. Blacks may be losing more than others simply because they are the most left-leaning group in a political environment that favors Republicans and conservatives.

Another somewhat unique aspect of African Americans' political preferences concerns their spending preferences. Blacks are more likely than other groups to favor spending increases. Blacks favor spending increases 49 percent of the time, while Whites only favor increases 40 percent of the time, according to the data set. The gap may not be huge, but any minority group that favors spending increases when the majority does not has a real chance of losing. Perhaps even more importantly, any group that regularly favors spending increases in a world in which budget constraints force governments to limit spending could lose disproportionately. Blacks may be losing more than others simply because they favor spending increases more than others.

The other potential non-racial explanation for the racial patterns in policy responsiveness is that race is correlated with many other demographic factors that are actually driving responsiveness. Given that race, class, and the other demographic characteristics are all interrelated, a simple count of winners and losers by group may overstate or understate the influence of a particular demographic characteristic. It could be that many of the racial effects shown in Figure 4.1 are driven by class, religion, and other dimensions.

Fortunately, one of the principal advantages of my research design is that I can incorporate all of these different factors into a single model that seeks to explain policy responsiveness. More precisely, I run a regression that not only controls for race, class, and all of the other demographic characteristics I have examined, but also incorporates the political orientation of each respondent.[28] In terms of political preferences, I include: the standard party identification scale, self-described placement on a liberal-conservative ideology scale, a measure of whether each respondent favors a spending increase or a spending decrease, and a measure of whether or not each respondent favors the most popular spending position on that issue in that year.[29]

The results of this analysis are displayed in Figure 4.2.[30] It shows the predicted effects of each variable on the probability of winning, holding all other variables constant.[31] The actual regression is included in the appendix.

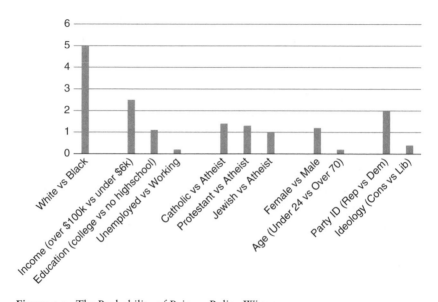

Figure 4.2. The Probability of Being a Policy Winner
Source: General Social Survey (1972–2000), Historical Tables (US Govt Printing Office)

The model demonstrates the uniquely powerful role of race in shaping political responsiveness. The model estimates that, all else equal, the probability of political responsiveness to a voter's priorities is 5.0 points higher for a White person than for a Black person. The figure clearly shows that race has the largest single effect on who government responds to. The effect of race on government responsiveness dwarfs the effects of class. Race is twice as powerful as income or education in explaining who wins in the policy arena. Race also overshadows the impact of religion and every other demographic characteristic.[32] And, perhaps most importantly, race even dominates politics in structuring policy responsiveness. Other factors, such as class, are certainly relevant in this picture, but the biggest part of why some Americans get what they want from government and others do not is a function of race. *Thus, any explanation of inequality in American politics must begin with a focus on race.*

The enduring role of race in Figure 4.2 also tells us that the connection between race and policy responsiveness cannot be easily explained away. African Americans are not losing in the policy arena because of their socioeconomic status or their political orientation. They are not losing because they are poor or less educated than others. They are not losing because they are more liberal or more Democratic than others. They are not losing because they favor more spending increases or oppose the public's favored position more than others. The disadvantage Blacks face in the American policy world seems to stem from much deeper causes. One real possibility is racial discrimination. We already know through randomized field experiments that members of Congress and state legislators are significantly more likely to respond to a request for help from a White constituent than from a Black constituent (Butler and Broockman 2011). These studies provide clear evidence of discrimination in access to the political arena. To believe that racial discrimination also plays a role in policy responsiveness would not require a massive leap of faith. Could it be that elected leaders simply dismiss Black voices more readily than others?

Race is, of course, not the only factor shaping policy responsiveness. In line with previous scholars, I also continue to find evidence of a class bias. Higher levels of educational attainment and higher income both increase the odds of ending up on the winning side of a policy battle. But after controlling for race these gaps are relatively small. The predicted gap between wealthy Americans (those earning more than $100,000) and poorer Americans (those earning less than $6,000) is only 2.5 points. The comparable gap between the highly educated (a college degree or higher) and the poorly educated (less than a high school degree) is only 1.1 points. Even when the effects of education and income are combined, the estimated class effect (2.7 points) is still dwarfed by the race effect. Following race and class, the next largest demographic factor is religion, with Catholics, Protestants, and Jews all about 1 point more likely than atheists to be winners.[33] Other demographic dividing lines, such as gender and age, tend to play an even smaller role.

Skeptics might wonder if I am measuring class in the right way. Perhaps the results would change if I were to focus on the top 1 percent, the group that the media so often highlight. Changing the measurements for class do not seem to matter. When I break down class into finer categories or merge education and income together into one scale, some of the tests reveal that those near the very top of the socioeconomic pyramid do better than those in the top third, but these differences pale in comparison to the racial differences.[34] Race trumps class, no matter how class is measured.

This is remarkable, and in many respects. Race is a more power-ful determinant of government responsiveness than class, even over a period of time in which economic inequality has grown to a striking degree. Race is a more powerful force in determining whether policies are likely to adhere to voters' wishes, despite the chasm between the lifestyles of the rich and poor. This finding also flies in the face of long-established political research into policy responsiveness. The best-known studies of class in American politics almost all conclude that class is central. Indeed, they contend that class is the most important factor driving representation. The work of Gilens (2012) and Bartels (2008), in particular, seems to show clearly that, when it comes to policy, the rich dominate at the expense of the poor.

The biggest problem is that all of the existing studies ignore race. Ignoring race makes class divisions seem sharper than they actually are. Yes, the rich and the poor do sometimes disagree, but not nearly as much as White and non-White Americans. On the vote (as analyzed in Chapter 2), divisions surface between working-class and middle-class voters, yet those class divisions pale in comparison to racial divisions. And on policy the same is true. Rich and poor Americans do not always want the government to spend money on the same things, but most of the time they do. In fact, when I dig deeper into policy preferences on spending, I find that across all of the different spending areas and all of the different years, the opi-nions of poorer and richer Americans closely mirror each other. The mean opinion of richer Americans across the eleven policy areas and years is correlated with the mean opinion of poorer Americans at 0.97. The fact that higher-class opinions match so closely with lower-class opinions means that class cannot determine who wins and who loses across most policy decisions.[35] Class only looks like an important factor if it is not compared to race.

Ignoring race also leads to false conclusions about how much class matters. Because race and class are so deeply intertwined, looking at class in isolation can be misleading. Many of the class divisions that have been observed in past research are, in fact, racial divisions at root. Once we control for race, the class divisions recede. Put another way, it is impossible to fully evaluate class or race without considering and incorporating the other. When both race and class are assessed simulta-neously, as the evidence in this book underscores, race eclipses class as the central force in American politics.

Of course, this will not and should not be the final word on class and representation. It is certainly possible that class matters in other, more subtle ways not incorporated here. Some might argue that well-off Americans win not by shaping larger, more prominent decisions on matters such as spending, but instead by winning in the fine details of policymaking. Wealthy Americans' influence might surface in other ways – for example, in influencing who benefits from government regulations, rather than in affecting government spending priorities. Alternatively, the policy influence of wealthier Americans might not be direct, but might instead work through lobbying and interest groups' pressure – elements of the policy process that the current analysis does not incorporate. Indeed, Gilens and Page (2014) have shown quite convincingly that the goals of corporations and other business interest groups better predict policy than even the preferences of the wealthy (but see Baumgartner et al. 2009). Economic power could still be a central factor in the American policymaking process. More work needs to be done. But if that work is to be telling, it will have to incorporate both race and class into the analysis.

Another interesting finding emerges from Figure 4.2: Politics, in the form of a voter's preferred political party, also very much shapes government responsiveness. Democrats win less often than do Republicans. That partisan tilt is not large, but it is real. All else equal, strong Democrats lose 2.0 percent more in the policy world than strong Republicans. I believe that this is the first evidence of this partisan policy gap. At this point, I can only speculate as to its source. Perhaps it is due to the fact that Republicans held the presidency during two-thirds of this period. Why largely Republican control of the presidency was not offset by largely Democratic control of the House and Senate over this period remains unclear. When I look for solutions to unequal representation in Chapter 7, I explore variation in responsiveness under Democratic and Republican administrations and look to see how partisan controls shape who wins and who loses in the policy arena.[36]

Do Certain Disadvantages Reinforce One Another?

Figure 4.2 does not tell us whether different dimensions, such as race and gender, interact with each other to further shape responsiveness. Does disadvantage on one dimension reinforce disadvantage on the other? Looking across subgroups, I found two key instances of such "intersectionality." First, Black women are particularly likely to be ignored in the policy arena. When government chooses policy, the voices of Black women are the most likely to be overlooked.[37] Second, race and class do interact to impact Blacks and Whites differently. Essentially, I find that the effect of class works in the opposite direction for Whites and Blacks. Whereas higher-income Whites are 1.9 percentage points more successful than low-income Whites, higher-income Blacks are actually marginally less likely than lower-income Blacks to get the policies they want (0.9 percent). Attaining higher status does not appear to be an avenue through which Blacks can narrow the responsiveness gap. No other two individual characteristics interacted to greatly shape responsiveness.

Variation Across Issues and Time

Looking at all of the different policy areas and all of the different years together in one big analysis – as I have done to this point – is important to evaluate policy responsiveness in an overall way. But this overall picture could conceal enormous variation. The winners and losers may change from year to year, and from policy to policy.

To really determine how disadvantaged African Americans are in the policy arena, one needs to know if they are consistent losers across time and across different policy areas. Do African Americans lose year after year and on policy after policy? Or are losses on some policies and in some years offset by victories on other policies at other times? Do any victories advance policies that Blacks care about most? If African Americans lose most of the time on most policies, but win on policies that concern them most, then this trade-off might mean that American democracy is working more favorably than the data initially suggested. And how do race and class compare? How do the disadvantages of race and class compare across different policies and different years?

To answers these questions, I repeat the previous analysis, but separate the eleven different policy areas and the twenty-eight different years in the data set. I begin with responsiveness across the eleven different policy areas in the data. Table 4.1 shows all the significant estimated effects of race and class in each policy area.[38]

Several important conclusions emerge from looking at each policy area separately. First and foremost, African Americans are significantly disadvantaged on *every issue*. Regardless of the government's policy focus, Black opinions hold significantly less sway than White opinions.

Table 4.1 Significant Gaps in Responsiveness by Race, Class, and Issue Area

	Race	Income	Education
	(Black vs. White)	(High vs. Low)	(High vs. Low)
Health Care	−1.7		
Welfare	−2.0		3.7
Foreign Aid	−2.7		4.5
Crime	−3.2	7.5	2.7
Environment	−3.2		−4.7
Transportation	−5.4		4.8
Defense	−5.7	4.6	−5.2
Education	−6.8		−5.1
Recreation	−6.8		1.8
Aid to Cities	−10.3	7.1	2.2
Space	−13.8	11.7	6.9

Source: General Social Survey (1972–2000), Historical Tables (US Govt Printing Office)

By contrast, class has a much less consistent impact on policy responsiveness. In more than half of all policy areas, income has no significant effect on who wins or loses. That suggests that for much of what government does, income plays little part in shaping whose voices are heard. Higher-income Americans, for the most part, have no better political megaphones that allow their voices to be more influential than lower-income Americans. On issues in which income does matter – on crime, aid to cities, space, and defense – lower-income Americans are significantly less influential than wealthier Americans.

The effects of education are even more mixed. Education is almost always significantly related to policy responsiveness, but whether education effect favors those who are better educated or those who have less education varies from policy area to policy area. Most of the time, educational effects favor those on the top. For seven of the policy areas, well-educated voices tend to hold more sway. But on three other policy areas – the environment, defense, and, notably, education itself – the effect is the reverse; policies favored by well-educated voters tend to lose. And finally, on one policy area – foreign aid – education plays no significant role in shaping policy responsiveness. Put succinctly, the effects of class are highly variable. Sometimes a bias favors well-off members of society. Sometimes a bias works against them. And sometimes class status is largely irrelevant. The message of these data is clear: *Race is much more of an ever-present barrier than class.*

Some interesting variation emerges across issues in the degree to which African Americans are disadvantaged. The size of the Black disadvantage diminishes somewhat in policy areas that appear to be particularly important to the Black community. Specifically, the degree to which Blacks fall behind Whites appears to be somewhat smaller on welfare (-2.0), health care (-1.7), and crime (-3.2), than on other policy areas. This is slightly encouraging in that Blacks succeed more on the issues that are especially critical to their community.[39] Whether it is because African Americans are pushing particularly hard to make their voices heard on these particular policy areas or because leaders in the federal government simply recognize that these are areas where Black voices should hold greater sway, this is a positive pattern.

When I look at variation over time, the pattern of results is fairly similar. Race matters more consistently than class. In twenty of the twenty-six years, African Americans fare worse than Whites to a statistically significant degree. By contrast, income is positive and significantly related to responsiveness in just three of the twenty-six individual years. The effects of education are similarly uneven. In most years, education is insignificant; in six years educational attainment has a positive effect on responsiveness, while in three years (1974, 1976, and 1988), it has a negative effect.

In the whole forty-year period analyzed, just one brief, three-year period (1975–77) surfaces during which government is *actually somewhat more responsive to Blacks than to Whites*. This interesting and potentially important anomaly prompts an obvious question: What is it about those years that led to better outcomes for African Americans? This is a subject I will explore in depth later when I look more directly at potential solutions to inequality in American politics. But overall it is clear that race, more than anything else, leads to consistent losing across time and policies.

The Biggest and Most Consistent Losers

To this point, I have been using a relatively simple measure of responsiveness. The measure has only two options. Either government does what you want, or it does not. But we might also care about the *distance* between an individual's policy preferences and government policy actions. How far does the policy outcome veer from one's ideal point? With the available data I cannot go too far down this road, but I can assess the distance between preferences and outcomes with a slightly more nuanced measure. With this alternate measure, if a voter gets exactly what he or she wants (e.g. a voter wants a decrease in spending, and spending subsequently declines), that voter is still coded as a winner. At the other end of the scale are big losers, who wind up with exactly the *opposite* of what they want. For example, a voter might want a spending increase, but government chooses to subsequently decrease spending. Finally, in the middle are those for whom government spending is slightly different from their preference. A voter might want no change in spending in a given category, but government might subsequently increase or decrease spending.

Analyzing the data this way essentially reinforces the earlier conclusions. Whites are about 6 percent more likely than African Americans to end up winning, and about 5 percent less likely than Whites to end up as "slight losers" – figures that dwarf gaps by class, religion, and other individual characteristics.[40]

All of the data I have presented so far could actually understate the magnitude of the problem. To this point, I have not looked at how many times each individual loses on policy. Yet that aspect might be the most important. No one always wins, of course, but if someone loses consistently across all or most issues, this suggests that an individual (group) is being shut out of the democratic process. Because each of the respondents is asked about his or her preferences on eleven different policy areas, the data can reveal who wins – and who loses – consistently across all areas. Do certain individuals always or almost always win or lose in the policy arena?

When I look simultaneously at each individual's preferences across all eleven policy areas, I find the same starkly racialized pattern. Overall, 13 percent of all African Americans can be characterized as "super losers," meaning that government fails to do what they want across all eleven policy areas. By contrast, only 9 percent of Whites could be considered super losers. The fact that across this range of different policy areas Blacks are consistently more likely to end up losers once again raises concerns about equity in American democracy.

At the other end of the spectrum, none of the Black respondents get what they want on all eleven policy areas. The end result is that

Blacks are grossly over-represented at the bottom and greatly under-represented at the top. Blacks make up 18 percent of all respondents who lose consistently and only 9 percent of respondents who win on six or more policy areas.

One important difference that emerges when I look for super losers is that class seems to rival race. Fully 15 percent of those with the lowest levels of education lose on all eleven policy areas. Likewise, just over 10 percent of those at the bottom end of the income scale lose consistently. Both race and class seem to help define the most disadvantaged in the policy arena.[41]

Latinos and Asian Americans

The analysis presented here contains a major omission: It fails to incorporate the opinions of Latinos and Asian Americans. The absence of these two groups is, unfortunately, driven by the data, which do not allow me to single out members of either group in most years. The main survey does not ask about either group until 2000. Given that I have only a few years of data for these two groups, I cannot offer anything close to firm conclusions about their place in the policy world.

Moreover, when I did try to look more closely at these two groups, the results were inconsistent. Different tests led to different conclusions. In most of the more rigorous regression models, I found that policy was slightly less responsive to Latinos than to Whites. This mirrors Griffin and Newman's (2008) analysis of the congruence between district public opinion and the voting records of individual Congress members. One might thus conclude that in the policy world Latinos fall somewhere near Blacks, at the bottom end of the racial hierarchy. But given that in many alternate tests Latinos were not significantly more likely than others to lose on policy, this is not yet a conclusion that I am ready to draw.

Meanwhile for Asian Americans, some small signs suggest that they are significantly advantaged in the policy world. In one or two key models, Asian Americans were actually more likely than Whites to end up winners. But in most tests I found no significant differences between Whites and Asian Americans.

Perhaps the most that can be said is that small signs suggest that Latinos may hold a less advantaged position in the policy world, and that few clear inferences can be drawn about Asian Americans. Firm conclusions about the status of these two pan-ethnic groups will likely have to await the accumulation of more data.

Interpreting the Patterns

To be fair, there are different ways of interpreting the results I have presented in this chapter. One read of the data is that the American policy world is fairly open. No single group appears to have anything resembling total control of the process.[42] And at the other end of the spectrum, no single group loses all of the time. There is some bias in who gets what they want from government, but American democracy is not totally shutting out the voices of its minorities. Government clearly responds to all groups to some degree. In short, things could be a lot worse. I cannot disagree with this conclusion.

A second view might see differences in responsiveness as real but argue that they are both unsurprising and justified. Under this view, differences in responsiveness are unsurprising – and justified – because Blacks represent a small minority of the population. It is little wonder that they win on policy less often than the White majority. Moreover, the inequalities are justified because Blacks, as a minority, should have less say than the majority-White population. Put simply, the median voter is White, and politicians should represent the median voter, both strategically and normatively.

In this second case, I would push back more forcefully. I would counter that while that majoritarian logic may be reasonable, it fails to explain why Blacks stand out even among small minorities. Blacks are the *only* minority group singled out in this way in American democracy. Other racial and ethnic minorities (namely Asians, the poor, the young, the unemployed, Jews, and Catholics) all get roughly equal influence or, in some cases, more influence than their numbers would suggest. Moreover, the smallest minority I examine, the wealthiest 1 percent, do exceptionally well in shaping policy. Other minorities do not lose disproportionately. Only Black voices are differentially ignored.[43]

The bottom line is that the differences I see in the policy world are both real and distressing. I have shown that when the government makes policy, it responds substantially more to advantaged interests than it does to the preferences of the disadvantaged. Blacks and to a lesser extent the lower classes lose out. Blacks lose by a larger margin than any demographic group, they lose more regularly over time, and they lose more consistently across issues. Those who need most, get the least.

But it is not just that Blacks lose more regularly than Whites. And it is not just that African Americans lose more in the policy world than any other demographic group. Critically, Blacks' disadvantage cannot be easily explained away. African Americans are not losing in the policy world because they identify overwhelmingly as Democrats or liberals. Blacks are not losing because they prefer greater spending. Even after I control for party identification, ideological orientation, whether someone opposes the national plurality on that issue, and a tendency to favor spending increases, Blacks still lose significantly more than any other group. This last point should be underscored. The lack of responsiveness to Black interests is not the result of party or partisanship. In this era, Democrats are certainly losing more than Republicans when it comes to policy, but African Americans are losing out even more. Moreover, class cannot explain the racial imbalance, either. Even when Blacks make it to the middle class, they still end up with limited policy influence. Middle-class Blacks have, by my estimates, less influence than poorer Blacks.

Ultimately, racial inequality in policy responsiveness seems to be driven by a deeper, more fundamental factor. I cannot say what it is but given that I have incorporated everything I think might explain it, I am left with little to point to other than racial discrimination. Perhaps politicians simply heed Black voices less. We already know from Dan Butler and David Broockman's field experiments that legislators discriminate. When Butler and Broockman (2011) contacted legislators via email, legislators responded to white-sounding names more than they responded to names they perceived to be Black. Moreover, White legislators were particularly likely to discriminate against their Black constituents. That pattern, coupled with the fact that roughly 90 percent of all elected officials are White, could easily explain why Black voices are less likely to be heard in the nation's policymaking process.

It is also quite likely that institutional structures impede Black interests in American democracy. Gerrymandering – as we have already seen – can help with other forms of representation, but it could be hurting Black interests when it comes to policy outcomes. The malapportionment of the Senate could also be a factor. Few Blacks live in the smaller population states that are over-represented by the very design of the Senate. It is also possible that politicians listen more to individual Americans who give them more money – a pattern that would also serve to negatively impact Black interests.

Regardless of whether these racial inequities can be explained, the fact that they exist is distressing. Their existence suggests that racial equality remains an elusive goal in the American political landscape. Political equality – a fundamental ideal for any democracy – is undercut if the color of one's skin is the most important determinant of who wins and who loses in the polity.

Part III

Immigration's Rising Impact on American Democracy

The story that I have written so far has ignored immigration. That is not an oversight. The Black-White divide remains the nation's largest. African Americans lose more than any other group – racial or otherwise – at almost every stage of the democratic process. America's old racial conflict is alive and well.

But the United States is changing. Over the past half-century 60 million new souls have joined the American experiment. Latinos now outnumber Blacks. Asian Americans are gaining fast. The reality is that immigration may not just be altering the US population, it may also be altering its politics.

In Part III of this book, I assess the political consequences of immigration. Anxiety about immigration is well documented. But until very recently scholars and observers have been skeptical that immigration is important enough to drive our core political identities or our major policy decisions. I contend that this is all changing. In the next two chapters, I look for signs of an immigrant backlash in our politics. Specifically, in Chapter 5, I examine whether the influx of millions of immigrants has sparked enough fear and anxiety to shift core partisan identities, and whether this fear, and the political tactics that exaggerate it and capitalize on it, are driving large numbers of White Americans to the Republican Party. Then in Chapter 6 I examine the policy consequences of this backlash at the state level. Immigration may not yet be the central dividing line in American politics, but it may be reshaping a wide range of policy challenges in the states.

5 IMMIGRATION IS RESHAPING PARTISAN POLITICS

"They're sending people that have lots of problems, and they're bringing those problems with us. They're bringing drugs. They're bringing crime. They're rapists. And some, I assume, are good people."[1]

With these now infamous lines about Mexican immigrants, President Trump set in motion his meteoric rise in the 2016 presidential campaign. Before giving that speech, Trump was floundering. Polls placed him near the bottom of the 16-candidate Republican field.[2] But just a month later – after almost non-stop coverage of his immigration remarks – Trump had skyrocketed to first place in the polls.[3]

Immigration appeared to fuel his candidacy throughout the primary and the general election. In the primary, Trump won over Republican voters who wanted to deport unauthorized immigrants, and he lost decisively among those who favored a pathway to citizenship. All told, 53 percent of those who preferred deportation supported Trump. By contrast, only 26 percent of those who backed a citizenship option voted for Trump (Tesler 2016b). In the general election, a similar pattern held. Three-quarters of Trump voters felt that illegal immigrants were "mostly a drain" on American society. Only 11 percent of Clinton supporters agreed.[4]

And immigration did not fade from the scene after Trump won the election. Trump's early presidency began with an attempted ban on immigration from seven predominantly Muslim countries and has continued with repeal of the Deferred Action for Childhood Arrivals (DACA) program, the elimination of Temporary Protected Status for tens of thousands of Central Americans, a limit on refugees, an increase in the number and scope of deportations, the shutdown of the federal government for a record-setting thirty-five days to gain funds to build a wall along the entire Southern border with Mexico, and, most recently, a declaration of a national emergency on border security to build the wall without congressional approval. It appears that Trump is set on fulfilling his commitment to a base of anti-immigrant supporters.

Trump's focus on immigration does not necessarily mean that immigration motivates voters. Nor does the correlation between immigration views and the vote prove that views on immigration played a pivotal role in bringing voters into the Trump fold. But the stark patterns of the Trump era are intriguing. They suggest that immigration could be emerging as a core force driving the sharp racial divide in American politics.

In this chapter, I assess the role that immigration plays in shaping the nation's partisan politics and its racial divides. I focus on White Americans because they are the primary audience for the immigrant-threat narrative. As the evidence here shows, immigration is a potent force. Immigration has not replaced race as the primary factor driving White partisan decisions, but it does represent a distinct and increasingly important dimension of American politics.

Why Immigration Matters: A Theory

Bill Storey, a White retired civil engineer, expresses his anger and anxiety about immigration this way: "The people who are coming across the border – as far as I'm concerned, they are common criminals" (Shear 2013). Ken Sowell, a White lawyer from the South has similar views and a clear solution: "What we need to do is put them [illegal immigrants] on a bus. We need to enforce the border" (Shear 2013). Bill and Ken are not alone. Across the country millions of White Americans in poll after poll have expressed anger and anxiety about the number and the character of immigrants crossing the border.

These feelings are well known. Less known is the impact of this anxiety on the politics of the nation. Are fears and concerns about immigration influencing the core political decisions of individual Americans? Or, put more pointedly, is the Republican Party using these fears to attract White Americans to the Party? On this question political scientists have had remarkably little to say.[5] Until Trump won election with a campaign that explicitly targeted immigrants, few thought that immigration was powerful enough to sway core partisan identities. And even after Trump's election, no researcher has been able to connect views on immigration to white partisan choice in a robust, causal way.[6]

Yet I think that just such a tie can and should be made. Indeed, the story is quite simple. Immigration and an immigrant-threat narrative stir anxiety. Then the Republican Party offers an easily identifiable home to those who are concerned about a changing America. In the next section, I expand on this story and argue that widespread concerns about immigration and the Republican Party's embrace of an anti-immigrant narrative have in recent years pushed large numbers of White Americans to the Republican Party. More than simply telling this new story, I will attempt to back up the argument with compelling analysis that illustrates just how immigration is changing the balance of partisan power in American politics.

Step 1. An Immigrant Influx

The first feature of immigration that sets it apart from most other issues is its magnitude. Americans are limited political animals in many ways. They tend not to follow the minute details of the day's political debates. They frequently show little interest in the candidates and the campaigns waged for their benefit. Their knowledge of basic political facts is often sorely inadequate (Delli Carpini and Keeter 1996). But immigration is no ephemeral phenomenon. Unlike many of the other political developments that US politicians debate, immigration is massive, local, and long term. I believe that one of the reasons immigration is so central in the politics of individual White Americans is its almost overwhelming magnitude. Over the last five decades, upwards of 1 million immigrants have arrived on this nation's shores annually. Immigrants and their children now represent almost 30 percent of the population (MPI 2019). The vast demographic change is impossible for White Americans to miss.

What makes the change so noticeable and, for some, more menacing is its diversity. Large-scale immigration has produced a sea change in the racial and ethnic composition of the nation. Immigration has moved the United States from a primarily Black-and-White world in which Whites dominated in almost every sphere to a much more racially complex one. The census estimates that somewhere around the mid-point of this century America will become a majority-minority nation.

Step 2. The Message: An Immigrant Threat

The second key force driving the impact of immigration on American politics is an "immigrant-threat" narrative that fuels individual fears and insecurities about Latinos and immigrants. This wideranging and often-repeated narrative casts immigrants and especially Latinos in a negative light, and highlights a host of pernicious fiscal, social, and cultural consequences of immigration. Candidate Trump's "They're bringing drugs. They're bringing crime. They're rapists ..." comes again to mind.

Within the economic sphere, there are claims that immigrants, particularly those in the country without legal status, are overly reliant on welfare, use considerable public resources in areas such as health and education, and fail to pay their fair share of taxes. The overall fiscal story, according to the narrative, is one of significant economic loss for the nation's taxpayers (Borjas 2001). Other versions of the narrative are more focused on the possibility that immigration will bring crime and disorder (Gimpel and Skerry 1999). The narrative typically also underscores the cultural dissimilarity of the Latino immigrant population and likelihood that continued immigration will lead to the demise of the traditional American way of life (Huntington 2005). In other forms, the narrative focuses on the "Sleeping Latino Giant" and the political threat posed by an increasingly large and increasingly demanding immigrant community.

All of these messages are regularly repeated in the media. Several reviews of recent national TV news coverage and magazine and newspaper stories suggest that the immigrant-threat narrative is ubiquitous and that images of immigrants clandestinely crossing the US–Mexico border, committing crimes, and accessing public services are common (Ana 2003, Chavez 2008, Pérez 2016, Valentino et al. 2013,). One analysis, for example, found that 85 percent of media stories on immigration mentioned "undocumented" or "illegal" immigrants (Pérez 2016). A study of all *New York Times* coverage of immigration from 1980 to 2011 likewise found that coverage was overwhelmingly negative in tone and content (Abrajano and Hajnal 2015). All told, negative stories on immigration outnumbered positive stories by four to one. When members of the public read or watch stories about immigration, they are likely to find a scant few that portray immigrants in a positive light.

Moreover, there is ample evidence that these messages can be effective. Experiments show that listening to right-wing media host Michael Savage discuss concerns about immigration, or reading an excerpt from *State of Emergency*, Pat Buchanan's anti-immigration book, led a random sample of Whites to hold to decidedly more negative stereotypes of Latinos (Barreto 2012).

Step 3. A Partisan Divide

Once aroused, that anxiety seeks a political home. The last critical development for the immigration backlash theory is the coupling of the immigrant threat with increasingly clear *partisan* choice. Driving this development is the growing policy gap between Democratic and Republican leaders on immigration. Although elites in both parties express a variety of views on immigration, the political entrepreneurs who have been most vocal about the immigrant-threat narrative have generally come from the Republican side.[7] Republican leaders such as Mike Huckabee and Tom Tancredo, along with conservative commentators such as Bill O'Reilly, Ann Coulter, and Rush Limbaugh, have repeatedly highlighted the ills of undocumented immigration, and have advocated for a range of reforms to push immigrants out of the country and to limit new immigration.[8] As Tancredo put it during his presidential bid, "We're not just talking about the number of jobs that we may be losing, or the number of kids that are in our schools and impacting our school system, or the number of people that are abusing our hospital system and taking advantage of the welfare system in this country ... We're talking about something that goes to the very heart of this nation – whether or not we will actually survive as a nation."[9]

Even Mitt Romney, who represents the more moderate faction of the party, adopted an anti-immigrant platform in his 2008 bid for president. His platform included self-deportation and opposition to the Dream Act – a law meant to protect children who came to the United States illegally with their parents. "We all know Hillary Clinton and the Democrats have it wrong on illegal immigration," he said in an ad that aired during the campaign. "Our party should not make that mistake. As Governor, I authorized the state police to enforce immigration laws. I opposed driver's licenses and in-state tuition for illegal aliens. As president, I'll oppose amnesty, cut funding for sanctuary cities and secure our borders" (Novak 2007). Some have gone so far as to say that the only things Republicans have offered Latino and Asian voters are "fear and hostility."[10]

By contrast, most Democratic leaders have either expressed support for immigrants' rights or avoided the issue altogether. Barack Obama is a case in point. He was often criticized for moving too slowly on immigration reform, and for deporting record numbers of undocumented migrants. Yet, as his public statements suggest, he offered a far more welcoming tone on immigration than his Republican colleagues: "America can only prosper when all Americans prosper – brown, Black, White, Asian, and Native American," he said during the 2008 presidential election. "That's the idea that lies at the heart of my campaign, and that's the idea that will lie at the heart of my presidency. Because we are all Americans. *Todos somos Americanos* [we are all Americans]. And in this country, we rise and fall together."[11] Eight years later, Hillary Clinton offered a similarly welcoming tone during her presidential bid: "I don't want to rip families apart. I don't want to send parents away from children. I don't want to see the deportation force that Trump has talked about in action in our country ... That is an idea that is not in keeping with who we are as a nation."[12]

These increasingly divergent policy stances are borne out by votes in Congress. As political science researchers Gary Miller and Norman Schofield have demonstrated, Republican support for immigrants' rights was reasonably strong during the Reagan era, and, as late as 1990, immigration-related legislation generated little noticeable partisan division. In fact, Ronald Reagan signed a law that granted amnesty to almost 3 million undocumented immigrants. But since that time, votes in Congress reveal an increasingly stark contrast, with Republican legislators repeatedly supporting tougher laws against immigrants, and Democrats favoring more admission and greater immigrants' rights (Jeong et al. 2011, Miller and Schofield 2008). Political scientist Tom Wong finds that between 2006 and 2012 Republican House and Senate members favored restrictive policies 98.4 percent of the time, while Democrats supported those measures only 66.4 percent of the time (Wong 2013). On any number of different immigration-related issues – erecting border fences, English as the official language, amnesty, government workers reporting undocumented immigrants, and so-called "anchor babies" (the US-born children of immigrants) – Republicans and Democrats are largely on opposite sides.

The same pattern of partisan divergence is evident at the state level. All the high-profile and controversial anti-immigrant state measures have been initiated and/or endorsed by state Republican leaders and largely opposed by Democrats. In Arizona, for example, no Democrat in the legislature supported SB 1070, an immigrant enforcement bill that required local law enforcement officials to investigate the status of anyone detained. By contrast, all but one Republican voted for the same bill (Archibold 2010). Similarly, partisan battle lines surfaced in California over Proposition 187, the 1994 ballot initiative to deny undocumented immigrants health care, education, and any state services. Republican governor Pete Wilson was one of the primary advocates of the "Save Our State" initiative when it passed, and Democratic governor Gray Davis was the primary actor challenging the measure in court five years later. Compelling evidence shows that Democratic and Republican leaders at the local level are just as sharply divided on immigration (Gulasekaram and Ramakrishnan 2015). One end of that local partisan polarization is epitomized by Joe Arpaio, the former Republican sheriff of Maricopa County, Arizona, who proudly proclaimed that "Nothing is going to stop me from cracking down on illegal immigration." Gavin Newsom, the former Democratic mayor of San Francisco, who fought vigorously for sanctuary cities to protect the undocumented, represents the other end of the local spectrum.

These divergent party stances on immigration are borne out by interest-group ratings. Interest groups universally rate Democratic members of Congress as distinctly liberal on immigration, and Republican members as strongly conservative. The Federation for American Immigration Reform (FAIR), for example, rates current Democratic House members on average as a 10 out of 100 on its immigration legislation scale, with 100 denoting the most restrictive position on immigration. By contrast, Republican House members average 99 on the scale. Significantly, FAIR's estimate of the partisan divide on immigration has grown sharply over time. As late as 1996, its ratings showed little partisan divide on immigration, with average scores of 44 for Democrats and 52 for Republicans. But by the early 2000s, FAIR's ratings by party sharply diverge.

A similarly anti-immigrant group, NumbersUSA, gave President Obama a failing grade on immigration, while offering passing grades for all the 2012 Republican presidential hopefuls. The National Latino Congreso sees the same large partisan gap, but as a pro-immigrant interest group, it gave Democrats high grades – an average score of 81 percent – while labeling Republican legislators as extraordinarily poor on immigration – an average rating of 7 percent.

All of this presents individual White Americans with a compelling partisan logic. Anyone who is anxious about immigration and the growing Latino population has a strong incentive to favor the Republican Party. And, of course, anyone who embraces immigration's benefits has a reason to align with Democrats.[13]

Summing it all up, many White Americans will see that America is changing, they will believe that it is changing in ways that are bad for the nation, and they will learn that one party, the Republican Party, is vigorously opposed to this development, while the other party, the Democratic Party, is largely supportive. For many White Americans, this may be a powerful motivation to defect to the Republican Party.

Just One in a Series of Nativist Episodes

This in many ways reprises a very old and quintessentially American story on immigration. America may be a nation of immigrants, but it has not always welcomed immigrants with open arms. Immigration has often sparked widespread fear and mobilization when the number of new arrivals has been large, or when the make-up of new Americans has differed from the native-born in obvious racial or ethnic ways (Daniels 2004, Fetzer 2000, Schrag 2011, Tichenor 2002, Zolberg 2009).[14] Indeed, the history of the nation can be told through a series of challenging immigrant-nativist confrontations. The rising tide of German and French migrants at the end of the eighteenth century sparked one of the first large-scale nativist movements. Numerous episodes followed: anti-Irish discrimination in the 1850s, a populist backlash against Chinese immigrants in the 1880s, prevalent anti-southern and eastern European sentiment in the early twentieth century, and a long history of animosity toward Mexicans dating back to the Mexican-American War (Fetzer 2000, Higham 1985, Zolberg 2009). World War II generated similarly widespread anti-immigrant concern, and led to the internment of more than 100,000 Japanese Americans. For the vast majority of Americans, and even for US Supreme Court justices, the threat posed by these immigrants – many of whom were American citizens – justified the clear violation of their rights. One could also include current-day US anxiety about and discrimination against Arab Americans in this lengthy list of nativist movements.[15]

Thus, contemporary concerns about immigrants are not new. They are just one example of a recurring, longer-term phenomenon. If Americans have so often rallied in large numbers against immigrants in the past, then there is a real possibility that the same kind of anti-immigrant mobilization may surface today – particularly with the near historically high levels of immigrants, the high share of immigrants from non-White ethnic groups, and the great tide of human mobility in the age of globalization.

Hope Rather Than Fear

Of course, fear and backlash are not the only possible outgrowth of large-scale immigration. Just as I point to fear, others might point to hope. The hope is that immigration will breed understanding and cooperation rather than division and conflict.

There are reasons to believe that immigration could, in fact, be fostering better relations. The positive economic impact of immigration is one of those reasons. Although the threat narrative often points to the negative fiscal consequences of immigration, the economic reality is very different. Economists generally agree that the long-term impact of immigration on the nation's economy is positive or at worst neutral. The reality is that most immigrants come to the country looking for jobs and opportunity. Most work hard, most pay taxes, and relatively few receive benefits (Bean and Stevens 2003). Their efforts help fuel the economy. Why would there be a backlash against a largely positive economic influence?[16]

Perhaps even more importantly immigrants today can point to an impressive record of assimilation. Despite starting on a relatively weaker economic and educational footing than previous immigrant waves, today's immigrants have by and large been able to make substantial intergenerational strides on almost every conceivable measure of economic and social incorporation (Alba and Nee 2005). By the third generation in the United States, newcomers have come close to matching or even exceeding the average American on English-language ability, educational attainment, patriotism, and other core US values (Bean and Stevens 2003, Citrin et al. 2007, Garza et al. 1996). The data also indicate that immigrants are less prone than natives to suffer long spells of unemployment, or to use public welfare (Bean and Stevens 2003). Today's immigrants are also less likely to commit crimes (Flagg 2018, Rumbaut 2006). Most of the elements of the immigrant-threat narrative are not actually true.

In this best-case scenario, the actions and efforts of immigrants in the economic, cultural, and social spheres will win over the hearts and minds of native-born White Americans, and ultimately lead to a nation in which racial divisions are muted, and inter-group conflict is rare. At least at first glance, there are compelling signs of positive shifts on the racial front. With increased immigration have come rapidly rising rates of interracial marriage along with newer, more complex, and much less rigid racial categories.[17] The relative simplicity and rigidity of the "one-drop" rule that governed the Black-White divide for much of US history has evolved into an era in which the census recognizes mixed racial identities, and the largest minority group, Latinos, can choose to identify with more than one race.

Thus, one real possibility is that immigration will lead us together rather than push us apart. In this vein, any Republican strategy of targeting immigrants might backfire, and could actually enhance the willingness of individual White Americans to support more liberal, Democratic, and pro-immigrant policies.[18]

Ignoring Immigration

A third possibility is that immigration makes little difference in the politics of the nation. Skeptics might contend that immigration is simply not important enough in the minds of individual Americans to generate the kinds of broad political consequences that I have envisioned. Supporting this view is the fact that individual Americans often downplay the importance of immigration. Surveys show that the public has seldom viewed immigration as the nation's most significant problem. Rarely have more than 10 percent of Americans cited immigration as the most pressing concern facing the country.[19] Furthermore, over the last few decades the nation has faced any number of other issues that have captured the lion's share of the public's attention. Many scholars would argue that terrorism, war, economic woes, and other worries have dominated recent political debates and the decision-making calculus of individual Americans (Adams 1997, Layman and Carmines 1997, Miller and Shanks 1996).

Immigration might also matter simply because partisan attachments are so rigid. Some scholars would contend that even if immigration were on a par with these other issues, it still would have little impact on party identification. There are those who believe that party identification is largely impervious to change (Campbell et al. 1960, Green et al. 2002). These scholars view party identification as the "unmoved mover," a core identity that itself drives a wide array of political perceptions and choices and remains largely unaltered by the politics of the day (Goren 2005). From this perspective Americans are socialized into one party or the other at an early age, and that first partisan lens colors their politics for the rest of their lives. Concerns about immigration, however widespread, will simply not be enough to substantially alter these deep-seated psychological attachments. If anything, attitudes on immigration will fall in line with pre-existing partisan attachments (Green et al. 2002). From this perspective, immigration is likely to be one of many issues that fail to make much of an impact on the fortress of partisanship.

Existing Answers

Who is right? Is immigration driving a widespread backlash by White Americans, as I contend? Is it leading to greater understanding and a blurring of racial divisions, as others insist? Or is immigration being eclipsed by larger and more pressing issues, such as foreign conflict and the economy?

Remarkably, little is known about how views of immigrants shape core political affiliations and basic voting decisions. Immigration is undoubtedly one of the most important demographic forces shaping the nation today, but scant information reveals how it affects the partisan balance of power.[20] Political scientists and other observers of US politics have done a great deal to try to assess how Americans feel about immigrants and immigration (Brader et al. 2008, Cohen-Marks et al. 2012, Hopkins and Hainmueller 2015, Schildkraut 2011). They have in various ways explored the *determinants* of immigration attitudes.[21] But somewhat surprisingly research has not systematically explored the *consequences* of attitudes about immigration. Do feelings about immigration ultimately influence how people feel about policies and the parties and candidates they support? Does immigration affect who Americans are politically? On these latter kinds of question, surprisingly few answers exist.[22]

Immigrant-Threat Narrative Received

Nevertheless, the immigrant-threat narrative clearly has been absorbed by a large cross section of White Americans, many of whom now express significant concerns about the costs of immigration. Extensive polling data reveal deep concerns about immigrants and the immigrant population among a substantial share of White America.[23] In a range of different surveys, almost half of all Americans believe that immigrants are a "burden" or feel that immigrants "hurt the country."[24] One-third to a half of the nation wants to see a decrease in the current levels of immigration, and anywhere from one-third to a half thinks "immigration is a bad thing for this country."[25]

Moreover, there are large segments of the population that have bought into each of the different elements of the threat narrative. Some 61 percent of Americans are concerned that undocumented immigrants are "putting an unfair burden on US schools, hospitals, and government services." Another 87 percent are concerned or quite concerned that immigrants "making low wages might make US employers less willing to pay American workers a decent wage."[26] Fully 58 percent feel that immigrants do not learn English quickly enough, and about one-third of Americans believe that Latino immigrants significantly increase crime.[27]

Attitudes toward undocumented immigrants are even more negative. When given the choice between "primarily moving in the direction of integrating illegal immigrants into American society or in the direction of stricter enforcement against illegal immigration," almost 70 percent choose stricter enforcement.[28] Two-thirds say that undocumented immigrants should not be eligible for social services.[29] Polls also show that well over 60 percent of Americans approve of Arizona's controversial SB 1070, commonly referred to as the "show me your papers" law because it enables law enforcement officials to stop anyone they suspect to be in the country without legal status. A clear majority would like to see a similar law requiring police to verify legal status in their state.[30] And almost half would like to see a wall built across the entire Southern border.[31] What makes these attitudes about undocumented immigration all the more alarming is that a majority of Americans (61 percent) believe that most current immigrants are here illegally – a view that is at odds with statistics showing that three-quarters of immigrants have legal residence.[32] In short, immigration has *not* gone unnoticed. And many Americans believe its consequences are anything but positive.[33]

None of this is to say that the United States or even White America is wholly united on immigration. Perhaps the fairest assessment is that the public is decidedly split. Many Americans hold positive views of immigrants, and support policies that would increase immigration, and would expand the rights and interests of immigrants.[34] Depending on the nature of the question and exact wording used, surveys can suggest reasonably widespread support for immigration. Roughly as many Americans believe that "immigrants strengthen the United States with their hard work and talents" as the number of Americans who believe that immigrants are harming the nation.[35] Similar proportions of people see immigrants on balance as an "economic benefit" rather than an "economic burden."[36] Americans appear to be especially supportive of earned legalization. In most surveys, a clear majority favors measures that would allow undocumented immigrants to remain in the country as temporary workers or, eventually, as citizens.[37] Overall, about one-third of Americans say they are "sympathetic" to the plight of undocumented immigrants. An equal number feel that "America should always welcome immigrants."[38]

All of this means that immigration could represent an important dividing line in US politics. If feelings on immigration – both negative and positive – are strong enough, immigration could drive many of the core political choices that Americans make.

Tying Immigration to Partisanship

Demonstrating that immigration really is driving large-scale White defection from the Democratic to the Republican Party is not an easy task. Indeed, tying immigration to changes in partisanship requires a multi-step process. I begin that process with what I believe to be the simplest, most direct, and most convincing test. I examine whether individual attitudes about immigration are correlated with party identification. That is, are Whites who feel more negatively about immigrants and immigration more likely to identify with the Republican Party?

Whites' views on immigration are, in fact, closely linked to their attachments to the Democratic and Republican parties. The connection is illustrated in Figure 5.1, which shows the relationship between individual Whites' views on undocumented immigrants and several key indicators of partisan choice.[39]

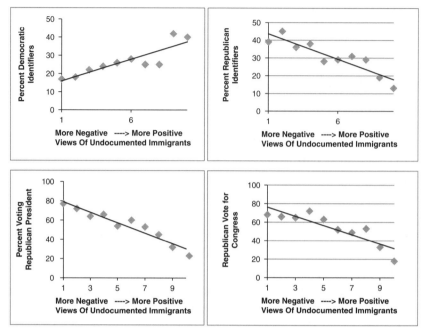

Figure 5.1. Immigrant Views and White Partisan Choice
Source: American National Election Studies 2008

For all of the core partisan decisions White Americans make – from the party with which they choose to align, to the candidates they vote for in presidential and congressional elections – a clear correlation emerges between attitudes toward undocumented immigrants and political choice.[40] What impresses is not the presence of the correlation but the magnitude of it. *Americans with the most positive views of undocumented immigrants almost never identify with the Republican Party –* only 13 percent of them do so. But almost half of those Whites with negative views toward undocumented immigrants – 45 percent – identify as Republicans. Similarly, as White attitudes shift from more negative to more positive, the probability of identifying as a Democrat increases from 17 to 40 percent. The figures for the vote are even starker. Few Americans with positive views of immigrants vote Republican for president or Congress – 18 percent and 23 percent, respectively. But a clear majority of those with negative views of undocumented immigrants favor Republican candidates – 68 percent in congressional elections, and 77 percent in presidential elections.

Moreover, the results are the same regardless of how one measures views on immigration. Whether I focus on questions on policy toward undocumented immigrants as I do in Figure 5.1, or instead focus on attitudes toward immigration more generally or on feelings toward Latinos – the largest immigrant group – I find that immigration views and party are linked. The partisan world of White America seems, at least at first glance, to be fundamentally shaped by attitudes on immigration.[41]

Equally importantly, it does not much matter which particular survey I use or how a particular poll was conducted. The analysis in the figure is from a standard phone survey of adult citizens – specifically the 2008 American National Election Survey – but if I instead analyze a face-to-face survey of 1,000 adults (GSS), an Internet survey of 30,000 Americans across 1,200 different zip codes (CCES), or a larger telephone survey of 98,000 adults (NAES), a similar picture emerges. Moreover, the data from the most recent elections show even sharper partisan differences on immigration.

A Stricter Test

The figures above show a correlation between attitudes on immigration and partisan choice. But before making causal claims about that relationship, I need to consider the possibility that the link between views on immigration and partisan choice is spurious – a by-product of a connection with a third factor such as attitudes on war, the economy, terrorism, gay rights, or race. In recent years, the two parties have squared off on many issues, any number of which could be driving the link between immigration and party.

One way to deal with this concern is to incorporate these other factors and to control for them in a regression model. My empirical strategy thus controls for all possible confounding issues to see if the relationship between immigration and political choice fades away. The list of potential confounding issues is long and for 2008, in particular, these issues include policy opinions on: intervention in Iraq and Afghanistan, security and terrorism, perceptions of the economy, attitudes toward income redistribution, racial attitudes, liberal-conservative ideologies, and a complete set of individual sociodemographic characteristics including class, age, gender, and religion.[42]

I start with an analysis of the 2008 election – a year in which the existence of comprehensive survey data allows me to incorporate almost all, if not all, of the potentially relevant confounding factors. Figure 5.2 shows the predicted impact of immigration views on party identification and presidential vote choice in 2008 after taking into account each of these many possible confounding issues.[43] The analysis shows that the inclusion of all these different factors does not eliminate the impact of immigration.

Even after I control for individual policy positions, ideological views, racial attitudes, and socioeconomic characteristics, attitudes on immigration are still closely and significantly linked with partisan choices. Immigration still matters, and to a striking degree. White Americans who hold negative views of undocumented immigrants are a full point to the right of Whites with less negative views on the 7-point party identification scale when all controls are included. To put this in context, a 1-point shift equals the difference between a voter who leans Democratic and one who is a pure independent. Thus, this finding suggests that immigration views have the potential to reshape US politics.

How White Americans think about immigrants is even more strongly related to how they vote. In the 2008 presidential contest, Whites with negative views of immigrants were – all else equal – 55 percent more likely to vote for John McCain than Barack Obama. Views on immigration mattered to a striking degree – eclipsing other issues in an election taking place against the backdrop of one of the nation's sharpest recessions, two wars in Afghanistan and Iraq, and with the nation's first Black presidential nominee on the ballot.[44]

Once again, it matters little how I measure views on immigration, or which factors I include in the model.[45] The patterns in Figure 5.2 use attitudes toward undocumented immigrants. But I get roughly similar results if I instead focus on feelings toward Latinos or attitudes toward legal immigration.

Racial Resentment vs. the Anti-Immigration Backlash

Immigration is, of course, not the only thing that matters. Looking deeper at the analysis, I find that how individual Americans feel about Blacks, and individual views on policies designed to help African Americans still very much matter.[46] The most racially resentful

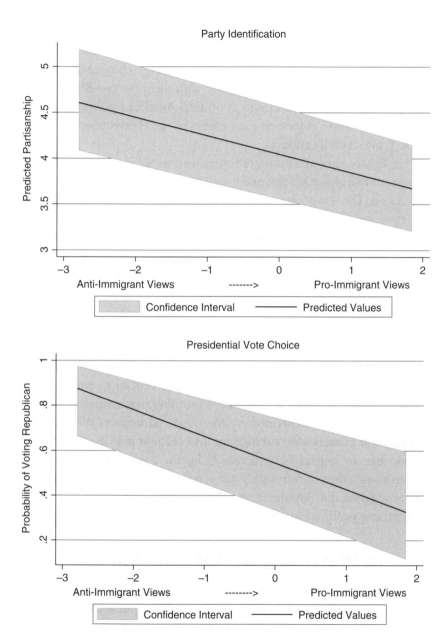

Figure 5.2. The Estimated Impact of Immigration Views on White Party Identification and Presidential Vote Choice (2008)
Source: American National Election Studies 2008

Americans were about 1 point to the right of the least racially resentfully Americans on the party identification scale. Likewise, Whites with the most anti-Black views were 45 percent more likely to favor McCain, the Republican candidate, than were those with the most pro-Black views. Immigration may be increasingly central to American politics, but it is not coming close to eliminating the effects of racial resentment. The old Black-White conflict endures.

In fact, race and immigration are connected in many ways. How Americans feel about Blacks, and how Americans feel about immigrants are related. Those who are anxious about immigration also often resent demands made by African Americans. I suspect that a lot of these feelings toward both groups have the same roots. Indeed, studies have shown that both attitudes on race and attitudes on immigration are closely linked to deep-seated psychological predispositions such as authoritarianism, intolerance, and ethnocentrism (Kinder and Kam 2012, Valentino et al. 2013).

However, immigration and race represent distinct dimensions, as the data make clear. Attitudes on race and immigration are correlated, as I have just mentioned, but the correlation is not all that strong. In this particular case, the correlation between racial resentment and anti-immigrant attitudes is just 0.28 – meaning that relatively little of one attitude can be explained by the other. Moreover, the fact that immigration matters *after* taking race into account indicates that immigration has an impact beyond race.[47] Further, the fact that the anti-immigration effects are roughly on a par with the racial resentment effects suggests that immigration represents not only a new dimension to American politics but an important one as well.

The Effect of Immigration Within Each Party

Another way to examine the interrelationships between immigration, party identification, and vote choice is to look closely at vote choice *within* each party. By focusing separately on Democrat and Republic identifiers, one gains another perspective on how attitudes toward immigration matter. As one might anticipate, views of immigrants and Latinos have the largest impact on non-partisans. White Independents with more negative views of immigrants were 67.7 percent more likely to vote for McCain than were White Independents with more positive views of immigrants. Even among those who claim ties to the Democratic Party, views of undocumented immigrants are moderately related to vote choice. The vast majority of Democrats voted for Obama, but those who have more negative views of undocumented immigrants were 6.5 percent less likely to support him than those with more positive views of undocumented immigrants. I did, however, find that views of immigrants matter less for Republicans. Immigration attitudes clearly have an effect on vote choice that goes well beyond partisan ties.

The Impact of Immigration Beyond 2008

The results from 2008 are compelling because the data and the underlying model are so comprehensive. But if I want to argue that immigration is fundamentally reshaping US politics, the data cannot be limited to a single election year. Instead, it should span an array of contests across a number of years using a range of surveys.

In order to offer a more general statement about immigration's role in American politics, I conducted parallel analysis of the vote using almost the entire range of survey data, years, and elections that were available. Specifically, that includes: the 2010 and 2016 Cooperative Congressional Election Survey (CCES); the 2010 Evaluations of Government and Survey; the 2000 and 2004 National Annenberg Election Surveys (NAES); the 1996, 2000, and 2004 General Social Survey (GSS); and the 1948–2008 Cumulative Files of the American National Election Study.

The different data sets all tell a similar story. A backlash against immigration is fueling White support for the Republican Party and Republican candidates. In each study, I found significant and substantial ties between immigration views and partisan choice. Across the range of studies, immigration views helped to shape vote choice at not just the presidential level but also at congressional and gubernatorial levels. Across the years of the ANES study, for example, I found that those who hold more negative views of Latinos are, all else equal, 35 percent more likely than those with positive views of Latinos to favor Republican gubernatorial candidates.[48] Only in two contexts – senatorial elections, and older years of the ANES – did a clear link between immigration and the vote fail to materialize.

These results closely match up with studies of the Trump-Clinton contest in 2016. Myriad studies (by Collingwood et al. 2017,

Gimpel 2017, Griffin and Teixeira 2017, and Sides 2017) find a close connection between support for Trump and immigration views. Indeed, these studies suggest that immigration may have been even more important in that contest – perhaps not surprising, given Trump's often overt and explicit anti-immigrant campaign. One of the most comprehensive studies found that immigration attitudes explained about 35 percent of the vote even after taking into account a range of other factors (Hooghe and Dassonneville 2018). Perhaps most compelling is this: Attitudes on immigration strongly predicted which Obama supporters defected from the Democratic Party to support Trump in 2016 (Collingwood et al. 2017, Sides 2017). Preliminary data from the 2018 midterm elections tell a similar story (Bacon 2018). In that election, fully 90 percent of those who thought current immigration policies were "too tough" voted for Democratic House candidates, while only 14 percent of those who thought US immigration policies were "not tough enough" did likewise (CNN 2018).

Immigration even played a role in partisan primaries. Only one of the surveys asked a large sample of White Americans about their primary vote choices, but in that one case – the 2000 presidential contest – concerns about immigration shaped the vote. In the Republican primary, those who saw immigration as the nation's most important problem were 7.3 percent more likely to support Bush over McCain – a pattern that fits Bush's comparatively tough stance on immigration in that contest. One striking feature of the Republican primary vote that year is that immigration was especially crucial to Democrats and Independents who voted in the Republican primary. Attitudes on immigration were roughly five times as powerful a predictor of the vote among non-Republicans who cast ballots in the Republican primary. That pattern suggests that Democrats and Independents who are especially concerned about immigration may be shifting to the Republican Party to favor anti-immigrant candidates. Interestingly, immigration did not appear to be a significant issue in the 2000 Democratic primary contest between Al Gore and Bill Bradley, both of whom offered relatively few clear proposals on immigration.

Overall, the effects of immigration are extraordinarily robust. Whites' partisan choices seem to flow from their immigration attitudes no matter when or how these attitudes are measured. The impact of immigration on American politics is not limited to a particular year, a particular measure, a particular methodology, or a particular type of election. In nearly every way I examined the issue, restrictive views on immigration led to substantially greater support for the Republican Party and Republican candidates. No matter how one looks at the issue, immigration is now a central feature of American politics.

Using all of these data, I also attempted to see how the impact of immigration is changing over time. The pattern of results strongly suggests that the influence of immigration on party identification is increasing over time. The most obvious sign that immigration is increasingly connected to partisanship is that the immigration views of Democratic and Republican supporters are increasingly diverging. In 1994, self-identified Democrats were just as likely as self-identified Republicans to say that immigrants are "a burden" on American society. But over time Democrats became more supportive of immigrants, and Republicans became less supportive. As a result, the "burden" gap between Democrats and Republicans grew to about 10 points by 2005, and is almost 35 points today (Jones 2019). Looking at different elections in different data sets, I also found that immigration views tend to be more significant and more robust predictors of the vote in more recent contests. For example, I found strong effects for immigration on all four presidential contests in the twenty-first century and more inconsistent effects in the 1990s and 1980s. At the same time, I cannot offer a definitive conclusion on this change because the quality and nature of the data change over time. In recent years, surveys have been asking more and better questions about immigration. Thus, it is difficult to know whether the increasingly significant results over time are real, or, at least in part, an artifact of better data.

Addressing Causality

Though White Americans' feelings about immigration are intricately connected to their partisan identities and electoral decisions, the complexity of the issue warrants further examination. Before one can be absolutely confident that attitudes on immigration are *actually driving* party identification and the vote, one more test is needed to rule out the possibility that party identification is itself the main driver of change.[49] Individual Americans could be taking cues from partisan leaders; that is, they could be adjusting their stances on immigration to match those of a party that they know, trust, and believe in. Indeed, much of the literature in US politics suggests that party identification stands near the beginning of a funnel of causality that drives factors such as issue positions and the vote (Bartels 2002; Campbell et al. 1960; Miller and Shanks 1996). From this perspective, party identification is a "durable attachment not readily disturbed by passing events and personalities" (Campbell et al. 1960:51). If party identification is as powerful a force as many believe, it could be the core identity driving people's thoughts and feelings about issues such as immigration.[50]

One way to examine this issue of "what causes what" is to analyze the same individual's views at different points over time. The key test is whether an individual American's position on immigration at one point shapes future changes in that individual's partisanship. That is, is it possible to predict who will shift to the Republican Party in the future based only on how those people think about immigration today?

For this causality test, I focus on panel data from the ANES that repeatedly asked the same respondents for their views and partisanship in 2008 and 2009. I look to see if views on immigration in 2008 (measured by a question about whether undocumented immigrants should be given a chance to become citizens) have a significant effect on changes in party identification between 2008 and 2009. The results demonstrate a clear temporal link. Individuals with anti-immigrant views in 2008 were more likely than individuals with pro-immigrant views to shift toward the Republican Party.[51] The effect of immigration views on party identification is also apparent in two earlier panel studies from 2000–04 and 1992–93.

The size of the effect is generally not large. Over the course of a single year (from 2008 to 2009), those with more negative views on immigration shift about one-quarter of a point more to the right on the 7-point party identification scale. That shows that attitudes on immigration are not leading immediately to a wholesale shift from strong Democrat to strong Republican. But if these small shifts accumulate over time, they could help to account for the large-scale partisan changes evidenced in recent decades.

The Bigger Picture

The patterns to this point are clear: Individual attitudes on immigration are driving individual changes in partisanship and the vote. At this point, I want to begin to tie this individual-level story to larger national patterns. If immigration is having a major impact on

White partisan politics, then changes at the national level should surface, as well. If growing fears over immigration are having a major impact, a noticeable decline should emerge in White support for Democrats over time.

Figure 5.3, which shows the share of White Americans voting for Democratic candidates in congressional elections since the 1980s, demonstrates that this trend is, indeed, taking place. Much has already been made of the defection of White Americans from the Democratic Party in the 1960s and 1970s in response to the Democratic Party's support of a civil rights agenda. But, as the figure shows, White defection has continued to the present day. As late as the early 1990s, Whites evenly divided between the Democratic and Republican parties. Since then, a slow and uneven but nevertheless relentless shift to the right has taken place. Today, White Republican voters outnumber White Democrat voters by a wide margin.

This shift is important, but does it have anything to do with immigration? Obviously, much is going on in US politics in this period. An almost endless array of events and issues could be responsible for shifts in White partisan ties. To see if these larger national patterns are linked to immigration, I examine whether the overall national mood on immigration at one point in time predicts changes in aggregate White partisanship in the next time period. If the immigration backlash story is true, periods of increased White anxiety about immigration should be closely followed by shifts in the share of White Americans attached to the Republican Party.

To perform the test, I combine data from two different data sets. One asks regularly about attitudes on immigration (the Gallup Poll).

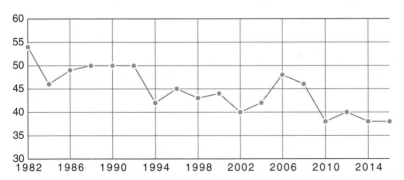

Figure 5.3. Declining White Support for House Democrats
Source: American National Election Studies (1982–2016)

The other asks frequently about partisanship (the *New York Times*/CBS News Poll). Attitudes on immigration are measured with the question, "Should immigration be kept at its present level, increased, or decreased?"[52] To determine aggregate immigration opinion, I subtract the portion that favors a decrease from the portion that favors an increase. To gauge partisanship, the *New York Times*/CBS News Polls ask a relatively standard 5-point party identification scale. To gauge aggregate White partisanship, I use the national average of White responses on that 5-point scale.[53]

The core test is to see if opposition to immigration in one quarter predicts greater identification with the Republican Party in the next quarter. It does. Strong White opposition to immigration in one quarter leads to a noticeable shift to the Republican Party in the subsequent quarter.[54] The size of the effect is, once again, far from large. The model predicts a little over a one-tenth-point shift on the 5-point party identification scale when the White public moves from a strongly pro-immigrant mood to a strongly anti-immigrant mood. That shift is quite small, but it could be meaningful. If White anxiety about immigration stayed at a relatively high level over multiple quarters, a real shift in aggregate White partisanship could follow. Immigration may not be the only factor driving changes in White party identification, but it is an important contributing factor.[55]

I see the same pattern if I focus separately on the proportion of Whites who identify as Independents. More negative attitudes on immigration lead to increased independence, a shift that should alarm the Democratic Party. All these relationships persist if I control for presidential approval and unemployment – the two factors typically viewed as most important in shaping aggregate partisanship (MacKuen, Erikson, and Stimson 1989).[56]

There is little doubt that many factors are contributing to the defection of White America from the Democratic Party. But one can make a plausible case that a backlash to immigration is helping drive one of the more significant developments in American party politics in the last half century. The striking feature of the empirical patterns here is not that immigration matters. US history amply demonstrates that many White Americans have felt threatened by different racial/ethnic groups at various times (Masuoka and Junn 2013, Olzak 1992, Tichenor 2002). The arresting feature is, instead, just how wide-ranging those effects remain today. In a political era in which many claim that the significance of race has faded, immigrant-related views impact the political orientation of many members of the White population. Party identification – the most influential variable in US politics – is at least in part a function of the way individual White Americans see immigrants. So, too, is the vote in national contests for president and Congress. In short, immigration substantially shapes Americans' political identities. The immigration backlash is real, and it is meaningful. And it has been a boon for the Republican Party. The willingness of Republican leaders to increasingly and vocally embrace an anti-immigrant narrative has rewarded the Party with a larger and larger slice of the White vote and widespread electoral victories from the local to the national level. Donald Trump, perhaps more than anyone else, knows this. As he told the *New York Times* editorial board: "I just say, 'We will build the wall!' and they go nuts" (Beinart 2016).

Latinos vs. Immigrants

Throughout this chapter I have been deliberately imprecise about defining exactly which immigrants or which aspects of immigration threaten individual Americans. In theory, Americans who are anxious about immigration and its impact on the United States could make important distinctions between different subsets of the immigrant population. The concerns of individual Americans could be driven by a subset of immigrants such as the undocumented, Latino immigrants, or Mexican immigrants. The reaction could also be broader – driven by and directed at the entire pan-ethnic Latino population or the entire Asian-American population. Each of the different categories – undocumented immigrant, documented immigrant, Mexican American, Latino, and Asian American – do after all represent distinct populations with often widely divergent structural positions in the American economy and life.

In reality, the data suggest that most Americans who are concerned about immigration tend not to make important distinctions between different segments of the Latino/immigrant population. In surveys, Americans tend to reserve their most negative sentiments for "illegal immigrants," but when also asked about "immigrants" overall, or specifically about Mexican Americans or Latinos, all of their answers tend to be highly correlated. In the American National Election Study, for example, I find that answers to questions specifically asking about undocumented immigrants, legal immigrants, and Latinos all cohere well together (alpha scale reliability of 0.73). Further proof of this muddling of immigrant, undocumented, and Latino is evident in the misperceptions that Americans have about the immigrant population. Surveys show that most Americans incorrectly believe that most immigrants are undocumented, even though less than one-quarter are undocumented (Enos 2010, Kaiser Family Foundation 2004). The end result is that when individual Americans think of an immigrant, the image they have in mind is likely to be of an *undocumented* immigrant (Brader et al. 2008, Pérez 2016, Valentino et al. 2013). Likewise, surveys show that perceptions about the size of the undocumented population are strikingly similar to estimates of the size of the Latino population, suggesting that Americans conflate the terms Latino and immigrant (Enos 2010, Kaiser Family Foundation 2004). For many White Americans, immigrant means Latino, and Latino means immigrant. All of this is also evident in the analysis that I undertake in this chapter. Whether I focus on questions that ask specifically about the undocumented population, those that ask more broadly about immigration, or those that ask for feelings about the entire Latino population, I find similar effects. Concerns about any one of these groups lead to an anti-immigrant backlash.

The distinction that individual Americans do appear to make is between Latinos and Asian Americans. The anti-immigrant backlash is decidedly not a backlash against Asian Americans – even though most of the nation's newest immigrants are Asian Americans. Attitudes toward Asian Americans contrast, often sharply, with attitudes toward Latinos. Matching their elevated economic standing and educational achievements, Asian Americans are seen as the "model minority" – intelligent, hardworking, law-abiding, and successful (Lee 2000). Latinos, in sharp contrast, tend to be stereotyped as less intelligent, welfare-prone, and violent (Bobo 2001).[57] These distinct stereotypes are also consistent with survey findings on overall feelings toward each group. Most Whites say they feel closer to Asian Americans than they do to Latinos. In one poll, 92 percent of Whites said they get along with Asians, while only 67 percent felt the same way about Latinos. In another, fully 48 percent of Americans believe there are too many immigrants from Latin American countries, but only 31 percent say the same thing about immigrants from Asian countries (Gallup 2019a). Survey experiments further demonstrate that images of Latinos, much more than images of Asian Americans, spark negative responses in the context of immigration (Pérez 2016, Valentino et al. 2013).

This focus on Latino immigration may be surprising in light of the nation's dark history on Asian immigration. The Chinese Exclusion Act of the late nineteenth century, and the internment of more than 100,000 Japanese citizens during World War II demonstrate that Asian Americans can be the target of White ire. It is also entirely possible that, with declining Latino immigration and growing Asian immigration, Asians will once again be the focus of White anxiety. But for now, the conclusion is clear: How individual White Americans think about Asian Americans today typically reveals little about how they think about immigrants.

Class and the Immigrant Backlash

This investigation into the White anti-immigrant backlash has, to this point, largely avoided mention of class. But there are reasons to believe that class could matter in shaping White Americans' response to immigration. Economists have shown that the negative economic effects of America's low-skilled immigrant labor force tend to be concentrated on low-skilled natives (Bean and Stevens 2003, Borjas 2001). Although the overall fiscal impact of immigration tends to be positive, these studies show that, within certain industries, the wages of lower-skilled, native-born Americans may have declined as a result of competition from immigrants. Moreover, in recent elections, lower-class Whites – more than middle-class Whites – have shifted to the Republican Party (Casselman 2017, Cohn 2016, McGillis 2016, Porter 2016). Could the two trends be connected?

To assess this possibility, I examined an array of different public opinion surveys to see if the effects of immigration are more pronounced among lower-class Whites. Even though class should matter, little evidence demonstrates that class greatly shapes the White reaction to immigration. Among Whites, views on immigration were at best marginally tied to class. Time and time again, the surveys revealed no clear link between Whites' incomes and their feelings about immigrants. In a few cases, less-educated Whites were more anxious about immigration than better-educated Whites, but the differences were inconsistent and never large. More importantly, when I looked to see if views on immigration interacted with class to impact partisanship, I found no clear relationship. Regardless of class status, holding negative views of immigrants led to more support for the Republican Party and Republican candidates. All of this echoes past research showing that reactions to immigration tend to be driven more by symbolic and cultural concerns than by concrete economic considerations (Citrin et al. 1997, Hainmueller and Hiscox 2010, Hainmueller and Hopkins 2014, but see Hanson 2005, Scheve and Slaughter 2001). Once again, class does not play a primary role in shaping the nation's politics.

Looking Forward

The big question, then, is whether immigration will be used to divide Americans even further. Has the nation finally reached the peak of an anti-immigrant backlash? Donald Trump's campaign and his presidency have pushed the immigration issue to new heights. Can Republicans push even further in the future? Will that backlash grow and increasingly pit an anxious White majority against a coalition of more sympathetic and perhaps equally scared racial and ethnic minority voters?

One side of that equation concerns White voters. The key issue here is whether even more Whites can be swayed to the Republican side by the immigrant-threat narrative. A quick glance at the immigration-related views of White Democrats suggests that there is, in fact, room for further partisan defections. At present, most White Democrats – but not all – express relatively understanding views toward immigrants. Even among White Democratic identifiers, some 44 percent feel that "to be truly American" it is very important or fairly important to "have been born in the United States."[58] Fully 64 percent believe it is at least somewhat likely that "immigrants will take away jobs from Americans" (ANES 2016). Republican leaders could try to use immigration to entice some of those White voters to their side. And, if the issue of immigration and the immigrant-threat narrative are broadened to include Muslim Americans, then even more White Democrats likely could be brought into the Republican fold. Finally, as the non-White population continues to grow, and as Whites slowly lose their majority status, the perceived threat may grow, too, making this Republican message increasingly attractive.[59]

The other side of that equation is the racial and ethnic minority population, a population that I have largely ignored in this discussion. Could these populations be swayed by the issue of immigration to support the Republican Party?

For Latinos and Asian Americans – two groups for whom immigration is core to their American experience – this seems a remote possibility.[60] Early research revealed some ambivalence on the issue of immigration among small segments of the Latino and Asian-American population – particularly for second- and third-generation Americans and those with higher economic status – but that ambivalence has faded over time. The widespread use of an anti-immigrant narrative seems to have led to a greater sense of solidarity and greater cohesion among both pan-ethnic groups (Abrajano and Alvarez 2010, Barreto and Segura 2014, Ramakrishnan 2014, Wong et al. 2011). To the extent that immigration drives Latino and Asian-American partisanship, it pushes firmly in the Democratic direction (Bowler et al. 2006, Fraga et al. 2012, Nicholson and Segura 2005). In fact, many would argue that the growth in Asian-American and Latino attachment to the Democratic Party over the last two decades is largely a direct result of the Republican Party's increasingly anti-immigrant stance (Barreto and Segura 2014). Pushing further on immigration will almost assuredly lose the Republican Party more Latino and Asian-American votes than it gains.

African Americans are also unlikely to represent a fruitful target for Republican efforts. There are certainly reasons to believe that Blacks, as a group, could be susceptible to an immigrant-threat narrative. African Americans, who fall disproportionately at the low end of the socioeconomic spectrum, tend to live in areas with high levels of in-migration, where Blacks are often forced to compete for jobs, housing, and other resources with the new immigrants (Johnson and Oliver 1989). Blacks, perhaps as a result, are clearly divided on the issue of immigration (Doherty 2006). Nonetheless, immigration has, as of yet, done little to help Republicans attract Black support. Opposition to the Republican Party's stance on racial issues and its overall conservative economic agenda has been more than enough to prevent large-scale Black defections from the Democratic Party (Dawson 1994, Hajnal and Lee 2011). If anything, Black support for the Democratic Party has solidified over the last few years.

In the near term it is possible that Republican inroads into the White population will outweigh Latino and Asian-American mobilization by the Democratic Party. If that is true, then the nation may not have quite reached the zenith of the anti-immigrant backlash. Trump won with this strategy in 2016, and fellow Republicans could win with a similar strategy in the next few electoral cycles. But the changing demographics of the nation suggest that the current anti-immigrant strategy will eventually backfire. Even if nothing changes in terms of partisan strategies, the growing size of the Latino and Asian-American population means that the Republican Party may lose more and more votes over time. As the non-White share of the electorate increases, the benefits of an anti-immigrant strategy are likely to diminish.

6 THE IMMIGRATION BACKLASH IN THE STATES

African Americans are the biggest losers in American democracy.[1] That is the bottom line for much of what I have written so far in these pages. That conclusion is correct, but it is also incomplete. Blacks are not the only losers in American democracy. Latinos and other immigrants are also regularly a target of our politics and our policy, as evidenced by Trump during his campaign (calling Mexicans rapists, and promising to build a wall on the Mexican border) and during his presidency (deciding to rescind DACA, and declaring a national emergency to move forward on the border wall in the face of congressional opposition). But the phenomenon is much broader than Trump and the presidential political arena. Anxiety about immigration is becoming more and more central to American politics. As I have already noted, one sign of that broad White backlash is the defection of so many Whites to the Republican Party. But other signs are surfacing. They have been "invisible" largely because my focus until this point has been on the national policy arena – which is certainly worthy of attention, but perhaps not the most visible political arena in which an anti-immigrant backlash may be visible.[2] Many of the basic policy decisions about Latinos and the immigrant community are made at the state level, and, particularly, in states where large concentrations of Latinos live. Thus, much of the immigrant backlash is emerging at the state level.

A defining feature of immigration in the American context is its uneven nature. Some Americans live in areas in which there is almost no direct experience of immigration, while others live in neighborhoods, cities, and states dramatically transformed by immigration. In other locations Americans are experiencing rapid demographic change as the result of immigration for the first time. I believe that this demographic variation matters. Individual White Americans who see larger, more rapid changes will feel more threatened, and they will be more likely to lash out against that change. Policy will follow. States that see more immigration and more change will pass more policies that target that new population. Thus, just as the reach of immigration is uneven, the political impact of immigration is also uneven.

Three states illustrate that pattern. In California, the state with the largest Latino population, immigration is a defining feature almost everywhere. The state's 15 million Latino residents represent almost 40 percent of the state's population. Immigrants dominate employment in restaurants, landscaping, housekeeping, and numerous other fields. Immigrants walk the streets. Signs and stores advertise to immigrants. California's long-term and large-scale experience with immigration thrust it into the forefront of states that actively targeted undocumented immigrants. With Proposition 187, the "Save Our State" initiative of 1994, the voters of California passed the first measure in the nation to seek to exclude undocumented immigrants from a range of public services, including health care and education. Many other states followed suit. But California was the first.

In Vermont, a state with one of the smallest Latino populations, the demographic, social and political story is very different. Overt evidence of immigration is rare. Fewer than 15,000 Latinos live in the state. Immigrants do not eclipse native-born citizens in any avenue of work. No neighborhood has a Latino-majority population.[3] Days, months, or even years are likely to pass before a typical citizen in the state will encounter an undocumented immigrant. Given the limited impact immigration has had on the state, Vermont, unsurprisingly, has been inactive on the immigration-oriented legislative front. Over a recent five-year period, the state adopted only one state law addressing immigration – a bill that urged Congress to authorize more visas for agricultural workers (NCSL 2019).

Finally, in South Carolina, a state with one of the fastest-growing immigrant populations, politicians and pundits regularly debate the merits and pitfalls of immigration in the state. With Latinos representing only 5 percent of the population, daily signs of immigration in the streets are rare. But discussions in the media and elsewhere often return to the subject of the state's rapidly growing immigrant population. That debate stirred widespread concern about the state's immigrant population, and eventually led to the passage of an omnibus Illegal Immigration Reform Act (H 4400). That 2008 Act increased penalties for businesses that hire undocumented immigrants, forced employers to check the immigration status of their workers, denied public assistance and attendance at public colleges to undocumented immigrants, and, in a variety of other ways, tried to make the state inhospitable to these immigrants.

The story of immigration and the story of this chapter are in essence the story of these three states. Immigration is having a real impact on policies enacted in America, but that impact is uneven. Where there is mass immigration and a larger concentration of Latinos, the policy backlash is more severe. In these states, policy has moved sharply in a more regressive and punitive way. By contrast, where the reach of immigration has been relatively limited, policy has changed little.

In this chapter I tell this story both by looking at what is already known about policies that *explicitly* target the immigrant population and by offering new analysis of an array of broader policies on education, criminal justice, and taxes – policy areas that are only *implicitly* tied to immigration. What I find is that in states with larger Latino populations, a widespread backlash is emerging, in terms of policies that both explicitly and implicitly target Latinos and immigrant communities. At the same time, signs of more positive and inclusive steps are also surfacing. I find that once the Latino population becomes large enough to cross a demographic threshold, politics and policy begin to shift back toward inclusion and generosity.

Why Context Matters

The context here merits further discussion. Why would living near a large out-group population lead to a negative reaction and more regressive policies? The underlying logic is relatively straightforward. Human beings naturally form groups (Tajfel 1981). Those on the outside of one's "tribe" can often be imbued with negative characteristics and can often represent a threat. The larger that out-group, the greater the threat. That threat can be real or perceived. In some cases, out-group members create competition for available jobs, a struggle for political offices, reductions in housing prices, increased pressures on schools, and clashes over any number of public services. In other cases, the threat is more imagined than real. Greater visibility of the out-group, in and of itself, sparks anxiety and nurtures stereotypes but does little to harm the native-born. But in either case, proximity should lead to heightened tension, more negative attitudes toward the out-group, and a backlash. The end result is that individuals in contexts with larger minority populations should feel more threatened, express greater animosity, and be especially supportive of a host of policies aimed at maintaining the in-group's social, political, and economic privileges.[4]

This racial threat model was first applied to Black-White relations in the United States (Blalock 1967, Key 1949). In the Black-White case, studies have demonstrated that Whites who live in proximity to larger Black populations tend to be more racially resentful, hold more stereotypes of Blacks, support more extreme White candidates, oppose policies such as affirmative action that are designed to aid Blacks, and, in earlier periods, engage in violence against Blacks (Black and Black 1973, Corzine et al. 1983, Dixon 2006, Giles and Evans 1986, Winter 2008). The effects of Black context extend even further. Larger Black populations have also been linked to more conservative views on a range of implicitly racial policies such as welfare and social security (Fellowes and Rowe 2004, Hero and Preuhs 2007, Johnson 2001, Keiser et al. 2004, Soss et al. 2001, 2006, Winter 2008), and to large-scale defection from the Democratic Party (Huckfeldt and Kohfeld 1989).

More recently, the theory has been applied to try to explain attitudes and behavior across a wider range of contexts and groups. Much of that research has demonstrated clear ties between White animosity and the Latino and immigrant context. Analysis in the United States has at times demonstrated a robust relationship between the size and growth of the local immigrant population, and more hostile views of immigrants. Higher concentrations of immigrants and/or growth in the local immigrant population have been linked to support for more security at the border, greater restrictions on immigrants once they are in the country, and increased efforts to repatriate immigrants to their home countries (Ayers et al. 2009, Campbell et al. 2006, Citrin et al. 1997, Ha and Oliver 2010, Hawley 2011, Hood and Morris 1998, Newman 2013; but see Scheve and Slaughter 2001, Tolbert and Hero 2001). Comparative research has also found that larger immigrant populations at the national level are associated with more negative views of immigrants, and more support for restrictionist immigration policy (Dustmann and Preston 2001, McLaren 2003, Quillian 1995).[5]

A racial-threat view is, however, far from the only possible under-standing of how out-group context could impact attitudes and actions. An alternative view contends that proximity should generally lead to greater understanding and acceptance (Allport 1954, Dixon and Rosenbaum 2004, Jackman and Crane 1986). This *contact hypothesis* argues that out-group animosity is more often the result of unfamiliarity and inaccurate perceptions about the out-group than about real competi-tion over resources. From this perspective, personal interaction with out-groups exposes majority-group members to new, more accurate information about out-group members that should refute negative stereo-types and allow for the development of more favorable views.[6] In many versions of this contact hypothesis, the nature of the contact is critical. Positive understanding is only likely to grow when individuals of similar status interact in a cooperative setting (Allport 1954, Jackman and Crane 1986). Although the bulk of the research looking at immigrant or Latino context points to White backlash, a few studies find positive relationships between the immigrant context and White views – especially when the out-group in question is composed primarily of Asian Americans (Fox 2004, Ha and Oliver 2010, Hood and Morris 1998, 2000).

Finally, a third possibility is that context has no independent effect on inter-group attitudes or policy outcomes. Geographic context might be largely irrelevant for understanding inter-group conflict and cooperation for any number of reasons. For example, how people feel about and interact with out-groups could be driven primarily by biases and stereotypes that are learned early in life, and that are unaffected by one's current neighborhood or context. Likewise, other individual char-acteristics such as education, economic class, or partisanship could be the main factors shaping attitudes and actions toward the out-group (Gulasekaram and Ramakrishnan 2015). In addition, larger institu-tional structures might be more important than context in determining how people interact with out-groups. If any of these alternate views is accurate, behavior toward out-groups – in this case, policies directed at immigrants and Latinos – will be unrelated to geographic context.[7]

The States and Policies Directed at Immigrants

Immigration policy has traditionally been viewed as the purview of the federal government, but with the number of immigrants in the country growing rapidly, and the federal government repeatedly failing to enact comprehensive immigration reform, states have become the primary actors legislating on the welfare of immigrants in this nation. After decades of passing almost no measures that explicitly dealt with immigration or immigrants, states have stepped full throttle into the policy void. In the last decades, states have passed more than 3,000 measures that dealt explicitly with immigration or immigrants (NCSL 2019).

Moreover, as an exacting analysis by Michael Rivera has shown, these measures follow a clear pattern, one that fits closely with a racial-threat story. To begin with, the clear majority of these substantively significant laws have served to limit rather than expand immigrants' rights or interests (Monogan 2013, Rivera 2015). During this period states have done everything from reducing or eliminating immigrants' access to public services in education, health, and welfare, to allowing the police to target individuals suspected of being undocumented.

More importantly, in terms of the racial-threat theory, the states with the largest Latino populations have been the most active and the most aggressive (Rivera 2015). Texas, perhaps more than any other state, exemplifies this pattern. A state with one of the highest shares of Latino and undocumented residents, Texas passed seven anti-immigrant laws between 2007 and 2009, including measures to detect and deter undocumented use of the state Medicaid program, to reduce eligibility for the state's Child Health Care Program, and to require private companies that work with the state to demonstrate that they do not employ unauthorized workers. But Texas is not alone. Arizona, a state in which Latinos make up 30 percent of the population, passed twelve anti-immigrant measures in that same period. Arizona's 2010 efforts included the passage of the well-known SB 1070, one of the strictest anti-illegal immigration measures ever passed. In the same time frame, Colorado ushered eleven anti-immigrants bills into law, including one requiring that employers be notified of the prohibition against hiring an unauthorized alien and another that tied unemployment insurance benefits to citizenship.

At the other end of the spectrum, the ten states with the smallest Latino populations passed on average only two anti-immigrant laws in the same period. Instead, states with few immigrants and Latinos tended to pass more pro-immigrant legislation. Vermont, for example, expanded welfare eligibility. New Hampshire passed stiffer penalties for cross-border sexual and labor exploitation. Montana passed a measure that eased ID restrictions on the undocumented. In fact, eight of the ten states with the smallest Latino population passed more pro-immigrant bills than anti-immigrant bills.[8] At least in terms of explicit measures that directly and explicitly target immigrants, a real backlash has emerged, and that backlash is most pronounced where the Latino population is largest and most visible.

Implicit Policy

These patterns, while important, may actually understate the influence of immigration on policy. Almost all of the work to date on immigration context examines policies that are *explicitly* focused on immigrants, and ignores everything else.[9] I think that is a mistake. I believe that the influence of immigration in the policy world extends much more broadly to a range of policy areas such as education, welfare, crime, health, and taxes that are only *implicitly* tied to immigration. Policies that defund schools or that criminalize certain behaviors may not explicitly focus on immigrants; nevertheless, such policies may galvanize support and gain passage with immigrants in mind – especially in locations where immigrants make up a large share of the individuals affected by the policies.

I suspect these broad-ranging issues provide a barometer of the influence of immigration context. The reason is simple: A number of these broader policy debates on issues that are ostensibly unrelated to immigration have increasingly been infused with references to immigrants and images of both legal and undocumented immigrants. As the immigrant population grows, immigrants almost naturally become an increasingly central focus of policy considerations. Republican leaders, in particular, have increasingly put immigration and Latinos at the center of their policy discussions. When Americans now talk about welfare, crime, education, and a number of other important policy arenas, they often also talk about some aspect of immigration. And I suspect that when they decide about policy, images of Latinos and undocumented immigrants figure prominently in their heads.

Welfare is perhaps the most obvious case of a policy area that has been colored by immigration and, in particular, by the images and presumed actions of Latino immigrants. That connection likely begins with a pervasive "immigrant-threat" narrative put forward by the media and by leaders in the Republican Party. This narrative repeatedly highlights the heavy reliance of immigrants on public assistance, and the related costs for the American taxpayer. The fact that Latinos now make up almost 30 percent of the population receiving Temporary Assistance for Needy Families (TANF) only reinforces this connection for Americans. And in states such as California, where the majority of residents on public assistances are Latino, that connection becomes even clearer. Many Americans have heard and incorporated the message. Just under 70 percent of Whites view Latinos as particularly prone to be welfare recipients (Bobo 2001).[10] Likewise at least some surveys show that more Americans believe that immigrants come "primarily to use government services and welfare benefits" than that immigrants come "primarily for jobs" (Polling Report 2019). It is thus not surprising that the few studies to have looked have found a close link between the share of a state population that is Latino and state welfare policy (Fellowes and Rowe 2004, Hero and Preuhs 2007, Soss et al. 2001, 2008). Welfare benefit levels tend to be lower in states with many non-citizens – precisely the states with the greatest perceived threat, and, potentially, the greatest concerns over the prospect of public resources being squandered on immigrants, rather than helping fellow native-born, White Americans (Hero and Preuhs 2007).

These findings on welfare are important. But the growing reach of immigration in the lives of individual citizens and in the political debates of the day suggests that this focus on welfare may still be too narrow. In this chapter, I take the research a step further by looking at the connection between Latino context and a broader range of policies in which immigrants are not the explicit target but could nevertheless be part of the policy equation. Specifically, I examine the impact of Latino context on criminal justice, education, health care, and tax policy. I choose these areas because each has increasingly been infused with images and references to the Latino population, to immigrants, or to both.

Criminal justice provides a powerful example. When Latinos and immigrants are in the news, the theme, more often than not, is crime. Studies have shown that fully 66 percent of network news coverage of Latinos incorporates crime, terrorism, or unauthorized immigration (NAHJ 2005). And, as with welfare, a disproportionate number of Latinos have been caught up in the criminal justice system. Latinos now, unfortunately, make up a little over one-fifth of all those incarcerated in the United States (Bureau of Justice 2019). One result is a clear association between crime and immigration by many members of the public.

Despite the fact that only about one-quarter of the foreign-born population is undocumented, the majority of Americans believe that most immigrants are in the United States without legal status (Citrin and Sides 2008, Kaiser Family Foundation 2004). Another result is widespread stereotyping of Latinos. Surveys reveal that a majority of White Americans view Latinos as being particularly prone to violence (Bobo and Johnson 2000).[11] As such, it should not be surprising to learn that 19 percent of all of the bills in state legislatures that explicitly mention immigrants also address criminal justice (NCSL 2019). Given these connections between Latinos and crime, one might reasonably assume that White Americans at least partly consider the immigrant or Latino population when they weigh criminal justice policy measures. If true, then it is not a stretch to expect that larger Latino populations will be linked with more punitive criminal justice policies.

Plenty of evidence also ties the immigration context to health-care policy. The immigrant-threat narrative often highlights the costs of immigrants' use of public health services. Anti-immigrant groups such as the Federation for American Immigration Reform (FAIR) loudly proclaim that undocumented immigrants cost federal and state governments $10.7 billion a year in health-care spending. Again, the message appears to have been accepted by the public. Fully 85 percent of Americans believe that providing services such as school and health care to undocumented immigrants costs taxpayers too much (NPR/Kaiser Family Foundation 2004). This connection between immigration and health care is also worth recalling in terms of the events that transpired during President Obama's September 2009 speech to Congress regarding his proposed health-care plan. When President Obama stated that the Democratic plan would not include coverage for undocumented immigrants, Representative Joe Wilson of South Carolina interrupted the president's speech by shouting, "You lie!" This outburst and the overall focus on undocumented immigrants made Latinos one of the main "target" groups of this policy. Shortly after the heated debate a Pew poll found that 66 percent of those opposed to the plan reported that they were opposed because the plan might cover undocumented immigrants (Pew 2009).

An equally plausible connection could be made between education and immigration. Deliberations about the merits of different educational reforms as well as access to public education itself have increasingly focused on Latinos. Especially in states with large immigrant and Latino populations, public discussions about education policy change have often centered on how the new policies might help or hurt the immigrant population. One of the core tenets of California's Proposition 187 was a provision that limited immigrants' access to public education.[12] Soon thereafter, the state passed Prop. 227, a measure that outlawed bilingual education. The debate continues today in a different form with arguments for and against the Dream Act to grant legal status to undocumented residents who were brought to the United States as children.

Similarly, images of the immigrant population at least occasionally undergird debates about broader issues like jobs and taxes (Tichenor 2002). The persistence of low wages and high unemployment rates are often linked to the flow of low-skilled, undocumented immigrants coming across the border (Borjas 2001). The story on taxes is analogous – more immigrants using public services but not paying taxes leads to the perception that law-abiding Americans are paying more than their fair share. Concerns about unauthorized immigrants not paying taxes and the long-term negative fiscal consequences of the United States' large immigrant population may already be shaping the willingness of White Americans to tax themselves to provide basic services in municipalities around the country (Hopkins 2009). Donald Trump's campaign and his effort to build an impenetrable wall are some of the most recent manifestations of this narrative, but they only continue a long-standing discussion about immigration and the economy. Given that large segments of the American population believe that immigrants are hurting wages and job prospects, many proposed economic policy solutions would likely be influenced by considerations about immigration.

If this premise is true, then there will be clear policy prescriptions in each of these areas for those who are concerned about immigration and the growing Latino population. Increased anti-immigrant sentiment in each case will likely lead directly to more conservative policy. The public's belief that immigrants disproportionately use public services, and that immigrants and their offspring represent a considerable share of the "receiving" population provide a strong motivation for retrenchment. Likewise, if the prevailing perception is that Latinos are prone to crime, and that many of the criminal offenders in the streets are Latinos and immigrants, then a likely solution is harsher sentencing. The overall hypothesis of this story is that anxiety and resentment generated by an increasingly large immigrant population likely leads to less generous and more punitive policy choices.

These are, however, only logical deductions. We do not yet know if state policy in any of these areas really is a function of immigrant context. No study that I know of has tried to make these empirical connections. Only a broader, geographically informed study can begin to illuminate the extent of immigration's impact on American politics.

Do Latinos Play a Role?

This immigration backlash story is only part of the policy story that I seek to tell. The second goal of this chapter is to incorporate the role that Latinos themselves play in this process. One of the implications of the argument so far is that Latinos can do little on their own to effect change. Up to this point, the only role that the Latino population has played is in sparking a negative White reaction. The mere presence of Latinos changes the attitudes and actions of the rest of the United States. That is an important part of the story – especially considering that White Americans make up the vast majority of the voting population.

At the same time, it is far from the entire story. In this chapter, I also begin to consider the other side of the equation – the role that racial and ethnic minorities play in American politics and how that role differs dramatically from that of Whites. I want to begin to dispel the notion that Latinos are powerless. In fact, I believe that Latinos do have some agency in the policy process. While I have argued that the immigrant backlash is a powerful force, I believe that, given sufficient numbers, Latinos and others can begin to overwhelm that force. Once the size of the Latino population passes a certain threshold, Latinos should be able to mobilize to influence policy outcomes, and policy should begin to shift back to the left.

I say this even though I know that there are real questions as to just how much influence the Latino population has in American politics at the national level. A range of factors limits Latino participation in the electoral arena to the point at which Latinos often participate at half the rate of Whites (Hajnal 2010, Verba et al. 1995). Foreign birth and undocumented status both limit the extent of Latino participation. Latinos are also hampered by limited economic resources relative to Whites. To the degree that money is a factor in American politics, Latinos simply have less of it to contribute to the process (Verba et al.

1995). The end result is that politicians may simply be less receptive to Latinos. Indeed, Griffin and Newman (2007) find that legislators are less responsive to the views of Latino constituents than they are to those of White constituents.

Yet, it is also worth noting that large numbers of the Latino community can and do mobilize to try to influence policy. The protests in 2006 that drew millions of Americans together to fight for immigrants' rights represent just one of the more prominent examples (Barreto et al. 2009). Scholars also point to the decisive role that Latino votes have had in some electoral contests (Abrajano and Alvarez 2010). The growing influence of the "Latino giant" is also evident in the halls of American democracy. In California and Texas, Latinos now make up about one-fifth of the legislature. Latinos represent almost 40 percent of the population in those two states, and they represent sizable and growing shares in many others. State legislators are unlikely to totally ignore the concerns and preferences of such a large group.

Thus, I believe that the pattern of immigration backlash should only hold until the Latino population becomes large enough to mobilize to effect policy change on its own. Once Latinos pass this threshold, a larger Latino population should be associated with more pro-Latino outcomes. The end result, I argue, is that the relationship between Latino context and policy should be a curvilinear one.[13]

Ultimately, the analysis will tell us one way or another whether Latinos do have some agency. If I can show that a more complex relationship exists and that Latinos can – if their numbers are large enough – sway policy in a more pro-Latino direction, then expectations about the future change radically. The backlash will persist to a certain point but over the long term as the immigrant population grows ever larger, a coalition of Latinos, other ethnic/racial minorities, and liberal Whites may win out.

Measuring Context

As I noted in the previous chapter, the data seem to suggest that concerns about immigration are focused on the Latino population. When Americans think about immigration, the image in their mind is likely to be of a Latino – often an undocumented immigrant (Brader et al. 2008, Pérez 2016, Valentino et al. 2013). Likewise, when Americans think about Latinos, the image is likely to be an immigrant.

In essence, immigrant and Latino are conflated. That is why estimates of the size of the local immigrant population closely mirror estimates of the local Latino population (Enos 2010). For this reason, in the analysis that follows I focus on the percentage of Latinos in a state as the primary measure of context.[14] Do larger concentrations of Latinos lead to policies that are more regressive, more punitive, and less generous?[15]

Government Spending in Heavily Latino States

Is a White backlash taking place against immigrants, or Latino populations? Does Latino context play a role in shaping state policy? The answers are clear. States with more Latinos tend to redistribute less and punish more.

The initial test of this basic idea is a simple one. I compare government spending in states with large and small Latino populations. I focus on spending because I think that is one of the most revealing indicators of a government's priorities.[16] More money for education, for example, suggests that the state cares about education, and is willing to invest its limited resources to try to improve educational outcomes. The analysis specifically focuses on the *proportion* of the state budget that goes to each policy area. By focusing on the proportion, I get a measure of the government's priorities *relative* to other functions, and I avoid some of the variation caused by the fact that some states are richer than others and are thus able to spend more money.[17]

I begin by looking at spending on health, education, and prisons – three policy areas that are, on the surface, unrelated to immigration and the Latino population. But as I have argued these "non-racial" policies could be very much driven by attitudes toward these groups – especially in states in which many if not most of the people impacted by the policies are Latinos and immigrants.[18]

There is a substantial difference in two of the three policy areas between spending in states with large Latino populations and states with relatively small Latino populations.[19] Just as the racial-threat theory would predict, in states with a large Latino population whose members could benefit from public services, Medicaid funding is significantly lower. Specifically, Medicaid falls from 3.7 percent of the budget in states with relatively few Latinos to 2.5 percent of the budget in states with large numbers of Latinos. At first glance, that might seem like a small drop but as the third column of Table 6.1 illustrates, it

Table 6.1 Government Policy in Heavily Latino States is More Regressive (Share of All State Spending)

	States With a Small Latino Population	States With a Large Latino Population	Proportional Difference in Spending
Spending			
Health care	3.7%	2.5%	−32%
Corrections	3.9	4.7	+21
Education	25.8	24.8	−4
Taxation			
Sales tax	27.5	36.4	+32
Property tax	5.8	1.3	−78

Source: National Association of State Budget Officers (1995–2011)
Small Latino Population <5% Hispanic; Large Latino Population >15% Hispanic

actually represents a pretty sizable shift in spending. Heavily Latino states spend 32 percent less on Medicaid than states with few Latinos.

Also, as expected, the pattern is exactly the opposite for spending on criminal justice. In states in which Latinos represent a large share of the population, and could be the target of tougher laws and harsher sentences, spending on prisons is substantially higher. Heavily Latino states spend 4.7 percent of their budget on prisons, while states with small Latino populations spend 3.9 percent of their budgets in the same way.[20] Again, that difference might at first seem small, but it represents a 21 percent increase in the share of the budget going to prisons. The difference is also large if I instead analyze spending on a per capita basis. Using this metric, I find that states with smaller Latino populations spend on average $89.75 per resident to operate prisons, while states with larger Latino populations spend fully $139.30 per resident annually.

The third policy area, education, also fits the pattern, but here the differences are small no matter how one looks at it. States with larger Latino populations spend less – but only 4 percent less – on education. At least judging by this one test, there is no major difference in education spending between states with differing Latino population shares. Other more advanced tests later in this chapter reveal a robust relationship, but for now I can make no strong claims about the link between the Latino population and educational policy decisions.

How governments spend their money is only half of the fiscal story. There can be no public services without taxes and fees. State governments also have to make weighty decisions about how they raise their revenues. On this front, tax decisions are the most important. States can choose to raise revenue through more progressive tax measures such as property taxes, or they can favor more regressive means such as sales taxes. Regressive taxes such as sales taxes will fall most heavily on immigrants, Latinos, and the poor for whom retail sales represent a large share of their spending. By contrast, progressive taxes such as property taxes do not place a burden on those at the lower end of the spectrum because the poor generally do not own property. Thus, the extent to which states favor sales over property taxes could say a lot about the groups they seek to penalize or benefit.[21]

What tax patterns do say is very clear. States that are heavily Latino tend to raise much more of their revenue through regressive sales taxes, and much less of their revenue through progressive property taxes. The differences are substantial. There is, in fact, a 32 percent increase in the share of revenue raised through sales taxes in states in which Latinos represent a large share of the population. Likewise, there is a 78 percent decrease in the share of revenue raised through progressive property taxes in those same states (compared to states with small Latino population shares).

All told, states with larger Latino populations tend to spend and tax in ways that appear to target the Latino community, and benefit other more advantaged segments of the population. The upshot? On the spending side, heavily Latino states spend less on public services when Latinos are the potential beneficiaries, and more on criminal justice when Latinos are the potential target. On the taxing side, heavily Latino states impose higher taxes on the poor and lower taxes on the rich. By contrast, in states with smaller Latino populations, public services are more generous, and taxes are more progressive. In short, the size of the Latino population very much appears to shape how states raise and spend their money.[22]

A More Definitive Test of the Racial-Threat Story

Basic comparisons of states with and without significant Latino populations are telling, but they are far from conclusive. A range of other factors might be driving the results. Heavily Latino states might also be facing difficult economic circumstances that effectively force them to be less generous. These same states – for reasons having nothing to do with the Latino population – might also have more conservative residents or more Republican legislators, either of which could easily account for the distinct spending patterns. Heavily Latino and non-

Latino states might also differ in educational levels, population size, region, or legislative professionalism. All of this means that the results could be driven less by the share of Latinos in the state and more by any number of other factors.

To help ensure that that is not the case, I performed a series of regressions on the data that controlled for other factors that might shape state government spending and taxation decisions.[23] Specifically, I controlled for: the share of citizens identifying as conservative, the share of state legislators who are Republican, the unemployment rate, median household income, the professionalization of the legislature, and several demographic factors including the proportion of residents with a bachelor's degree, and the share of residents who are African American and Asian American.[24]

The results are even more powerful after taking into account all of these other factors.[25] I find that, all else equal, states with larger Latino populations are significantly less likely to spend money on education, significantly less likely to provide Medicaid, and significantly more likely to devote money to prisons.[26] In essence, Latinos are affected by policy but cannot and do not influence the choice of policy.[27]

These more complex regressions also confirm the link between Latino population share and tax policy.[28] Controlling for a range of factors, states with more Latinos rely more heavily on regressive taxes, and utilize progressive taxes much less often. Finally, if I go back and look at welfare spending, as other scholars have done in the past, the same pattern surfaces. As the share of Latinos in the population increases, the amount of money that states spend on welfare diminishes. (Regression results are included in the appendix.)

All of this indicates that the United States' increasingly diverse population is generating a real, wide-ranging backlash. As the Latino population grows, Americans become less willing to invest in public services such as education, health, and welfare, and they become more willing to fund prisons. In other words, when the policy is more apt to impact Latinos, benefits decline, and punishments increase.[29]

Latino Agency

The conclusions so far suggest that Latinos are really just a pawn in a game played by the rest of the American population. But are Latinos really without any agency in the policy world? What about

California, where 23 percent of state legislators are Latino, or New Mexico, where 40 percent of the eligible voter population is Latino? Do Latino numbers eventually matter?

I believe that Latinos do have some power, and can begin to have a say when their numbers are large enough. Once Latinos make up 30 percent or 40 percent of the population, they may be able to provide the swing vote that turns the tide, and leads to the election of more pro-Latino legislators or governors. If large enough and active enough, the Latino population might be able to begin to push policy back toward a more pro-Latino agenda. Can Latinos begin to assert themselves when their numbers grow sufficiently large?

Testing this more complex model is fairly straightforward. I need only include an additional measure of the size of the Latino population that singles out these larger Latino populations in the regression models. When I do that, I confirm that Latinos do play a role in the policy world and that they can begin to decide their own fates when their numbers are sufficient.[30] In Figure 6.1 I illustrate the relationship between the Latino population share and spending on corrections from the regression model. The figure shows that growth in the Latino population first leads to a rise in the proportion of state funds that go to corrections, but as Latinos become a larger and larger share of the state population, the amount of corrections spending declines substantially.[31] Once Latinos pass a particular threshold, Latino population growth begins to be associated with increasingly liberal policy outcomes on corrections. The increasingly liberal trend in corrections spending begins roughly when Latinos reach one-third of a state's population, and slopes significantly downward by the time Latinos are 40 percent of the population. Of course, this is only an average effect. Exactly when Latinos will begin to win on policy in any given state will depend on a more complex set of factors that likely includes the share of Whites who are racially and politically liberal, the size and views of other racial and ethnic minorities in the state, and the state's institutional structure and electoral laws.

This relationship does not only hold for corrections spending. I find a similar pattern on education spending. State funds for education decline as the share of the Latino population grows – all else equal – but that decline begins to ebb away after the Latino population increases beyond the one-third threshold. After that point, Latinos appear to be large enough in number to help sway policy outcomes, and education spending begins to grow.

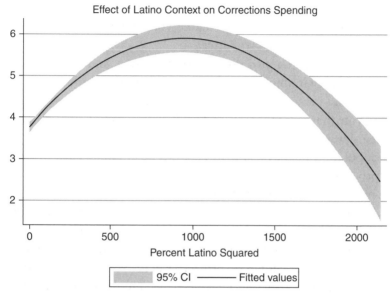

Figure 6.1. The Effect of Latino Context on Corrections Spending
Source: National Association of State Budget Officers (1995–2011)

Latinos also appear to impact tax policy. States with larger Latino populations are more likely to favor regressive means of raising revenue, such as the sales tax, but the effect of the Latino population size is attenuated after it reaches a certain threshold (roughly about one-third Latino). Beyond that threshold, the Latino population is large enough to influence policy and larger Latino populations are associated with more progressive tax policy.

Taken together, this suggests that the Latino population serves as more than just a threat to the rest of the community. Latinos, themselves, appear to have an impact on policy. If Latinos grow to one-third of the national population and become majorities in many states – as they are expected to do by the middle of the twenty-first century – then Latinos might have much more of a say than they do now, and state policy might look very different than it does now.

California's Turnaround on Immigration

California's history with immigration and its policy response aptly illustrate this complex relationship. As one of the first states to face large-scale Latino immigration, California was also one of the first to try to actively impose restrictions on services for undocumented immigrants, as evidenced in 1994 with the now infamous Proposition 187. Over time, Whites in the state became more conservative, with more and more moving to the Republican Party. Policy on immigration, education, and corrections shifted decidedly to the right. California fell from among the top half of all states in per-pupil education funding in 1980, when Whites represented the overwhelming majority of schoolchildren, to near the bottom (forty-fourth place) in 2009, when Latinos were the single largest racial/ethnic group among school-age children (Kaplan 2010). Likewise, corrections funding more than tripled as a proportion of the budget from only about 2.9 percent of the budget in 1980 to well over 10 percent in 2005 (California Budget Project 2011). Driving this growth in prison spending was a series of stricter sentencing laws such as California's famous 1994 "Three Strikes Law," which imposed mandatory life sentences for all three-time felons.

As the Latino population has grown and amassed enough influence to be an important part of the state's Democratic majority, policy has shifted back to the left. With the active support of Latinos, who now account for 38 percent of the population, and with the strong backing of Latino legislators, who now hold 23 percent of the seats in the state legislature, a series of pro-immigrant measures has passed the legislature. These measures include offering undocumented immigrants in-state tuition, drivers' licenses, and the opportunity to practice law. Education and corrections funding are also now slowly following suit. In the last few years, state education funding has experienced a slight but noticeable uptick. With voters passing Prop. 30, a tax measure that is expected to raise billions for K-12 education, the state is likely to see even more growth in education spending. At the other end of the spectrum, corrections funding has dropped markedly, and the state has initiated a number of steps to gain early release of prisoners. In addition, the state has shifted resources from imprisonment to rehabilitation. Over the last three decades, California has transformed itself from a leader in anti-immigrant policymaking to a leader in providing creative, forward-thinking policies on immigration (California Immigrant Policy Center 2015).[32] A range of different factors has contributed to these policy changes in California, but Latino context and the immigrant-threat narrative appear to be an important part of the story.

What About States With Rapidly Expanding Latino Populations?

It is important to distinguish between the *size* of a minority population and the *rate of growth* of that population when thinking about context and perceptions of racial threat. A spate of recent anti-immigrant legislation in new destination states, such as South Carolina and Alabama, suggests that rapid growth in the Latino population may be particularly threatening. Judging by at least some media accounts, rapidly expanding immigrant communities are sparking heated reactions in areas throughout the South and Midwest that have not previously experienced much in-migration (Severson 2011, Sulzberger 2010).[33] Is the overall size of the Latino population driving policy, as the results so far have suggested? Or does rapid growth of new immigrants have a more pronounced effect?

To assess this possibility, I tested a range of measures that capture different aspects of Latino/immigrant population growth.[34] In the end, I did find some effects, but the results were far from robust. In particular, I found that changes in state welfare spending could be tied to changes in the size of a state's Latino population. In new immigrant destination states in which the overall number of immigrants might still be small but where rapid growth is occurring, cutbacks in welfare spending became more commonplace.[35]

At the same time, despite testing all kinds of different measures of population change and assessing these population measures against a range of different policy areas, I could find few other significant effects. Rapid population growth surely matters – as demonstrated by sudden surges in explicitly anti-immigrant legislation in states that were until recently fairly racially homogenous. But population growth appears to have a less consistent and less robust impact on broader state policy-making than does the overall size of the Latino population. Conflict can and does occur in new immigrant destinations, but it seems to be more prevalent in states with larger, long-standing immigrant populations.[36]

Race vs. Immigration and Race vs. Citizenship Status

It is also worth digging deeper into the question of whether the backlash is directed at the entire Latino population – as the analysis has implied – or whether most of the fear, anxiety, and backlash are driven by the undocumented population. There is at least some reason to believe that all of this is being driven by the undocumented population. Many – if not most – of the explicitly anti-immigrant policy measures passed by states have specifically targeted the undocumented population. Unauthorized immigrants were targeted by Proposition 187 back in the 1990s in California. They were also the target of more recent policies in Arizona, Georgia, and South Carolina. Moreover, when Americans are asked about immigration in surveys, they reserve their most negative assessments for the undocumented population. Individual White Americans are often ambivalent about legal immigration. They seem much less divided by illegal immigration.

Given that so much of the immigration debate over the last three decades has focused on the undocumented population, testing reactions to this specific group is an important next step. To determine if it is the population of *undocumented* immigrants, rather than *all* immigrants, that drives policy reaction, I substituted a measure of the size of a given state's undocumented population into the empirical models. No official records exist for the actual size of the unauthorized population by state, so I rely on the estimates provided by Passel and Cohn (2009) and the Pew Hispanic Center (2018b).

I could, however, find no clear link between the estimated size of the undocumented population and policy at the state level.[37] These results suggest that policy changes are driven more by the larger Latino population than they are by the smaller undocumented population per se. In many ways, this is exactly what I expected. Americans regularly conflate immigration and illegal immigration. Indeed, the majority of Americans think that most of the nation's immigrants are here illegally. In the minds of many White Americans, the terms Latino, immigrant, and illegal tend to be muddled together. Immigration is changing the United States, but those changes appear often to be noticed and filtered through the lens of race. The group targeted more than any other is Latinos.

Discussion

As this chapter demonstrates, America's racial divide has consequences far and wide.

Those consequences extend beyond the national-level decision-making that determines how the federal government will choose to spend its money; and beyond the effects on African Americans – the group that loses the most on national policy. The consequences of a racially divided America extend – as I have just demonstrated – to state-level policies and to other groups such as Latinos. The pattern across states is clear. A large Latino population is perceived as a racial threat and sparks a backlash that leads to decreased funds for education, a larger criminal justice apparatus, and a more regressive taxation system. All of this could have very real and very negative consequences. Latinos already lag far behind Whites and Asian Americans in nearly every indicator of educational performance (graduation rates, standardized test scores, etc.) and are already over-represented in the criminal justice system, so the decision to reduce education funding, and to increase corrections funding in states with a large Latino community may exacerbate the problem even further. This rightward policy shift also runs counter to the preferences of the bulk of the Latino population (Bowler and Segura 2011, Fraga et al. 2012). As Latinos grow in number, policies are less likely to reflect what they want.

For many, this is unsurprising. Many have suspected that immigration and the growing Latino population are generating a harsh reaction. Trump's campaign only underscored those suspicions. Nevertheless, something novel emerges here. These comparisons show just how wide-ranging the consequences are when policymaking takes place in the context of perceived racial threats. In a political era in which many claim race is less important than it once was, I find that larger concentrations of Latinos are leading what appears to be a fundamental reordering of political preferences. States are reacting to immigrant arrivals not simply by making laws that explicitly target immigrants but also, more fundamentally, by changing the core priorities of state government across a broad range of ostensibly non-racial policies such as education, health, criminal justice, and taxes. The patterns in this chapter suggest that the nation's increasingly diverse population is having a profound impact on the politics of the United States. Who wins and who loses in the battle over state policy is very much a function of racial context and the immigrant threat.

Thus, the evidence powerfully shows that context matters, and that it matters a great deal. What is less clear is the mechanism behind the relationship between Latino population size and state policy: Is the driving force personal interactions with Latino immigrants, negative media coverage of Latinos, or political campaigns that target Latinos?[38] I am doubtful that individual interactions play a big role – partly because state context is such a poor proxy for interracial contact. I am also doubtful that personal interactions drive negative White reactions to Latinos because studies that are able to measure and test the effects of personal interactions find that they generally lead to more tolerant rather than less tolerant views (Dixon and Rosenbaum 2004).

Increasingly negative media coverage seems more plausible. In other research, Marisa Abrajano, Hans Hassell, and I have shown that media outlets do cover immigration with an overwhelmingly negative tone, and that the public responds to that immigrant-threat narrative. At the national level, we found that after a period of particularly negative media coverage, aggregate White partisanship becomes more Republican (Abrajano and Hajnal 2015). A similar pattern could be happening regarding policy at the state level.

I suspect that political elites in the Republican Party also play an important role in driving the reaction to immigration and the Latino population. In California, for example, the widespread backlash against immigration in the 1990s seemed to gain steam only after the Republican governor, Pete Wilson, actively campaigned against the influx of immigrants, and led the fight for Prop. 187. Nationwide, as more and more Republican leaders have taken anti-immigrant stances over time, the backlash against immigration has become increasingly pronounced. For many, Trump's campaign against immigrants served to fuel that fire even further.

This story is not, however, a purely negative one. Latinos, despite all of the barriers they face, also have some agency, and are able to shift policy in a pro-Latino direction if their numbers are large enough. If the Census Bureau's population projections are correct, and if Whites lose their majority status in a few decades, then this emerging pattern bodes well for Latinos in the long term. The nation may experience more anxiety, more conflict, and more backlash in the near term. But in the longer term, the influence of Latinos and other minorities should only grow more pronounced, and policy should become more aligned with their preferences. California may be just the first domino to fall. As the state's former governor, Jerry Brown, recently proclaimed "Just as California's changed, Arizona's going to change. And Texas . . . we're part of a great and grand transition" (Feliz 2015).

Part IV
Seeking Greater Equality

It is extremely difficult to find effective and attainable solutions to real-world political problems such as those outlined in this book. Nevertheless, in Part IV, I seek to identify changes that could alleviate the racial inequities documented throughout this book. The analysis shows that one change – the election of more Democrats to positions of power – holds promise for altering the fate of racial and ethnic minorities in American democracy and their well-being in American society. This section ends with a discussion of expectations for the future.

7 DEMOCRATIC PARTY CONTROL AND EQUALITY IN POLICY RESPONSIVENESS

America's democracy is uneven and racially imbalanced. Whites and White interests tend to prevail. Racial and ethnic minorities and their interests are more apt to lose out in the policy arenas at local, state, and national levels.[1] That is the story of this book so far. But it need not be the final word. If Americans are concerned about equality within the democratic process and ultimately about the well-being of all, then they need to think about ways to correct for that racial imbalance. One place to start is with the two major political parties.

A quick glance at the nation's last two presidents highlights the enormous importance that partisanship seems to make. Barack Obama's signature policy achievement was the passage of the Affordable Care Act (Obamacare). Donald Trump's first major policy initiative was to attempt to repeal the act. Barack Obama responded to the Black Lives Matter movement by vigorously prosecuting local police forces, and mandating agreements that included major reforms of local police practices. Donald Trump has tried to revoke those agreements. President Obama signed the Paris Agreement to address climate change. President Trump initiated the withdrawal from the agreement. Under Obama, Deferred Action for Childhood Arrivals (DACA) was born to give those immigrants who arrived in the United States as undocumented children an opportunity to seek work permits and, ultimately, citizenship. Under Trump, DACA is dying. Obama's administration sharply expanded the number of refugees allowed to enter the country. Trump's administration limited refugees. Barack Obama nominated a staunch liberal for the Supreme Court. Donald Trump appointed one of the most conservative Supreme Court judges in recent history. It is only a slight exaggeration to state that the two men and their policies could not be more different. Donald Trump and his (Republican) presidency are in many ways the antithesis of Barack Obama and his (Democratic) presidency.[2]

Barack Obama and Donald Trump differ on almost every dimension but perhaps the most significant is partisanship. One is a Democrat. The other a Republican. That party divide drives much of their policy differences. It shapes their agendas in office. And if we are looking for factors that might mitigate or exacerbate racial imbalances in responsiveness, partisanship is a logical place to start.

Partisan differences are, of course, not limited to the presidency. Democratic and Republican leaders differ on their policy positions at every level. Democrats tend to seek a more liberal policy agenda, while Republicans pursue a more conservative one. That raises an important question. Do more minority-friendly policies emerge when Democrats are in office than when Republicans hold power? And more broadly, could Democratic Party control be an answer to the racial imbalance in American democracy?

The answer, as I show in this chapter, is that it matters who controls the levers of power. An examination of policy responsiveness over time shows that policy responds to African-American interests to a much greater degree when Democrats occupy the White House or are the majority in Congress. When Democrats control both institutions, almost all of the racial imbalance disappears. By electing Democrats into office, deep racial inequalities in democratic responsiveness could be eliminated.

Why Democrats Might Be Better for Minorities

Why might one expect Democratic control to matter? One reason to expect minorities to fare better under Democrats is the overwhelming support racial and ethnic minorities give to the Democratic Party in American elections. The 90 percent of Blacks, 77 percent of Asian Americans, and 69 percent of Latinos who voted for Democratic House candidates in 2018 must be voting Democratic for some reason.[3] Likewise, the fact that Whites tend to favor the Republican Party and Republican candidates suggests that Republican control may be better for White America. The 60 percent of all White voters who sided with

Republican candidates must believe that Republicans are the better option.[4] Surely all of these Americans – both White and non-White – cannot be wrong.

Moreover, when asked directly which party is better for minorities, Americans are generally in agreement. More than 70 percent of African Americans contend that the Democratic Party "works hard on issues Black people care about" (Dawson 1994). Latinos by an almost three to one margin believe that the Democratic Party better represents the views of Latinos (Dade 2011).[5]

Asian Americans are only a little less likely to believe that the Democratic Party is particularly responsive to issues that affect their pan-ethnic group. Even among White Americans, two-thirds claim that the Democratic Party provides more aid to minorities than the Republican Party.[6] If the vast majority of Americans – both White and non-White – believe that the Democratic Party serves the interests of racial and ethnic minorities more than the Republican Party, switching the party in power must matter.

In addition, the Democratic Party itself makes the same claims. Democratic leaders regularly contend that their policy platform will benefit the minority community. As the party of greater redistribution, increased affirmative action, and tougher anti-discrimination measures, Democrats assert that their agenda is a pro-minority one. They repeatedly assert that their more liberal policies on race, welfare, education, poverty, and crime are bound to help minorities who fall disproportionately on the lower half of the socioeconomic spectrum. Democrats also contend that Republican policies will serve to leave minorities further and further behind. As Vice President Joe Biden recently put it, the GOP's approach to financial regulation would "put y'all back in chains" (Sullivan 2012).

Are Democrats Really Better?

But do minorities really gain when Democrats rule? The notion that Democrats are more responsive to the interests and preferences of minorities might not be so clear as it first appears. The assertion that all of these Democratic policies, when passed, have led to better outcomes for minorities is just that – an assertion. Most critically, Republicans make almost exactly the same claims about their policies. Republican leaders contend that greater efficiencies associated with more conservative policies and smaller government ultimately lead to more growth and higher incomes for all. During the 2016 presidential debates, Donald Trump claimed "I will do more for African Americans and Latinos than [Hillary Clinton] can ever do in ten lifetimes. All she has done is talk to the African Americans and to the Latinos" (Desmond-Harris 2016). Trump's comments echo a Republican theme that goes back to Ronald Reagan and beyond.

Reagan once argued in a speech to the NAACP that "A strong economy returns the greatest good to the Black population. It returns a benefit greater than that provided by specific federal programs. By slowing the growth of government and by limiting the tax burden and thus stimulating investment, we will also be reducing inflation and unemployment" (Reagan 1981). That appears to be the logic behind the recent Republican tax cuts. During his time as House Majority leader, Paul Ryan argued: "Passing this bill is the single biggest thing we can do to grow the economy, to restore opportunity, and to help middle-income families that are struggling" (DeBonis and Paletta 2017).

Republicans also argue that the absence of policies targeting minorities reduces race-based stigmatization, and results in a more just, color-blind society.[7] Finally, Republicans can also claim to offer a more socially conservative policy agenda that fits with the stated preferences of many minority voters. On issues as diverse as abortion and gay marriage, the policy platform of the Republican Party may be closely aligned with relatively large religiously conservative segments of the Black, Latino, and Asian-American populations. According to African-American presidential candidate Herman Cain, Blacks and others do not support the Democratic Party because it is better for them, but rather because they have been "brainwashed into not being open-minded, not even considering a conservative point of view" (Bouie 2016). The two parties often offer starkly different paths, but both can clearly and logically claim to aid racial and ethnic minorities.

It is also worth noting that although the clear majority of non-Whites currently favor the Democratic Party and most Whites oppose the Democratic Party, no racial group is totally unified when it comes to assessing the relative merits of the two parties. Typically, almost 40 percent of Whites side against the majority position of the White community, and instead favor Democratic candidates. Some 20 percent to 40 percent of Latino and Asian-American voters likewise vote

Republican, and oppose their group's preferred party. Even African Americans, the most cohesive group politically, are far from unanimous. Anywhere from 10 percent to 20 percent of Black voters favor the Republican Party in a typical electoral contest. Could these contrarian voters know more than others?

Even among scholars, assessments about the relative responsiveness of the two parties are decidedly mixed. Most scholars wholeheartedly believe that Democratic Party control is beneficial to minorities. The belief – albeit one not confirmed – is that a more liberal economic agenda and a more liberal racial platform will help minority communities. But a second, less common viewpoint holds that the Democratic Party, though more liberal than the Republican Party, has been half-hearted in its efforts to pursue racial equality.[8] Democratic non-responsiveness is perhaps best explained by Paul Frymer (1999). Frymer contends that Blacks have been "captured" by the Democratic Party. Since Blacks tend to fall on the liberal fringe of the Democratic Party, they essentially have nowhere to go. Most Blacks will not ever consider voting Republican. That means that Democrats do not need to actively appeal to Blacks, and it follows that Republicans will not bother to appeal to Blacks, either. And the problem could be even worse. Because moderate White voters who often decide electoral contests in American politics may be resentful of Black demands for more resources, Democrats and Republican may even have an incentive to actively favor White interests over Black preferences. The end result is likely to be a lack of responsiveness to the African-American population from *both* parties.

Black voters are not the lone group prone to being ignored. Paul Kim suggests that the same strategic imperatives of the United States' two-party system are likely to work systematically to exclude the interests of Asian Americans, as well. Plenty of political observers have lamented the reluctance of either major party to put forward meaningful reforms on immigration and other issues of particular concern to the Latino community. The bottom line from this perspective is that neither party should be viewed as particularly pro-minority.

Still other scholars believe that the more color-blind agenda espoused by the Republicans has ultimately benefited minorities more than the Democratic Party's color-conscious policies. Representative of this viewpoint is work by Stephan Thernstrom and Abigail Thernstrom, arguing that Black economic gains were more pronounced in the period before the initiation of the Democrats' racially liberal policy agenda in the 1960s than afterward (Thernstrom and Thernstrom 1997).

What Do Current Studies Show?

What, then, is the reality? Is one party actually better than the other party for minorities? Surprisingly, data addressing this point are limited. Scholars have clearly demonstrated close ties between race, party, and well-being in earlier periods in American history. Indeed, Desmond King and Rogers Smith have compellingly shown that competition between two parties – one more closely associated with a White supremacist order, and the other tightly linked to an egalitarian transformative order – has at times had enormous consequences for minority well-being (King and Smith 2005). The Republican Party's efforts to end slavery under Abraham Lincoln provide the most obvious example of one party favoring a radically more egalitarian agenda than the other (Klinkner and Smith 1999). Racial inequality also clearly declined in the years after the Democratic Party put the New Deal in place (Thernstrom and Thernstrom 1997). Others have lauded the Democratic Party for the key part it played in advancing the Civil Rights Act, the Voting Rights Act, and other transformative civil rights legislation of the 1960s (Klinkner and Smith 1999).[9]

Whether either party's policies can or should be viewed as being more responsive to minorities in recent decades is less clear. Despite the fact that race has been such a strong dividing line in modern-day American politics, surprisingly little work has sought to directly test the racial consequences of Democratic and Republican control. One of the biggest hurdles has been the availability of data. Until very recently, national surveys did not have samples that were large enough to accurately measure Black, Latino, and Asian-American opinions on the issues of the day. This gap made gauging policy responsiveness to minorities almost impossible. As a result, much of the research has been largely anecdotal and piecemeal. Scholars might point to the Republican Party's embrace of tougher criminal sentencing in the 1970s and 1980s as being particularly harmful to minority well-being in the last few decades. More recently, some would point to President Obama's executive order legalizing millions of undocumented immigrants as a sign that Democrats are more responsive to minority interests than Republicans. Those same scholars might also point to the fact that Republicans challenged the executive order as another strong sign that Republican policy is, in fact, anti-minority.

But these kinds of pronouncements single out extreme cases and overlook larger patterns. Focusing on Obama's executive order, for example, ignores the fact that Reagan signed into law a much broader amnesty law in the 1990s. It also overlooks the fact that Obama deported more undocumented immigrants than any other president. Signature accomplishments cannot be examined in isolation. Any credible analysis needs to look at the broader array of policies enacted by both parties over a broad sweep of time to assess systematically whether and how parties matter for minorities.

Fortunately, these data limitations have begun to fade in recent years. That has allowed John Griffin and Brian Newman to directly assess partisan responsiveness on a national scale (Griffin and Newman 2007). Their work reveals important patterns. They find that the votes of Democratic legislators are more responsive to Latino opinion than those of Republican legislators. At the same time, they find no difference between Democratic and Republican legislators in responsiveness to Black opinion. While an important step forward, their research only looks at how party allegiance affects the votes of individual legislators. They do not examine which policies actually pass through the legislature, or how party control of the entire legislature impacts responsiveness. As such, no direct test has assessed how partisan control impacts minority interests or minority well-being.[10]

The closest scholars have come to measuring this stems from the extensive literature on class and responsiveness.[11] Here again the data are decidedly mixed. Many find, at best, limited differences in how well the two parties represent the lower classes. In perhaps the most thorough empirical analysis of class and policy responsiveness, Martin Gilens finds that Democrats and Republicans are both disproportionately responsive to privileged segments of the electorate. As Gilens concludes, "... the broader expectation that the preferences of low- or middle-income Americans would be reflected more strongly in policy outcomes under Democratic than Republican control is not met" (2012:178).[12] These findings seem to be reflected in economic outcomes for different classes. Jacob Hacker and Paul Pierson (2011) show that inequality has grown over the last few decades regardless of the party in power. Page (1983) similarly points to the failure of both parties to effectively counteract inequality. From this perspective, neither party should be viewed as particularly pro-minority or particularly effective in improving minority well-being.

But not everyone agrees. In what is undoubtedly the closest to a direct test of the hypothesis, Larry Bartels finds that greater economic gains for lower-income Americans are associated with Democratic control of the presidency than with Republican control. Benjamin Page and James Simmons (2000) provide additional evidence that the Democratic Party's support of liberal welfare policies has benefited the poor and working classes. Ellis (2013) similarly finds that Democratic legislators are relatively more responsive than Republican legislators to the policy interests of lower-income Americans. Given that minorities fall disproportionately toward the lower end of the class scale, one could infer that the Democratic Party benefits racial and ethnic minorities.[13]

At this point the answer is unknown. With no direct test to show how partisan control impacts policy responsiveness to racial and ethnic minority public opinion, or how partisan control affects minority well-being, the jury is very much still out.

Two Steps to Assessing Party Control

In the next two chapters I attempt to see if, in fact, Democratic or Republican party control matters for racial and ethnic minorities. I do so by breaking the question into two distinct and equally critical parts. First, I look at *policy responsiveness*. In terms of the policies a party in control passes, is one party more *responsive* to minority preferences than the other? To answer this question, I add Democratic and Republican control to the analysis of policy responsiveness that I undertook in Chapter 4, and look to see if control by the Democrats or Republicans reduces the racial biases that I uncovered.

Second, in the next chapter I look at *economic well-being* under differing partisan regimes. Once all is said and done, do minority incomes and job prospects improve more when the Democrats control the presidency and the Congress or when the Republicans do? I answer this second question by compiling annual data on basic indicators of income, poverty, and employment for each racial group every year over the last half-century, and then look to see how racial inequality changes under Democratic and Republican regimes. Only after looking at both questions can I tell if either Democratic or Republican control represents a viable solution to America's uneven democracy.

Party Control and Policy Responsiveness

As Chapter 4 shows, a real imbalance exists in the nation's policy responsiveness. The federal government heeds the wishes of Whites more than those of Blacks. Policy actions across a forty-year period, and across an array of different policy areas, clearly demonstrate that Blacks lose out significantly more than Whites. Moreover, that racial gap dwarfs other gaps by class, religion, gender, age, and any other demographic variable that I could examine. Race, more than any other factor, determines whose opinions matter.

But in conducting that analysis, I also noticed that racial gaps in responsiveness varied by year. Blacks almost always lost out more than Whites, but the size of the gap waxed and waned from year to year. That variation suggests that who is in power might matter. Perhaps when Democrats dominate the halls of power, the racial gap declines, and American democracy becomes more evenhanded.

To test that possibility, I return to the policy responsiveness data to see whether the party in office alters the patterns of bias.

The Presidency and Congress

To assess the effects of partisan control I look at which party controls the two most powerful institutions in American democracy: Congress and the presidency.[14] The political relevance of these two offices should be clear. The president stands at the top of American democracy. The president can veto any piece of legislation passed by Congress. As such he may have the institutional power to sway the direction of policy (Cameron 2000). As the only leader elected by all of the people, the president may also have the bully pulpit and hence the ability to push American government in one direction or another (Kernell 1997, Neustadt 1980). As the sharp contrast between policy outcomes under President Obama and President Trump suggests, control of the presidency by one party or the other could have real implications for the fate of racial and ethnic minorities in American democracy.

I also cannot ignore Congress. Given its prominent role in the Constitution as the primary lawmaking body in the polity, Congress may have equally strong influence over the well-being of different groups in society. There is, in fact, a long-standing debate about the relative influence of Congress and the presidency (Cameron 2000,

Edwards 2003, Kernell 1997, Kiewiet and McCubbins 1985). With this in mind, I consider the partisan make-up of the House and the Senate as well as the partisanship of the presidency in the analysis that follows.

There is no guarantee that the actors who control either office will be able to effect real change in policy and outcomes. The framers of the Constitution sought to ensure that the power of the president and the powers of Congress were checked both by each other and by the judiciary. Federalism and the states further limit the purview of the presidency and Congress. It also may be the case that no matter who controls the presidency or Congress, generating changes to the nation's economic trajectory may be beyond the ability of government.

Beyond this first question – asking which office has the power to alter outcomes in American democracy – is a second: does *partisan control* really matter? There are long-standing debates about whether the power primarily flows from parties and partisan control, or from individual legislators (Cox and McCubbins 2004, Krehbiel 1998). As such, the tests I perform should help answer several questions. They provide insight into the relative importance of Congress and the presidency for shaping responsiveness and the importance or irrelevance of partisan control; moreover, this information may reveal a way to increase responsiveness to minority interests in American democracy.

Measuring Responsiveness Under Different Partisan Regimes

Is policy responsiveness different when Democrats are in control? To answer this question, I examine policy outcomes – specifically patterns in federal government spending – over the last half-century to compare outcomes when Democrats are in charge to outcomes when Republicans are in charge. Recall that in Chapter 4, to examine responsiveness, I focused on surveys that asked Americans for their preferences on federal government spending. I then looked to see whether subsequent federal government spending matched individual preferences. In each case I matched individual spending preferences on a given issue in a given year with changes in government spending on that same issue in the *following* fiscal year. That one-year time difference is important because a central aspect of this investigation is understanding whether public opinion actually leads to policy change.

All told, the surveys asked more than 400,000 individuals for their spending preferences across eleven core policy areas between 1972 and 2010.[15] The eleven spending areas are: welfare, national defense, education, foreign aid, parks and recreation, law enforcement, improving and protecting the nation's health, solving the problems of big cities, improving and protecting the environment, the space exploration program, and highways and bridges. These eleven areas address many of the most important spending decisions the government makes. Collectively, they cover more than half of the federal budget. As noted earlier, I focus on spending because it is one of the most important indicators of government priorities. Decisions about where to invest money, and where to cut, say a lot about how much government values each policy area. It should, however, be clear that spending is not the only dimension of policy.

The surveys asked Americans whether they think the government should increase spending in a particular area, decrease spending, or keep spending at about the same level. To see if they get what they want, I match those individual preferences with actual federal government spending outcomes in the following year in each area. Combining individual preferences and government spending patterns, I can observe whose policy preferences are enacted by government and whose are not. If, for example, a particular individual favored a decline in health care, and if the federal government chose to significantly decrease health-care spending in the following year, that individual is a policy "winner."[16] Because the sample of opinion is large and representative and the policy areas cover most of the federal budget, the data should provide a relatively broad window into policy responsiveness in American democracy.

Does Democratic Control Reduce Racial Inequality in Responsiveness?

The first answer to this question comes from a simple tabulation of policy winners and losers by race under Democratic and Republican regimes over the past half-century. Across all of the years and all of the respondents, a clear pattern emerges. The racial gap in responsiveness declines considerably when Democrats are in charge. Figure 7.1 provides a snapshot of that pattern. The figure shows how much more responsive the government is to Whites than to Blacks under different partisan regimes. Specifically, it shows the racial gap in policy responsiveness under Democratic and Republican presidents and under Democratic and Republican Congresses.

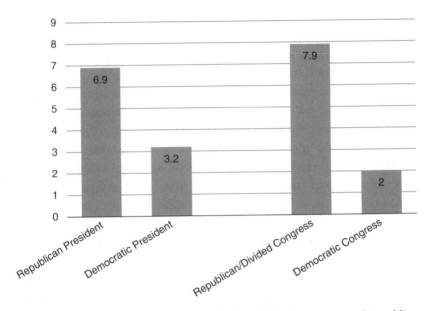

Figure 7.1. Gaps in Policy Responsiveness by Race Under Democrats and Republicans
Source: General Social Survey (1972–2000), Historical Tables (US Govt Printing Office)

When Republicans control the White House, White Americans are almost 7 points more likely than Blacks to see their preferences met in policies. But most of that imbalance fades away when the nation has a Democratic president. In those years, Whites are 3.2 percent more likely than African Americans to see their spending preferences translated into governmental policy. Likewise, the racial gap in responsiveness drops from an average of 7.9 points when Democrats do not control the House and Senate to 2.0 points when Democrats control both houses of Congress. Judged at least by this first test, partisan control is a critical factor shaping who wins and who loses in the policy arena. Under Democrats the racial imbalance in responsiveness largely disappears, and American democracy becomes much more evenhanded.

I began by focusing on the Black-White gap because I have data on Black policy preferences for almost half a century. By contrast, I only have about ten years of data on Latino and Asian-American spending preferences. As such, I have much less confidence in the analysis of these two minority groups – especially when looking for changes over time or across partisan regimes. Indeed, given the paucity of data, and given the lack of change in partisan control of Congress over that ten-year period,

I cannot test the effects of Democratic control of Congress on policy responsiveness to Latinos and Asian Americans.

Nevertheless, it is interesting to look at the patterns in responsiveness to Latinos and Asian Americans across Democratic and Republican presidencies. I find, once again, that policy outcomes for both of these minority groups appear to improve under Democrats. Specifically, Latinos are disproportionate policy losers under a Republican president; they lose on policy 2.2 points more often than Whites. By contrast, Latinos are slightly more likely than Whites to be policy winners when a Democratic president is in office – although the difference is slight. Under Democratic presidents, Latinos win on policy 1.1 percent more than Whites. Asian Americans are slightly more likely than Whites to win on policy regardless of who controls the presidency, but here, too, the outcomes are better under a Democratic administration. The Asian-American advantage over Whites grows from 2.6 points under a Republican president to 3.5 points under a Democrat one. All of this suggests that party control does matter, and that Latinos and Asian Americans do better under Democrats.

I underscore that these particular results on Latinos and Asian Americans should be read with caution. The limited data mean that I am essentially comparing Latino and Asian-American outcomes only under two administrations: those of Bill Clinton and George W. Bush. To the extent that those two presidencies are representative of other Democratic and Republican administrations, the patterns will be informative. To the extent that they are not, the results will be misleading.

A Stricter Test

A simple count of policy winners and losers by race and year makes intuitive sense and is, no doubt, a telling test. But it ignores several other factors that could be impacting responsiveness and distorting the patterns in Figure 7.1. Blacks could be losing disproportionately because government ignores Black preferences more than others, and that racial imbalance could indeed be reduced when Democrats hold office. But Blacks are different from other Americans on many different dimensions. They are more likely to be from the lower end of the socioeconomic spectrum. They are more likely to be liberal and to favor spending increases. They likely have more "extreme" spending preferences than the average American. All of these other, non-racial factors could contribute to the pattern in Figure 7.1. Likewise, the years that Democrats and Republicans govern could be different for reasons that have nothing to do with the Party in charge. Perhaps Democrats are lucky, and they tend to inherit strong economies that allow them to spend more. Black policy losses and the relative gains that Blacks experience under Democrats could have nothing to do with race or racial bias, and could instead be related to changes in the economy that just happen to coincide with Democratic or Republican control. To know if Democrat control and racial bias really are driving the results, I need to control for a range of other factors.[17]

Fortunately, this research design allows me take into account all of these different factors. More precisely, I run a regression that not only controls for the race, class, and other demographic characteristics of each respondent, but also incorporates: the party identification and political ideology of each respondent, a measure of whether each respondent favors a spending increase or a spending decrease, and a measure of whether each respondent favors the most popular spending position on that issue in that year. In addition, I control for overall economic conditions in each year; this step ensures that results that take place under Democratic leadership are not different simply because Democrats inherent different economic conditions. By including this range of controls, I can be more confident that race really is driving any of the differences in responsiveness and that Democratic or Republican control minimizes those imbalances.

The results of this analysis are displayed in Figure 7.2 The figure shows the predicted racial gaps in policy responsiveness under different partisan regimes, controlling for all of the other factors I have mentioned.[18] This more definitive test confirms the original story. When Democrats hold office, much of the racial imbalance in American democracy disappears.

As the figure illustrates, having a Democratic president or a Democratic Congress both matter. All else equal, having a Democratic president cuts the Black-White gap in policy success in half. Democratic control of Congress is an even more powerful factor in reducing racial imbalances. The racial gap declines from a robust 8.1 points when Democrats do not control Congress to a relatively small 1.9 points when they do. The combined effect of having Democrats in both offices is even more powerful. When a Democrat is president and Democrats also control Congress all of the policy bias against Blacks fades away. In fact, when

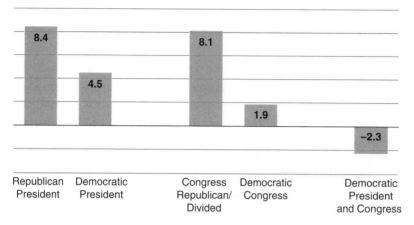

Figure 7.2. Predicted Black-White Gaps in Policy Responsiveness Under Democrats and Republicans
Source: General Social Survey (1972–2000), Historical Tables (US Govt Printing Office)

Democrats are fully in charge, policy responsiveness tilts very slightly in favor of African Americans. In those years when Democrats are in the White House and in the majority in Congress, the model predicts that policy follows the preferences of Blacks about 2.3 percent more often than it follows the preferences of Whites. Under Democrats, African Americans receive a full and fair say in the policies that our government pursues.[19]

Imbalance on Policies Minorities Care About

One concern about this analysis stems from its failure to consider how much individual citizens care about each policy area.[20] Does Democratic control improve outcomes for racial and ethnic minorities on the policy areas they care most about?

Blacks, for example, may not care at all about spending on space exploration, but might be deeply troubled by losing on welfare or education. I sought to test this by focusing only on the five spending areas that tend to be most often associated with Black interests (welfare, health, education, crime, and aid to cities).[21] The results suggest that the effect of having Democrats in office is even more pronounced in those five areas. All else equal, on the issues that Blacks care most about, Blacks lose 16.6 percent more than Whites lose when Republicans control the presidency and Congress. But that racial gap declines to 1.3 percent when Democrats are in charge. The party determining policy, indeed, matters.

That overall pattern is just as clear if I dig deeper and look at key policy decisions enacted by Republican and Democratic administrations over the last few decades – both those in years within the data set as well as those in the most recent years. On the core policies that they care deeply about, racial and ethnic minorities across the nation often win big when Democrats are in charge, and often lose even bigger when Republicans control all of the major offices. One can see that pattern most recently with the Republican tax cut of 2017 – considered by many to be the premier policy achievement of Donald Trump's first years in office. As I have previously noted, that measure instituted major tax cuts that focused disproportionately on the wealthiest Americans. The package passed despite polling showing that only 1 percent of African Americans supported the policy.[22]

That contrasts sharply with 2010, the last year that Democrats occupied the White House and held majorities in both the House and the Senate. The signature policy initiative that year was the Affordable Care Act (ACA, otherwise known as Obamacare). The passage of that Democratic-led legislation not only heralded a dramatic decrease in the number of uninsured Americans, it provided a big political win for African Americans. In 2009, 71.8 percent of African Americans favored an increase in health-care spending. When Barack Obama and the Democrats passed the ACA, and subsequently increased spending on health care by a substantial 10.3 percent, individual African Americans experienced a policy response they wanted. On that core issue in that year when Democrats controlled all three levers of power, government proved to be highly responsive to the African-American community.

Shifting back to 2006, the last year when Republicans had that same political combination – a majority in House and Senate and control of the presidency (with George W. Bush in office) – a sharp contrast in outcomes emerges. At that time, African Americans overwhelmingly favored increases in welfare spending (81 percent), education spending (88 percent), and health-care spending (92 percent), alongside cuts in military spending (73 percent). Under Republican leadership, African Americans did not get what they wanted on any of these critical policy areas.

Backtracking further to 1994, when Bill Clinton was in office and Democrats controlled Congress, African Americans were once again major policy winners. Democratic control of the House and

Senate and a Clinton presidency resulted in major increases in welfare spending (up 12 percent), educational investment (up 19 percent), and health-care outlays (up 7 percent). Democratic control also led to a 3-percent decline in defense spending. That pattern aligned almost perfectly with African-American preferences.

Shifting back again in time, the next most recent period of largely Republican control follows the same script. The year 1987, the last year of Republican control of both presidency and Senate, was also one of the worst years in the analysis for African-American interests in American democracy. That year, 91 percent of African Americans did not have their preferences met on welfare, 86 percent lost out on defense, 85 percent were denied on health care, and 80 percent were policy losers on education.[23] Whether I look at all of the years and all of the policies together, or whether I focus on the most important policies in key years, the pattern that emerges is the same. When Republicans are in charge, African-American interests tend to be ignored. Democratic control, by contrast, leads to much greater responsiveness to African-American interests. Critically, Black gains do not necessarily mean White losses. When Democrats control the policy agenda, Whites are just as likely as African Americans to have a say in policy. Put in more direct terms, American democracy would be far fairer and more broadly responsive if Democrats were always in control.

One cannot know if this pattern will persist. It is worth noting, however, that recent developments in American politics do not herald any major change. Survey data asking Americans for their spending preferences for 2018 or 2019 are not yet available, but the current period of largely Republican control will likely do little to alter the pattern of minority losses under Republicans. The 2018 Republican budget called for deep cuts in welfare and health-care spending, and sharp increases in military spending. That is almost the mirror image of what African Americans across the country want. Across all of the survey years, the overwhelming majority of African Americans have always favored increases in spending on welfare and health care, and always opposed increases in military spending. Under Trump and a Republican Senate, African Americans may have to wait on the sidelines.[24]

Democratic Party Control and Responsiveness to Lower-Class Whites

The data show clearly that Blacks do better under Democrats. That helps to explain the overwhelming support African Americans give to the Democratic Party. And it points to the election of Democrats as the best way to rectify racial imbalances in American democracy. But what about Whites and, in particular, lower-class Whites? Can their largely Republican votes be explained by better representation under Republicans?

The short answer is no. When I limit the analysis to White Americans and look to see if policy responsiveness is greater when Republicans are in charge, I find the opposite to be true. The analysis shows that the Democratic Party is, in fact, more responsive to White preferences than is the Republican Party. And the difference is real. The federal government is 3.2 percent more responsive to White interests when Democrats control Congress.[25] If Whites were voting for the Party that more often acted on their policy preferences, they would be far more supportive of the Democratic Party.

This is particularly true for lower-class Whites. Further analysis shows that any bias in responsiveness against working-class Whites goes away when Democrats are in charge. In general, as I showed in Chapter 4, a slight bias against lower-class preferences is evident when the federal government makes decisions about spending. But when Democrats control Congress, that bias goes away, and, in fact, slightly reverses. On spending, Democratic-controlled congresses are actually slightly more responsive to the bottom third of the White population than they are to the top third of the White population.[26] Again, control of the presidency appears to make little difference in terms of the segments of the White population that win on policy. If lower-class White Americans were voting based on which party responded more proactively to their policy positions, they would be aligning much more closely with the Democratic Party.

Combined, these different results tell us that Democrats are simply more responsive to the public's preferences as a whole than are Republicans. Democrats are responding not just to Black interests but also to those of Whites and ultimately to a broader array of interests.

Conclusions

American democracy is often uneven. Over the last half-century, when it comes to matters of policy, African Americans are more apt than Whites to lose out. However, this need not always be the case. Indeed, this chapter demonstrates that that racial imbalance in responsiveness fades away at certain times. A deeper look at the patterns that underlie these changes indicates that Democratic Party control is primarily responsible for that shift in responsiveness. When Democrats control the White House, the racial gap in responsiveness declines. When Democrats control Congress, the racial gap in responsiveness fades even further. When Democrats control both the presidency and Congress, the racial gap in responsiveness disappears. At such times, there is no bias; policy responses treat White and Black interests equally.

This is a finding that is worth underlining. By most measures that I have examined in this book, Blacks are the group that is most likely to lose in American democracy. Especially in the arena of policy, Blacks lose more than any other racial or demographic group, and they lose more consistently across issues and across time than any other group. Yet, by electing Democrats into office, those deep patterns of inequality can be eliminated. In American democracy, some groups lose more consistently than others. They lose over long periods of time. They are, in short, less well represented in the American political system. Do such outcomes raise concerns? If so, and if the nation wants to change this pattern, then a critical first step is knowing in which direction to head. The analysis in this chapter shows the way forward if the nation wants to achieve greater racial equality in government responsiveness. At least over the last half-century, greater racial equality emerges when the Democratic Party is in control.[27]

It is important to note that Democratic control does not presage an era of special privilege for African Americans. Under no circumstances do African Americans win more often than White Americans. When Democrats control either the White House or Congress, African Americans still lose more regularly than Whites. And even when Democrats control both the legislative and executive branches of power, their outcomes basically *match* those of Whites. Democratic control is really only correcting a racial imbalance that occurs most of the time in American politics. It does not overcompensate. It merely levels the playing field.

African Americans are not the only group that appears to be better off when Democrats are in control. The data, while limited, suggest that other racial and ethnic minorities fare well under Democrats. Additional analysis shows that the racial gap in responsiveness between Whites and Latinos appears to decline when Democrats hold the Oval Office, and any advantage that Asian Americans hold over other minority groups in policy successes may even increase when

Democrats take over. Racial and ethnic minorities as a whole do better when Democrats control the central levers of power. Benefits are not exclusive to minorities. Additional models reveal that Democratic incumbents are significantly more responsive than Republican leaders to lower-class voter preferences, to Democratic identifiers, and to liberals. In other words, the most disadvantaged and those on the left have more say when Democrats are in charge. Moreover, data show that Democrats are more responsive, not just to these individual groups, but to Americans as a whole. Having a Democrat in the White House not only means more responsiveness to African Americans, it means more responsiveness to voters overall. On average, more Americans win what they want in policy terms when Democrats govern. One can rightly voice concern about the limited knowledge that the average American has about policy and government; one can also reasonably express a deep reluctance about government following every whim of the public. Nevertheless, the fact that more Americans get what they want out of policy when Democrats are in charge is unlikely to be a bad outcome.[28]

8 DEMOCRATIC PARTY CONTROL AND MINORITY WELL-BEING

Clementine Matthias, a single African-American mother, was told that her son would most likely never walk on his own.[1] Born prematurely and weighing barely more than a pound, Frankie had little chance of surviving a week. But with his mother's tireless efforts, Frankie now walks and attends a specialized high school. Life for the family, however, is a real struggle. Indeed, they are never far from being destitute. They lost their Section 8 subsidized apartment in the Bronx in late 2013, and were forced into a homeless shelter. The fraught situation led Ms. Matthias to take desperate measures. She was caught shoplifting, and she then spent time in a correctional facility. She nearly lost custody of Frankie and her daughter, Nevaeh. But Ms. Matthias fought her way out of the shelter and out of the crisis. The family now has an apartment, and Nevaeh is thriving in school, but finances are exceptionally tight. They live largely off of disability, welfare, and food stamps. They could use much more. They are hanging on, but who knows for how much longer?

Thais Marques, a Latina immigrant, was brought to the United States illegally from Brazil when she was just five years old.[2] Thais' parents – both undocumented – have worked hard for almost two decades in the United States, trying to fulfill the American dream. Her father cleans parking lots at night. Her mother is a housekeeper. But as Thais puts it, "They don't get paid very well. Every month was just a question about whether we were gonna make ends meet." Receiving work authorization through the Deferred Action for Childhood Arrivals (DACA) made all of the difference. With papers in hand, Thais immediately became the highest earner in the family. The family was financially stable. But with the end of DACA looming, Thais does not know what will happen.[3] She does not know Brazil, and she does not know what her future in the United States looks like. She wants to support her family, but she does not know if she will be able to.

Both the Matthias family and the Marques family work hard, and both have tried against tough odds to succeed. Both families continue to live on the edge. They desperately need support. In both cases, government policy appears to be critical to the families' well-being. What government does or does not do going forward could determine whether the families prosper or fail.

These two families illustrate broader patterns in American society. There are deep racial inequalities in the political process – as I have shown – but equally importantly, there are severe racial inequalities beyond the political arena. Economic well-being is not evenly distributed across the racial and ethnic spectrum. Instead, a robust racial hierarchy exists, with Whites more likely to be on the top and racial and ethnic minorities more likely to fall below. The statistics are telling. Blacks and Latinos earn only two-thirds as much as Whites. Blacks and Latinos are twice as likely as Whites to be poor, twice as likely to be unemployed, and between three and five times more likely to be arrested. They accumulate less than one-tenth of the wealth that Whites acquire (Lewis and Burd-Sharps 2010, Pew 2016).

This is not to say that race totally determines one's life chances. The underlying story is much more complicated. The pattern of Whites on top and non-Whites at the bottom is not universal. Asian Americans, another largely immigrant minority group, tend to end up closer to the top end of the racial hierarchy, with incomes and educational outcomes that roughly match those of Whites on average (Lewis and Burd-Sharps 2010). And within each racial and ethnic minority group there is tremendous diversity in outcomes. For example, many within the Asian-American population suffer from poverty and other social disadvantages, despite generally positive patterns of assimilation and economic success within the group as a whole. Whites also do not all fit neatly into a hierarchy driven exclusively by race. Many Whites cannot be called privileged. With dead-end, low-paying jobs, limited education, and almost hopeless economic circumstances, large swaths of White America do not fit the racial narrative. As the 2016 election so dramatically exposed, working-class Whites are struggling in many profound ways.

Nevertheless, racial differences in material well-being are very real, very large, and very much in need of redress. Those economic disparities are the subject of this chapter. I attempt to determine if there is anything we can do to address America's racial hierarchy in well-being.

Up until now, this book has focused almost exclusively on the democratic process. Who votes? Who wins office? What policies are passed? These are critically important subjects. The patterns discussed here reveal a great deal about how fair American democracy truly is. At the same time, these tests are in some sense second-order concerns. They generally overlook the outcome that citizens are likely to care most about: their well-being. The most fundamental question has yet to be addressed. Which regimes make people better or worse off?

In this chapter, I take the next and arguably the most critical step of assessing the effects of different governing regimes on group well-being. The focus shifts squarely to material well-being. Can politics make any difference in the core economic outcomes of individual Americans? And can it impact the deep racial inequalities in well-being that I have just highlighted?

The previous chapter showed that Democratic control can make a real difference – at least in terms of the policy process. Overall, there is a clear racial imbalance to policy responsiveness. Whites get more of the policies they want than do racial and ethnic minorities. But much of that changes when Democrats win office. When Democrats are in charge of the presidency and Congress there is little to no racial imbalance in policy responsiveness.

Could Democratic control have even broader effects? Could it actually change the material well-being of different racial and ethnic groups? Could it reduce the sharp racial inequalities that define American life? In the rest of this chapter, I attempt to answer those questions to see if a solution to America's racial hierarchy can be found.

Assessing the Impact of Party on Well-Being by Race

To help answer these questions, I offer a simple, direct test that examines the connection between party control and minority well-being. I trace the well-being of racial and ethnic minorities over time using objective, empirical measures, and then compare the relative progress of these demographic groups under different partisan regimes. Specifically, I test to see if Blacks and other racial and ethnic minorities fare better on basic indicators of well-being such as income, poverty, and unemployment when Democrats or Republicans control the presidency (and Congress).

The test is neither novel nor complex. Others have used it to assess the impact of partisan control on well-being by class in the American context (Bartels 2008, Hibbs and Dennis 1988). And it has been used widely in comparative work in other countries to study democratic responsiveness (Holmberg et al. 2009, Lijphart 1999). But remarkably this test has not been employed in the United States to study the impact of Democratic and Republican control on the well-being of racial and ethnic minorities.

There is a long and well-established literature assessing the impact of having racial and ethnic minorities in office but that literature rarely, if ever, looks at basic indicators such as income, employment, and poverty. Instead it focuses – like almost all of the political science literature – on the democratic process itself (Barreto 2011, Fraga et al. 1997, Grose 2011, Kerr and Mladenka 1994, Meier and England 1984, Tate 2003).[4]

Claims about whether racial and ethnic minorities gain or lose under Democrats and Republicans thus lack the empirical validation that would make them meaningful.[5] To know how partisan control impacts minority well-being, a direct test of the relationship is essential.

To assess well-being, I focus on the most fundamental markers of economic status: income, employment, and poverty. All are measured annually through the American Community Survey (conducted by the Census Bureau). All measures can be compiled for each racial and ethnic group.[6] In all cases, the analysis examines *change* in well-being from year to year. This helps to directly pinpoint the impact of the current administration.

Once again, the political focus is on the presidency and Congress. Although there is a healthy debate about the ability of either the president or Congress to effect change, if government can impact economic well-being, these are the elected offices most likely to make a difference.[7] Because government regimes are unlikely to impact well-being immediately upon entering office – policies take some time to be passed and to be implemented – I attribute conditions in the first year of a term to the previous regime. For example, even though Barack Obama entered office in January 2009, changes in Black poverty in 2009 are credited to the previous administration of George W. Bush.[8]

To assess partisan control across different governing regimes, and to help minimize the confounding influence of other non-political factors, I compile data on well-being for as many years as possible. All told, the data cover more than sixty years from 1948 to 2010.

African-American Well-Being

I start with the impact of Democratic and Republican control on Black well-being. I do so for two reasons. First, there is ample reason to be concerned about the well-being of African Americans in American democracy and life. Evidence in this book demonstrates that African Americans are more disadvantaged in the policy arena than any other group. Federal government decisions about policy weigh Black preferences less heavily than those of other racial groups, or those of different economic classes or religions. Blacks are severely under-represented in office, and their favored candidates end up on the losing side of American elections more regularly than any other demographic group. More broadly, African Americans have faced and continue to face difficult life circumstances. Evidence shows that racial discrimination against African Americans is widespread (Bertrand and Mullainathan 2004, Butler and Broockman 2011). The particularly disadvantaged economic status of the African-American population today – poverty and unemployment rates twice those of the national average – also justifies the close attention to Black outcomes.

A second, practical reason to focus first on African Americans is that many more years of data are available for Blacks than for Latinos or Asian Americans. The census reports outcomes for Asian Americans dating back only to 1988 and for Latinos extending back only to 1970. With fewer years and thus less variation in political leadership for Latinos and Asian Americans, any conclusions about these two groups will be much more tentative.

The Presidency and Black Well-Being

Do Democrats really help minorities? Or does Republican control actually do more to improve minority well-being? I begin to answer these questions by comparing gains in Black well-being under Democratic and Republican presidents. Table 8.1 presents the average annual change in Black well-being for income, poverty, and

Table 8.1 Party of the President and Black Economic Well-Being

	Average Annual Change for Blacks			Average Annual Gain Relative to Whites		
	Under Democrats	Under Republicans	Dem. vs. Rep. Difference	Under Democrats	Under Republicans	Dem. vs. Rep. Difference
Income	$895	$142	$754 (299)**	$613	$276	$337 (197)*
Poverty Rate	−2.41	.150	−2.56 (.94)**	−2.06	.23	−2.29 (.74)**
Unemployment Rate	−.359	.391	−.751 (.429)*	−.195	.206	−.401 (.232)*

*** p<.001 ** p<.01 * p<.05 Standard error in parentheses
Source: Current Population Survey (1948–2010)

unemployment. The first three columns look at annual change for Blacks alone. The last three columns present figures for Blacks relative to Whites.

The pattern of results is clear. African Americans tend to experience substantial gains under Democratic presidents, whereas they tend to incur significant losses or remain stagnant under Republicans. On every basic economic indicator, tests show that gains under Democrats were significantly greater than gains under Republicans.[9] In terms of income, Black families gained on average $895 annually under Democrats but only managed $142 in annual income growth under Republicans. The difference in income growth of $754 is not only highly significant (p<.01), it is substantial. The pattern for poverty is even starker. Under Democratic presidents, Black poverty declined by an average of 2.41 points per year. In sharp contrast, Black poverty actually grew under Republicans – by 0.15 points annually. Finally, the difference is most remarkable for unemployment. The Black unemployment rate declined by more than one-third of a point (0.36) annually under Democratic presidents, while it grew by more than one-third (0.39) under Republicans.

Moreover, as the second half of the table shows, African Americans were also much more likely to catch up with Whites under Democratic administrations.[10] Black gains relative to Whites in terms of income, unemployment, and poverty were all significantly greater under Democrats than they were under Republicans. Again, the starkest contrast is in terms of unemployment. On average the Black-White unemployment gap declined by 0.20 points annually under Democrats, while it grew by 0.21 points annually under Republicans. Substantial differences also emerged in trends in Black-White well-being on measures of poverty and income. Under Democrats, Blacks made real gains in terms of narrowing the Black-White poverty gap. Annually, the Black-White poverty gap declined by just over 2 points under Democratic administrations. By contrast, under Republicans there was a 0.23-point annual increase in the Black-White poverty gap.

This sharp partisan contrast exists no matter how one measures income, poverty, or unemployment. The patterns are essentially identical, for example, regardless of whether one focuses on: mean or median income, family or household income, adults or all persons in a household, the gap between or ratio of Black and White outcomes. By any of these measures, Republican administrations were, on average,

Table 8.2 The Cumulative Effects of Democratic and
Republican Party Presidential Control on African
American Well-Being

	All Democratic Years	All Republican Years
Poverty rate	−38.6	+5.3
Unemployment rate	−7.9	+13.7
Income	$23,281	$5,032

Source: Current Population Survey (1948–2010)

bad for African Americans, and Democratic administrations were, on average, good for them, both in absolute and relative terms.

As Table 8.2 demonstrates, the cumulative effects of these partisan differences are immense for the Black population. If I simply add up all of the changes in Black well-being under Democratic presidencies in the data set and compare the total to a summary of all of the changes under Republican presidencies, dramatic differences emerge. Across the sixteen years of Democratic leadership in the data the Black poverty rate declined by a net 38.6 percentage points. By contrast, over the twenty-one years of Republican presidencies, the rate of poverty for Blacks grew 5 points. The figures for unemployment are just as pronounced. Across thirty-five years of Republican presidencies, Black unemployment went up by a net 13.7 percentage points. Across twenty-two years with Democrats, the Black unemployment rate fell 7.9 points. Putting those two numbers together and making the heroic assumption that the rest of the world would not have changed, one can speculate that Black unemployment would be 21.6 points higher if Republicans had been in charge for the entire period than if Democrats had held the presidency for the duration. Finally, across twenty-six years of Democratic administrations, Black incomes grew by $23,281 (as measured by constant 2008 dollars). Black incomes also grew under Republicans, but much more slowly – roughly $5,000 across twenty-nine years. Moreover, the cumulative effects are equally striking if I concentrate instead on Black well-being relative to White well-being. Blacks made enormous gains relative to Whites under Democrats, and typically fell further behind Whites under Republicans.[11] The results suggest that which party controls the presidency may be one of the most important influences on who wins and who loses in America.

The consistency of this partisan divergence over the last half-century is stark and compelling. Across the different years and different administrations, relatively few exceptions to the basic partisan pattern surface. Generally speaking, in the years when Democrats were in office, Black economic well-being improved. Black incomes grew in 77 percent of the years that Democrats held the presidency, Black poverty declined in 88 percent of those years, and Black unemployment fell in 71 percent of those years. In sharp contrast, Blacks, more often than not, lost under Republican administrations. In fact, during the majority of years of Republican presidential leadership Black poverty increased and Black unemployment grew. Only in terms of income did Blacks tend to make annual gains under Republicans. The same consistent partisan divergence appears whether I focus on Black well-being in isolation, or, instead, on Black well-being relative to White well-being. However measured, Blacks made consistent gains under Democratic presidents, and suffered regular losses under Republicans.

A More Inclusive Test

These patterns are striking, but one wonders whether they tell the whole story. Could these trends be coincidental? Perhaps Democratic presidents have merely been lucky, presiding over expanding economies while Republican leaders have led in less economically vibrant times. What about the impact of other political actors? Presidents undeniably wield considerable power, but many would claim that Congress, as the main lawmaking body in the nation, has more influence over basic economic outcomes. Might Congress also play a role?

In Table 8.3 I begin to consider these and other factors. To further test the role of the presidency and to see if Congress, the other main legislative actor in American politics, helps to shape well-being by race, I include a range of different political and economic measures in a series of different regression models, the results of which are displayed in Table 8.3. The table presents six different regressions, three of which examine changes in Black income, poverty, and unemployment in isolation, and three of which focus on Black outcomes relative to those of Whites.[12]

To assess the impact of partisan control in Congress, each of the regression models includes measures for which political party controls the House and the Senate.[13] Years of Democratic control are singled out.[14]

Table 8.3 Party of the President and Annual Change in Black Economic Well-Being: Regression

	Average Annual Change for Blacks			Average Gain of Blacks Relative to Whites		
	Income	Poverty	Unemployed	Income	Poverty	Unemployed
Democratic President	1031 (276)***	-2.61 (.85)**	-.87 (.38)*	403 (193)*	-2.41 (.82)**	-.57 (.24)*
Median Income	.071 (.054)	.000 (.000)	.000 (.000)	.007 (.038)	.000 (.000)	.000 (.000)
Inflation	-213 (63)***	.48 (.18)*	.24 (.09)*	-54.4 (44.1)	.22 (.18)	.14 (.06)*
Change in Labor Force	753 (518)	-1.59 (1.75)	-2.10 (.69)**	-31.4 (363)	-.60 (1.69)	-1.02 (.43)*
Change in Oil Prices	.24 (6.07)	.002 (.016)	.011 (.008)	5.80 (4.26)	-.005 (.015)	.001 (.005)
Time Trend	-2110 (2054)	-.281 (6.32)	-1.20 (2.90)	-865 (1442)	-2.89 (6.12)	-1.15 (1.82)
Democratic House	974 (500)	1.80 (1.90)	-.44 (.70)	921 (351)*	.63 (1.84)	-.31 (.44)
Democratic Senate	-240 (388)	-.26 (1.06)	.10 (.50)	-489 (272)	.67 (1.03)	-.13 (.31)
Constant	-2273 (1523)	-22.5 (11.6)	.34 (2.61)	-729 (1070)	-22.7 (11.3)	.13 (1.64)
Adj R. Squared	.29	.39	.35	.19	.29	.19
N	57	40	51	57	40	51

***p<.001 **p<.01 *p<.05 Standard error in parentheses
Source: Current Population Survey (1948–2010)

To try to ensure that any partisan effects I find are not due to economic conditions that are outside the control of either the presidency or Congress, I control for a range of basic economic indicators. Because oil is one of the most volatile and economically critical commodities, and because it is generally viewed as largely beyond the control of American political actors, I control for the annual increase in the real price of oil (from the Federal Reserve Bank). Because the measures I use to examine changes in well-being may be sensitive to changes in workforce participation, I also include a control for the annual change in the proportion of adults in the labor force (from the Bureau of Labor Statistics). Likewise, to account for other basic economic forces, I add controls for lagged median income, the current rate of inflation, and, in alternate tests, GDP and changes in GDP.

In addition, a number of broader changes occurring over time may impact relative group well-being. For example, educational outcomes have risen steadily over time. So, too, have divorce rates. Over time, Americans have increasingly begun to have children later in life and have chosen to have smaller families. One could also cite the increasing impact of globalization on American economic fortunes. Fortunately, because these factors are changing slowly and relatively constantly over time, they are unlikely to be confounded with the numerous alterations in partisan control of the presidency that we have seen over the past five decades.[15] Nevertheless, I can take steps to address these broader trends by including a linear trend term in the analysis.

As Table 8.3 shows, presidential partisanship continues to be a critical predictor of Black well-being. Even after controlling for a range of other factors, I find that under Democratic presidents the Black population is significantly more likely to experience growth in income, declines in poverty, and decreases in unemployment. The regression estimates in the first three columns of the table suggest that the gains are substantial. Black family incomes grew more than $1,000 faster annually under Democratic leadership than they did under Republican presidents. Likewise, the Black poverty rate declined 2.6 points faster under Democrats and the Black unemployment rate fell almost 1 point faster. Moreover, as the last three columns indicate, all of these gains also occur relative to Whites. Under Democratic presidents Blacks significantly close the gap with Whites in terms of income, poverty, and unemployment.

In many ways these findings are not that surprising. This pattern fits neatly with earlier work by Douglas Hibbs, who found that from 1948 to 1978 economic inequality grew markedly more under Republican administrations than it did under Democratic administrations (Hibbs 1987). It also parallels work by Larry Bartels, who concludes that Democrats did more than Republicans for the lower classes (Bartels 2008).

There are also signs, albeit extraordinarily limited ones, that Congress matters as well. The most obvious is the significant and substantively large relationship between a Democratic majority in the House and changes in Black incomes. Specifically, under Democratic majorities the Black-White income gap declines $921 faster than it does under Republican majorities. At the same time, the results on Congress are mixed. As Table 8.3 shows, Congress appears to have no impact on other measures of Black well-being. Alternate tests that measured Democratic control in different ways were equally inconclusive.[16] Limited variation in Democratic and Republican control of Congress may be to blame, at least in part. Democrats controlled Congress continuously for the vast majority of this period (from 1955 to 1994); thus, congressional partisan effects may be confounded with broader economic trends.[17]

What are the effects of a divided government? Given that Congress and the president have to work together to get major policy changes enacted, one might expect the president to be less influential when Congress and the presidency are controlled by two different political parties (Niskanen 2003, but see Mayhew 1991). To test this proposition, I substituted in a dummy variable that singled out years with both a Democratic president and a Republican Congress. That analysis reveals that Democratic administrations are less effective at raising Black incomes when they have to work with a Republican Congress. In fact, the results show that Black family income did not grow significantly under Democratic presidents facing a Republican-controlled Congress. However, divided government had no clear effects for Black poverty or Black unemployment. In short, the evidence suggests that the presidency is generally more important than Congress for these core economic outcomes.

More Rigorous Tests

The multivariate analysis in Table 8.3 strongly suggests that the strikingly divergent paths that African-American economic fortunes follow under Democratic and Republican administrations are no mere coincidence of the timing of Democratic and Republican electoral victories. To try to confirm the robustness of these partisan patterns, and to increase confidence in the role that presidential administrations play in shaping America's racial order, however, I explored a range of additional tests.

First, I considered the role of economic growth. Growth rather than partisan control could be driving minority gains. However, when I added measures for GDP and annual changes in GDP to the models in Table 8.3, no appreciable change surfaced in the size or significance of the party effects. The robustness of the Democratic-presidency effect to the inclusion of economic growth is important because it begins to help reveal what does or what does not drive minority gains under Democrats. Given claims by Larry Bartels and Douglas Hibbs that Democrats have been better at fostering growth, one might suspect that minority gains under Democratic administrations are largely a function of increased growth (Bartels 2008, Hibbs 1987). But, at least at first glance, that does not appear to be the case. Other more racially specific policies may instead be driving the gains under Democrats.

Another possibility is that the different paths taken by Democrats and Republicans are largely reactions to the policies of their predecessors. Republican administrations might, for example, have to counter the excesses of previous Democratic administrations by reining in spending. Likewise, Democrats might feel the need for expansionary policies in reaction to Republican belt-tightening. If this were the case, we would expect partisan divergence to be greatest when a president of one party succeeds a president of the other party. However, I find essentially the opposite pattern. That is, the greatest change emerges under administrations in which the president is in his second term, or when he belongs to the same party as his predecessor, rather than under presidential administrations that are part of a partisan transition in power political. Rather than reacting to the actions of the other party, each party seems to push its particular agenda more forcefully with longer time in office. Democratic administrations appear to help African Americans experience greater economic gains as the president's time in office increases; the longer Republican presidential administrations hold office, the more the fortunes of Blacks appear to fall. A range of other tests confirmed the core relationship.[18] There is, in short, a consistency in the impact of partisan control strongly suggesting that the divergence in economic fortunes of African Americans under Democrats and Republicans is real.

A Role for the Courts?

Does the third branch of the federal government – the judicial system – play a role in this policymaking picture? Although the courts are sometimes ignored in discussions of policymaking in the federal system, many have argued that in the realm of race, court decisions have played a critical role in protecting minorities, and in fostering real gains in minority well-being.[19] Landmark decisions by the courts have arguably altered the economic and social trajectory of African Americans and other minorities – although some dispute the efficacy of these kinds of court decisions.

In light of the potentially important role played by the federal courts, I added several different measures of court ideology in alternate regression models. However, I found little connection between the ideology of the courts and Black well-being. Regardless of what measures I employed, court ideology was insignificant when added to all of the models in Table 8.3 (Bailey 2007, Epstein et al. 2007, Martin and Quinn 2002).[20]

Beyond Economic Well-Being

I was also able to assess the effects of partisan control on one other potentially important outcome: contact with the criminal justice system. When I extended the study beyond the economic sphere to criminal justice, one of the more highly partisan and politicized policy areas, I once again found substantial differences in Black outcomes depending on the party of the president. As before, Black outcomes improve under Democrats, while under Republicans they deteriorate. For Blacks, the overall arrest rate for adults, the homicide arrest rate, and the juvenile arrest rate all decline significantly faster under Democrats than under Republicans. Just as importantly for Blacks, who are much more likely than Whites to be caught up in the criminal justice system, the racial gap in arrest rates declines significantly and substantially under Democrats, while it grows under Republicans.[21]

The cumulative effect on the racialized patterns of criminal justice in America that stem from these partisan differences is large. Across the twelve years of Democratic presidencies in the data, the Black-White arrest gap (the number of Blacks arrested in comparison to the number of Whites arrested) experienced a net drop of sixty-one arrests per 1,000 residents. By contrast, across the twenty-two years of Republican leadership that same gap grew by a total of thirty-six arrests. Today, the Black-White arrest gap stands at sixty-nine arrests per 1,000 adult residents. These figures suggest that the racial divide in arrest rates would be considerably smaller if Democrats had been in control for the entire period.[22]

As a final test I looked to see if presidential partisanship impacts outcomes where one might expect to find less of a partisan effect. Because the federal government traditionally has limited purview over education policy, for example, no link should emerge between presidential partisanship and changes in educational outcomes.[23] Indeed, this is what I found when I examined educational outcomes by race. Regardless of who holds the office of the president, Black high school and college graduation rates increase slowly and steadily over time. Given the ever-increasing technological gains and medical advancements that have led to slow and relatively steady improvement in health outcomes over time, health care might represent another policy area in which the impact of partisan control could be less pronounced. Here, too, I found no link between health outcomes, as measured by infant mortality and life expectancy, and presidential partisanship. The bottom line of this set of analyses is that the pattern of results fits expectations. I find partisan effects where we would expect them, and I find no partisan effects where they should be largely absent.

Measuring the Well-Being of Other Minority Groups

Blacks have been the racial group most closely associated with the Democratic Party, and, perhaps, the group most likely to benefit from the Democratic Party's racially liberal policy agenda. However, they may not be the only racial group that stands to gain from Democratic control of the presidency.

Should one expect Latino and Asian-American outcomes to be shaped by partisan control in a parallel fashion to Blacks? On one hand, all three minority groups share certain experiences and characteristics.

As with Blacks, Latinos and Asian Americans face widespread and often negative stereotyping from the White population, and have, at times, been subject to deeply racist and exclusionary practices. Also, like Blacks, Latinos and Asian Americans have generally favored Democrats in the voting booth. But a range of important dissimilarities among the groups suggests they may follow different paths. First, the experiences of the Latino and Asian-American populations are shaped much more by the process of immigration. As such, their structural location in the American economy and in American society may differ fundamentally from the position of African Americans. Second, the population of both pan-ethnic groups is extraordinarily diverse. As scholars from Pei-Te Lien to Lisa Garcia Bedolla point out, neither pan-ethnic population should be viewed as a cohesive entity (Bedolla 2009, Lien et al. 2004). Disparate socioeconomic circumstances within each group, distinctive paths to arrival in the United States, and different levels of incorporation once in the United States all imply that the same policy could affect members of each pan-ethnic group in sharply divergent ways. Third, although Asian Americans and Latinos tend to support Democrats, they do so in a less unified fashion than African Americans. To the extent that political parties seek specific policies to reward particular constituent groups, one might expect Blacks to experience greater benefits because their support of the Democratic Party has been unstinting as compared to the support from other minority groups. Finally, and perhaps most critically for the study, the Asian-American case may be particularly divergent from the Black case because Asian Americans hold a less disadvantaged economic position in American society. The economic status of the Asian-American population as a whole falls much closer to the status of Whites than to the status of either Blacks or Latinos. Asian Americans also report much lower levels of racial discrimination against their group than do Blacks or Latinos.

For these reasons one might expect a similar pattern of partisan effects to emerge in an examination of the fortunes of Latinos. For Asian Americans, by contrast, one might expect that the more advantaged economic position that many members of that pan-ethnic group hold may influence the outcomes.

In Table 8.4, I begin to assess the link between presidential partisanship and the welfare of these two other racial and ethnic minority groups. The table presents figures for mean annual changes in

Table 8.4 Party of the President and Latino and Asian-American Economic Well-Being

	Average Annual Change for Each Group			Average Annual Gain Relative to Whites		
	Under Democrats	Under Republicans	Dem. vs. Rep. Difference	Under Democrats	Under Republicans	Dem. vs. Rep. Difference
LATINOS						
Income	$628	$-197	$825 (482)*	$783	$-118	$900 (619)
Poverty Rate	-.425	.330	-.755 (.789)	-.350	.278	-.628 (.671)
Unemployed Rate	-.246	.325	-.571 (.569)	-.208	.133	-.341 (.279)
ASIANS						
Income	$991	$142	$849 (1387)	$117	$-7	$123 (1020)
Poverty Rate	-.813	-.154	-.659 (.962)	-.288	-.115	-.172 (1.08)
Unemployed Rate	—[1]	—[1]	—[1]	—[1]	—[1]	—[1]

** p<.01 *p<.05 [1]Too few years available. Standard error in parentheses

Source: Current Population Survey (1948–2010)

income, poverty, and unemployment for both groups, and shows whether the changes occurred under Democratic or Republican presidencies. The first three columns once again report the average annual change for each group in isolation, and the second three columns present data on how changes in Latino and Asian-American outcomes compare to changes in White outcomes.

The overall pattern of results for Latinos mirrors what we saw earlier for Blacks. Latinos appear to benefit from Democratic leadership, and they often suffer losses under Republicans. For Latinos, Democratic presidencies are associated with large annual gains in income, substantial declines in poverty, and real drops in unemployment. By contrast, under Republican administrations Latinos tend to lose income, become poorer, and experience greater unemployment. This is true whether I look at Latinos in isolation, or whether I compare Latino gains and losses to those of Whites. Moreover, the magnitude of these partisan differences is once again quite substantial. Latino incomes grew an average of $628 annually under Democrats, while they declined by an average of $197 annually under Republicans. Similarly, Latino poverty declined at an average rate of about half a point under Democrats and grew at a rate of about one-third of a point under Republicans. Finally, the unemployment rate for Latinos averaged a one-quarter point decline annually under Democrats, and a one-third point increase annually under Republicans. The gains and losses are even more dramatic if I compare Latino to White well-being. Latinos closed the gap on White income about $900 per year faster under Democrats than under Republicans. The comparable annual figures for the Latino-White poverty gap and the Latino-White unemployment gap are 0.63 points and 0.34 points, respectively.

I have far fewer years of data for Latino outcomes than I do for Black outcomes. Nevertheless, the cumulative partisan difference for the available years of Republican and Democratic leadership is still dramatic. Across the years of Democratic administrations in the data, Latino incomes grew a total of $7,531, the Latino poverty rate dropped 5.1 points, and Latino unemployment fell 3.2 points. By contrast, adding all of the available Republican years shows that Latino family income suffered a net $4,728 decline, Latino poverty increased 7.6 points, and Latino unemployment grew 7.8 points. Had the patterns of racial progression that occurred under Democrats been in effect throughout the entire period, Latinos might be in a very different economic position in American society.

The figures for Asian Americans, while not so stark, point in the same directions: greater gains under Democrats and periods of stagnation under Republicans. Asian-American family income grew by almost $1,000 annually under Democrats, but only by $142 annually under Republicans. That means that Asian Americans closed the income gap on Whites in Democratic years but failed to make any progress in Republican years. Similarly, annual declines in Asian-American poverty were greater under Democrats (0.81 points) than they were under Republicans (0.15 points). Overall, it appears that Democratic presidential leadership enhanced the well-being of America's racial minorities, while Republican administrations tended to enlarge the gap between Whites and minorities.[24]

While the partisan trends for both Latinos and Asian Americans are relatively clear, the partisan differences are generally not statistically significant. I do not have enough years of data on these two pan-ethnic groups.[25]

The consistency of the patterns for Latinos and Asian Americans and Blacks across most of the different indicators of well-being suggests that the differences are based on substance, rather than some statistical quirk. Nevertheless, without more data definitive conclusions are not possible. In short, Latinos and Asian Americans also appear to benefit considerably from Democratic administrations, and they appear to lose under Republican presidencies.

Do Whites Lose?

The dramatic gains that racial and ethnic minorities experience under Democratic presidents raise questions about White Americans and their well-being under Democrats. Are minority gains under Democrats coming at the expense of Whites? That is, do Whites lose when Democrats win? Alternatively, does a rising Democratic tide raise all boats?

These questions are all the more important in light of the growing racial divide in the vote highlighted throughout this book. Have White Americans been defecting from the Democratic Party to the Republican Party in such large numbers because their economic

Table 8.5 Party of the President and White Well-Being

	Average Annual Change for Whites		
	Under Democrats	Under Republicans	Dem. vs. Rep. Difference
Income	$959	$507	$452 (304)
Poverty Rate	-.35	.16	-.51 (.31)
Unemployment Rate	-.16	.19	-.35 (.25)

** p<.01 *p<.05. Standard error in parentheses
Source: Current Population Survey (1948–2010)

fortunes are declining under Democrats? Does this economic motivation underlie the movement of working-class Whites toward the Trump presidency? Are the economic fortunes of White Americans, and particularly those of lower-class White Americans, now enhanced by the Republican Party?

In Table 8.5, I begin to answer these questions. The table shows average annual changes for White Americans under Democratic and Republican administrations in the core economic outcome areas in which Blacks and other minorities made real gains under Democrats.

Table 8.5 is clear on one important point: White Americans do not lose under Democrats. On average, under Democrats, White incomes have grown, White poverty has declined, and White unemployment has diminished.[26] Thus, minority gains are unlikely to come largely at the expense of White gains. Democrats appear to be able to aid minorities without inflicting any major losses on the White community. Whether Democratic administrations actually benefit White Americans more than Republican administrations do is less clear. On the three measures of well-being in Table 8.5, the average gains under Democrats are larger than the average gains under Republicans. But the partisan differences here do not quite attain statistical significance, and they are all much smaller than they were for Blacks and other minorities.

It would also be informative to look at the pattern of gains and losses for working-class Whites under Democrats and Republicans. The data on White well-being are, unfortunately, not broken down by class. But earlier work by Bartels (2008) shows quite definitively that lower-class Americans gain substantially more under Democrats on basic indicators of economic well-being than they do under Republicans.

This suggests that even lower-class Whites have little reason – at least economically – to vote for Republicans.

Combined, this suggests that the policies enacted by Democratic presidents benefit all Americans regardless of race, but that those benefits may disproportionately accrue to the minority population.

What are Democrats Doing to Help Minorities?

What have Democrats done that has enabled them to raise the welfare of racial and ethnic minorities? What are Democratic administrations doing that improves the economic standing of the minority population? By contrast, what are Republicans failing to do? There is no shortage of policy differences between Democrats and Republicans, and thus no shortage of potential explanations for minority gains under Democrats. Overall economic growth likely undergirds many of the gains seen during these periods, as underscored by the economic gains experienced by all groups under Democratic presidents. Indeed, Larry Bartels and Douglas Hibbs have both already shown that the policy agenda of the Democratic Party during the second half of the twentieth century more effectively created economic growth than the competing policies of the Republicans (Bartels 2008, Hibbs 1987).[27] But it is important to note that these racial patterns are not solely driven by economic growth. When I controlled for GDP, substantial partisan differences persisted.

A second category of racially explicit policies that directly target minorities may also help minorities (Massey and Denton 1993). The efforts of the Democratic Party to enact a range of racially explicit, racially egalitarian policies may have contributed to minority gains. Although landmark anti-discrimination measures, such as President Harry Truman's executive order to desegregate the armed forces, the Fair Housing Act, and the Civil Rights Act are particularly worthy of study, more recent initiatives to expand affirmative action in government hiring may be important as well.

Major partisan differences have also emerged on a range of policy programs that are neither explicitly redistributive nor explicitly racial, such as those governing criminal justice and immigration. These may also disproportionately impact the minority community, and could help explain the patterns we see.

Finally, scholars have made strong claims about redistribution and the efficacy of various transfers to the poor (e.g. President Lyndon Johnson's "War on Poverty," or President Bill Clinton's expansion of the earned income tax credit). The American Political Science Association (APSA) Taskforce on Inequality in American Democracy, in particular, highlights the important role that tax policy can play in expanding or mitigating economic inequality (APSA 2004). Because these kinds of redistributive efforts (e.g. taxing and spending) tend to fluctuate extensively from administration to administration, they are, in my opinion, among the most logical sources of minority gains and losses across different administrations. The fact that Republicans under the Trump presidency recently passed one of the largest and one of the least progressive tax cuts in history only serves to underscore the partisan differences in this area, and the potential for tax policy to shape economic well-being – for good or for ill.

Unfortunately, very few studies have been able to systematically tie the passage of a particular policy or set of policies to quantifiable gains or losses in minority well-being or even to the overall well-being of the population (APSA 2004). So many policies are passed every year that it is hard to isolate the effects of any one policy. Nevertheless, the problem is too important to ignore. If we can identify and highlight specific policies that reduce or exacerbate the economic divide between White and non-White Americans, we may be able to greatly reduce America's racial inequality.

I also acknowledge that voters might want more information about the non-economic effects of partisan control before passing judgment on either the Democratic or Republican parties. Economic indicators (such as income, employment, and poverty) and social outcomes (such as criminal justice) might be less important to some voters than moral, environmental, or foreign policy concerns. Many voters certainly express strong views about homosexuality, abortion, and other social morality issues (Layman and Carmines 1997). Evidence also suggests that international events and actions can affect the electoral calculus of voters (Kernell 1997). I do not claim that the outcomes that are the focus here are, or should be, the only issues citizens care about. Future studies could certainly benefit from incorporating outcomes in these other areas. Nevertheless, knowing that the Democratic Party has to this point been more effective in reducing racial gaps in economic well-being is certainly an important factor for voters to consider.

Implications for Parties and Institutions

Knowing that racial and ethnic minorities do better materially under Democrats than under Republicans also has obvious relevance for political discourse in the United States. It suggests that, however much racial inequality persists, such inequalities would be much greater were it not for periods of Democratic Party dominance. The stark patterns presented here suggest that it is, indeed, accurate to view American partisan conflict as partly a contest between two political orders, one of which is racially egalitarian and transformative, and the other of which is racially restrictive (King and Smith 2005).

These results do not directly contradict less sanguine assessments of the Democratic Party. One could still argue, as Paul Frymer does, that the Democratic Party often takes minorities – especially Blacks – for granted (Frymer 1999). It may also still be fair to claim, as Robert Lieberman and Ira Katznelson do, that the Democratic Party's implementation of a liberal agenda has at times been marred by inordinate attention to lower-class Whites' welfare (Lieberman 1998, Katznelson 2005). And one could still reasonably argue that the Democratic Party could and should have done more to advance an economically progressive and racially transformative platform.

The results presented here do, however, directly contradict scholarly claims by Stephan and Abigail Thernstrom and others about the ability of the color-blind politics of the Republican Party to advance minority well-being (Thernstrom and Thernstrom 1997). The enactment of the Republican agenda at different points in recent decades has clearly not helped minority interests, and may have actually hurt them.

This study also has wide-ranging implications for our understanding of American political institutions. Perhaps most obviously, the results presented here suggest that politics matters. There has been an ongoing debate – particularly in the economics literature – about the ability of governments to raise the welfare of their citizens (Hayek and Hamowy 2011, Keynes 1936). The stark gains for minorities on core measures of well-being under Democratic administrations reinforce the view that governments can do a lot to positively impact the welfare of their constituents (Hacker and Pierson 2011, Page and Simmons 2000).

Similarly, ample evidence here indicates that political parties matter. My results show that parties in American politics are far from empty shells. The two major parties may have fewer resources than they once had, and they may be much more candidate-centered than they once were, but the results indicate that party differences are very real, and that leadership by either major party can dramatically affect individual and group well-being (Aldrich 1995). Indeed, judging by the magnitude of the partisan effects observed here, party control may be one of the most important influences on who wins and who loses in American democracy.

The results presented here also offer some insight into the relative impact of different institutions within American democracy. The president, it appears, has fairly robust power. Even though each presidential administration is subject to any number of arbitrary and uncontrollable events, and even though presidents have to negotiate with an often unruly Congress, their words and actions appear to have a substantial impact on the well-being of individual Americans. Presidents' choices – how they deal with the economic conditions and issues of the day, and, more broadly, the policy agendas they pursue – have wide-ranging consequences, as illustrated by core measures of well-being for all Americans, and the relative standing of America's racial and ethnic groups.

Some limited signs suggest that Congress and in particular the presence of a divided government have implications for America's racial hierarchy. The effects, while inconsistent, nonetheless indicate that Black income grows more when a Democratic president is coupled with a Democratic Congress than when a Democratic president faces a Republican Congress. As for the third branch of federal government, the courts do not appear to significantly impact minority well-being – at least as far as I have been able to measure such potential influence. However, I believe that this interpretation of the relatively minor roles of Congress and the federal courts warrants caution. Such conclusions should be tempered because the relatively long stretches of Democratic congressional control during this period make analysis of Congress somewhat problematic, and because I have not examined all aspects of the judicial process, such as the effects of landmark decisions. In short, I believe I have shown that presidents and partisanship matter, but the roles of Congress and the courts in shaping America's racial order warrant greater examination.

Finally, there may also be some guidance for those interested in broader questions of democratic theory. Objective assessments about the responsiveness of different leaders to constituent groups are indispensable to democracy. Voters cannot choose effectively if they do not know which candidate or party best serves their interest. Yet political scientists often prefer not to take partisan sides in their scholarly work, deeming such conclusions insufficiently "objective." We tend to pride ourselves on remaining above the partisan fray. But in shying away from taking sides, we neglect one of the core elements of democracy – evaluation. Democracy rests, almost more than anything else, on the electorate's ability to evaluate the responsiveness of those who govern. Elected leaders act and constituents then evaluate those actions. Have they done a good job or not? If voters cannot tell whom government has helped and whom it has hurt, they will not know which party to reward and which to punish. Without effective evaluation, elections lose much of their purpose, and democracy is diminished. This chapter demonstrates that academics can and should provide effective evaluation. By evaluating outcomes and illustrating the relative gains and losses of different groups under different regimes, scholars can make a major contribution to the improved functioning of democracy.

9 WHERE WILL WE GO FROM HERE?

"This is the meaning of our liberty and our creed, why men and women and children of every race and every faith can join in celebration across this magnificent mall, and why a man whose father less than 60 years ago might not have been served at a local restaurant can now stand before you to take a most sacred oath." – Barack Hussein Obama, Inauguration speech, 2009.

Over a decade and three presidential elections ago, America bore witness to a historic moment. The National Mall teemed with people, all longing to be part of a transition that had seemed unimaginable not so long before, both for a man and for a nation. The man was Barack Hussein Obama – the offspring of a Black father from Kenya and a White mother from Kansas whose family tree includes slave owners, among them, Jefferson Davis, the president of the Confederacy. The moment was the Presidential Inaugural – taking place on a cold, bright and breezy day 146 years after Abraham Lincoln signed the Emancipation Proclamation and forty-six years after the Rev. Martin Luther King Jr.'s delivered his "I Have a Dream" speech.

Anand Thomas, a thirty-two-year-old nurse from Westchester County, New York, who rode a crowded, early-morning bus to the ceremony with camera, sandwiches, and tissues in tow, expressed the views of a world struck by the power of the moment, when she said, "Today, we're hoping to see history" (Stout 2009).

For the first time in human history, a largely White nation had elected a Black man to be its leader. When Obama rested his hand on the same bible that Lincoln had used, the last racial barrier was said to have fallen. The utter elation of many Americans of all races, but, in particular, of African Americans and civil rights campaigners, many of whom had feared they would never live to see the day, made for an emotional scene. The bywords of the campaign – "Yes We Can," "Hope," and "Change" – seemed to transcend mere slogans. The evidence of how much a nation could change and hope to achieve stood before them under the bright noonday sun taking the oath to become the Forty-Fourth President of the United States of America. To many, Obama's victory meant that the future of the nation looked bright. Writers around the country heralded a better, fairer, more harmonious future. One headline in Forbes proclaimed, "Racism in America is Over" (McWhorter 2008). The *Washington Post* talked about the possibility of a "post-racial society" (Prose 2008).

Dangerously Divided

That hope of a post-racial America was not realized with Barack Obama's first or second election. Instead, racial division continued, and perhaps even grew during and after his eight years in the office. The failure to overcome the obstacle of race is the story of this book. As chapter after chapter has demonstrated, Americans have not yet surmounted their deep racial differences. In election after election, in year after year, from local to national elections, the overwhelming majority of racial and ethnic minority voters stand on one side of the democratic fault line opposed to the clear majority of White Americans. Our racial identities, more than any other demographic factor, determine who we are politically.

Hope for a less racialized polity has been replaced with the realization that racial divisions are growing rather than receding. Since Barack Obama's election, the data reveal sharpened racial divisions in the vote and heightened racial tensions.[1] Donald Trump's campaign and his time in office appear to have exacerbated such divisions.[2]

More broadly, across a longer arc of time, as this book has documented, a massive reorganization of American politics around race has occurred. A little over half a century ago, the two parties

248 / Dangerously Divided

were almost indistinguishable in their racial make-up. African Americans and White Americans were both split between the Democratic and Republican parties. But over time, racial fissures have opened and slowly but inexorably expanded. After the Democratic Party embraced a pro-civil rights agenda and the Republican Party countered by advancing a "Southern Strategy" that sought to limit Black gains, Whites and Blacks grew further and further apart politically. By 1990, the overwhelming majority of Blacks were firmly entrenched on the Democratic side, and any advantages the Democrats had previously held among Whites had disappeared. Then as the nation moved into the twenty-first century, the Republican Party shifted toward an anti-immigrant agenda, and Democrats followed suit by offering a more welcoming stance on immigration. As a result, the racial divide grew into a racial chasm. More and more Asian Americans and Latinos became attached to the Democratic Party, and more and more Whites defected to the Republican Party. At present, the Republican Party is almost exclusively a party of White Americans. In the last few elections, roughly 90 percent of all of its supporters have been White. In sharp contrast, the Democrats are now a party of diversity, with almost half of their followers identifying as racial and ethnic minorities. *Arguably, we are now more divided by race than at any other time in modern American history. Ironically, as the nation has become more diverse, it has become more divided by that diversity.* This is the first conclusion of this book, and it is a troubling one.

A Peripheral Role for Class

Remarkably, the rise of racial division has occurred while the nation has been experiencing extraordinary economic upheaval. Over the last half-century, economic inequality has been steadily on the rise. The life experiences of the wealthy have increasingly diverged from the travails and uncertain circumstances of the unskilled laborer. In 1978, America's CEOs earned roughly 30 times what their workers earned. Today that figure is closer to 300 (Umoh 2018). It now takes the typical worker more than two months of toil to match what their CEOs earn in an hour (Krantz 2015). The three wealthiest Americans now own assets worth more than the assets of half of the United States' 330 million citizens combined (Kertscher 2018). These are large, perhaps unprecedented, economic gaps between haves and have-nots.

And the situation does not appear to be improving. The financial crisis of 2007 and 2008 led to the worst economic downturn in the United States since the Great Depression, with millions losing homes, jobs, and, in many cases, hope. The subsequent recovery has been sustained but it has also been uneven. Some 95 percent of all economic gains have gone to the top 1 percent (Reich 2012). All of this is why former US Secretary of Labor Robert Reich calls inequality the defining issue of the day (2012), and why economist Robert Shiller, a Nobel laureate, calls rising economic disparities, "the most important problem we are facing" (Wilkins 2013).

Yet my analysis of the vote in 2016 and in most American elections over the last few decades indicates that, even in the face of these trends, class plays only a *secondary* role in American politics. The choices that voters make are far more likely to diverge by race than by class. The wealthy do not differ that much from the poor when it comes to choosing between a Democrat and a Republican. In 2016, those making more than $200,000 annually were only 4 percent more likely to favor Trump over Clinton. Likewise, the gap in 2016 between those with a college degree and those without a high school degree was only 6 points. And critically, the better-educated were actually less likely to vote for the Republican candidate – a slight reversal of decades of upper-class Republican voting. American democracy is now hardly divided by class.

These conclusions seem to fly in the face of much of the media coverage of American politics and, especially, of the 2016 election. Story after story following that election highlighted the fact that working-class Whites made up the bulk of those who shifted from Obama to Trump. Time and time again the theme of the coverage was all about "how Trump won the White working class" (Stern 2017). From this perspective, Democrats were doomed in the future if they did not do more to recapture the White working class (Ball 2017, Greenberg 2018).

How is it that class attracts so much attention when the overwhelming wealth of data presented in this book so clearly demonstrates that class plays a marginal role in the vote? The answer lies in part on the narrow focus of many of these studies. Many studies that emphasize the role of class tend to focus on a narrow segment of the electorate that switched support from one political camp to another – from Obama to Trump, for example.[3] These voters are critical in helping to explain the outcome of a tight election, but they are not representative of the larger electorate. Less than 5 percent of the electorate switched from Obama to Trump.

If one instead looks at the entire electorate, as I do in this book, the overall patterns are clear. Despite the enormous focus on working-class support for Trump, lower-income Americans were actually slightly *less* likely than upper-income Americans to vote for Trump. All told, there is only a little correlation between class and the vote. When America votes, the outcome is hardly shaped by wealth or poverty.

Moreover, even when we look more closely at who did and did not switch, the argument for class as the central motivation is hardly convincing. If economic disadvantage is the driving force behind the Trump vote, then the most pronounced shift toward Trump should have taken place not among White voters but among the nation's most disadvantaged populations, its racial and ethnic minorities. Blacks and Latinos are much more likely than Whites to suffer economically, and to live in depressed neighborhoods cut off from recent economic gains. Yet, they are not turning to the Republican Party. *In the face of the same economic circumstances, Whites and non-Whites are making the opposite partisan choices. That should tell us something about the racial nature of our politics.* It is also worth noting that several recent studies have found that racial attitudes, much more than economic concerns, predicted who would switch from Obama to Trump. According to one prominent panel study that tracked Obama voters over time, "No other factor predicted changes in White partisanship during Obama's presidency as powerfully and as consistently as racial attitudes" (John Sides, quoted in Porter 2018).

It is also easy to highlight the effects of class, when class is examined in isolation. Class divides can look reasonably large on their own. But comparing class divisions and racial divisions makes clear which one lies at the core of the nation's politics. As I have shown time and time again in this book, the class divide pales in comparison to the racial divide.

The outsized importance of race does not deny or diminish the importance of economic change in the American political picture. Mobility is declining (Chetty et al. 2017). America is now profoundly unequal. People are angry. People are suffering. This new state of affairs in some ways marks a symbolic end to the American dream. It suggests that America is no longer the land of opportunity. It hints that we may no longer be able to legitimately claim to live up to the core motto of the

Declaration of Independence of "Life, Liberty, and the pursuit of Happiness." President Obama may in fact be absolutely correct when he stated that income inequality is "the defining challenge of our time."[4] This is a situation that all Americans should recognize and seek to change.

What is truly remarkable is this: *Amid such profound economic tumult, race and immigration are the primary forces shaping our politics. Economic anxiety, real as it is, has not resulted in class warfare or even class politics.* Instead economic anxiety appears to beget racial insecurity and angst about immigration. As has so often happened in the past in American politics, racial and ethnic minorities and immigrants are being used as scapegoats for Whites who are concerned about their role in the economy and in American society more broadly (Daniels 2004, Higham 1985, Key 1949, Kousser 1999, Tichenor 2002, Zolberg 2009). Anger must find a target. Thus, increasing racial diversity and burgeoning immigration are dividing the nation.

Beyond Race and Class

Despite all of the talk about a new and distinct generation of millennials, little evidence supports the notion that a generational divide is increasingly shaping our partisan politics (Hochschild et al. 2012, Norris 2017, Taylor 2014, Teixeira 2009). *Once I control for race, age plays a secondary role* in shaping our partisan attachments and electoral choices. Discussion of the growing urban-rural divide in American politics warrants consideration (Cramer 2016, Kurtzleben 2016, Skelley 2016). *But once again, after I control for race and other demographic factors, the urban-rural gap largely fades away.*

One demographic factor that is increasingly impacting our politics and is therefore contributing more and more to our partisan polarization is gender. A half-century ago, there were almost no differences in the partisan choices of men and women. If anything, women were slightly more likely than men to identify as Republicans. That has slowly but inexorably changed over time. Women are now substantially more likely than men to favor the Democratic Party. Gender is now very much relevant to the partisan equation (Rakich and Mehta 2018). But despite the growing importance of the divide between male and female voters, *gender still pales in comparison to race.* A roughly 10-point gender gap in party identification is small when compared to 30- or 50-point racial gaps.[5]

If there is a competitor to race's dominant role in dividing the two parties, it is religion. Religion plays an increasingly prominent role in dividing Democrats from Republicans. White Evangelicals have over time become more and more attached to the Republican Party and are now one of the Republican Party's most reliable supporters.[6] More broadly, those who indicate that religion is important in their lives and who attend church consistently have shifted to the Republican Party. As part of that shift, more and more Protestants and Catholics are moving from the Democratic Party to the Republican Party. At the other end of the religious spectrum atheists and those who do not go to services are increasingly linked to the Democratic Party. The end result is *that religion has become a critically important dividing line in American politics. Even religion is, however, generally overshadowed by race.*

All told race not only overshadows class, but its effects dwarf those of almost every other conceivable demographic factor.

Explaining the Racial Divide

Why is race, more than any other factor, shaping American democracy? And why is that racial divide growing in an age of rising economic inequality? As with any major societal phenomenon, many different factors are surely contributing. It is easy to see that our politics are increasingly being driven by economic anxiety, views on just how much government should be involved in our lives, and social issues such as abortion and gay rights (Abramowitz 1994, Adams 1997, Carsey and Layman 2006). Scholars have clearly demonstrated that each of these factors has contributed to the defection of some White Americans from the Democratic Party to the Republican Party, and thus each factor has contributed to the racial imbalances that now characterize American democracy. I do not dispute any of these conclusions.

Nevertheless, in this book, I focus on two other explanations that cannot and should not be ignored. These explanations, which stubbornly surface again and again, are race and immigration. Some aspects of the racial story are well known and well documented. As observers of American politics have so clearly illustrated, the diverging positions of the Democratic and Republican parties on matters of race over the last half-century have given Americans of all racial stripes an increasingly clear choice between support of a racially progressive agenda that favors government action to try to rectify racial inequities and allegiance to a more color-blind platform that views racial and ethnic minority demands as excessive and unwarranted (Edsall and Edsall 1991, King and Smith 2005). That stark partisan choice has unambiguously resulted in partisan defections by both majority and minority populations (Carmines and Stimson 1989, Parker and Barreto 2013). For many White Americans, racial considerations – namely a sense of racial threat and racial resentment – have increasingly drawn them to the Republican Party (Abramowitz 2018, Carmines and Stimson 1989, Sides et al. 2018, Tesler and Sears 2010). A sense of linked fate with their racial or pan-ethnic brethren has, likewise, brought much of the racial and ethnic minority population into the Democratic fold (Barreto and Collingwood 2015, Dawson 1994, Hajnal and Lee 2011, Kuo et al. 2017, Lien et al. 2004, Nicholson and Segura 2005, Ramakrishnan et al. 2009). There should be little doubt that we are racially divided in large part because of race itself.

These conventional explanations do not, however, tell the whole story. They do not fully explain the more recent, large-scale defection of White Americans from the Democratic to the Republican Party in the first decades of the twenty-first century. That recent shift, I contend, is at least in part driven by anxiety over immigration. The Republican Party has since the mid-1990s increasingly seized on the issue of immigration to define itself as the protector of America's culture and prosperity in the face of an immigrant onslaught. The data put forward in this book show that the anti-immigrant narrative has been widely successful for the Republican Party. A range of tests – some simple and others more complex – show that White Americans' views about immigration strongly predict where they stand on the partisan scale. Those concerned about immigration and its impact on the nation – a sizable share of the White population – have increasingly shifted to the Republican Party. The end result, as I have also shown here, is a broad White backlash against immigrant and minority interests.

America's Unequal Democracy

The narrative of the first part of this book – that America's partisan divide is increasingly shaped by race – is not an entirely new one. Scholars of racial politics have long documented and lamented the deep and troublesome racial divisions plaguing this nation. My analysis goes further than most, and contrasts race with other demographic divides more than most, but it tells essentially the same story. We are deeply divided by race.

The narrative of the second part of this book – that outcomes in America's democracy are racially uneven – is much more novel. Studies have shown that at certain times and in certain places, outcomes have been skewed by race. But scholars have largely been unable to offer a broader, overall assessment of outcomes in American democracy. We do not yet know what the consequences of this racial divide are for who wins and who loses in American democracy.

This lack of understanding represents an important omission for two reasons. First, while we should care about the inputs in American democracy, what ultimately matters are the outputs of that process. True understanding of democracy and its consequences for the public relies on knowing who wins when the votes are counted, which kinds of candidates control the levers of power, and whose voices are heard when government chooses to spend the trillions of dollars it manages. Second, as I have argued here, the consequences of a racially divided vote are worrisome. The logic of a majoritarian democracy is clear. If a White majority wants to elect candidates and pass policies at the expense of racial and ethnic minorities, it has the power to do so. But is this the kind of democracy and society that Americans want? Doesn't this prospect fall well short of the ideals Americans hold? Is the creation of a political underclass beneficial for anyone?

My examination of outcomes across American democracy thus breaks important new ground. The results are troubling. I find that there is a strong racial element in play determining who wins and who loses in American democracy. America's racial fault lines have wide-ranging consequences. When America elects its leaders, it rarely chooses racial and ethnic minorities. At almost every level, from the local to the national, roughly 90 percent of all officials elected to office are White – a striking figure in a nation that is only 60 percent White. *Immigration and other factors have greatly increased the diversity of the nation's halls of power over the last half century, but our political leadership remains overwhelmingly White.*

And it is not just racial and ethnic minority *candidates* who lose. Racial and ethnic minority *voters* also lose disproportionately when the votes are tallied. Across the nation, most members of most groups – racial or otherwise – end up voting for candidates who do ultimately win. African Americans are the lone exception. Across the hundreds of offices and decades of elections examined in this book, in most cases the clear majority of Black voters end up on the losing side of the vote. Blacks are more than four times as likely as Whites to consistently lose across all of the different offices I examine. This is a disparity that no previous researcher has uncovered. It is one that should raise deep concerns.

The policies that we pass are also skewed. Congress and the president do listen to the public when they make decisions about policy, but they respond to some voices more than to others. Race – more than class, age, gender, or any other demographic factor – determines whose voices are heard. Blacks, more than any other group, tend to be ignored. On important matters of policy, African Americans are the most likely to be left out of the policy process. This is an important new finding that is well worth underlining. Many people who study race – and perhaps Black Americans who experience this frustration directly – will not find this surprising. Nevertheless, it is troubling. And now that understanding of our political system has emerged and been recognized, the question that follows is whether the nation can summon the will to do something about it. Is America willing to work to find ways to be a full democracy, responsive to and benefiting all groups of people?

As the pages of this book demonstrate, race and immigration also impact policy outcomes at the state level in ways that target the underprivileged. A White backlash against immigration means that when the Latino population grows, and when policies are more likely to impact Latinos, benefits decline and punishment increases. More precisely, states with larger Latino populations are less willing to invest in public services such as education, health, and welfare. Instead, they are more likely to funnel greater resources to criminal justice, and to institute regressive taxation systems. Scholars have already known that immigration creates widespread anxiety but not how broadly those feelings impact policy. The data I put forward here demonstrate for the first time that immigration and race are fundamentally altering the core priorities of state governments.

Why We Should Be Concerned

This book shows that American democracy is uneven. Some groups – especially Blacks and Latinos – lose more than others. What it does not show is overwhelming tyranny of the majority. There is no group – including Blacks and Latinos – that is totally shut out of the political process. Many members of every group – including Blacks and Latinos – end up on the winning side of the democracy. The racial imbalances that I uncover are real but not enormous. Blacks, for example, are only about 5 percentage points less likely than Whites to have their preferences met on policy.

At first glance, these patterns might not seem all that problematic. They might even be reassuring to some. After all, America is a majoritarian democracy. Shouldn't the majority have more of a say than the minority? Shouldn't Blacks, who only represent 13 percent of the population, and Latinos, who only represent 18 percent of the population, have less of a say than Whites, who represent 61 percent of the population? By this logic, slightly imbalanced outcomes might be viewed as reasonable or even democratic.

Here is why we, as members or observers of American democracy, should be concerned. First, the groups that lose the most are always the same. They are always racial and ethnic minorities. In a contentious democracy there will always be losers. Any minority group could conceivably end up on the losing side of the democratic process at any point. Poorer Americans, younger Americans, older Americans, rural Americans, or any other group that represents less than half of the population could sometimes end up as the big losers. But the reality is that they do not. As the analysis presented in this book makes clear, in American democracy it is almost always racial and ethnic minorities that lose the most. Across all of the different outcomes we examine, Blacks and Latinos lose more consistently than any others. Losing is fine, in some respects. One cannot really expect to be a perpetual winner. But when time and time again, across issue after issue, in context after context, the losers are from the same racial and ethnic minority groups, concerns about resentment build, and the chances of conflict increase. In any democracy – but especially in one with a history of racial exclusion and racial conflict – that is problematic.

The other troubling aspect of the patterns uncovered in this book is that the racial imbalance cannot be easily explained. Race not only matters more than anything else, it matters after factoring in everything else. Race matters after taking into account class, gender, age, religion, and all of the other demographic factors that tend to structure American politics. Blacks and Latinos are not losing simply because they are poorer or less educated than others. Even more critically, race matters after taking into account partisanship and ideology. Blacks and Latinos are not losing because they are largely liberal or overwhelmingly Democratic. They are not losing because their preferences are different or unique. Indeed, I find that government weighs the preferences of Blacks less, even when they hold the same preferences as Whites. I have not been able to control for every structural feature of American democracy, but to this point racial inequality in American democracy is unexplained. Blacks and Latinos may be losing more than any other group solely because they are Black or Latino – a relationship that, if true, should be worrying, both for its potential consequences for society and for its obvious divergence from basic democratic principles.

Finally, we should be concerned because the analysis shows that when it comes to outcomes in American democracy race tends to matter even more than partisanship and ideology. There is little doubt that partisanship and ideology represent the primary dividing lines in American democracy (Abramowitz and Saunders 1998, Campbell et al. 1960, Green et al. 2002). One's place in American democracy is largely defined by whether one identifies as a Democrat or a Republican, or as a liberal or a conservative. Yet, race more than partisanship or ideology best predicts whether one is a winner or loser in American democracy. Over the last three decades, liberal, Democratic voters lost more often than conservative, Republican voters, but no one lost more frequently than African-American voters. Over the last four decades, federal government spending mirrored the preferences of Republicans and conservatives more than Democrats and liberals, but even after considering partisanship and ideology, Blacks were the biggest losers. When race, not politics, most determines who wins and who loses, we should be alarmed.

A Nation Torn Apart by Race?

Given both the consistency with which racial and ethnic minorities lose across different aspects of American democracy and the fact that those losses are hard to explain, the emergence of racial tensions and racial conflict outside of politics would seem unsurprising. When skin color, more than anything else, predicts who wins and who loses in our democracy, the potential for the nation to tear itself apart becomes all too real.[7]

This book has not and will not provide a detailed assessment of either racial tension or racial conflict in this country. But in this last chapter, it is worth briefly looking beyond the voting booth at the deeper and darker elements of our racial divide. Unfortunately, every indication suggests that racial divides in the ballot box have spilled over into racial animosity and racial conflict outside of it.

In spite of the widespread optimism that marked the historic election of Barack Obama just over a decade ago, events on the ground in the intervening years have served as reminders of how far the nation has yet to go. In the ensuing decade incidents of racialized violence have been all too common. Trayvon Martin in Florida, Michael Brown in Missouri, Eric Garner in New York, Walter Scott in South Carolina ... the roster of the names of Black men dying in the wake of troubling confrontations with police and security has grown ever longer. And deaths are not coming exclusively in confrontations with authorities. When a White man named Dylann Roof shot and killed nine African Americans at the Emanuel African Methodist Episcopal Church in Charleston, South Carolina, on June 17, 2015, the nation was shocked and horrified. Perhaps it should not have been surprised. That attack was just the latest in a long line of assaults on Black churches.[8] And when James Fields rammed his car into protesters demonstrating against a White supremacist rally in Charlottesville, Virginia, killing thirty-two-year-old Heather D. Heyer, the event was equally shocking but, again, it should not have been surprising. At the time of these horrific events, the nation was in the midst of a surge in hate crimes and an explosion in the number of hate groups (Chen 2017). In 2017 more than 7,000 hate crimes were reported – a 30 percent increase since 2014 (FBI 2018).[9]

Reactions to these kinds of encounters can be just as telling. On one side protest banners of "I Can't Breathe," "Hands Up, Don't Shoot," and "Black Lives Matter" reveal how angry and aggrieved members of the Black community feel. In 2017, after his Los Angeles home was painted with racial slurs, professional basketball player Lebron James, one of the most privileged members of the African-American population, observed, "Hate in America, especially for African-Americans, is living every day" (North 2017). On the other side, viral videos urging Blacks to "Get Over Slavery," demonstrations in favor of the Confederate flag and Confederate war memorials, and "White Lives Matter" rallies reveal how angry and resentful many Whites feel. When our nation's first Black president sent out his first, cheerful Twitter post – "Hello, Twitter! It's Barack. Really!" – replies filled with racial slurs, one using an image of the president with his neck in a noose, arrived within minutes. Protesters chanting "Bye, bye Black sheep" at a speech in Arizona, signs showing the "Primate in Chief," and bumper stickers and T-shirts that read, "NIGGER, PLEASE!! It's a WHITE house" all reveal a deep-seated aversion to Black empowerment (Merrill et al. 2013).

And while it may be convenient to blame the tension solely on the arrival of the nation's first Black president, it is clear that the vitriolic rhetoric from the far right did not stop with the departure of the forty-fourth president. Rather, the opposite occurred. White nationalism and hate groups in many forms seemed to be reinvigorated by the election of a presidential candidate who verbally attacked Mexican immigrants, who almost singlehandedly created the Birther Movement that questioned the authenticity of Obama's birth certificate, and who banned immigration from a number of Muslim-majority countries. Trump's victory seemed to embolden racists around the country. The Southern Poverty Law Center uncovered almost 900 incidents of hate or bias in the ten days after the 2016 election. In the month after, the group counted 1,094 incidents, and one month later the figure grew to 1,863 (North 2017). In 2017, the first year of Trump's presidency, law enforcement reported 7,175 incidents of hate crime, an increase of 17 percent over the five-year high reached in 2016 (FBI 2018).

Let's also be clear that this animosity and violence is not solely targeted at the Black community. Incidences of violence and aggression against immigrants seem, at least by the headlines, to be just as common. Just last year, ten undocumented immigrants died from dehydration after being abandoned in a sweltering tractor trailer in San Antonio. That incident recalled another Texas smuggling case years earlier in which nineteen would-be immigrants died. Stories of White paramilitary volunteers patrolling the border reveal just how deep the hatred runs. One *Newsweek* article recounted how B.J., a fifty-three-year-old woman who patrols the South Texas border, relishes a "manhunt" in which she first identifies tracks, then speeds through the trails to find the migrants, and finally chases after them in her truck until they tire out.

"You can't tell me this isn't fun," she told one reporter (Zabludovsky 2014). The fact that hundreds of immigrants die each year trying to cross the border does not seem to faze members of the Texas Border Volunteers, a 300-strong force that dresses in fatigues and tries to catch "illegals" (Zabludovsky 2014).

When a relatively mainstream conservative thinker like Ann Coulter can write, "The rape of little girls isn't even considered a crime in Latino culture ... Another few years of our current immigration policies, and we'll all have to move to Canada to escape the rapes," it is clear that animosity toward immigrants is broadly accepted (Beinart 2016).

The most troubling aspect of this climate is that we seem to be going in the wrong direction, and one that seemed unlikely a decade ago. On the eve of Barack Obama's inauguration a record 77 percent of Americans offered a positive assessment of race relations (Dann 2017). The victory of a Black man proved not only to ourselves but also to the world just how far we had come from the dark days of our racial past. But in the ensuing years, the nation experienced a stunning reversal in our racial outlook. Optimism on the racial front has slowly but surely been replaced with pessimism. By 2018, a near-record share of the population – again, 77 percent – called race relations "bad" or "fairly bad" (Dann 2017). Fully one-third of the population (36 percent) says that racism and bigotry are an "imminent threat to the country" (Whitesides 2017). Relatively few Americans expect things to get better in the future. Only about one-quarter of Americans predict that racial relations will improve going forward (McClatchy-Marist poll 2017).[10]

Adding to the dilemma is the fact that we are, as a nation, also deeply divided in our assessments of the fairness of American society. More than one-third of Whites (38 percent) believe the country has already done enough to achieve racial equality. By contrast, only 8 percent of Blacks believe the same. Latinos fall halfway in between (Pew 2017c). Americans are equally divided over what causes racial inequality. The vast majority of African Americans (70 percent) cite racial discrimination as a major reason that Blacks have a harder time getting ahead. Only a small minority of Whites (36 percent) agree. Latinos, once again, fall in the middle (58 percent agree). Whites are also much less likely than African Americans to believe that Blacks are treated unfairly by the police, by the courts, by the housing industry, at the workplace, and by the electoral system.

The racial divide is perhaps sharpest when Americans think about the future. Almost half of all African Americans (43 percent) believe that the country will never make the changes needed for Blacks to achieve equal rights. By contrast, White Americans overwhelmingly believe that the nation will achieve or has already achieved racial equality. Only 11 percent of Whites believe that racial inequality will persist (Pew 2017c).

A barrier fell when Barack Obama entered the White House, but the issue of race did not go away. Far from it. Hate crimes, violence, and pessimism about the future have only grown. With the benefit of hindsight, the euphoria and idealism of election day 2008 can now seem to be little more than hyperbole or naïveté, or both.

The turn of events is remarkable. More than half a century after the nation passed the landmark Civil Rights Act outlawing discrimination based on race, decades after outlawing segregation in schools, years after enforcing the constitutional right to vote, we are riven by race, the very issue that these laws and actions sought to address. Our democratic system is sharply tilted in favor of Whites, and our society is experiencing wide-ranging and growing racial tensions and racial violence.

Hope

America's increasingly sharp racial divide and its uneven democracy are troubling. If we care about equality within the democratic process and, ultimately, about the well-being of all Americans, then we need to think about ways to correct for these racial imbalances. Fortunately, America's history suggests that progress is possible. Over the long arc of history, America's democracy has become more open and more even. From the nation's founding, when only land-owning white men could vote and slavery was sanctioned, to today, when all citizens – bar some felons – can participate, the United States has made remarkable progress.[11] That progress has been uneven and there have been notable periods of backlash and regression – Reconstruction and the Jim Crow Era come to mind – but there is no doubt that the steps forward have been real (Klinkner and Smith 1999). The arc of American history, replete with progress and setbacks, suggests that the nation can do even better.

But for those who care and who want to create a more equitable democracy, what can be done? The data that I have presented in this book demonstrate that minorities fare worse than Whites in American democracy. But the data also show that there are exceptions. At specific times and in particular contexts, outcomes for minorities improve and their interests in democracy begin to be advanced. By analyzing that variation, I have been able to show that one change – moving to Democratic Party control – could radically reduce racial inequities in American democracy. An examination of federal spending over almost four decades reveals that Democratic Party control of the presidency and Congress eliminates most of the racial imbalance in policy responsiveness. When Republicans are in charge, policy largely follows White interests. Racial and ethnic minority preferences are more apt to be ignored. But when Democrats take control, policy outcomes weigh the preferences of White and non-White Americans in roughly equal measure. Again, this may not come as a surprise to many observers of American politics, but it is a critical new finding because it documents what has heretofore been largely limited to belief. In the face of facts, the situation warrants attention and action.

This is true not only at the national level but also at the state level. My deeper examination of state policy reveals that states with Democratic control of the legislature and the governor's office spend more in areas such as health and education – areas that could directly benefit a disadvantaged minority population – and likewise spend less in areas such as criminal justice that could potentially target minorities.

Even more importantly, I find that Democratic control helps to shape a deeper, more fundamental outcome: the economic well-being of racial and ethnic minorities. When the nation is governed by Democrats, racial and ethnic minority well-being improves dramatically. A Democrat in the White House means growing incomes, declining poverty, and declining unemployment for the nation's racial and ethnic minority population. By contrast, under Republican administrations, Blacks, Latinos, and Asian Americans generally suffer losses. Moreover, the gap in well-being between Whites and minorities declines appreciably under Democrats. If sustained over a long enough period, and if Democratic control leads to a continuation of policies that address the issues that directly affect minority populations, *Democratic control might eventually erase most of the economic inequality between Whites and non-Whites.*

Of all the findings generated in this book, this might be the most important. Researchers have had difficulty finding viable and effective solutions to the problem of minority under-representation in American democracy. These patterns suggest that they might not need to look any further. A solution to racial inequality is readily available. Electing Democrats has the potential to reverse much of the racial inequality in American democracy, and to erase most of the racial inequality in economic well-being. Electing Democrats is not a straightforward or easy task, as the Trump election most recently evidenced, and as the wide expanse of "red" states and congressional districts suggests. There is also some uncertainty involved. The Democratic agenda could shift in the future. Long-term power for any political party could lead to corruption, incompetence, and a lack of responsiveness.

Nevertheless, a move to the "blue" approach that Democrats have put forward offers the potential to bring minorities in from the margins of democracy. Advocacy for wider participation in democracy must almost certainly begin with advocating for a party that aims for, and in many respects achieves, this goal.

On this point, again, it is also crucial to highlight the fact that White Americans do not lose under Democrats. In fact, the opposite is true. I find that White well-being improves under Democrats, and perhaps even more quickly than it does under Republicans. When Democrats win, much of America wins.

Democratic Party control is not the only change that could impact America's uneven democracy. Throughout the book, other factors that in different ways might tilt the balance back toward minorities are identified, if not fully investigated. On the institutional level, addressing the issue of gerrymandering seems to have promise. There is a scholarly debate about how beneficial majority-minority districts have been in the past, and open questions remain about what the ideal makeup of districts is for minority interests (Cameron et al. 1996, Lublin 1997, Shotts 2003). Gerrymandering is often viewed in a negative light because it can be used for antidemocratic aims, to protect incumbents, to undercut the viability of challenges, to solidify the power of a certain party, and to dilute the power of some groups. Nonetheless, the data presented here make clear that racial and ethnic minority voters – Blacks, Latinos, and Asian Americans alike – are all much more likely to end up on the winning side of the vote when they are grouped together with other minorities and like-minded Whites. Black voters typically lose more often than they win. But in House elections, where district boundaries are often drawn to concentrate minority voters, their success rates soar. Descriptive representation also rises when racial and ethnic minority voters are concentrated together in the same district. I found that the under-representation of racial and ethnic minorities was decidedly less pronounced in the US House of Representatives and in state legislatures – institutions whose membership has been decidedly influenced by redistricting.[12]

Some other ideas read less like concrete reform and more like aspirations. Underlying much of the data presented here is the notion that if we could just change White attitudes, we could erase the racial tilt of American democracy. If Whites could recognize that immigrants are a benefit financially, socially, and culturally, as many studies suggest they are, the immigrant backlash would recede, and state policy would more closely align with minority interests. If Whites did not view African-American gains as a threat to their own interests, the racial divide in the vote would almost certainly decline, and more minorities would end up on the winning side of democracy. If Whites believed that policies that benefit minority populations also benefit the most vulnerable White populations, they might change their stance on many political issues. Of course, nothing presented here tells us how to change White attitudes. If there is one area in which political scientists need to do more work, it is in terms of persuasion and education.[13] How do we convince the declining White majority that America's diverse population is not a threat to them? How do we teach White America to embrace rather than fear diversity? How do we provide people of every color with the analytical tools to distinguish fact from inflammatory political rhetoric?

Understanding the Future

Many believe that a solution to America's uneven democracy is already on the horizon. That solution is demographic change. A rapidly expanding racial and ethnic minority population will ultimately win out over a declining White population. That scenario will also eventually bring about the demise of the Republican Party. Pundits and prognosticators and maybe even most social scientists tend to support this view.

There is much to this argument. The demographic projections are clear. White Americans will lose their majority status, and they will lose it relatively quickly. As Figure 9.1 illustrates, the US Census predicts that the White share of the population will continue to decline to the point where non-Hispanic Whites will themselves become a minority sometime around the midpoint of this century.

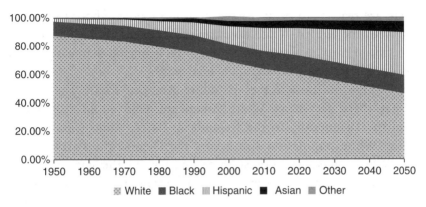

Figure 9.1. America's Changing Racial Demographics
Source: US Census Bureau

These numbers are powerful. They indicate that White power is likely to diminish over time. Moreover, this trend is already happening in the nation's most diverse states. As this book makes clear, states with the largest Latino populations tend to spend more on education, health, and welfare, which could benefit Latinos; and less on criminal justice, which could target Latinos. Once the Latino population of a state passes a population threshold, policy typically begins to swing to this more inclusive and liberal Democratic agenda. California provides perhaps the best example. California led the early backlash against immigrants with the passage of Proposition 187, the "Save Our State" measure that was designed to prevent undocumented immigrants from accessing public services. But years later, shortly after California became a majority-minority state, it instituted a set of more inclusive policies designed to help assimilate and aid immigrants. With the backing of the Democratic Party, those efforts included substantial new funding for education and health care – spending that would greatly and positively impact the disadvantaged minority community. If the Golden State is any guide, the future is clear. America will become a much more liberal and a much more Democratic nation. I agree that all of this is a very real possibility.

The Short-Term Future

But I also believe that the nation's future is far from set in stone. Demography is not the only factor that drives the nation's destiny.

There are reasons to be at least a little bit skeptical about the inevitability of the end of White dominance as well as the decline of the Republican Party. At least in the short term, I contend that many forces could counteract this demographic tidal wave.

One of those forces is White America itself. The reality is that there are many White Americans who could still defect from the Democratic to the Republican Party. Almost 40 percent of the White population still favors the Democratic Party. Given that Whites make up almost three-quarters of the national vote, White Democrats represent a lot of potential new Republican supporters.

Moreover, there are reasons to expect more White defections to the Republican Party. Even after all of the White flight of the past few decades, some Whites with nativist views or concerns about racial change remain in the Democratic Party. The majority of White Democrats today express relatively sympathetic views toward immigrants, but many others within the party are anxious about the changes the country is experiencing. Fully 41 percent of White Democrats agree that "to be truly American it is important to have been born in the United States."[14] Some 40 percent feel that current border security is inadequate, and most (68 percent) would like to see fewer than 1 million legal immigrants admitted to the country each year (Harvard-Harris Poll 2018). Even after President Trump repealed the Deferred Action for Child Arrivals (DACA) program, eliminated Temporary Protected Status for tens of thousands of Central Americans, put limits on the number of refugees entering the country, increased the number and scope of deportations, and started building a massive wall along the entire Southern border with Mexico, fully 21 percent of Democratic identifiers indicated that they approved of the job Trump was doing on immigration (Harvard-Harris Poll 2018). In short, a large share of Democrats remains skeptical about immigration. The poll numbers on race are not all that different. Most White Democrats express compassionate views toward racial minorities. But a large share of White Democrats are ambivalent about race. Most White Democrats (58 percent) believe that there is at least "a little" discrimination against Whites in America (ANES 2016).[15] One-third thinks that Blacks should work their way up without "special favors" (ANES 2016). Overall, about one-third of White Democrats scored as racially resentful on the most recent version of the American National Election Survey. Republican leaders might hope to use immigration and race to attract some of these White voters.

There is also reason to expect these White attitudes on immigration and race to harden in the future. As the non-White population continues to grow, and as Whites slowly lose their majority status, the threat that Whites perceive from the non-White population may grow as well. As a result, Republican messages may be increasingly attractive. Indeed, a long line of research demonstrates this racial threat dynamic (Blalock 1967, Key 1949). Researchers have shown that as the size of the Black population increases, Whites become more negative toward Blacks, increase their support for racist candidates, move toward more conservative views on a range of implicitly racial policies like welfare, and increasingly identify as Republican (Giles and Hertz 1994, Glaser 1996, Hero and Preuhs 2007, Huckfeldt and Kohfeld 1989, Soss et al. 2006, Taylor 1998). Other studies have demonstrated links between Latino or immigrant context and animosity toward immigrants, efforts to decrease taxes and public services, and support for more restrictive immigration policies (Campbell et al. 2006, Citrin et al. 1997, Ha and Oliver 2010, Hood and Morris 1998, Hopkins 2010, Newman 2013).[16] One especially important experiment found that simply informing Whites that America was about to become a majority-minority nation led White Americans to express greater political conservatism and lean more toward the Republican Party (Craig and Richeson 2014). The policy backlash against Latinos in this book echoes these findings on racial threat. If immigration and diversity have led to a White backlash in states in the past, they could lead to a greater backlash and greater affinity with the Republican Party in the future.

Even if White Americans do not shift their views on race and immigration or their partisanship identities, a range of institutional barriers are likely to help Whites dominate well into the future. Partisan gerrymandering in many states ensures that Republicans hold more seats than their popular support warrants (McGann et al. 2017). The fact that racial and ethnic minorities are disproportionately concentrated in the largest states means that Whites hold disproportionate sway over the Senate (Malhotra and Raso 2007). The proliferation of strict voter identification laws and other barriers to participation have further enhanced the advantage that White voters have (Hajnal et al. 2017). More broadly, the advantages of higher socioeconomic status mean that White Americans participate in the electoral arena and contribute financially at higher rates than racial minorities (Leighley and Nagler 2013). Taken together, this means that a shift in the balance of electoral power may take much longer than a shift in racial demographics implies.

A Republican Choice

The Republican Party is a key actor on this particular political stage. Republican leaders face a choice with major future implications. They can continue to use immigration and race to appeal to the White majority, or they can moderate their tactics on immigration and race to try to appeal to a more diverse audience. How they deal with that choice is likely to determine whether the nation continues down a path of increasingly racialized politics, or shifts to an alternate path that leads to less racial polarization and more inclusive policymaking.

Republican leaders are, of course, not ignorant of the demographic tsunami ahead. Officials within the party have already begun some serious soul-searching about race and the long-term future of their party. As early as 2008, elites within the party called for a more moderate Republican Party and an end to racial scapegoating. Four years later the Republican National Committee issued a report entitled the "Growth and Opportunity Project," which recommended greater investments in and outreach to the minority community. These leaders recognized that the future – especially in presidential elections – was likely to be in the hands of racial and ethnic minority voters. A number of Republican senators – most notably Marco Rubio – have signaled a desire to move to the center on immigration. More moderate voices in the party have begun to push for comprehensive immigration reform, and they say they are now willing to support some form of amnesty (Preston 2012).

But the racially conservative wing of the party remains adamantly opposed to these moves. Many current incumbents in the Republican Party owe their own success to the existing campaign strategy. If they move to the middle on race and immigration, they are likely to face primary challenges on the right. And, in relatively safe districts and states, they have little chance of losing to Democrats on the left. These incumbents are largely beholden to a race-baiting strategy. Convincing them to shift away from it will be hard.

Moreover, it is important to remember how successful this strategy has been for the Republican Party. Republicans may have lost most of the minority vote as a result of this strategy, but they have garnered most of the White vote. Over the last half-century White America has gone from largely favoring the Democratic Party to largely supporting the Republican Party. With the help of White voters, Republicans now reside in most of the governor's mansions (27 states); they control far more state legislatures than do the Democrats (30 versus 19); they are the majority in the Senate; and they currently hold the presidency. Trump's success with an explicit anti-immigrant campaign has only reinforced the view that scapegoating immigrants and race-baiting work. For the time being, many incumbent Republicans and perhaps the party as a whole stand to gain from a White backlash.

Thus, over the short term, I believe the Republican Party is likely to send a somewhat mixed and incoherent signal on race and immigration. Forward-thinking elites intent on winning the presidency and securing the party's future will attempt to move the party away from the anti-minority, anti-immigrant strategy and toward a more inclusive agenda. But other leaders, recognizing the immediate power of that divisive strategy, will likely hold on to it.

The Long-Term Future

But what happens when Whites eventually become a relatively small minority, vastly outnumbered by a diverse array of racial and ethnic minorities? If the current strategy begins to fail, can Republicans radically alter course and resurrect their fortunes?

Many believe that the die is already cast and that it is too late for Republicans to have any hope with the minority vote. As one *Slate* magazine article put it: "Republicans crossed a point of no return. Raw ethnonationalism is their future, even if they don't want it" (Bouie 2016).

But that conclusion misses a fundamental attribute of the immigrant population – its ambivalence about *both* major parties. Despite the growing attachment of Latinos and Asian Americans to the Democratic Party, Democrats have a relatively tenuous hold on this population. Analysis of national survey data indicates that the majorities of both the Asian-American and Latino populations claim to be non-partisan (Hajnal and Lee 2011). When Latinos and Asian Americans vote, they overwhelmingly favor Democrats, but most Latinos and Asian

Americans do not vote. These non-voters could vote in the future. They are overwhelmingly non-partisan. They might represent a fruitful target for the Republican Party. In short, when one looks more broadly at the entire immigrant population, Democratic ties do not run so deep.

Surveys also suggest that if Republicans change tactics on immigration, they could make major inroads with the Latino and Asian-American populations. A 2013 Latino Decisions poll asked Latino respondents "if they would be more or less likely to vote for a Republican candidate in the future if the Republicans take a leadership role in passing comprehensive immigration reform including a pathway to citizenship": 43 percent of Latinos who had previously supported Obama said that they would be more likely to vote for the Republican candidate.[17] Another Latino Decisions poll revealed that half of all Latino registered voters have cast a vote for a Republican in the past (Vavreck 2014). In the words of the *New York Times*, "Latino voters are not dead set against Republicans" (Vavreck 2014). Experimental studies also show that emphasizing or de-emphasizing racial discrimination can induce large shifts in Asian-American partisanship (Kuo et al. 2017). This picture suggests that both pan-ethnic groups are still up for grabs politically.

African Americans represent a far tougher case for the Republican Party (Dawson 1994). Yet even among African Americans, signs of ambivalence toward the Democratic Party are palpable. Many African-American commentators have expressed frustration with the Obama administration and the party's lack of action on reducing racial inequality. In surveys, almost 30 percent of Blacks feel that the Democratic Party does not "work hard for Black interests."[18] Put simply, many racial and ethnic minorities are not particularly enthralled with the Democratic Party.

History also suggests that racial and ethnic minorities have not been blindly loyal to one party. Their allegiances tend to shift when partisan programs shift. As Dawson (1994) has aptly demonstrated, African Americans have generally supported the party that presents the most racially liberal policy agenda, and they have shifted in large numbers when the two parties have reversed their positions on race. More recently, in 2004 Latinos gave a historic 40 percent of their votes to George W. Bush when he advocated comprehensive immigration reform. When it comes to politics, memories can be short. Transgressions of the past can be forgotten and promises for the future can be effective. If the Republican Party does choose to embrace a more pro-immigrant, pro-minority stance, that strategy could be successful.

Critically, the Republican Party may be able to attract minority support without realizing overwhelming losses among White Americans. White Republicans are far from universally fearful of immigration or completely antagonistic on race.[19] Many within the Republican Party express relatively positive feelings about immigrants, and they are sympathetic to African Americans. Almost half of Republicans – 42 percent – do not think that immigrants hurt American culture. Fully 70 percent would allow Dreamers (the undocumented immigrants brought to the United States as children) to stay in the country. On race, 95 percent of Republicans admit that there is at least a little discrimination against Blacks. Roughly one in five scores relatively low on a racial resentment scale. This heterogeneity means that the Republican Party may be able to retain support from White Americans even if it shifts to a more minority- or immigrant-friendly agenda.

Other wildcards might help to shape the long-term future. The end of large-scale Hispanic migration to the United States could erode the effectiveness of the immigrant-threat narrative and reduce anxiety about racial change. Less immigration also implies greater assimilation. Latinos could become less culturally and economically distinct, and they could eventually be viewed as White. Such changes could erode White angst, greatly increase the size of the White population, and alter the balance of the nation's racial demographics. The growth of multiracial identities could also impact America's racial politics in the future. Already 17 percent of all new marriages are interracial (Livingston and Brown 2017). If racial lines continue to blur, racial divisions might follow suit. In addition, increasing conflict with the Muslim world, and attention to Muslim Americans, could distract America from traditional racial fault lines, and reshape its politics. Attitudes on Muslims were already one of the most important predictors of a Trump vote in 2016 (Klinkner 2016, Lajevardi and Abrajano 2019, Tesler 2016b). Media attention to Muslims is very much on the rise (Lajevardi 2017). If Muslims become the main target of White America's ire, America's racial divisions might change. The longer one looks into the future, the greater the uncertainty.

A Democratic Choice

It is also important to highlight the fact that the Democratic Party has a choice as well. Moving forward, the Democratic Party can choose to actively embrace the White working-class vote. Many strategists are advocating for this strategic change. This class-based strategy calls for a de-emphasis on race, and a shift to more moderate policies on immigration and race. If successful, the strategy could bring back the roughly 5 percent of voters who defected from Obama to Trump. The news website, Vox, in putting forward headlines such as "The Math is Clear: Democrats Need to Win More Working-Class White Votes," is not alone in highlighting the need for this strategy.

Alternatively, the Democratic Party can opt to embrace racial diversity more fully. This second strategy would entail more vocal support for racial and ethnic minority causes. To date, many Democratic leaders have been reluctant to fully articulate a pro-minority agenda for fear of driving more Whites to the Republican Party. As the number of minorities grows, and the share of Whites declines, that calculation could shift. This strategy could also incorporate a large effort to mobilize minorities, who have traditionally participated in elections at much lower rates than Whites. This is a consequential choice for the Democratic Party.

Two Futures

I do not profess to know what the future holds, or even which pathways the Democratic and Republican parties will choose. What I do know is that the nation stands at a crossroads. America faces two radically different futures. In one scenario, the worrisome racial divide between an almost exclusively White Republican Party and a disproportionately non-White Democratic Party shrinks, the racial imbalance in American democracy declines, and wide-ranging racial conflict is averted. In that scenario, Beau and Malik, the representative White and Black voters I introduced at the beginning of this book, begin to find some common ground. They cease to view each other as enemies or threats. They see that policies that benefit one might benefit the other. They see potential for compromise, rather than staking out and adhering to positions at the extremes. They start to work together to repair a broken democracy.

But in a more ominous scenario, an increasingly anxious and aggrieved White population fights against a rising tide of minority voters, who in turn flock in ever larger numbers to the Democratic Party. The racial divide in American party politics expands to an ever deeper racial chasm. American democracy tilts even more in favor of White America. In that second, more troubling scenario, Beau and Malik grow ever more distant in their politics. Malik becomes ever more resentful of his diminished status in American democracy. He wonders whether voter participation is a farce, and he thinks about other, more effective ways to express his anger. Beau also grows angry. He becomes ever more fearful of losing his privileged status. He, too, may feel more likely to resort to extra-democratic means of expression. Ironically, as the two become more entrenched at the polar extremes of the American political system, they also may find common ground. Both are likely to feel under threat, a growing sense of anger, and an urge to fight in some way for a place in an American society and political system that seems to thwart their beliefs and positions.

Hanging in the balance is the fate both of American democracy and America's racial and ethnic minority populations. The different pathways will determine whether the Democratic Party rises or the Republican Party continues to govern. The different pathways will also determine whether racial and ethnic minorities remain largely on the outside looking in when it comes to power and representation in American democracy. And, finally, the choices that Republican and Democratic leaders make will determine whether the racial gap in well-being remains real and robust, or whether the long arc of American history really will lead to full equality.

NOTES

Introduction

1. For more information on the rare cases in American democracy that do not employ majoritarian voting, see www.fairvote.org/jurisdictions_using_fair_rep#full_list_of_fair_voting_jurisdictions.
2. It is also quite conceivable that the Republican Party will shift direction as the nation's electorate becomes more and more racially diverse.
3. This class inequality narrative is not, however, without its detractors. Comparative studies find that class divisions in American politics are less pronounced than they are elsewhere (Giedo et al. 2013, Powell 1986). Longitudinal studies using objective indicators of class and the vote show no measurable increase in class voting and, if anything, find declining ties between class and the vote (Evans 1999, Giedo et al. 2013). Some even suggest that a new post-materialist culture is emerging (Inglehart 1990). Others argue that the notion that American democracy tilts toward the well-off is overstated – in large part because the upper and lower classes generally agree on policy (Brunner et al. 2013, Soroka and Wlezien 2008, Ura and Ellis 2008).
4. By mobilizing and advocating for change, racial and ethnic minorities also played a critical role (Lee 2002). Those efforts were sometimes successful but also bred resentment on the part of many Whites. Bids for things like busing and affirmative action were often viewed as overly demanding (Kinder and Sanders 1996).
5. Descriptive representation is a standard measure of minority representation, and, as a result, numerous studies examine descriptive representation by race (Brown-Dean et al. 2015), class (Carnes 2013, 2015), gender (Center for American Women in Politics 2015), and religion (Pew 2013).
6. There have been prolonged periods in American history during which the primary target of White ire was not Black America, as exemplified by: Indian removal in the early nineteenth century, the maltreatment of Mexican landholders in the mid-nineteenth century, the widespread abuse of Chinese immigrants at the end of the nineteenth century, and the internment of more than 100,000 Japanese Americans during the World War II era.
7. As the Pete Wilson ad showed footage of Mexican migrants racing across the border, a narrator intoned, "They keep coming" (Hemmer 2017). The anti-immigrant

playbook has changed little over the years. In his failed bid to be elected to the US Senate from New Hampshire, Republican candidate Scott Brown ran an ad with an almost identical video of a horde of people rushing the border fence (Haberman 2014). And Donald Trump's contention that a crisis exists on the nation's southern border fits well into the same narrative.

8. Griffin and Newman (2008) come closest by looking at the responsiveness of individual legislators. They find that Democratic Congress members are more responsive to Latino opinion.

What Divides Us? Race, Class, and Political Choice

1. President-elect Trump actually held two Bibles – the second was given to him as a child by his mother.
2. Data reported from the National Exit Poll.
3. Clinton also lost ground relative to Obama in forty-seven of the fifty counties with the lowest rate of completed bachelor's degrees. She gained in most of the best-educated counties (Silver 2016).
4. Bill Maher, as quoted in Tesler 2016c.
5. Data for 2016 are primarily from the National Election Pool exit poll (NEP) but analysis of the 2016 Cooperative Congressional Election Study (CCES) leads to similar conclusions about electoral divides. The NEP provides the best early estimate of the preferences of voters from different demographic groups. There are, however, concerns with the methodology used by national media organizations to conduct the exit poll and in particular some criticisms of the nature of the sample of racial and ethnic minorities (Latino Decisions 2016). Therefore, for the Latino vote estimate I use the Latino Decisions Election Eve Poll. The Asian American vote estimate is from the Asian Decisions Election Eve Poll. These two election eve polls interview in multiple languages and offer much larger and more representative samples of the two racial and ethnic minority groups.
6. The 75 percent figure from Asian American Decisions differs significantly from the 65 percent figure reported by the National Election Poll exit poll but matches closely with the 79 percent figure from the much larger Asian American sample in a fourteen-state exit poll conducted by the Asian American Legal Defense and Education Fund. Lee (2016) has convincingly shown that the Asian American Decision poll figure is a better estimate of the Asian American vote.
7. The National Election Pool exit poll conducted by Edison Research found that 65 percent of Latino voters favored Clinton but as Latino Decisions (2016) details, there are serious concerns with the Latino sample in that exit poll.
8. In line with media reports, the exit polls did reveal that White working-class Americans were disproportionately likely to favor Trump. But, as we will see, much of that pattern is driven by race rather than class.
9. The education gap does grow slightly toward the educational extremes. Some 58 percent of Americans with postgraduate degrees voted for Clinton.
10. To do this analysis and to combine these categories, I used data from the 2016 CCES.
11. Importantly, both the National Exit Poll and the 2016 CCES show that the pattern of the vote by race, class, religion, and other demographic factors in the vote for the House, the Senate, and Governor's race in 2016 was strikingly similar to the presidential contest. Race was just as consequential in these other contests. The Trump-Clinton matchup was not all that unusual by these metrics.
12. The figure for Asian Americans is from an Asian American Decisions poll. The National Exit Poll sampled a small and unrepresentative segment of the Asian

American population. Lee (2016) has convincingly shown that the Asian American Decision poll figure is a better estimate of the Asian American vote.

13. Preliminary analysis of the 2018 exit polls suggests a strikingly similar pattern. Some 44 percent of Whites voted Democratic compared to 90 percent of Blacks, 77 percent of Asian Americans, and 69 percent of Latinos (CNN 2018).

14. Those in the educational middle, by contrast, were slightly more likely to favor Republicans than they were to side with Democrats, but the gap was small – 45 percent Democratic vs. 54 percent Republican.

15. Race also dominated class in congressional elections in 2018, although preliminary data show a slight increase in 2018 in education-based voting. The racial divides were equally large: 56 percent (between Black and White voters), 30 percent (Asian American vs. White), and 25 percent (Latino vs. White). Income divided Americans at the same level (a 16-point gap between those earning less than $30,000 and those earning more than $200,000). Gaps by education grew significantly (a 17-point gap between those without a high school degree and those with a postgraduate education) (CNN 2018).

16. The data on party identification are from the 2006–14 Cooperative Congressional Election Study. The pattern of results is similar if I instead use the American National Election Study or other recent, major surveys.

17. Party identification figures include partisan leaners as partisans since research shows that these leaners regularly vote with their partisan leaning (Keith et al. 1992). Dropping leaners does little to alter the basic pattern of divides.

18. I was not able to include a measure of urban or rural voters in the 2012 analysis, but various measures of urban-rural location are available in many of the surveys I examine. When I incorporate a measure that distinguishes between urban, sub-urban, and rural Americans, I generally find that the urban-rural divide has grown significantly in recent years (up to about a 27-point gap in the 2016 presidential contest). But I also find that most of this gap is explained by other demographic factors. Once I control for education, income, religion, and the like, I often find no significant gap between urban and rural voters.

19. Once again I use data from the 2006–14 CCES, but the results do not markedly diverge if the focus is on the ANES in 2016 or earlier years, or on other major surveys.

20. A similar analysis that instead looks at a 7-point scale of where Americans fall across the entire party identification spectrum from strongly Democrat to strongly Republican leads to an almost identical pattern of results.

21. The conclusion is the same regardless of how party identification and ideology (as standard 7- or 3-point scales, or as a series of dummy variables) are measured. Race mattered a lot after taking into account partisan ties and ideological positions.

22. The data set includes not only mayoral vote choice (23 elections) but also candidate choices in city council (26 contests), city comptroller (2), city attorney (2), city clerk (1), and public advocate elections (2) and preferences on ballot propositions (6).

23. Given concerns about the small number of cities and the generalizability of this data set, I sought to evaluate the role of race in a larger and more diverse set of elections. Specifically, using a variety of methods including exit polls, public opinion surveys, precinct analysis, and ecological inference, I was able to get the vote by race for 254 candidates in 96 mayoral primary and general elections in 25 of the largest cities between 1985 and 2014. The results from this larger set of cities and elections confirm the original findings about the local vote. Across this broader set of cities, this longer time frame, and this greater number of elections, race continues to greatly shape the urban vote. The racial divides across this larger set of elections are, if

anything, larger than the divides we see for the five cities in Figure 1.7. In the average mayoral election, the percentage of Blacks who supported the winning candidate differed by 43 points from the percentage of White voters supporting that same candidate. The Latino-White and Asian American-White divides are smaller but still substantial – 22 points and 21 points, respectively. No matter which elections we look at, race greatly shapes the urban vote.

24. Specifically, for each election in the data set, I run a single logistic regression with all of the individual voters in the exit poll as cases predicting support for the winning candidate. Then for each election, I use Clarify to calculate the marginal effect of shifting from one category (e.g. Black respondent) to the comparison category (e.g. White respondent) for each independent variable in each election. I then calculate the average predicted effect of each independent variable across the different elections in the exit poll data set. Figure 1.8 displays the mean predicted effect for each independent variable across the elections.

25. Moreover, race is consistently important across the sixty-three individual contests. Across the sixty-three different elections' specific regressions, the Black-White divide is almost always significant. In fully 80 percent of the contests, the coefficient on Black voters is significant, indicating that the Black vote differs significantly from the White vote. By contrast, income, education, and employment status were all significant predictors of the vote in less than one-third of the elections. By this measure, religion was once gain the second most important demographic factor. Religious denomination significantly predicted vote choice a little more than half of the time. At the urban level, only political party and ideology rivaled race in terms of the consistent nature of its impact. Party identification and liberal-conservative ideology significantly impacted the vote in just over 70 percent of all contests.

26. To further assess the importance of race in these contests, I conducted one other test (analysis not shown). I assessed intra-group divisions within the Black, Latino, and White electorate (the Asian-American sample was generally too small to allow for intra-group analysis). Specifically, I looked to see if there were substantially different electoral preferences across class or other demographic factors *within* each racial and ethnic group. In the majority of elections, there were no major within-group divides. Within each of the minority groups, substantial differences of opinion were rare.

27. The conclusions I reach about race and class and other demographic factors and their roles in American democracy do not depend on which data set I use to examine individual choices. I tend to focus on the best available sources (the ANES for over-time change, the CCES for analysis of a range of recent elections, and National Exit Polls for the vote in 2014), but I arrive at strikingly similar results if I instead analyze the General Social Survey (1972–2010), the National Annenberg Election Survey (2000–04), Gallup Polls (1960–2014), or surveys tailored to understand minority preferences (the 2008 National Asian American Survey, the 2006 Latino National Survey, Pew surveys of Latinos and Asian Americans, or the 1994 National Politics Study). The one key difference, as I have already noted, is that the two most recent National Exit Polls likely understated the Latino and Asian-American Democratic vote.

28. The numbers for Latinos and Asian Americans in Figure 1.9 do, however, conceal an important pattern in Latino and Asian-American partisanship – namely, the non-attachment of so many Latinos and Asian Americans to either political party. Surveys that include non-citizens indicate that half of the Latino and Asian-American populations claim no ties to either party (Hajnal and Lee 2011).

29. To cite just one example on the White side of the question, the ANES shows that White support for Republican senatorial candidates grows from an average of 47.2 percent in the 1970s, to 50.8 percent in the 1980s, 51.9 percent in the 1990s, and 53.7 percent in the 2000s.

30. Although Figure 1.11 does not reveal it, two important and likely related changes occurred over the period of time covered by the figure. On the income side, the party preferences of the very rich evolved from slightly Republican to slightly Democratic, while the less well off shifted from sharply Democratic to more mixed partisan preferences. At the same time, the effect of education on the vote and on partisanship shifted in the opposite direction with the best educated increasingly moving to the Democratic Party (Drutman 2016, Piketty 2018).

31. Similarly, it is important to recognize that there has been a substantial shift in the rural vote toward the Republican Party in recent elections (Cramer 2016, Kurtzleben 2016). But that does not mean the urban-rural divide is a major factor driving American politics. In fact, as I noted briefly earlier in this chapter, once I control for class, age, and other demographic factors, I typically find that urban vs. rural status has few significant effects on the vote.

32. Barack Obama has mixed racial heritage but generally identifies as Black and was viewed almost universally as the nation's first Black president.

33. In the conventional version of the story, the role played by elite leaders in the party was critical. A more nuanced account suggests that White voters were repelled not just by the actions of Democratic Party leaders but also by the actions of African Americans themselves (Hood et al. 2012, Lee 2002). As more and more Blacks joined the Democratic Party and as more and more Blacks mobilized for ever greater rights, Whites felt that their central position in the party and in the nation was threatened (Huckfeldt and Kohfeld 1989).

34. Carmines and Stimson (1989) present the best evidence of the increasingly polarized racial positions of Democratic and Republican elites and party activists.

35. An array of other types of studies point to race as the main motivation driving White defections from the Democratic Party. Some find that White defections to the Republican Party were more pronounced in areas with larger African-American populations (Huckfeldt and Kohfeld 1989). Others have shown White Americans switched to the Republican Party in large numbers when Blacks mobilized in large numbers (Hood et al. 2012). As Hood, Kidd and Morris note, "It is the concomitance of Black mobilization and Republican growth that is so striking" (Hood et al. 2012:8).

36. Unfortunately, coming up with a direct and decisive test of what exactly has driven shifts in partisanship and electoral choice over the last half-century has proven to be difficult. Part of the problem is complexity. Different segments of the electorate almost certainly have different motivations and different ways of reaching conclusions about the political world. Even the same person can have different motivations at different times or even contrasting considerations in the same political instant. The other problem is methodological. The methodological tools at our disposal are imperfect and often unable to effectively and definitively distinguish the effect of one motivation from another. Once we cross the threshold from dealing in demographic characteristics to focusing on attitudes and perceptions, firm statements about what is driving what are harder to make.

37. There are, of course, other issues such as terrorism, war, trade, and the deficit that could conceivably be linked to the racial divide. Also, a number of non-issue-based sources of partisan attachments including childhood socialization (Campbell et al. 1960, Niemi and Jennings 1991), values or predispositions (Jacoby 2014),

retrospective evaluations (Fiorina 1981, MacKuen et al. 1989), and candidate characteristics (McCurley and Mondak 1995) could feasibly contribute to the racial divide. It is, however, difficult in each of these cases to come up with a theory that could account for the massive, growing racial divide we are witnessing in American politics today.

38. There are also obviously concerns about conflict. It seems unlikely that Americans can be so divided politically without also feeling some sort of racial antipathy.

Who Wins Office?

1. On the relative benefits of proportional representation for minorities see for example Lijphart (1997) and Taagepara and Shugart (1989).

2. E.g. Bowler et al. 2003, Bullock and Dunn 1999, Davidson and Grofman 1994, Menifield 2001.

3. For evidence on the effectiveness of descriptive representation see Griffin and Newman (2007), Grose (2011), Juenke and Preuhs (2011), and Kerr and Miller (1997). At the same time, the evidence suggests that most of the change is relatively modest (Hero and Tolbert 1995, Swain 1995).

4. For excellent summaries of the different dimensions of representation, see Mansbridge (1999) and Phillips (1998).

5. At the same time it should be noted that no similar change in White attitudes occurred under Barack Obama (Tesler 2016a).

6. I will elaborate on the limits of descriptive representation in subsequent chapters.

7. The one historical exception is that African Americans were well represented in office in the period immediately after the Civil War. In 1872 there were 324 Blacks elected to state legislatures and Congress in the former Confederate states. But Whites – especially Southern Whites – mobilized in large numbers and used an array of violent and non-violent tactics to intimidate Black voters and reduce the number of Black elected officials. White Southerners instituted a program of unprecedented violence, poll taxes, new residency and registration requirements, and at-large elections to great effect (Davidson and Grofman 1994, Foner 1984, Holt 1979, Parker 1990). In Louisiana, for example, in less than one year, Democrats killed more than 1,000 people in their effort to regain control of the political process (Kousser 1974). Over a thirty-year time span White Southerners wiped out virtually all of the gains made by Black voters. By 1900, only five of the 324 Black elected officials in the South were still in power (Kousser 1992).

8. That includes three Black senators (Kamala Harris, Cory Booker, and Tim Scott) and forty-four Black House members.

9. Admittedly much of that fear and mobilization has subsided as the number of African Americans in office has grown and Americans have become more familiar with Black elected officials but that does little to minimize the meaning of these early victories.

10. Quoted in Hajnal 2006.

11. Quoted in Rivlin 1992:155.

12. Quoted in Eisinger 1980:15.

13. Quoted in Keiser (1997:305). This phenomenon is of course not confined to Black mayoral candidates. When Harvey Gantt ran for the Senate in 1990, Jesse Helms countered with an ad depicting a White worker losing a job to a less-qualified Black man. Analysts felt that the ad was the turning point of the campaign. "The ad scared some Whites, convincing them that Gantt was a threat to their future and . . . propelled Helms to victory" (Frisby 1991:14). Years earlier, George Wallace, as

a gubernatorial candidate, was much more direct: "If I don't win, them niggers are going to control this state" (quoted in Black and Black, 1973:736).

14. Black mayoral challengers who won office in their cities for the first time in the 1960s and 1970s confronted turnout that averaged over 70 percent – unheard of for local elections that typically average 20–30 percent turnout – and a united White vote: More than 80 percent of White voters opposed them on average (Hajnal 2006).

15. Quoted in Donze, 1998:A14.

16. Data on minority representation comes from the following sources: Figures on Black representation are generally from the Joint Center for Political and Economic Studies (JCPES 1974–2001). Latino representation is derived largely from the National Association of Latino Elected Officials (NALEO 1984–2018). Numbers on Asian-American representation are produced by the University of California Los Angeles Asian American Studies Center (APALC 1978–2014). Data on city council positions are from a 2011 survey of city clerks conducted by the International City/County Management Association (ICMA 2011). For data on Blacks before 1970 and data on Latinos prior to 1984, see Garza et al. (1986). Data on the total number of elected officials by office across the nation come from the Census of Governments.

17. Here I measure each racial group's share of the national population. I do this because one might want all residents – regardless of citizenship or age – to be represented. If I instead focus on the share of voting-age citizens in each group, the overall conclusion is exactly the same. Racial and ethnic minorities are greatly under-represented at every level.

18. We have much less data on Native American representation in office but the little data we do have suggest that this group is equally under-represented in office. In 2015 there were only two Native American members of Congress (Tom Cole, a Republican House Member who is Chickasaw, and Markwayne Mullin, a Republican House Member who is Cherokee) and in 2012 only fifty-nine Native Americans state legislators (Bowler and Segura 2011).

19. The under-representation of Blacks, Latinos, and Asian Americans appears to be just as pronounced or even more pronounced for other local positions. The most recent figures at the mayoral level suggest that of all the nation's mayors, only about 2 percent are Black, less than 1 percent are Latino, and a tiny fraction are Asian American (APALC 1978–2014, JCPES 1974–2011, MacManus and Bullock 1993, NALEO 1984–2018). Combining all local offices together, the best estimate is that African Americans only hold 2.9 percent of all local offices, while Latinos and Asian Americans are even worse off, holding 1.2 percent and 0.2 percent of all offices respectively.

20. For decades, there was a significant and systematic difference between what White Americans said in pre-election polls and their behavior in the voting booth when a Black candidate was running for office. Whites were apparently reluctant to admit that they were not voting for a Black candidate. This so-called Bradley effect – named because Tom Bradley, an African-American gubernatorial candidate in California, won the election-day polling by a significant margin, but lost the actual vote – was substantial before 1990 but has faded over time (Hopkins 2009)

21. Gallup 2015: survey from June 2015. An equally high share – 91 percent – indicated they would vote for a Hispanic candidate.

22. The only individual trait for which Whites rated Black candidates higher than the White candidate on average was in terms of being religious (Williams 1990).

23. Studies can examine how racial prejudice predicts vote choice in real-world elections. Several studies have done this. There is little doubt that Whites' racial attitudes greatly shape the vote in bi-racial contests. Every study that looked at the Obama

vote, for example, found the more prejudiced White Americans were significantly less likely to vote for Obama (Kinder and Dale-Riddle 2011, Kinder and Kam 2012, Lewis-Beck et al. 2010, Tesler and Sears 2010). But it is not clear if this is all due to the race of the candidate. Racial attitudes are correlated with vote choice in most White-vs.-White elections, and it is not clear how much more prejudice mattered in the Obama case than it typically does in White-vs.-White elections (Citrin et al. 1990).

24. See Colleau et al. (1990), McConnaughy et al. (2010), Reeves (1997), Sigelman et al. (1995), Terkildsen (1993), Visalvanich (2017), Weaver (2012).

25. Highton (2004) is the most comprehensive and compelling study, but Bullock and Dunn (1999) find roughly similar patterns. On the other hand, one important, new study found a significant bias against Black candidates and a smaller bias against Latino candidates (Visalvanich 2017).

26. There were also two weaker White candidates who each garnered about 10 percent of the vote.

27. Not surprisingly, these same minority candidates received strong support from members of their own group. On average 71 percent of Black voters, 56 percent of Latino voters, and 52 percent of Asian-American voters favored the candidate from their own race in these contests.

28. I can also examine the presidential vote. In both of Barack Obama's elections a clear majority of White voters opposed his candidacy (57 percent in 2008 and 61 percent in 2012). Likewise, 60 percent of Whites opposed him in the 2008 Democratic Primary. Decades before Barack Obama's bid, the vast majority of White primary voters opposed Jesse Jackson's presidential bid. The 2016 presidential bids of Marco Rubio and Ted Cruz tell a similar story.

29. No Asian-American mayors won office in the data set. But almost all of the break-through big-city Asian-American mayors (e.g. Edwin Lee in San Francisco and Jean Quan in Oakland) won office in majority-minority cities.

30. The data I have on city councils indicate that there is an extremely strong negative correlation between the share of Whites in the population and minority representa-tion, suggesting that minorities tend to win city council positions largely when the White population is small, and thus when minority candidates can rely on the minority vote to win office.

31. The figures are calculated from the International City-County Managers Association Form of Governments Surveys (1986–2011). Data from more recent elections in California reveal that blue-collar workers won well under 5 percent of all positions at the school-district, city, and county levels (Carnes 2015).

Which Voters Win Elections?

1. This chapter is derived from the article "Who Loses in American Democracy: A Count of Votes Demonstrates the Limited Representation of African Americans," in *Perspectives on Politics*. I wrote the article with co-author Jeremy Horowitz, who was an essential partner in that project.

2. By discounting representation from leaders from the majority group, we also dis-count the influence that minority voters can have on majority leaders. Yet, the evidence suggests that minority voters can influence the policy positions of leaders who are from the majority group. In the case of race and ethnicity, a range of scholars have demonstrated a positive relationship between the size of the Black community and the degree to which elected leaders support minority interests (Cameron, Epstein, and Halloran 1996; Lublin 1997). Discounting minority

influence in majority-White districts is especially problematic in the American case, where the vast majority of racial and ethnic minorities live within districts or political boundaries in which Whites are the dominant majority and few minority candidates ever run for office, and where representation is almost always White. Over 70 percent of all Blacks, for example, live in state and federal districts that are majority-White, and across the nation only about 1 percent of all of these majority-White districts have ever elected a Black candidate to office (Handley and Grofman 1994, Lublin 1997). If these racial and ethnic minorities do influence their White leaders, studies of descriptive representation may be missing most of the influence that minority voters have in America.

3. To highlight just one extreme example of the flaws of this view; by this standard, President Lyndon Johnson, who helped pass some of the nation's most significant Civil Rights legislation, would be ruled out as a champion of racial and ethnic minority representation simply because he was White.

4. Swain (1995) and Hero and Tolbert (1995) both find little difference between White and non-White Democrats representing minority districts, but others find real differences, both substantive (Casellas 2007, Minta 2011, Whitby 1998) and symbolic (Barreto 2007, Gay 2001, Hajnal 2006).

5. In some ways this measure is akin to the seats-to-vote ratio that is the frequent focus of comparative politics scholars (e.g. Benoit and Shepsle 1995). A measure of the seats-to-votes ratio can, however, only assess partisan representation, not group-level representation.

6. There are important studies of minority electoral success in particular locales or specific policy areas (Browning et al. 1984, Eisinger 1982, Kerr and Mladenka 1994, Meier and England 1984) and some broader studies of the fate of the minority vote in the South in past decades (Kousser 1999, Parker 1990).

7. A lesser concern is that those who do not vote may have different preferences from those who do vote, and thus focusing on voters alone may skew results. This is less of a problem here because the analysis looks at each demographic separately. It need only be the case that voters from a (racial) group have similar preferences to non-voters from the same (racial) group. On this point, limited data suggest that voters and non-voters from the *same* racial group typically have similar preferences (Hajnal 2010).

8. Each VNS survey contains a fairly representative sample of the nation's voters. Voters are asked about their race (White, Black, Hispanic/Latino, Asian American, or Other), whether they view themselves as Hispanic, and an array of other demographic characteristics including income, education, age, gender, religion, work status, and sexuality. The demographic characteristics of the national sample closely match national demographics. The average number of people interviewed for each poll is more than 13,000. Each poll also generally includes a large enough sample of African-American, Latino, and Asian-American voters to allow for analysis of each group. There are, on average, 1,486 African-American, 868 Latino, 214 Asian-American, and 10,290 White respondents in each poll. Another important quality of the *Voter News Service* exit polls is their accuracy. The VNS estimated Democratic vote share correlates with the actual Democratic vote share at .99 in presidential elections, .88 in gubernatorial elections, .86 in gubernatorial elections, and .63 in US House of Representatives elections.

9. Estimates of the vote by race came largely from exit polls or pre-election polls (within a week of the contest), but in some cases I also used ecological inference or homogenous precinct analysis (for more information, see Hajnal and Trounstine 2005). Since some mayoral data are aggregate rather than individual votes, for all of

these elections I calculated the percentage of each racial and ethnic group that wound up losers and averaged that number across the twenty cities to obtain the figures presented in Table 3.1. Two factors limit the generalizability of the mayoral findings. First, I was only able to obtain estimates of the vote by race for about half of all elections in these cities. Second, these twenty cities have slightly different racial demographics (fewer Whites) than the nation as a whole.

10. One study of winners and losers in direct democracy suggests that the patterns are not all that dissimilar when citizens vote directly on policy (Hajnal et al. 2002). That study found that across a wide array of recent policy initiatives in California, racial minorities were significantly more likely than Whites to end up as losers in the vote. One important difference was that in California Latinos, rather than Blacks, were the minority most likely to lose.

11. Fully 64 percent of voters in these cities chose John Kerry in 2004.

12. If I focus specifically on mayoral primaries, the same racial hierarchy emerges. Across the eight Democratic primaries for which I have data, African-American voters lose (48 percent of the time) more often than Whites (37 percent), Latinos (41 percent), and Asian Americans (38 percent). At least at the mayoral level, African Americans are failing disproportionately at all stages of the electoral process. They are, in essence, doubly disadvantaged. Admittedly, much more work needs to be done across a broader array of primary contests to offer an overarching assessment of primaries in American democracy. However, none of these limited primary results would lead one to dismiss the concerns that emerge out of the general election analysis.

13. Because the VNS collected House votes in separate state-level files, those votes cannot be added to this analysis.

14. Though available data do not allow for an examination of how often the same voter loses over time, indications are that many Black voters may be consistent losers over time, especially in the South. The worst case appears to be Alabama, where the clear majority of Black voters lose almost every year in contests for the Senate, governor, and the House. Likewise, the data in Texas show consistent losses over time for the bulk of African-American and Latino voters. An admittedly non-systematic search found no other demographic group (class, gender, age) that lost as consistently over time in any other region.

15. Likewise, being unemployed was not closely tied to losing.

16. There are, indeed, some signs of a rightward tilt in outcomes during this time period. In these presidential elections, most liberals (60 percent) and most Democrats (64 percent) end up on the losing side of the vote. The partisan or ideological skew is not, however, nearly as consistent as the racial skew. In the other three types of elections for which data are available, most Democrats and liberals end up winners. Moreover, in these senatorial, gubernatorial, and House elections, those on the left and those on the right win at about the same rate.

17. The appendix contains the regression model underlying the figure. The regression models do not include variables for sexual orientation, urbanicity, or education because the VNS did not ask about sexual orientation or urbanicity in every year of the survey, and because it asked about education for only half of the respondents. The same is true for religion in the congressional analysis. For this analysis, I pool the responses of every respondent for all elections of the same type (e.g. all Senate contests in all VNS years).

18. Predicted effects for gender, religion, and age are generally much smaller.

19. To some extent the presidential results are skewed by the fact that they include two Republican victories and only one Democratic victory. However, if I include one

more Democratic victory (using the recalled 1992 presidential votes of respondents from the 1994 VNS survey), the results are the same. African Americans are still significantly more likely than Whites to support the losing candidate in presidential contests.

20. Additional analysis reveals that the urban-rural divide also has no consistent effect on winning and losing once I control for other demographic factors. In some types of elections (presidential and gubernatorial contests), rural voters were marginally more successful, in others (Senate contests), rural voters were not significantly different from urban voters, and in others (House contests), rural voters were slightly less successful than urban voters.

21. Importantly, the success of Black voters in House elections does not only point to success in majority-Black districts: Since around 70 percent of Black voters in House elections live in majority-White districts, the present results imply that even in predominantly White districts outcomes regularly favor Black voters. One likely explanation is that Black voters are being grouped with liberal or Democratic White voters who help elect minority-favored candidates.

22. It is also worth noting a potential downside to pro-minority gerrymandering. By packing racial ethnic minorities together and creating a majority-minority district that leads to minority success within the district, one may reduce minority influence outside the district (Cameron et al. 1996).

23. There is only one "context" in the presidential elections (the nation). So it is less informative to look at geographic variation in the case of the presidency. Since the vast majority of Black voters (71 percent) win in congressional elections, there is less to explain here as well. Given the aggregate nature of the mayoral data, I cannot look at how context affects individual success for the mayoralty.

24. Since African Americans stand out as consistent losers, I focus on understanding variation in Black outcomes. However, the same analysis could be done for any other demographic or political group.

25. In terms of felon disenfranchisement, states are coded as barring: (1) any current prisoner from voting, (2) any current prisoner or parolee barred, or (3) anyone who has ever been convicted a felon (Manza 2006). State data sources are: ideology and partisanship (Wright 2014) and felony laws (Sentencing Project 2019).

26. All predicted probabilities shift the variables of interest from the 10th to the 90th percentile.

27. Time also matters. Black voters tend be much more successful in periods of Democratic dominance. Thus, 2006 stands out as the best year for Black voters in Senate elections. In gubernatorial elections, outcomes are more likely to favor Blacks in years that coincide with presidential elections.

28. The effects of individual demographic characteristics on Black outcomes are either negligible or inconsistent – likely due to the near-total unity among Black voters across most of these elections.

29. Of course, gerrymandering can also be used to concentrate racial and ethnic minorities in a small number of districts and therefore limit their broader influence.

30. Other comparative work has highlighted the negative implications of majoritarian systems for minority interests (Taagepara and Shugart 1989).

Who Wins on Policy?

1. The core of this chapter is from an article in *Politics, Groups, and Identities*, entitled "Political Inequality in America: Who Loses on Spending Policy? When is Policy Less

Biased?" I co-authored that chapter with John Griffin, Brian Newman, and David Searle. I greatly appreciate their willingness to use the material here.

2. Quinnipiac Poll. 2017.poll.qu.edu/national/release-detail?ReleaseID=2508. Accessed May 21, 2019.

3. Not everyone wants government to be totally responsive to the preferences of the public. Some would prefer that elected leaders perform in part as trustees who make independent decisions and use their own judgment about what is best for their constituents. But almost all agree that government policy should at least partly reflect public preferences.

4. Public opinion even seems to drive policy on foreign affairs, a policy area that few Americans follow closely (Bartels 1991). Others have shown that the overall national direction of policymaking follows the overall public policy mood (Stimson et al. 1995). There is, however, a real debate about how much politicians and the public affect each other's positions. Some, such as Page and Shapiro (1983), maintain that public preferences drive the actions of elected officials, while others contend that elected leaders are able to shape public opinion (Jacobs and Shapiro 2000, Zaller 1992). In practice, it is extremely difficult to determine in which direction influence flows.

5. Government responsiveness has been demonstrated using a range of different methods (Erikson et al. 2002, Wlezien and Soroka 2009) and at different levels including the state (Caughey and Warshaw 2017, Erikson et al. 1993, Lax and Phillips 2011) and the city level (Browning et al. 1984, Dahl 1961, Mladenka 1981).

6. Scholars and activists have, of course, long held concerns that the political system advantages the wealthy over the poor (e.g. Piven and Cloward 1977, Schattschneider 1970). That concern has motivated countless studies over the years (APSA 2004). However, only very recently have researchers been able to closely assess the link between the political preferences of different economic classes and policy outcomes. In essence, we are learning for the first time what we have long suspected: The system is skewed toward the rich.

7. A number of methodological critiques have, however, raised doubts about whether the rich really do dominate in the public opinion realm (Ura and Ellis 2008, Soroka and Wlezien 2008).

8. Using a variety of different methods and approaches, several other studies have similarly demonstrated that government action responds to high-income earners' preferences, and essentially ignores the preferences of low-income earners (Druckman and Jacobs 2011, Ellis 2012, Flavin 2012, Gilens and Page 2014, Page and Jacobs 2005, Rigby and Wright 2013). Some, however, suggest that the bias is overstated because the upper and lower classes generally agree on policy (Brunner et al. 2013, Soroka and Wlezien 2008, Ura and Ellis 2008).

9. The quote is in Greenberg (2012) and is from Amin Husain, one of the organizers of the protest.

10. There have been many other studies of policy responsiveness to racial and ethnic minorities. These studies are important in that they have generally found that Whites hold undue influence. The problem is that these studies have tended either to focus on a narrow range of policies or limit their analysis to a particular city or state. For example, important research has looked at the effects of an expanded Black electorate on policy outcomes in specific states (Keech 1968, Parker 1990) or the effect of expanded descriptive representation on a particular policy outcome across cities (Browning et al. 1984, Eisinger 1982, Kerr and Mladenka 1994, Meier and England 1984). More recently, studies have been able to examine the correspondence between minority opinion and the voting records of individual legislators (Griffin and Newman 2007, Lublin 1997, Whitby 1998). These studies provide insight into

one office, one location, or one aspect of policy but they offer little in the way of an overall evaluation. Judging by these studies, it is hard to know how well members of minorities – or any other group – are doing in American democracy.

11. Figures for the "poor" are for those below the official poverty threshold, while "wealthy" refers to the top 1 percent of income earners.

12. Similarly, racial and ethnic minorities are rarely of one mind on policy choices. Often, large segments of the minority community favor one kind of policy, while other segments favor a very different policy.

13. Group-level analysis can get around this problem by choosing groups of the same size. It is possible (although not necessarily ideal) with income, but impossible with race and many other demographic characteristics.

14. The GSS is a nationally representative survey administered in most years. The average sample each year is 1,967.

15. To be precise, I have 414,250 individual policy preferences. To get to that figure, I pool together all 28 GSS surveys fielded between 1972 and 2010.

16. In each case, the exact prompt is: "We are faced with many problems in this country, none of which can be solved easily or inexpensively. I'm going to name some of these problems, and for each one I'd like you to tell me whether you think we're spending too much money on it, too little money, or about the right amount."

17. The official budget categories and their codes are: income security (604, 605, 609), national defense (050), education (501–503), international affairs (151, 152), recreational resources (303), administration of justice (750), health (550), community development (451, 452), conservation and land management (302), space flight, research and supporting activities (252), and ground transportation (401). All spending data are from the government budget historical tables, and are converted to real dollars.

18. Those who wanted no change when government spending did not change, and those who sought an increase when spending increased, were likewise coded as winners.

19. It could be that elected leaders shape public preferences rather than the reverse.

20. In alternate analyses I use cut-offs of spending increases/decreases that are (a) greater than 2 percent of the budget for that policy area, and (b) greater than 5 percent of the budget for that policy area. All of the different specifications lead to similar results.

21. Converse (1964) and Zaller and Feldman (1992) have clearly shown that public opinion can be highly variable and error-prone.

22. If anything, the effects of race are slightly more pronounced.

23. Data on Hispanics and Asian Americans are limited to 2000–10 and are not strictly comparable to the other figures in the figure.

24. In alternate tests, I controlled for the mean spending preferences of each individual. In other words, I estimated whether individuals tend to favor spending increases across all areas, or whether they lean toward spending decreases across most areas. Those who favor spending increases in general are slightly more likely to have their preferences met – not surprising since government is growing over this time period. But inclusion of mean spending preferences does little to impact the overall findings on race.

25. Finally, if I use a different, lower cut-off to define spending increases/decreases, the percentage of winners in all groups rises slightly.

26. I recognize that these measures of religion are unrefined, and that more nuanced measures may generate larger differences. Unfortunately, such measures are not available in the GSS datasets I examine.

27. The GSS sample of Asian Americans is typically small (often less than 100), and the surveys have historically been offered only in English. Thus, the GSS data on Latinos and Asian Americans are not particularly reliable.

28. The main dependent variable – policy winning – is coded as 1 if a subsequent government action in a particular policy area matched the respondent's preferences; it is 0 otherwise. Because I incorporate each respondent's preferences for eleven spending areas, I cluster errors by respondent. I also include fixed effects for each policy area.

29. Each respondent is asked to describe his or her partisan attachment and is placed on a scale from 1 (strongly Democrat) to 7 (strongly Republican), with independents and non-partisans placed in the middle. Likewise, ideology ranges from 1 (strongly liberal) to 6 (strongly conservative).

30. Because the data set only identifies Hispanics and Asian Americans for the last ten years, I could not incorporate them in the main analysis, even though I wanted to do so. I briefly examine their policy success later in this chapter.

31. In the regression model, income is measured as real family income. Education is the number of years of schooling completed. Age is measured in years. Spending preferences, voting with the plurality, marital status, and fixed effects for each policy area are also included in the regression model, but are not displayed in the figure due to space limitations.

32. Additional analysis reveals that rural voters win marginally more on policy than urban voters.

33. I admit that if I could single out Evangelicals and born-again Christians, I might demonstrate even stronger effects for religion. Unfortunately, the data set does not always include these kinds of questions.

34. I explored several alternate measures of class, including logged income and an alpha factor combining income and education. None revealed a larger effect for class than race and most suggested a smaller or even insignificant effect for class. Given the possibility of non-linearities in the effect of class, I also used dummy variables for each income quartile and for different levels of education (e.g. high school vs. college). This also did not affect the overall results with respect to race, but did suggest that the gains in responsiveness are greatest near the top of the income and education scales, as Bartels (2008) and Gilens and Page (2014) found.

35. This is the same critique that a number of scholars have raised about the major studies of class bias (Brunner et al. 2013, Soroka and Wlezien 2008, Ura and Ellis 2008).

36. To help ensure that the overall story is accurate, I undertook a series of different checks on the analysis. In one set of these tests, I increased the lag between the time of a respondent's expressed spending preferences and the measure of subsequent change in government spending. Up to this point, I have focused on spending changes in the fiscal year after each GSS survey. But it is far from clear how quickly governments can react to shifts in public opinion. The government budgeting process is a complicated, drawn-out affair. It may take more than a year to transmit preferences to policy. Thus, in another set of tests, I looked for changes in spending two years after each respondent expressed his or her policy opinions. This did little to alter the overall conclusions.

37. The gaps are relatively small in the bivariate analysis but when I add an interaction term for Black and gender to the regressions, it is significant and negative – indicating that Black women are doubly disadvantaged.

38. I use the standard p<.05 as a cut-off for significance. Regressions are included in the appendix.

39. There is no way to definitively determine which spending areas are most important for African Americans. However, when I repeated the analysis focusing only on the five spending areas that surveys suggest are priorities for the Black community

(welfare, health, education, crime, and aid to cities), the overall racial imbalance in responsiveness remained. All else equal, Blacks are 4.9 percent more likely to lose across the five policy areas that appear to be most important to the group. Not surprisingly, when I re-tested the data focusing on the three policy areas in which Black and White opinion most differed (welfare, crime, and education), the racial imbalance in responsiveness became slightly more pronounced.

40. I reach the same conclusions, if I do more rigorous regression analysis that simultaneously controls for each of the different individual characteristics. In the regression models, big winners are coded 1, middle outcomes 0, and big losers -1.

41. Another way to test the model is to vary how one measures change in government spending. The cut-offs for defining an increase or decrease in spending, as opposed to no change in spending, are arbitrary. So I want to demonstrate the robustness of the results across different cut-off points. So far, I have defined changes in spending as any change in spending that is greater than a one standard deviation shift in annual spending in that policy area. This definition highlights large or out-of-the-ordinary changes in spending. But I might also want to focus on smaller, more regular spending changes. To do that, I defined an increase/decrease in spending as any change that is greater than 2 percent of the previous year's spending in that policy area. This alternate analysis led once again to very similar results. By any measure, government was least responsive to Blacks. The one change that was apparent is that neither income nor education had a statistically significant effect in a multivariate regression model when I used this alternate dependent variable. At least as measured by small changes in spending, policy responsiveness is primarily about race and not about class.

42. I have not, however, incorporated and assessed every conceivable set of interests. Perhaps most importantly I have not measured the influence of interest groups. Given the findings of Gilens and Page (2014) about the undue influence of interest groups over the policymaking process, this is a major omission.

43. Another way to engage this small minority argument is to see if Blacks who have the same kinds of preference as Whites garner less policy influence. I do that in the following manner: Instead of focusing on policy congruence, I look instead at policy outcomes. Does spending on that policy go up, stay flat, or go down? Then I use each individual's spending preferences (prefer an increase, decrease, or flat spending) to predict government spending. Finally, I interact those spending preferences with different demographic characteristics. In essence, I ask if different types of individuals who hold similar preferences are more or less likely to influence policy. This different method leads to the same conclusion about the racial imbalance in responsiveness. This alternate testing method shows that government policy was generally responsive to Americans' spending preferences but was significantly less responsive to Blacks' spending preferences. In fact, this alternate method indicates that policy outcomes are responsive to differences in White preferences and largely unresponsive to differences in Black preferences. A shift from favoring a spending increase to favoring a spending decrease for a White respondent was associated with a 4 percent increase in the probability of getting a spending decrease. The same shift for a Black respondent made no noticeable difference in the probably of getting a spending decrease. Once again, I found no biases across income and only marginal differences across education. Even when Americans want the same things, it is Black voices that are most muted.

Immigration is Reshaping Partisan Politics

1. Phillips (2017). Much of this chapter is derived from my *American Journal of Political Science* article, "Immigration, Latinos, and White Partisan Politics: The

New Democratic Defection." That article was written with Michael Rivera. I owe a deep debt of gratitude to Michael who was critical at all stages of the process from the initial idea to completion of the project.

2. Polling data from Real Clear Politics: www1.realclearpolitics.com/epolls/2016/pre sident/us/2016_republican_presidential_nomination-3823.html. Accessed May 22, 2019.

3. One study found that 58 percent of all Trump news coverage in the month after his infamous speech focused on immigration (Parker 2015). That was in no small part because Trump continued to talk about immigration. Lamont et al. (2017) found that Trump talked about immigration more than any other subject.

4. Poll results from 2016 Voter Survey: www.voterstudygroup.org/publications/2016-elections/data. Accessed May 22, 2019.

5. There are also three studies which looked at the impact of Prop. 187, California's famous anti-immigrant measure on subsequent White partisanship in the state. The three studies, however, reached opposite conclusions about its impact (Bowler et al. 2006, Dyck et al. 2012, Hui and Sears 2018).

6. However, since 2016 a virtual cottage industry of studies has looked for and found a close correlation between attitudes on immigration and the vote in both the primary and the general election in 2016 (Collingwood et al. 2017, Gimpel 2017, Griffin and Teixeira 2017, Hooghe and Dassonneville 2018, Sides 2017).

7. Admittedly, many Democratic leaders are reluctant to publicly support immigrants' rights issues, while many Republicans recognize the benefits of cheap labor to business.

8. Business interests within the Republican Party beholden to cheap immigrant labor clearly favor less regressive immigration reforms, but their views have been less and less likely to be vocalized by party leadership.

9. 2007 GOP debate at Saint Anselm College, June 3, 2007.

10. Editorial, "Immigration in the House." *New York Times*, July 7, 2013. www .nytimes.com/2013/07/08/opinion/immigration-in-the-house.html?hp&_r=0. Accessed May 22, 2019.

11. "Obama's Remarks to NALEO." Real Clear Politics, June 28, 2008. www .realclearpolitics.com/articles/2008/06/obamas_remarks_to_naleo.html. Accessed May 22, 2019.

12. Hillary Clinton, Third 2016 Presidential Debate in Las Vegas, October 19, 2016.

13. Again, I do not claim that the elites within either party are fully unified on the issue of immigration. Indeed, they are not. Some prominent Republicans (former president George W. Bush and Senator Marco Rubio) have tried various tactics on immigration to try to garner greater support from Latino voters. And as I write this book, Republican leaders appear to be engaged in an internal debate about the proper course for their party on immigration. Likewise, many Democrats offer at best lukewarm support for immigrants, and many couple support for amnesty with even more vigorous support for increased border security and deportations. But there seems little doubt that on average, the two major parties present Americans with divergent alternatives on immigration.

14. Pushing the analogy even further, the current backlash could be compared to any number of other historical episodes in which racial and ethnic minority efforts to attain social, economic, or political rights were actively and often violently rebuffed by large segments of the White population (Foner 1984, Klinkner and Smith 1999, Kousser 1999, Parker 1990).

15. Critically, many of these nativist episodes have had a real impact on the partisan politics of the day. In the 1850s, for example, a nativist backlash against Irish

Catholic immigrants helped spur the Know Nothings and the American Party to electoral success (Anbinder 1992).

16. At the same time, economists and demographers tend to agree that the consequences of immigration are uneven across the native-born population. There is evidence that the wages of less skilled workers who often compete with immigrants for jobs have been negatively impacted by large-scale immigration (Bean and Stevens 2003, Borjas 2001).

17. Today, 15 percent of all new marriages are interracial or interethnic – a figure that seems well-nigh impossible given the sharp dividing lines that only recently governed the US South (Passel et al. 2010).

18. That same strategy is, of course, likely to push the increasingly large immigrant population away from the Republican Party. Indeed, there is evidence that it is already happening (Hawley 2012, Nicholson and Segura 2005; but see Abrajano et al. 2008).

19. Gallup 2019b.

20. We do know more about the actions and allegiances of immigrants themselves. Various studies have demonstrated the growing strength of the minority vote, and in particular the Latino electorate (Abrajano and Alvarez 2010). Many others have demonstrated the increasing attachment of immigrants and their offspring to the Democratic Party (Hajnal and Lee 2011). These are certainly crucial developments in the course of US political history. Nevertheless, the votes of immigrants still represent a small fraction of the nation's electorate. Foreign-born residents still represent fewer than 5 percent of the voters in this country. If immigration is going to have a deeper impact on the politics of the nation, it will be with the larger, native-born population.

21. We know, for example, that cultural and racial considerations, more than personal economic interests, often seem to shape attitudes toward immigration (Brader et al. 2008, Citrin et al. 1997, Hainmueller and Hiscox 2010, Hainmueller and Hopkins 2014, Schildkraut 2005, Wright and Citrin 2011; but see Hanson 2005 and Scheve and Slaughter 2001).

22. Scholars have found clear evidence that immigration fundamentally shapes the views of Latinos (Hawley 2012, Nicholson and Segura 2005; but see Abrajano et al. 2008, Alvarez and Garcia Bedolla 2003). And as already noted several recent studies have revealed a correlation between immigration views and the 2016 vote (Collingwood et al. 2017, Gimpel 2017, Griffin and Teixeira 2017, Sides 2017).

23. Unless otherwise indicated, all polling figures are compiled from Polling Report 2019.

24. Poll figures from Pew Research Center poll in 2013 and Fox News poll 2013 as reported in Polling Report 2019.

25. Poll figures from Pew Research Center poll in 2013 and Gallup poll in 2012 as reported in Polling Report 2019.

26. Poll figures from USA Today poll in 2010 as reported in Polling Report 2019.

27. Pew 2006.

28. Poll figures from Quinnipiac survey in 2010 as reported in Polling Report 2019.

29. Pew 2006.

30. Polling Report 2019.

31. Quinnipac University Poll in 2019 as reported in Polling Report 2019.

32. The best estimates indicate that only about one-quarter of immigrants are undocumented (Pew Research Center 2006).

33. It is worth noting that all these figures understate White fears and concerns about immigration. National polling data, of course, include large numbers of Latino and

Asian-American respondents who are decidedly more pro-immigrant on every one of the questions that I highlight here. Typically, White views are 5–10 percent more anti-immigrant than these national figures suggest.

34. Another almost equally large segment of the US public appears to be ambivalent about immigration. For example, roughly one-quarter of the population feels unsure whether immigrants hurt or help the country (Fox News 2010 survey in Polling Report 2019). One-third think we should "welcome some" immigrants but not all (*New York Times* 2010 poll reported in Polling Report 2019). Likewise, 42 percent of Americans feel that we should pursue both increased border security and a pathway to citizenship equally vigorously (Pew Research Center 2012 from Polling Report 2019). For this segment of the population, in short, there appears to be real mix of admiration and concern.

35. Pew Research Center 2006.

36. From Pew Research Center 2008 survey, reported in Polling Report 2019.

37. Polling Report 2019.

38. From *New York Times* 2010 survey, reported in Polling Report 2019. In addition, the most recent polls have shown a substantial uptick in support for immigration.

39. The analysis in the figure uses four questions on illegal immigration from the 2008 ANES to measure views on immigration. For the figures, I divide respondents into ten evenly split groups based on their views on the undocumented immigration scale. The four questions are: a standard feeling thermometer that asks how one feels about "illegal immigrants" and ranges from 0 (meaning extremely cold or negative feelings) to 100 (for extremely warm or positive feelings); "Should controlling and reducing illegal immigration be a very important [or] . . . not an important foreign policy goal?"; "Do you favor/oppose the US government making it possible for illegal immigrants to become US citizens?"; and "Do you favor, oppose, or neither favor nor oppose allowing illegal immigrants to work in the United States for up to three years, after which they would have to go back to their home country?" To reduce error in measurement and get an overall measure of attitudes toward undocumented immigration, I combine the four questions and create an alpha factor score for each respondent. The four items cohere well, with a scale reliability of 0.70 and an average inter-item correlation of 0.36.

40. The correlation with immigration views and vote choice is just as strong for Senate elections. Fully 80 percent of White Americans with negative views of undocumented immigrants vote Republican in Senate elections, while only 30 percent of those with positive views of immigrants do so.

41. It also doesn't matter whether I combine the questions on immigration to create a factor score as I do in the figure, or whether I use a simpler additive scale or look at each question separately. The pattern of results is similar.

42. Specifically I include measures for: *basic ideology* – the standard 7-point liberal-conservative self-placement scale (from "extremely liberal" to "extremely conservative"); *war, terrorism, and security* – "Do you approve/disapprove of the way the US federal government has handled the war in Afghanistan?", "Do you approve/disapprove of the way the US federal government has handled the war in Iraq?", and "Should federal spending on the war on terrorism be increased, decreased, or kept about the same?"; *the economy and retrospective evaluations* –"Do you approve/disapprove of the way George W. Bush is handling his job as president?" and "Would you say that over the past year the nation's economy has gotten better, stayed about the same, or gotten worse?"; *redistribution* – "People who make more money should pay a larger percent of their income in taxes to the government than people who make less money," and "Should federal spending on welfare be

increased, decreased, or kept about the same?"; *morality and religion* – "Do you strongly favor [or] ... strongly oppose laws to protect homosexuals against job discrimination," and "Is religion an important part of your life?"; *racial attitudes* – four different questions from the racial resentment scale that ask for responses to "If Blacks would only try harder, they could be just as well off as Whites," "Blacks should [work their way up] without special favors," "Blacks have gotten less than they deserve," and "Generations of slavery and discrimination have created conditions that make it difficult for Blacks to work their way out of the lower class"; and *feelings toward racial minorities* – standard feeling thermometers that ask how warmly or coldly you feel about "Hispanics," "Asian Americans," and "African Americans."

43. I employ an ordinary least squares (OLS) regression for the 7-point party identification scale, and a logistic regression for vote choice.

44. Given claims that much of the instability in party identification comes from measurement error (Goren 2005, Green and Palmquist 1990, Green et al. 2002), I looked to see if immigration still predicted vote choice after taking into account measurement error in party identification. To do so, I turned to the main 2008 ANES data set, as well as the 2010 and 2012 CCES. With the 2008 ANES, I corrected for measurement error by creating a latent party identification alpha factor score that incorporated the same three different indicators employed by Paul Goren (2005) – a standard party identification scale, a feeling thermometer toward the Democratic Party, and a feeling thermometer toward the Republican Party. Inserting this latent measure of party identification into the 2008 analysis did almost nothing to alter the results. Immigration still significantly predicted partisanship and vote choice net other factors. Likewise, when I turned to the 2010 and 2012 CCES, and utilized a measure of latent party identification that was based on two standard party identification questions spaced several months apart (pre- and post-election), I discovered that all the statistically significant immigration-related results from the 2010 and 2012 CCES remained robust.

45. Alternate tests indicate that it matters little which other issues I include, or how I measure issues, ideology, and retrospective evaluations. When policy questions on health care, crime, foreign aid, schools, women's rights, the environment, and science are added to the model, the impact of immigrant-related views on partisan attachments is largely unaffected. Further, immigrant-related views remain significant when I substitute in alternate measures of economic policy preferences or retrospective evaluations. Regardless of one's opinions on the economy, war, abortion, and other factors, views of undocumented immigrants are strongly associated with being a Republican and voting Republican. I also assessed different party-based dependent variables. That is, instead of relying on the standard 7-point party identification scale, I used feeling thermometers toward each party, a dummy variable for Republican identity, a dummy variable for Democratic identity, and an unordered 3-point party identification scale. Views of undocumented immigrants in each case remained statistically significant and the effects were generally substantial.

46. This is true for the regression models that underlie Figure 5.2. And this has been demonstrated repeatedly by other researchers (Tesler 2016a, Tesler and Sears 2010).

47. Immigration matters beyond race in more recent elections, as well. In fact, several studies focused on the 2016 vote found that immigration attitudes rivaled racial considerations in explaining the vote (Gimpel 2017, Hooghe and Dassonneville 2018).

48. There is no question on immigration in most years of the ANES, so I instead focused on a question asking about feelings toward Hispanics.

49. However, the analysis has already shown that immigration views are not totally a function of partisan attachments. When I looked at the vote, I evaluated the impact of immigration views *after* controlling for party identification. Here I found that attitudes toward immigrants have a relationship with the vote that goes beyond partisanship. Similarly, by showing that immigration views matter in party primaries, I demonstrated that immigration matters when party does not.

50. There is incontrovertible evidence concerning the strength and stability of party identification (Campbell et al. 1960, Green et al. 2002). But there is also clear evidence that partisanship changes and slowly aligns with issue positions over the course of one's lifetime (Niemi and Jennings 1991). The reality is that sometimes party drives policy and at others the effect is reversed (Carsey and Layman 2006). Likely, the direction of effects depends on the issue and the context. I believe that because immigration – like race – is a relatively simple, symbolic, and emotional issue, it is a prime candidate for driving partisanship.

51. That effect persists even when I control for a range of other major issues typically linked to partisanship.

52. Gallup asked this question twenty-one times between 1993 and 2011.

53. In line with Michael MacKuen and his colleagues, as well as others who study aggregate partisanship, I average the party identification score for all respondents in a given survey and then average across surveys in a given quarter of a given year (MacKuen, Erikson, and Stimson 1989). I have included 169 *New York Times*/CBS News polls. The average sample size per quarter is 3,729.

54. This aggregate, over-time analysis serves a second purpose in that it can help establish the direction of the causal relationship between immigration attitudes and partisanship. When I reverse the test, I discover that aggregate White partisanship does not significantly predict changes in attitudes on immigration. Immigration is driving shifts in party identification rather than the other way around.

55. Because I was concerned about the limited number of data points, I reran the analysis after incorporating data from every question in the Roper Center Archives that asks about the preferred level of immigration. Combining all the different survey houses doubles the number of quarters for which I have immigration attitudes (forty-two quarters), but it also introduces considerable error as each survey house uses different question wording and different samples. The results for this larger data set roughly mirror the results here.

56. Alternative Prais-Winsten AR(1) and vector autoregressive models lead to similar results.

57. As Bobo (2001), has documented, almost 70 percent of Whites rate Latinos as especially welfare-prone and almost half see them as less intelligent than Whites on average. By contrast, less than 15 percent of Whites hold the same negative stereotypes of Asian Americans. Instead, when Whites stereotype Asian Americans, it is often for being economically successful. Almost half of all Whites believe that Asian Americans are especially hardworking. Only 5 percent of Whites feel the same way about Latinos (Bobo 2001, Lee 2000). Other survey data concur. A Pew survey from 2006 reports that Whites were roughly twice as likely to believe that Latinos were prone to end up on welfare, to increase crime, and to do poorly in school than they were to have similar sentiments about Asian Americans (Pew 2006).

58. Figures are from my analysis of the 2016 American National Election Study.

59. Some might argue that declining Latino immigration and in particular net negative migration from Mexico will make it harder for an immigrant-threat narrative to be effective, but Trump's success at a time when few immigrants are crossing the

Southern border indicates that the threat need not to be real or present to be politically effective.

60. Today 34 percent of Latinos and 59 percent of Asian Americans are foreign-born (Pew 2017 a, b). Moreover, family members or close friends of almost every Latino and Asian American have recently experienced immigration to the United States.

The Immigration Backlash in the States

1. Much of this chapter mirrors a chapter that I wrote with Marisa Abrajano for our book, *White Backlash: Immigration, Race, and American Politics*. I thank Marisa for all of her contributions and her willingness to use that material here.

2. This is not to say that an anti-immigrant backlash is not occurring at the national level. It may, however, be that because the Black-White divide has had a much longer history and is simply more entrenched in our national politics, we have seen clearer evidence of African-American interests being ignored.

3. As of 2017, the total population in Vermont is 623,657.

4. Racial threats need not be driven exclusively by the numbers in the population. It appears also to be contingent on the power of the out-group or the efforts of the out-group to garner more power. Historically, the nation has been especially likely to experience periods of White backlash when the African-American population has been particularly vocal or active in trying to secure greater rights (Klinkner and Smith 1999). During Reconstruction, the expansion of Black political representation was countered with massive resistance as White Southerners turned to widespread violence and instituted an array of new institutional barriers (Kousser 1999). Over a century later, the Civil Rights Movement was met with a similarly broad array of defensive White actions (Parker 1990).

5. A different line of research has shown a robust relationship between racial diversity in any form and the provision of public goods. In contexts with greater diversity, Americans appear to be less willing to pay for and provide public services (Alesina et al. 1999, Hero and Preuhs 2007, Hopkins 2009, Keiser et al. 2004, Soss et al. 2001).

6. It is important to note that in the analysis that follows I do not directly test the contact hypothesis. The primary measure of context – state racial demographics – is probably correlated with contact but only weakly. It is entirely possible for Whites living in extremely diverse states to engage in few personal interactions with members of minority out-groups, especially given the high rates of residential segregation in the nation (Massey 2001).

7. Supporting this view, some researchers have found that immigrant or Latino context has few significant implications (Burns and Gimpel 2000, Dixon 2006, Fennelly and Federico 2008, Taylor 1998).

8. Mississippi and Kentucky were the two exceptions.

9. An important exception is work by Hopkins (2010), which finds that local tax rates are tied to growth in the local immigrant population.

10. Work by Gilens (1999) found no clear link between attitudes toward Latinos and policy views on welfare in the 1990s, but more recent work by Fox (2004, 2012) suggests a tightening relationship.

11. Implicit attitude tests also now show that the American public associates being Latino with being undocumented (Pérez 2010).

12. More recently, Alabama enacted the Beason-Hammon Taxpayer and Citizen Protection Act in 2011 in an attempt to restrict undocumented immigrants from attending public schools. While the law does not prohibit undocumented youth from

enrolling in school, immediately after its passage the percentage of Latino students enrolled in Alabama schools dropped by 5 percent. The courts have at least temporarily blocked this provision: Robertson 2011.

13. The actual relationship is likely to be an even more complicated one that will also depend on the size and interests of other minority groups as well as of the liberal White population. I cannot, unfortunately, effectively model a demographic process that is so complex, and thus I choose to model a simpler curvilinear relationship that puts aside the role of these other groups. In the analysis, I do, however, control for the size of the Black and Asian-American populations, and I incorporate the political leaning of the entire state population.

14. However, because it is not clear in advance whether Americans are reacting to immigrants' presence or Latinos' presence and thus it is not clear how best to measure context, I repeat the analysis with a number of different measures. Specifically, as I describe later, I assess context by looking first at racial or pan-ethnic groups, but I then also consider the undocumented population, the total foreign-born population, and the foreign-born Latino population.

15. An ever-present concern with contextual analysis is that individual residents do not actually know much about the demographic profile of their area (Wong 2007). However, this problem may actually be less severe at the state level. Survey data indicate that Americans do tend to overestimate the absolute number of immigrants and minorities in their state (Enos 2010). However, the same data show that Americans tend to know the size of the state immigrant/minority population relative to other states. There is, in fact, a reasonably close correlation between individual perceptions and actual state rankings (Enos 2010). Ultimately, to the extent that Americans do not know the racial make-up of their states, the results should be biased downward. This "noise" in the contextual measure should only serve to reduce significance levels.

16. Alternatives might include tests that assess specific, concrete policies. For example, I could have looked at sentencing for drug violations or for violent crimes in each state. It is, however, difficult to come up with a single policy that accurately encompasses the state's overall policy record in any given area.

17. However, in a series of robustness tests I also look at per capita spending in each area.

18. Information on budget expenditures for all fifty states is available from annual reports provided by the National Association of State Budget Officers (NASBO). The data are available for more than a decade, spanning 1995–2011. For education, I only include K-12 education, and I exclude higher education spending since post-secondary education tends to be much less clearly associated with the immigrant or Latino population. On average, 20.5 percent of state expenditures go to K-12 education, but that figure varies widely from a high of 32.2 percent to a low of 3.8 percent. The measure of corrections funding incorporates spending to build and operate prison systems. Corrections expenditures are considerably lower, comprising only 4.1 percent of state spending on average. The measure of health-care spending is admittedly less encompassing, and may therefore be a less accurate portrayal of state efforts. Specifically, I look at the proportion of all state funds that go to Medicaid, a means-tested program that provides medical care for low-income individuals. Overall about 2.5 percent of all state funds go to Medicaid.

19. Specifically, I compare the top quarter of states based on the share of the population that identifies as Latino with the bottom quarter of states. The twelve heavily Latino states are (in descending order): New Mexico, Texas, California, Arizona, Nevada, Florida, Colorado, New Jersey, New York, Illinois, Connecticut, and Rhode Island.

The twelve states with the smallest share of Latinos are (in order): Maine, Vermont, Mississippi, Kentucky, New Hampshire, North Dakota, Montana, and Ohio, South Dakota, Missouri, Alabama, and Michigan.

20. One could argue that this increase in corrections spending in states with larger Latino populations is a function of Latinos being more prone to crime – and that criminality leading to higher costs. However, there is little indication that this is true. Nationally, Latinos are over-represented in the prison population (Pew 2018a). But most of that appears to be driven by racial disparities in the criminal justice system itself including lesser sentences for drug-related infractions that Whites are more likely to commit and imprisonment for immigration-related offences (Nellis 2016). Immigrants and areas with higher immigration areas are, in fact, associated with lower crime rates after controlling for other factors (Flagg 2018, Rumbaut 2006).

21. Aside from property and sales taxes, most other tax revenue comes from income taxes, which can range from regressive to progressive, and are harder to characterize.

22. One could argue that Latino voters are driving this conservative policy shift, but survey data show quite clearly that Latinos are more liberal than Whites on each of these policy areas (Barreto and Segura 2014).

23. The model of state spending/taxing is estimated using a cross-sectional time-series regression model that includes all years from 1995 to 2011, and employs a random effects model. Each of the time-varying independent variables is lagged by one year in order to address potential concerns about the direction of causality.

24. Data on the partisan composition of each state legislature are from the US Statistical Abstract (1990–2011). The ideological leaning of each state's citizenry is drawn from Erikson et al. (1993), who use public opinion survey data to estimate the percentage of a state population that is liberal, conservative, or moderate. The professionalization of each legislature is from Squire (2007). Unemployment data are from the Bureau of Labor Statistics: www.bls.gov/lau/home.htm. Average individual income is from the US Bureau of Labor Statistics, "Employment and Wages Online Annual Averages, 2009," www.bls.gov/cew/cewbultn09.htm. Also, in alternate tests I build on the research by Hero and Preuhs (2007) by controlling for regional variations across states that might affect their support for public goods spending on immigrants. Specifically, they argue that states along the US-Mexico border, as well as those with an international port, may have distinct policy regimes, and may be especially sensitive to the amount of state funds allocated to immigrants.

25. I also performed a number of other different robustness tests. To see if the results might be driven by one or two exceptional states with particularly large or particularly small Latino populations, I re-ran the analysis, dropping each state one at a time. Including a large number of states with a negligible Latino population could also be skewing the results. In alternate tests, I therefore excluded from the analysis those states in which Latinos comprise less than 3 percent of the total population; these states include Maine, New Hampshire, North and South Dakota, Vermont, West Virginia, and Mississippi. Even when these seven states are dropped from the sample, it leads to no substantive change in the main findings. Finally, I also incorporated a range of alternate measures of politics (dummy variables for which party controls the Senate, the House, and governor's office) and geography (controls for border states and various regional dummies). None of these alternative specifications affected the basic conclusions.

26. For regression outputs, see the appendix.

27. The regressions also show that partisan control of state government also matters. Democratic-led states tend to spend more on education, health, and welfare. Partisan control had a less clear impact on tax policy.

28. This pattern persists if I instead shift to an analysis of per capita spending, per pupil spending, or total dollars spent in each policy area.

29. I find, as do Gulasekaram and Ramakrishnan (2015), that politics also matters a great deal. States with more Republican legislators and more conservative voters are more likely to engage in policymaking that limits funds and services that might go to Latinos.

30. Specifically, I find that the percent Latino squared term is statistically significant indicating that there is a robust curvilinear effect to Latino population size.

31. Though the effect of Latino context on corrections spending is no longer statistically significant at larger values

32. See California Immigrant Policy Center, "The California Blueprint: Two Decades of Pro-Immigrant Transformation." ncg.org/sites/default/files/resources/The-California-Blueprint-1.pdf. Accessed June 11, 2019.

33. Some academic studies also point to growth as a key variable driving White behavior (Hopkins 2009, Newman 2013).

34. Because it is not clear exactly which aspect of growth over which time period is most likely to shape White reactions, I introduced a range of different measures that assessed Latino population growth and foreign-born population growth over the previous year, the past two years, or over the past five years.

35. It is also important to note that adding these different measures of population growth did little to affect the main results on the effects of Latino population size on state policy.

36. In the models I also looked at the effect of the size of the Black and Asian-American populations on policy. The findings here are far less clear and consistent. Larger Black populations were associated with lower welfare spending – a pattern that is consistent with existing research (Hero and Preuhs 2007, Soss et al. 2001). But no other policy outcomes were significantly related to Black population size. The Asian-American population was also more often than not unrelated to policy. But in a few cases, being in a state with a larger Asian-American population actually had a liberalizing effect. In particular, states with larger Asian-American populations spent more on welfare and had less regressive taxes. In other words, policy seemed to be more generous when Asian Americans were more visible. This seems to fit with earlier work that has at least on occasion found that proximity to large Asian-American communities is associated with more positive views about Asian Americans or policies related to Asian Americans (Hero and Preuhs 2007, Hood and Morris 2000, Tolbert and Hero 1999).

37. Likewise, I could find no robust relationship between the foreign-born population of a state and its policies. Given that Whites tend to react differently to Asian Americans and Latinos – the two main immigrant groups – this is perhaps not surprising. But it does reinforce the view that the overall patterns are driven more by race than by place of birth.

38. What I do know is that individual attitudes are part of the sequence. Other research I have undertaken shows quite clearly that in states with larger Latino populations, White residents hold especially critical views of Latinos, and these White residents are particularly likely to favor cuts in public services and to support tougher criminal sentencing (Abrajano and Hajnal 2015). The policy changes I see in this chapter fit neatly with this change in individual White attitudes.

Democratic Party Control and Equality in Policy Responsiveness

1. Much of this chapter uses material from an article entitled "Political Inequality in America: Who Loses on Spending Policy? When is Policy Less Biased?" that I co-

authored with John Griffin, Brian Newman, and David Searle. I am indebted to John, Brian, and David for allowing me to present the research here.

2. This is, of course, only a partial list of the stark policy differences between these two presidents. Trump and Obama differ sharply on any number of other issues including voting rights, abortion, criminal sentencing, gun control, taxes, and relations with Russia.

3. Data from the 2018 National Exit Poll.

4. Party identification is almost as lopsided in recent years. Among Whites, Republican identifiers outnumber Democratic identifiers (34 percent vs. 30 percent). Among non-Whites, Democratic identifiers (54 percent) outnumber Republican identifiers (15 percent) by almost four to one.

5. MSNBC Poll, December 2015: www.pollingreport.com/dvs.r.htm.

6. This figure is from a question in the American National Election Study on the efforts of both parties to "help Blacks."

7. The 2004 Republican National Committee platform states: "[W]e reject preferences, quotas, and set-asides based on skin color, ethnicity, or gender, which perpetuate divisions and can lead people to question the accomplishments of successful minorities and women."

8. Both Ira Katznelson and Robert Lieberman, for example, show in different ways that liberal efforts to expand welfare and to aid the disadvantaged were at least over some periods undercut by racism in the writing and implementation of policy. A slightly different interpretation holds that although the Democratic Party has actively tried to lift minorities and the working class, it has had little tangible impact. Supporting this perspective, Jacob Hacker and Paul Pierson show that inequality has grown over the last few decades regardless of the party in power (Hacker and Pierson 2011). Further underscoring this point are data from the APSA Taskforce on Inequality and American Democracy and critical studies by Martin Gilens and Larry Bartels showing that both political parties are especially responsive to and engaged with more privileged segments of the electorate. (See APSA 2004, Bartels 2008, Gilens 2012; Katznelson 2005; Lieberman 1998, Page 1983.)

9. See also Donahue and Heckman (1990) on this point, and Valelly (2004) on the Voting Rights Act.

10. There is, however, one study that finds that Democratic governors cause a decrease in the Black-White wage gap by helping to increase the number of hours worked by Blacks (Beland 2015). A similar study finds that Democratic governors also help to increase immigrant employment (Beland and Unel 2018).

11. Also relevant is a line of research that examines whether party control makes any difference at all (Caughey and Warshaw 2017, Erikson et al. 2002).

12. Bartels (2008) does, however, find that the bias in the favor of the well-off is in some cases slightly more muted under Democrats.

13. At the same time, given that Blacks, Latinos, and Asian Americans all represent extremely economically diverse populations, that inference is a far from certain one.

14. Since it takes some time to enact policy, presidential party control and congressional party control are lagged one year.

15. The data are from the General Social Survey which is a nationally representative survey. See Chapter 4 for more details on the survey questions, corresponding federal government spending categories, and the methodology I employ.

16. Those who wanted no change when government spending did not change and those who sought an increase when spending increased were likewise coded as winners.

17. Given the limited data on Latino and Asian-American spending preferences, I do not undertake this more rigorous analysis on either group.

18. The underlying regression is included in the appendix.

19. Alternate models reveal that Democratic leaders were significantly more responsive than Republican leaders to the lower class, Democratic identifiers, and liberals.

20. I conducted a series of robustness checks to help ensure that the results we see in Figures 7.1 and 7.2 are real. First, I focused on a different dependent variable that measured the *distance* between an individual's policy preferences and government policy actions. This new measure distinguishes between those who lost a little (e.g. individuals who wanted a spending increase but then saw no change in spending) vs. those who lost a lot (e.g. individuals who wanted a spending increase but then witnessed a decrease in spending). Analyzing the data this way essentially reinforces the same conclusions. I also employed different cut-offs to identify spending increases and decreases. The main analysis singles out changes that are greater than one standard deviation in annual spending for each particular policy area. In alternate tests, I looked at smaller cut-offs of 2 percent and 5 percent shifts in spending. It made little difference to the overall conclusions.

21. Similarly, I re-tested the data focusing on the three policy areas in which Black and White opinion most differed (welfare, crime, and education). Once again, I found that Democratic control was critical in eliminating racial bias in responsiveness.

22. By contrast, one-third of Whites surveyed favored the tax cut: Quinnipiac Poll (2017), poll.qu.edu/national/release-detail?ReleaseID=2508.

23. The year 1982, the first year in which Republicans held both a majority in Senate and the presidency (with Ronald Reagan in office), was no different. African Americans were once again overwhelming policy losers. That year education spending decreased by 12 percent (even though 82 percent of Blacks did not want a spending cut on education), defense spending increased by 18 percent (even though 86 percent of Blacks opposed that increase), and welfare and health-care spending both declined (despite the fact that 77 percent of African Americans favored increases on welfare, and 82 percent sought increases in health-care spending).

24. One other important factor that has been largely ignored in this chapter is the economy. There is, however, reason to expect that economic conditions could impact the responsiveness of government to different groups in American society. During periods of robust economic growth, governments generally have greater revenues, and thus can choose to spend those additional resources to try to accommodate the interests of citizens. And if minorities want greater spending – as the data show they do – government action coinciding with the policy preferences of racial minorities may be more likely to occur during periods of economic expansion. That is exactly what additional analysis finds. When I interact race with real per capita GDP growth, I find that racial imbalances in responsiveness decline when the economy is growing. Economic growth tends to boost responsiveness to everyone, but this is particularly true for Blacks. Responsiveness to Blacks grows significantly when GDP is growing. If one could manufacture more growth, some of the inequities in American politics could likely be reduced or eliminated. In other words, economic growth represents a second avenue to minority gains.

25. Interestingly, on this measure, partisan control of the presidency makes no difference.

26. By contrast, Republican administrations are significantly more responsive to the top third of the White population than to the bottom third.

27. Of course, parties and their platforms do change. It is certainly possible that the Republican Party could become more responsive to a broader segment of the public in the future. Likewise, Democrats could cease to pursue policies that garner wide public support.

28. There are also some broader implications for how we think about power in American politics. The most obvious is that these results demonstrate that parties matter. It is perhaps not surprising to learn that, in an age of heightened partisan polarization, which party controls the main levers of political power in this country matters. It is important to note just how much change in partisan control results in changes in the fundamental relationship between government and the governed.

Democratic Party Control and Minority Well-Being

1. Sections of this chapter come from an article co-authored with Jeremy Horowitz that is entitled, "Who Loses in American Democracy: A Count of Votes Demonstrates the Limited Representation of African Americans." That article was published in *Perspectives on Politics*. The Matthias family story is detailed in Otis (2018).

2. Thais Marques was interviewed by WBUR on September 5, 2017. www.wbur.org /hereandnow/2017/09/05/dreamer-trump-daca. Accessed June 11, 2019.

3. As of the writing of this book, the future of DACA was still in the hands of the courts, with several lawsuits against President Trump's decision to try to end DACA still pending.

4. Likewise, there is a smaller and less-developed literature looking at how control by one mayoral regime or another impacts policy at the local level, and a broader set of studies looking at how partisan control translates into policy outcomes at the state and local levels (Benedictis-Kessner and Warshaw 2016, Browning et al. 1984, Caughey and Warshaw 2017, Dye 1984, Erikson et al. 2002, Ferreira and Gyourko 2009, Garand 1988, Gerber and Hopkins 2011).

5. One important exception is Beland (2015), who finds that having a Democrat control the governor's office leads to increases in the number of hours worked by African Americans in the state.

6. I measure income primarily as median family income in constant 2008 dollars. As robustness tests, I repeat the analysis focusing on mean family income, and mean and median household income. For poverty measures, I focus on the overall poverty rate for families in each racial and ethnic group. Unemployment is the adult unemployment rate for each group. All economic data are from the US Census.

7. On the power of the presidency see Edwards (2003), Howell (2003), Kernell (1997), Kiewiet and McCubbins (1985), and Neustadt (1980).

8. More precisely, I lagged the measure of political control by one year. Alternate lags of two or three years produce slightly less consistent results.

9. Significance tests are a basic t-test for differences in means.

10. As an example, to see if the gap is closing or increasing, I subtract the Black unemployment rate from the White unemployment rate in the previous year, then subtract Black unemployment from White unemployment in the current year, and finally subtract the gap in the current year from the previous year.

11. The Black-White poverty gap grew by a net total of 6.2 points under Republicans, and fell by a whopping 33 points under Democrats. Similarly, the Black-White unemployment gap grew by 7.2 points under Republicans, and fell by 4.3 points under Democrats.

12. As an alternative, I also tested a time-series model with a lagged dependent variable that focused on annual group well-being instead of changes in group well-being. The results from that model are essentially identical to those I present here.

13. All Congress variables are lagged one year. In alternate tests, I also assess the proportion of Democrats in each legislative body, as well as the median ideological score in each body. Additional tests also consider the roles of divided government and partisan polarization. Few significant results emerged from these alternate tests.

14. All years with a Democratic administration in office are coded as 1 and all years with a Republican administration are coded 0.

15. Presidential partisanship is not significantly correlated with year. In other words, there are not more or fewer Democrats in office over time.

16. I found no significant effects for Congress when I substituted the percentage of the Democrats in the House and the Senate, and when I replaced the dummy variables for Democratic majorities with ideal point estimates (using the methodologies of Keith Poole and of Michael Bailey) for the median legislator in each body. The results for Congress change only marginally when I drop presidential partisanship from the model.

17. Democratic control of both the House and the Senate is negatively and significantly correlated with time. However, House and Senate effects are still insignificant when the time trend is dropped from the model.

18. Additional analysis shows that dropping one or two administrations at a time from the regressions, omitting partisan transition years, dropping presidential election years, or taking out years with unusually high or low economic growth has no appreciable effect on the overall pattern of results. The results are also robust to the inclusion of war dummy variables. If anything, including a Vietnam dummy variable leads to an increase in the estimated effect of a Democratic presidency. I also added an interaction between the party of the president and time to see if the effect of partisan control might be changing over time. In all but one case the interaction was not significant, suggesting that, generally speaking, the impact of presidential partisanship is not changing over time. In the one significant case, I found that the impact of partisan control on changes in the gap between Black and White incomes diminished over time, perhaps suggesting that the ability (or effort) of Democratic presidents to close the racial gap in incomes has diminished over time, or that Republican presidents are becoming more willing and able to do so.

19. On the efficacy of the judicial system see Parker 1990. On the limitations of the Supreme Court see Rosenberg 1991.

20. Whether I measured court ideology using Michael Bailey's or Andrew Martin and Kevin Quinn's estimates of the median ideological position of the Supreme Court, Lee Epstein et al.'s Judicial Common Space median scores, or the percentage of all active US Courts of Appeals judges nominated by Democratic presidents, court ideology was insignificant when added to all of the models in Table 8.3 (Bailey 2007; Martin and Quinn 2002, Epstein et al. 2007). It is also important to note that the inclusion of these different indicators of the politics of the Supreme Court and the US Courts of Appeals had no noticeable impact on the other relationships evident in Table 8.3.

21. Data on criminal victimization are less consistent and available over a shorter time period but analysis of the available data suggests a small and not quite significant drop in Black victimization rates under Democratic administrations. Black victimization rates did not, however, fall more quickly than White victimization rates under Democrats. This suggests that the diminished imprisonment of minorities relative to

Whites under Democrats is less about crime rates and more about criminal sentencing policies.

22. Even if I control for underlying trends in the criminal justice system in a multivariate model, I find (at least in the case of juvenile arrest rates) a significant connection between presidential partisanship and Black outcomes. All else equal, Black youth arrests increase (and increase relative to Whites) more under Republicans than they do under Democrats.

23. Of course, recent presidencies have seen more federal involvement in education. Measures like the No Child Left Behind Act or Obama's efforts on student loans and Trump initiatives on Charter schools suggest that federal influence over educational outcomes could be increasing. The federal government was also at least somewhat involved – if largely unsuccessfully – in the integration of schools after Brown v. The Board of Education in 1954 (Rosenberg 1991).

24. As was the case with Blacks, the gap in arrest rates between Asian Americans and Whites declines under Democrats and increases under Republicans. Moreover, these partisan divides are both statistically significant and substantial. For Asian Americans, adult arrest rates (per 1,000 residents) drop 3.3 percent under Democrats, and increase 1.0 percent under Republicans, on average. Long-term historic arrest data for Latinos are, unfortunately, not available.

25. Even though the magnitude of the partisan differences for Latinos is roughly on a par with those for Blacks on almost every indicator, only one of the ten cases in Table 8.4 – changes in the income of Latinos – passes a significance test (p<.05).

26. Alternate tests also reveal that the likelihood of Whites being arrested declined more under Democrats than under Republicans.

27. Blinder and Watson (2016) find that the accelerated economic growth under Democrats is in part due to factors beyond their control, including benign oil shocks and a more favorable international environment.

Where Will We Go from Here?

1. The fact that Obama's victory and presidency heightened the impact of racial views on policy preferences and the vote is now extraordinarily well documented (Ansolabehere and Stewart 2009, Highton 2011, Hutchings 2009, Jackman and Vavreck 2010, Kalmoe and Piston 2013, Kinder and Dale-Riddle 2011, Lewis-Beck et al. 2010, Pasek et al. 2009, Piston 2010, Ramakrishnan et al. 2009, Schaffner 2011, Tesler 2016a, Tesler and Sears 2010).

2. That Donald Trump's campaign and election further amplified the effect of racial attitudes and immigration-related views on the vote is also well documented (Sides 2017, Sides et al. 2017, Tesler 2016b, 2016d).

3. For example, see Altik et al. (2018). In prior elections, the focus was on Democrats who didn't vote for Obama.

4. Barack Obama, "Remarks by the President on Economic Mobility." December 4, 2013. obamawhitehouse.archives.gov/the-press-office/2013/12/04/remarks-president-economic-mobility. Accessed June 1, 2019.

5. As I have shown here and as others have also demonstrated (Cassese and Barnes 2018), it is also important to note that much of the gender gap is driven by other demographic factors, such as race.

6. Greater religiosity is not always associated with Republican Party support. Jews have remained steadfastly Democratic. And although the data are sparse, some evidence suggests that non-White Evangelicals are much more mixed in their partisan proclivities, and that Muslims are increasingly Democratic (Wong 2018).

7. It is likely not a coincidence that as race has increasingly sorted Americans into different partisan camps, hostility across those partisan lines has grown more severe (Haidt and Hetherington 2012, Iyengar et al. 2012, Mason 2018). With Whites largely on one partisan side and racial and ethnic minorities largely on the other, it is not surprising to find that Americans now tend to view fellow partisans as patriotic, well informed, and altruistic while perceiving members of the opposite party as unpatriotic, ignorant, and greedy (Iyengar et al. 2012). Today, Democrats and Republicans alike reveal a sharp desire to discriminate against each other (Iyengar and Westwood 2015).

8. In an eighteen-month period in 1995 and 1996, more than thirty Black churches were burned, leading Congress to pass the Church Arson Prevention Act.

9. Academic studies also demonstrate that the impact of racial prejudice on the presidential vote has been increasing significantly over time (Enders and Small 2016, Highton 2011, Jackman and Vavreck 2010, Kalmoe and Piston 2013, Tesler 2016a).

10. See maristpoll.marist.edu/wp-content/misc/usapolls/us170215/Complete%20Survey%20Findings_McClatchy_Marist%20Poll_Race%20Relations_March%202017.pdf

11. This does not mean that all barriers to voting are gone. In addition to felon disenfranchisement, the move to strict voter identification laws, the presence of a sometimes arduous registration process, and many other institutional features limit participation (Manza 2006, Hajnal et al. 2017).

12. Although not the subject of this book, researchers have identified a wide range of other institutional levers that could be employed to improve minority representation. These include universal voting, automatic registration, dropping strict voter identification laws, and shifting the timing of local elections (Fowler 2013, Hajnal 2018, Hajnal et al. 2017)

13. Important new work is emerging but more much needs to be done (e.g. Glaser and Ryan 2013, Hopkins et al. 2019).

14. Author's analysis of the 2016 ANES.

15. Fully 65 percent of White Democrats believe that it is at least "slightly likely" that Whites will be unable to find jobs because employers hire minorities (ANES 2016).

16. Findings on the Latino context are, however, less uniform than studies of the Black context. Some studies have found little connection between Latino or immigrant contexts and White vote views (Dixon 2006, Fennelly and Federico 2008, Scheve and Slaughter 2001, Tolbert and Hero 2001).

17. Another 2014 survey found that 41 percent of Asian Americans would consider switching their support from one candidate to another based on the candidates' stance on immigration (Ramakrishnan 2014).

18. Source: 1994 National Black Politics Study.

19. Even Hillary Clinton's provocative statement that "you could put *half* of Trump's supporters into what I call the basket of deplorables" (see www.nbcdfw.com/news/politics/Hillary-Clinton-Puts-Many-Trump-Backers-in-Basket-of-Deplorables–392985511.html?fb_comment_id=1537040606322023_1537367969622620) admits that half of Republicans are not racist or sexist or nativists (emphasis mine).

APPENDIX

Chapter 3

Table A3.1 Where and When Do Black Voters Lose?

	Losing vote for	
	Senate	Governor
STATE POLITICS		
Percent Democratic	−.03 (.01)**	−.04 (.01)**
Percent Republican	.17 (.01)**	−.02 (.01)
Mean Citizen Ideology	−.08 (.01)**	−.05 (.01)**
Voting Rights Act State	.64 (.13)**	1.1 (.23)**
STATE DEMOGRAPHICS		
Percent Black	.23 (.02)**	.07 (.02)**
Percent Black Squared	−56 (4.6)**	−33 (7.0)**
Percent with High School Education	.03 (.01)**	.13 (.02)**
STATE ELECTORAL INSTITUTIONS		
Felon Disenfranchisement Laws	.36 (.03)**	−.20 (.05)**
Registration Deadline	.02 (.01)**	−.03 (.01)**
Eligible Voter Turnout	2.8 (.74)**	−2.0 (1.1)**
ELECTION YEAR		
1994	2.7 (.19)**	1.2 (.16)**
1996	1.4 (.17)**	−1.7 (.37)**
1998	2.2 (.14)**	.30 (.11)*
2000	1.5 (.15)**	−2.4 (.49)**
2002	2.1 (.14)**	.46 (.10)**
2004	1.7 (.17)**	−.13 (.22)
INDIVIDUAL DEMOGRAPHICS		
Income	−.07 (.02)**	−.01 (.02)
Sex	−.06 (.05)	.14 (.07)*

Table A3.1 (cont.)

| | Losing vote for . . . .. | |
	Senate	Governor
Age	−.00 (.01)	−.02 (.02)
Catholic	−.06 (.11)	.21 (.16)
Protestant	−.10 (.08)	.11 (.10)
Jewish	.00 (.06)	−.06 (.08)
Atheist	.02 (.09)	.08 (.12)
Democrat	.06 (.07)	−.03 (.09)
Independent	−.24 (.12)**	−.64 (.16)**
Liberal	.14 (.07)	−.25 (.10)**
Moderate	.09 (.06)	−.21(.08)**
Constant	−14 (1.4)**	−7.3 (1.9)**
Chi Squared	2838**	744**
N	8964	4541

Logistic Regression ** $p < .01$ * $p < .05$
Source: Voter News Service Exit Polls, 1994–2006

Chapter 4

Table A4.1 The Determinants of Policy Responsiveness: Different Regression Models

	Demographics Only	With Political Controls	Controlling for Voting
Black	−0.21	−0.22	−0.22
	(0.01)***	(0.01)***	(0.01)***
Other Race	0.05	0.01	0.02
	(0.02)***	(0.02)	(0.02)
Income	0.11	0.11	0.11
	(0.03)***	(0.03)***	(0.03)***
Education	0.13	0.14	0.14
	(0.03)***	(0.04)***	(0.04)***
Sex	0.03	0.05	0.05
	(0.01)***	(0.01)***	(0.01)***
Age	0.05	−0.01	−0.02
	(0.02)**	(0.02)	(0.02)

Table A4.1 (cont.)

	Demographics Only	With Political Controls	Controlling for Voting
Unemployed	−0.02	−0.01	−0.01
	(0.02)	(0.02)	(0.02)
Married	−0.00	−0.00	−0.00
	(0.01)	(0.01)	(0.01)
Catholic	0.04	0.06	0.07
	(0.02)**	(0.02)***	(0.02)***
Jewish	0.02	0.04	0.05
	(0.03)	(0.04)	(0.04)
Protestant	0.04	0.06	0.06
	(0.02)**	(0.02)***	(0.02)***
No Religion	−0.01	−0.00	0.01
	(0.03)	(0.03)	(0.03)
Party ID		−0.09	−0.09
		(0.02)***	(0.02)***
Ideology		−0.00	−0.00
		(0.03)	(0.03)
Favor Spending Increase		−0.02	−0.02
		(0.01)***	(0.01)***
Member of Plurality		−0.62	−0.62
		(0.01)***	(0.01)***
Voted			0.01
			(0.01)
Constant	−0.19	0.25	0.24
	(0.03)***	(0.04)***	(0.04)***
N	457,808	399,535	395,215

* $p < 0.1$; ** $p < 0.05$; *** $p < 0.01$
Source: Voter News Service Exit Polls (1994–2006)

Chapter 6

Table A6.1 The Effect of Latino Context on State Spending

	Proportion of State Spending Going to:		
	Education	Corrections	Health
LATINO CONTEXT			
Percent Latino	−.65 (.23)**	.09 (.04)*	.10 (.07)
Percent Latino Squared	.02 (.005)**	−.002 (.001)*	−.002 (.001)
OTHER RACIAL CONTEXT			
Percent Black	.00 (.09)	.02 (.02)	.05 (.03)
Percent Asian	.87 (.51)	−.08 (.09)	−.72 (.16)**
POLITICAL			
Rep/Dem Ratio Legislature	−4.1 (3.3)	.10 (.54)	−.07 (.88)
Liberal Citizen Ideology	.08 (.06)	−.01 (.01)	−.01 (.02)
Professional Legislature	−18.5 (6.1)**	−2.6 (1.0)**	−.69 (1.66)
SOCIOECONOMIC STATUS			
Percent College Degree	.09 (.15)	.05 (.02)*	.11 (.04)**
Household Income	−.01 (.00)*	−.02 (.01)*	−.00 (.01)
Unemployment Rate	.26 (.13)	−.00 (.02)	.22 (.03)**
Total Population	.03 (.02)	.06 (.04)	.02 (.01)*
N	745	742	745
R squared	.06	.22	.14

Note: **p < .01; *p < .05
Source: Census of Government Finances and Census

Table A6.2 The Effect of Latino Context on State Taxation

	Percent of State Taxes Coming from:	
	Sales Taxes	Property Taxes
LATINO CONTEXT		
Percent Latino	.46 (.13)**	-.46 (.13)**
Percent Latino Squared	-.01 (.00)**	.01 (.00)*
OTHER RACIAL CONTEXT		
Percent Black	-.11 (.15)	-.09 (.06)
Percent Asian	-1.22 (.31)**	.43 (.31)
POLITICAL		
Republican/Democratic Ratio Legislature	-.03 (.01)*	.02 (.02)
Liberal Citizen Ideology	.03 (.02)	.11 (.02)**
Professional Legislature	-.07 (.03)**	.05 (.03)
SOCIOECONOMIC STATUS		
Percent College Degree	.07 (.06)	.28 (.08)**
Household Income	-.02 (.00)**	.03 (.03)
Unemployment Rate	.11 (.04)**	.09 (.07)
Total Population	.08 (.01)*	-.03 (.01)*
N	751	751
R squared	.08	.13

Note: **p < .01; *p < .05
Source: Census of Government Finances and Census

Chapter 7

Table A7.1 The Impact of Democratic Control on Policy Responsiveness

Partisan Control and Race Interacted	
Black* Dem President	0.17 (0.03)***
Black* Dem Congress	0.29 (0.03)***
Partisan Control	
Dem President	0.04 (0.01)***
Dem Congress	0.11 (0.01)***
Race	
Black	-0.37 (0.02)***
Other Race	0.04 (0.02)*
Class	
Income	0.07 (0.03)***
Education	0.20 (0.03)***

Table A7.1 (cont.)

Misc.	
Male	0.05 (0.01)***
Age	0.01 (0.02)
Unemployed	−0.02 (0.02)
Married	−0.00 (0.01)
Religion	
Catholic	0.06 (0.02)***
Jewish	0.04 (0.04)
Protestant	0.05 (0.02)**
No Religion	−0.01 (0.03)
Political Orientation	
Ideology	−0.01 (0.02)
Party ID	−0.11 (0.01)***
Majority	0.06 (0.00)***
Plurality	−0.62 (0.01)***
Constant	0.20 (0.04)***
N	381,606

$* \ p < 0.1$; $** \ p < 0.05$; $*** \ p < 0.01$

Source: General Social Survey (1972–2000), Historical Tables (US Govt Printing Office)

REFERENCES

Abrajano, Marisa, and Michael Alvarez. 2010. *New Faces, New Voices: The Hispanic Electorate in America*. Princeton, NJ: Princeton University Press.

Abrajano, Marisa, and Zoltan Hajnal. 2015. *White Backlash: Immigration, Race, and American Politics*. Princeton, NJ: Princeton University Press.

Abrajano, Marisa, R. Michael Alvarez, and Jonathan Nagler. 2008. "The Hispanic Vote in the 2004 Presidential Election: Insecurity and Moral Concerns." *The Journal of Politics* 70 (2):368–82.

Abramowitz, Alan I. 1994. "Issue Evolution Reconsidered: Racial Attitudes and Partisanship in the US Electorate." *American Journal of Political Science* 38 (1):1–24.

   2018. *The Great Alignment: Race, Party Transformation, and the Rise of Donald Trump*. New Haven, CT: Yale University Press.

Abramowitz, Alan I., and Kyle L. Saunders. 1998. "Ideological Realignment in the U.S. Electorate." *The Journal of Politics* 60 (3):634–52.

Abramowitz, Alan I., and Ruy Teixeira. 2009. "The Decline of the White Working Class and the Rise of a Mass Upper-Middle Class." *Political Science Quarterly* 124 (3):391–422.

Adams, Greg. 1997. "Abortion: Evidence of Issue Evolution." *American Journal of Political Science* 41:718–37.

Adorno, Theodore W., Else Frenkel-Brunswick, Daniel J. Levinson, and R. Nevitt Sanford. 1950. *The Authoritarian Personality*. New York, NY: Harper and Row.

Alba, Richard, and Victor Nee. 2005. *Remaking the American Mainstream: Assimilation and Contemporary Immigration*. Cambridge, MA: Harvard University Press.

Albritton, Robert B., George Amedee, Keenan Grenell, and Don-Terry Veal. 1996. "Deracialization and the New Black Politics." In *Race, Politics, and Governance in the United States*, ed. Huey L. Perry. Gainesville, FL: University of Florida Press.

Aldrich, John H. 1995. *Why Parties? The Origin and Transformation of Political Parties in America*. Chicago, IL: University of Chicago Press.

Alesina, Alberto, Reza Baqir, and William Easterly. 1999. "Public Goods and Ethnic Divisions." *The Quarterly Journal of Economics* 114 (4):1243–84.

Allport, G. W. 1954. *The Nature of Prejudice*. Menlo Park, CA: Addison-Wesley.

Almaguer, Tomas. 1994. *Racial Fault Lines: The Historical Origins of White Supremacy in California*. Berkeley, CA: University of California Press.

Altik, Jacob, Lonna Rae Atkeson, and Wendy Hansen. 2018. "Economic Voting and the 2016 Election." rubenson.org/wp-content/uploads/2018/09/Hansen-tpbw18.pdf. Accessed May 14, 2019.

Alvarez, R. Michael, and Lisa Garcia Bedolla. 2003. "The Foundations of Latino Voter Partisanship: Evidence from the 2000 Election." *The Journal of Politics* 65:31–49.

Ana, Otto Santa. 2003. *Brown Tide Rising: Metaphors of Latinos in Contemporary American Public Discourse*. Austin, TX: University of Texas Press.

Anbinder, Tyler. 1992. *Nativism and Slavery: The Northern Know Nothings and the Politics of the 1850s*. New York, NY: Oxford University Press.

Anderson, Carol. 2016. *White Rage: The Unspoken Truth of Our Racial Divide*. New York, NY: Bloomsbury.

Anderson, Christopher J., and Christine A. Guillory. 1997. "Political Institutions and Satisfaction with Democracy: A Cross National Analysis of Consensus and Majoritarian Systems." *American Political Science Review* 91 (1):66–81.

Anderson, Christopher J., and Andrew J. LoTempio. 2002. "Winning, Losing, and Political Trust in America." *British Journal of Political Science* 32:335–51.

ANES (American National Election Studies). 2016. Time Series Data Set. https://electionstudies.org/. Accessed July 16, 2019.

Ansolabehere, Stephen, and Charles Stewart III. 2009. "Amazing Race: How Post-Racial Was Obama's Victory?" *Boston Review*, January/February.

APALC. 1978–2014. "National Asian Pacific American Political Almanac."

APSA (American Political Science Association). 2004. "American Democracy in an Age of Rising Inequality." www.apsanet.org/portals/54/Files/Task%20Force%20Reports/taskforcereport.pdf. Accessed June 4, 2019.

Apuzzo, Matt, and John Eligon. 2015. "Ferguson Police Tainted by Bias, Justice Department Says." *New York Times*, March 4.

Archibold, Randal C. 2010. "Side by Side but Divided Over Immigration." *New York Times*, May 11.

Autor, David, David Dorn, Gordon Hanson, and Kaveh Majlesi. 2017. "Importing Political Polarization? The Electoral Consequences of Rising

Trade Exposure." National Bureau of Economic Research Working Paper no. 22637.

Ayers, John, C. Richard Hofstetter, and Bohdan Kolody. 2009. "Is Immigration a Racial Issue? Anglos' Attitudes on Immigration Policies in a Border County." *Social Science Quarterly* 90 (3):593–610.

Bacon, Perry. 2018. "Why Fights over Immigration Keep Shutting the Government Down." fivethirtyeight.com. fivethirtyeight.com/features/why-fights-over-immigration-keep-shutting-down-the-government/. Accessed May 28, 2019.

Bailey, Michael A. 2007. "Comparable Preference Estimates Across Time and Institutions for the Court, Congress and Presidency." *American Journal of Political Science* 51:433–48.

Ball, Krystal. 2017. "Democrats Have a Classism Problem." *The Hill*, November 2.

Barreto, Matt. 2007. "Si Se Puede! Latino Candidates and the Mobilization of Latino Voters." *American Political Science Review* 101:425–41.

———. 2011. *Ethnic Cues: The Role of Shared Ethnicity in Latino Political Participation*. Ann Arbor, MI: University of Michigan Press.

———. 2012. "Anti-Latino Stereotypes and the Media: Results of Two National Studies." National Hispanic Media Coalition, www.latinodecisions.com/blog/wp-content/uploads/2012/09/NHMC_webinar_slides.pdf. Accessed June 10, 2019.

Barreto, Matt, and Lauren Collingwood. 2015. "Group-Based Appeals and the Latino Vote in 2012: How Immigration Became a Mobilizing Issue." *Electoral Studies* 40:490–99.

Barreto, Matt, and Gary Segura. 2014. *Latino America: How America's Most Dynamic Population Is Poised to Transform the Politics of the Nation*. New York, NY: Public Affairs.

Barreto, Matt, Sylvia Manzano, Ricardo Ramírez, and Kathy Rim. 2009. "Mobilization, Participation, and Solidaridad: Latino Participation in the 2006 Immigration Protest Rallies." *Urban Affairs Review* 44:736–64.

Bartels, Larry M. 1991. "Instrumental and 'Quasi-Instrumental' Variables." *American Journal of Political Science* 35:777–800.

———. 1996. "Uninformed Votes: Information Effects in Presidential Elections." *American Journal of Political Science* 40 (1):194–230.

———. 2002. "Beyond the Running Tally: Partisan Bias in Political Perceptions." *Political Behavior* 24 (2):117–50.

———. 2008. *Unequal Democracy: The Political Economy of the New Gilded Age*. Princeton, NJ: Princeton University Press.

———. 2014. "Rich People Rule!" *Washington Post*, April 8.

Baumgartner, Frank R., Jeffrey M. Berry, Marie Hojnacki, David C. Kimball, and Beth L. Leech. 2009. *Lobbying and Policy Change: Who Wins, Who Loses, and Why*. Chicago, IL: University of Chicago Press.

Bean, Frank D., and Gillian Stevens. 2003. *America's Newcomers and the Dynamics of Diversity*. New York, NY: Russell Sage.

Bedolla, Lisa Garcia. 2009. *Latino Politics*. Cambridge, UK: Polity.

Beinart, Peter. 2016. "The Republican Party's White Strategy." *The Atlantic*, July. www.theatlantic.com/magazine/archive/2016/07/the-white-strategy /485612/. Accessed May 29, 2019.

Beland, Louis-Philippe. 2015. "Political Parties and Labor-Market Outcomes: Evidence from US States." *American Economic Journal: Applied Economics* 7:198–220.

Beland, Louis-Philippe, and Bulent Unel. 2018. "Governors' Party Affiliation and Unions." *Industrial Relations* 57 (2):177–95.

Benedictis-Kessner, Justin de, and Christopher Warshaw. 2016. "Mayoral Partisanship and Municipal Fiscal Policy." *The Journal of Politics* 78:1124–38.

Benoit, Kenneth, and Kenneth A. Shepsle. 1995. "Electoral Systems and Minority Representation." In *Classifying by Race*, ed. Paul E. Peterson. Princeton, NJ: Princeton University Press.

Berman, Mark and Wesley Lowery. 2015. "The 12 Key Highlights from the DOJ's Scathing Ferguson Report." *Washington Post*, March 4.

Bertrand, Marianne, and Sendhil Mullainathan. 2004. "Are Emily and Greg More Employable Than Lakisha and Jamal?" *American Economic Review* 94 (4):991–1013.

Bigg, Matthew. 2008. "Election of Obama Provokes Rise in US Hate Crime." Reuters, November 24. www.reuters.com/article/us-usa-obama-hatecrimes-idUSTRE4AN81U20081124. Accessed May 15, 2019.

Black, Earl, and Merle Black. 1973. "The Wallace Vote in Alabama: A Multiple Regression Analysis." *The Journal of Politics* 35:730–36.

  1987. *Politics and Society in the South*. Cambridge, MA: Harvard University Press.

  2002. *The Rise of Southern Republicans*. New York, NY: Belknap.

Blais, André. 2006. "What Affects Voter Turnout?" *Annual Review of Political Science* 9:111–25.

Blalock, Hubert M. 1967. *Toward a Theory of Minority-Group Relations*. New York, NY: Wiley.

Blau, Francine and Lawrence Kahn. 2017. "The Gender Wage Gap: Extent, Trends, and Explanations." *Journal of Economic Literature* 55 (3):789–865.

Blinder, Alan, and Mark Watson. 2016. "Presidents and the US Economy: An Econometric Exploration." *American Economic Review* 106:1015–45.

Blodget, Henry. 2013. "The Average CEO Earns More in an Hour Than Their Employee Earns in a Month." *Business Insider*, April 10.

Bobo, Lawrence. 1983. "Whites' Opposition to Busing: Symbolic Racism or Realistic Group Conflict." *Journal of Personality and Social Psychology* 45 (6):1196–210.

2001. "Racial Attitudes and Relations at the Close of the Twentieth Century." In *America Becoming: Racial Trends and Their Consequences*, eds. Neil Smelser, William Julius Wilson and Faith Mitchell. Washington, DC: National Academy Press. 21–39.

Bobo, Lawrence, and Franklin D. Gilliam. 1990. "Race, Sociopolitical Participation, and Black Empowerment." *American Political Science Review* 84:377–93.

Bobo, Lawrence, and Vincent Hutchings. 1996. "Perceptions of Racial Group Competition: Extending Blumer's Theory of Group Position to a Multiracial Social Context." *American Sociological Review* 61: 951–71.

Bobo, Lawrence, and Devon Johnson. 2000. "Racial Attitudes in a Prismatic Metropolis: Mapping Identity, Stereotypes, Competition, and Views on Affirmative Action." In *Prismatic Metropolis: Inequality in Los Angeles*, eds. Lawrence Bobo, Melvin Oliver, James Johnson and Abel Valenzuela. New York, NY: Russell Sage Foundation.

Bobo, Lawrence, Melvin Oliver, James Johnson, and Abel Valenzuela, eds. 2000. *Prismatic Metropolis: Inequality in Los Angeles*. New York, NY: Russell Sage Foundation.

Borjas, George J. 2001. *Heaven's Door: Immigration Policy and the American Economy*. Princeton, NJ: Princeton University Press.

Borosage, Robert. 2016. "Inequality is Still the Defining Issue of Our Time." *The Nation*, October 12.

Bouie, Jamelle. 2016. "It Lost Black Voters. Now it's Losing Latinos. What's Left is a Broken, White GOP." *Slate*, November.

Bowler, Shaun, and Todd Donovan. 2006. "Reasoning About Institutional Change: Winners, Losers, and Support for Electoral Reforms." *British Journal of Political Science* 37:455–76.

Bowler, Shaun, and Gary Segura. 2011. *The Future Is Ours: Minority Politics, Political Behavior, and the Multiracial Era of American Politics*. Washington, DC: CQ Press.

Bowler, Shaun, Todd Donovan, and David Brockington. 2003. *Electoral Reform and Minority Representation: Local Experments with Alternative Elections*. Columbus, OH: Ohio State University Press.

2009. *Beyond Representation: Local Experimentation with Alternative Electoral Systems*. Columbus, OH: Ohio State University Press.

Bowler, Shaun, Stephen P. Nicholson, and Gary M. Segura. 2006. "Earthquakes and Aftershocks: Tracking the Macropartisan Implications of California's Recent Political Environment." *American Journal of Political Science* 50 (1):146–59.

Brader, Ted, Nicholas Valentino, and Elizabeth Suhay. 2008. "What Triggers Public Opposition to Immigration? Anxiety, Group Cues, and Immigration Threat." *American Journal of Political Science* 52 (4):959–78.

Brewer, M. D., and J. M. Stonecash. 2001. "Class, Race Issues, and Declining White Support for the Democratic Party in the South." *Political Behavior* 23 (2):131–55.

Brown-Dean, Khalilah, Zoltan Hajnal, Christina Rivers, and Ismail White. 2015. "50 Years of the Voting Rights Act: The State of Race in Politics." Joint Center for Political and Economic Studies. jointcenter.org/sites/default/files/VRA%20report%2C%203.5.15%20%281130%20am%29%28updated%29.pdf. Accessed June 4, 2019.

Browning, Rufus R., Dale Rogers Marshall, and David H. Tabb. 1984. *Protest Is Not Enough*. Berkeley, CA: University of California Press.

Brunner, Eric, Stephen Ross, and Ebonya Washington. 2013. "Does Less Income Mean Less Representation?" *American Economic Journal: Economic Policy* 5:53–76.

Bullock, Charles S., and Richard E. Dunn. 1999. "The Demise of Racial Districting and the Future of Black Representation." *Emory Law Journal* 48:1209–53.

Bureau of Justice. 2019. "Prisoners in 2017." www.bjs.gov/content/pub/pdf/p17.pdf. Accessed June 5, 2019.

Burns, Peter, and James G. Gimpel. 2000. "Economic Insecurity, Prejudicial Stereotypes, and Public Opinion on Immigration Policy." *Political Science Quarterly* 115 (2):201–25.

Butler, Daniel M., and David E. Broockman. 2011. "Do Politicians Racially Discriminate against Constituents? A Field Experiment on State Legislators." *American Journal of Political Science* 55 (3):463–77.

Button, James. 1993. "Racial Cleavage in Local Voting: The Case of School and Tax Issue Referendums." *Journal of Black Studies* 24 (1):29–41.

California Budget Project. 2011. "Steady Climb: State Corrections Spending in California."

California Immigrant Policy Center. 2015. "Immigrant Health Advocates Applaud Efforts to Expand Healthcare for Undocumented and Uninsured Californians." caimmigrant.org/press-room/immigrant-health-advocates-applaud-efforts-to-expand-healthcare-for-undocumented-and-uninsured-californians/. Accessed June 5, 2019.

Cameron, Charles. 2000. *Veto Bargaining: Presidents and the Politics of Negative Power*. Cambridge, UK: Cambridge University Press.

Cameron, Charles, David Epstein and Sharyn Halloran. 1996. "Do Majority-Minority Districts Maximize Substantive Black Representation in Congress?" *American Political Science Review* 90:794–812.

Campbell, Andrea, Cara Wong, and Jack Citrin. 2006. "'Racial Threat', Partisan Climate, and Direct Democracy: Contextual Effects in Three California Initiatives." *Political Behavior* 28:129–50.

Campbell, Angus, Philip E. Converse, Warren E. Miller, and Donald E. Stokes. 1960. *The American Voter*. Chicago, IL: University of Chicago Press.

Carmines, Edward G., and James A. Stimson. 1989. *Issue Evolution: Race and the Transformation of American Politics*. Princeton, NJ: Princeton University Press.

Carnes, Nicholas. 2013. *White-Collar Government: The Hidden Role of Class in Economic Policy Making*. Chicago, IL: University of Chicago Press.

2015. "Does the Descriptive Representation of the Working Class Crowd out Women and Minorities?" *Politics, Groups, and Identities* 3:350–65.

2017. "Adam Smith Would Be Spinning in His Grave." *The Form* 15:151–65.

Carsey, Thomas M., and Geoffrey C. Layman. 2006. "Changing Sides or Changing Minds? Party Identification and Policy Preferences in the American Electorate." *American Journal of Political Science* 50 (2):464–77.

Casellas, Jason P. 2007. "Latino Representation in Congress." In *Latino Politics: Identity, Mobilization, and Representation*, eds. Rodolfo Espino, David L. Leal and Kenneth J. Meier. Charlottesville, VA: University of Virginia Press.

Casselman, Ben. 2017. "Stop Saying Trump's Win Had Nothing to Do with Economics." fivethirtyeight.com, January 9. fivethirtyeight.com/features/stop-saying-trumps-win-had-nothing-to-do-with-economics/. Accessed May 14, 2019.

Cassese, Erin C., and Tiffany D. Barnes. 2018. "Reconciling Sexism and Women's Support for Republican Candidates: A Look at Gender, Class, and Whiteness in the 2012 and 2016 Presidential Races." *Political Behavior*: 1–24.

Caughey, Devin, and Christopher Warshaw. 2017. "Policy Preferences and Policy Change: Dynamic Responsiveness in the American States, 1936–2014." *American Political Science Review* 112:249–66.

Center for American Women in Politics. 2000–19. "Women in Elective Office." Center for American Women in Politics, cawp.rutgers.edu/facts/levels_of_office. Accessed May 29, 2019.

Chalabi, Mona. 2018. "The Key Midterms Voter Trends: High Turnout and Youth Surge for Democrats." *The Guardian*, November 7.

Chavez, Leo. 2008. *The Latino Threat: Constructing Immigrants, Citizens, and the Nation*. Palo Alto, CA: Stanford University Press.

Chen, Michelle. 2017. "Donald Trump's Rise Has Coincided with an Explosion of Hate Groups." *The Nation*, March 24.

Chetty, Raj, David Grusky, Maximilian Hell, Nathaniel Hendren, Robert Manduca, and Jimmy Narang. 2017. "The Fading American Dream: Trends in Absolute Income Mobility since 1940." *Science* 356:398–406.

Citrin, Jack, and Jonathan Sides. 2008. "Immigration and the Imagined Community in Europe and the United States." *Political Studies* 56:33–65.

Citrin, Jack, Donald P. Green, Christopher Muste, and Cara Wong. 1997. "Public Opinion Toward Immigration Reform: The Role of Economic Motivations." *The Journal of Politics* 59 (3):858–81.

Citrin, Jack, Beth Reingold, and Evelyn Walters. 1990. "The 'Official English' Movement and the Symbolic Politics of Language in the United States." *Western Political Quarterly* 43:553–60.

Citrin, Jack, Donald P. Green, Christopher Muste, and Cara Wong. 1997. "Public Opinion toward Immigration Reform: The Role of Economic Motivations." *The Journal of Politics* 59 (3):858–81.

Citrin, Jack, Amy Lerman, Michael Murakami, and Kathryn Pearson. 2007. "Testing Huntington's Who Are We? Empirical Evidence Regarding the Linguistic and Political Assimilation of the New Immigrants." *Perspectives on Politics* 5:31–48.

Cleveland Plain Dealer. 2008. "America Begins its Journey into a Post-Racial Era." *Cleveland Plain Dealer*, November 5.

CNN. 2018. "National Exit Polls." www.cnn.com/election/2018/exit-polls. Accessed May 28, 2019.

Cohen-Marks, Mara, Stephen A. Nuno, and Gabriel R. Sanchez. 2012. "Look Back in Anger? Voter Opinions of Mexican Immigrants in the Aftermath of the 2006 Immigration Demonstrations." *Urban Affairs Review* 44 (5):695–717.

Cohn, Nate. 2016. "Why Trump Won: Working-Class Whites." *New York Times*, November 9.

2017. "A 2016 Review: Turnout Wasn't the Driver of Clinton's Defeat." *New York Times*, March 28.

Colleau, Sophie M., Kevin Glynn, Steven Lybrand, Richard M. Merelman, Paula Mohan, and James E. Wall. 1990. "Symbolic Racism in Candidate Evaluation: An Experiment." *Political Behavior* 12 (4):385–402.

Collet, Christian. 2005. "Bloc Voting, Polarization and the Panethnic Hypothesis: The Case of Little Saigon." *The Journal of Politics* 67:907–33.

Collingwood, Loren, Tyler Reny, and Ali Valenzuela. 2017. "Flipping for Trump: Immigration, Not Economics, Explains Shifts in White Working Class Votes." Semanticscholar.org.pdfs.semanticscholar.org/091e/4256c8cefc f54af4a47f474de8bc34c2a438.pdf?_ga=2.161009021.178760401 .1559644384-1665753000.1559122099. Accessed May 29, 2019.

Converse, Philip E. 1964. "The Nature of Belief Systems in Mass Publics." In *Ideology and Discontent*, ed. David E. Apter. New York, NY: Free Press.

Corzine, Jay, James Creech, and Lin Corzine. 1983. "Black Concentration and Lynchings in the South: Testing Blalock's Power-Threat Hypothesis." *Social Forces* 61:774–96.

Cox, Gary W., and Mathew D. McCubbins. 1993. *Legislative Leviathan: Party Government in the House*. Berkeley, CA: University of California Press.

2004. *Setting the Agenda: Responsible Party Government in the US House of Representatives*. Cambridge, UK: Cambridge University Press.

Craig, Maureen A., and Jennifer A. Richeson. 2014. "On the Precipice of a 'Majority-Minority' America: Perceived Status Threat from the Racial Demographic Shift Affects White Americans' Political Ideology." *Psychological Science* 25 (6):1189–97.

Craig, Stephen C., Michael D. Martinez, Jason Gainous, and James G. Kane. 2006. "Winners, Losers, and Election Context: Voter Responses to the 2000 Presidential Election." *Political Research Quarterly* 59:579–92.

Cramer, Katherine. 2016. *The Politics of Resentment: Rural Consciousness in Wisconsin and the Rise of Scott Walker*. Chicago, IL: University of Chicago Press.

Dade, Corey. 2011. "New Poll Suggests Latino Voters See 'Hostile' GOP." NPR, December 11. www.npr.org/blogs/itsallpolitics/2011/12/12/143601214/new-poll-suggests-latino-voters-see-hostile-gop. Accessed June 5, 2019.

Dahl, Robert A. 1961. *Who Governs? Democracy and Power in the American City*. New Haven, CT: Yale University Press.

Daniels, Roger. 2004. *Guarding the Golden Door: American Immigration Policy and Immigrants Since 1882*. New York, NY: Hill and Wang.

Dann, Carrie. 2017. "NBC/WSJ Poll: Americans Pessimistic on Race Relations." NBC News, September 21. www.nbcnews.com/politics/first-read/nbc-wsj-poll-americans-pessimistic-race-relations-n803446. Accessed June 10, 2019.

Davenport, Lauren. 2018. *Politics Beyond Black and White: Biracial Identity and Attitudes in America*. New York, NY: Cambridge University Press.

Davidson, Chandler. 1999. *Minority Vote Dilution*. Washington, DC: Howard University Press.

Davidson, Chandler, and Bernard Grofman. 1994. "The Voting Rights Act and the Second Reconstruction." In *Quiet Revolution in the South: The Impact of the Voting Rights Act, 1965–1990*, eds. Chandler Davidson and Bernard Grofman. Princeton, NJ: Princeton University Press. 378–87.

Dawson, Michael C. 1994. *Behind the Mule: Race and Class in African-American Politics*. Princeton, NJ: Princeton University Press.

2011. *Not in Our Lifetimes: The Future of Black Politics*. Chicago, IL: University of Chicago Press.

DeBonis, Mike, and Damian Paletta. 2017. "House Passes GOP Tax Bill, Upping Pressure on Struggling Senate Effort." *Washington Post*, November 16.

Delli Carpini, Michael X., and Scott Keeter. 1996. *What Americans Know About Politics and Why It Matters*. New Haven, CT: Yale University Press.

Desmond-Harris, Jenée. 2016. "Why Donald Trump Says 'the' before 'African Americans' and 'Latinos.'" Vox. October 20. www.vox.com/2016/10/20/

13342646/donald-trump-african-americans-latinos-race-racism-inner-city. Accessed June 5, 2019.

Dixon, Jeffrey. 2006. "The Ties That Bind and Those That Don't: Toward Reconciling Group Threat and Contact Theories of Prejudice." *Social Forces* 84 (4):2179–204.

Dixon, Jeffrey C., and Michael S. Rosenbaum. 2004. "Nice to Know You? Testing Contact, Cultural, and Group Threat Theories of Anti-Black and Anti-Hispanic Stereotypes." *Social Science Quarterly* 85:257–80.

Doherty, Caroll. 2006. "Attitudes Toward Immigration: In Black and White." Pew Research Center, April 25. www.pewresearch.org/2006/04/25/ attitudes-toward-immigration-in-black-and-white/. Accessed June 4, 2019.

Donahue, John J., and James Heckman. 1990. "Continuous Versus Episodic Change: The Impact of Civil Rights Policy on the Economic Status of Blacks." *Journal of Economic Literature* 29 (4):1603–43.

Donovan, Todd. 2010. "Obama and the White Vote." *Political Research Quarterly* 63:863–74.

Donze, Frank. 1998. "Dutch Morial's Historic 1978 Victory Recalled." *Times-Picayune*, May 3. A14.

Druckman, James N., and Lawrence R. Jacobs. 2011. "Segmented Representation: The Reagan White House and Disproportionate Responsiveness." In *Who Gets Represented?*, eds. Peter K. Enns and Christopher Wlezien. New York, NY: Russell Sage. 166–88.

Drutman, Lee. 2016. "How Race and Identity Became the Central Dividing Line in American Politics." Vox, August 30. www.vox.com/polyarchy/2016/8/ 30/12697920/race-dividing-american-politics. Accessed June 4, 2019.

Du Bois, W. E. B. 1949. *The Souls of Black Folk*. New York, NY: Bantam Books.

Dustmann, C., and I. Preston. 2001. "Attitudes to Ethnic Minorities, Ethnic Context, and Location Decisions." *Economic Journal* 111:353–73.

Dyck, Joshua J., Gregg B. Johnson, and Jesse T. Wasson. 2012. "A Blue Tide in the Golden State Ballot Propositions, Population Change, and Party Identification in California." *American Politics Research* 40:450–75.

Dye, Thomas R. 1984. "Party and Policy in the States." *The Journal of Politics* 46:1067–116.

Edelman, Benjamin, Michael Luca, and Dan Svirsky. 2017. "Racial Discrimination in the Sharing Economy: Evidence for a Field Experiment." *American Economic Journal: Applied Economics* 9 (2):1–22.

Edsall, Thomas B. 2013. "How Much Does Race Still Matter?" *New York Times*, February 27.

2016. "The Great Trump Reshuffle." *New York Times*, May 4.

2018. "The Democrats' Gentrification Problem." *New York Times*, April 19.

Edsall, Thomas B., and Mary D. Edsall. 1991. *Chain Reaction: The Impact of Race, Rights, and Taxes on American Politics*. New York, NY: W. W. Norton and Company.

Edwards, George C. 2003. *On Deaf Ears: The Limits of the Bully Pulpit*. New Haven, CT: Yale University Press.

Eisinger, Peter K. 1980. *Politics and Displacement: Racial and Ethnic Transition in Three American Cities*. Institute for Research on Poverty Monograph Series. New York, London, Toronto, Sydney, San Francisco: Academic Press.

   1982. "Black Employment in Municipal Jobs: The Impact of Black Political Power." *American Political Science Review* 76 (2):380–92.

Ellis, Christopher. 2012. "Understanding Economic Biases in Representation: Income, Resources, and Policy Representation in the 110th House." *Political Research Quarterly* 65:938–51.

   2013. "Social Context and Economic Biases in Representation." *The Journal of Politics* 75 (3):773–86.

Enders, Adam, and Steven Small. 2016. "Racial Prejudice Not Populism or Authoritarianism Predicts Support for Trump over Clinton." *Washington Post*, May 26.

Enos, Ryan D. 2010. "Are Illegal Immigrants Everywhere? Will It Change Your Vote?" YouGov.com, November 1. today.yougov.com/topics/politics/articles-reports/2010/11/01/illegal-immigration-might-be-election-issue. Accessed June 4, 2019.

Epstein, Lee, Thomas G. Walker, Nancy Staudt, Scott A. Hendrickson, and Jason M. Roberts. 2007. "The U.S. Supreme Court Justices Database." *Law and Courts* Spring:14–15.

Erikson, Robert S., Michael B. Mackuen, and James A. Stimson. 2002. *The Macro Polity*. New York, NY: Cambridge University Press.

Erikson, Robert S., Gerald C. Wright, and John P. McIver. 1993. *Statehouse Democracy: Public Opinion and Policy in the American States*. Cambridge, UK: Cambridge University Press.

Evans, Geoffrey. 1999. *The End of Class Politics? Class Voting in Comparative Context*. New York, NY: Oxford University Press.

FBI. 2018. "Uniform Crime Reports: Hate Crime Statistics." ucr.fbi.gov/hate-crime/2017. Accessed June 1, 2019.

Feliz, Wendy. 2015. "California Leads the Transition in Pro-Immigrant State Lawmaking." Immigrationimpact.com, May 18. immigrationimpact.com/2015/05/18/california-leads-the-transition-in-pro-immigrant-state-lawmaking/. Accessed May 29, 2019.

Fellowes, Matthew C., and Gretchen Rowe. 2004. "Politics and the New American Welfare States." *American Journal of Political Science* 48:362–73.

Fennelly, Katherine, and Christopher Federico. 2008. "Rural Residence as a Determinant of Attitudes Toward US Immigration Policy." *International Migration* 46:151–90.

Ferreira, Fernando, and Joseph Gyourko. 2009. "Do Political Parties Matter? Evidence from U.S. Cities." *The Quarterly Journal of Economics* 124:399–422.

Fetzer, J. 2000. *Public Attitudes Toward Immigration in the United States, France, and Germany.* Cambridge, UK: Cambridge University Press.

Fiorina, Morris P. 1981. *Retrospective Voting in American National Elections.* New Haven, CT: Yale University Press.

Flagg, Anna. 2018. "The Myth of the Criminal Immigrant." *New York Times,* March 30.

Flavin, Patrick. 2012. "Income Inequality and Policy Representation in the American States." *Public Opinion Quarterly* 40:29–59.

Foer, Franklin. 2017. "What's Wrong with the Democrats?" *The Atlantic,* July/August. www.theatlantic.com/magazine/archive/2017/07/whats-wrong-with-the-democrats/528696/. Accessed May 15, 2019.

Foner, Eric. 1984. *Reconstruction: America's Unfinished Revolution, 1863–1877.* New York, NY: Harper and Row.

Fowler, Anthony. 2013. "Electoral and Policy Consequences of Voter Turnout: Evidence from Compulsory Voting in Australia." *Quarterly Journal of Political Science* 8:159–82.

Fox, Cybelle. 2004. "The Changing Color of Welfare? How White's Attitudes Toward Latinos Influence Support for Welfare." *American Journal of Sociology* 110 (3):580–625.

   2012. *Three Worlds of Relief: Race, Immigration, and the American Welfare State from the Progressive Era to the New Deal.* Princeton, NJ: Princeton University Press.

Fraga, Bernard. 2016. "Candidates or Districts? Reevaluating the Role of Race in Voter Turnout." *American Journal of Political Science* 60:97–122.

Fraga, Luis R. 1992. "Latino Political Incorporation and the Voting Rights Act." In *Controversies in Minority Voting: The Voting Rights Act in Perspective,* eds. Bernard Grofman and Chandler Davidson. Washington, DC: The Brookings Institution. 278–83.

Fraga, Luis R., John Garcia, Rodney Hero, Michael Jones-Correa, Valerie Martinez-Ebers, and Gary Segura. 2012. *Latinos in the New Millennium: An Almanac of Opinion, Behavior, and Policy Preferences.* Cambridge, UK: Cambridge University Press.

Fraga, Luis Ricardo, Kenneth J. Meier, and Robert E. England. 1997. "Hispanic Americans and Educational Policy: Limits to Equal Access." In *Pursuing Power: Latinos and the Political System,* ed. F. Chris Garcia. Notre Dame, IN: University of Notre Dame Press.

Frank, Thomas. 2004. *What's the Matter with Kansas? How Conservatives Won the Heart of America*. New York, NY: Metropolitan Book.

Frisby, Michael K. 1991. "The New Black Politician." *Boston Globe*, July 14. 14.

Frymer, Paul. 1999. *Uneasy Alliances: Race and Party Competition in America*. Princeton, NJ: Princeton University Press.

Gallup. 2015. "In US, Socialist Presidential Candidates Least Appealing." www.gallup.com/poll/183713/socialist-presidential-candidates-least-appealing.aspx. Accessed May 20, 2019.

2019a. "In Depth: Race Relations." news.gallup.com/poll/1687/race-relations.aspx. Accessed May 28, 2019.

2019b. "In Depth: Immigration." news.gallup.com/poll/1660/immigration.aspx. Accessed May 28, 2019.

Gamio, Lazario. 2016. "Urban and Rural America Are Becoming Increasingly Polarized." *Washington Post*, November 16.

Garand, James C. 1988. "Explaining Government Growth in the U.S. States." *American Political Science Review* 82:837–49.

Garza, Rodolfo O. de la, Angelo Falcon, and F. Chris Garcia. 1996. "Will the Real Americans Please Stand Up: Anglo and Mexican American Support for Core American Political Values." *American Journal of Political Science* 40:335–51.

Gay, Claudine. 2001. "The Effect of Black Congressional Representation on Political Participation." *The American Political Science Review* 95:603–18.

2002. "Spirals of Trust? The Effect of Descriptive Representation on the Relationship between Citizens and Their Government." *American Journal of Political Science* 46:717–32.

Gelman, Andrew. 2009. *Red State, Blue State, Rich State, Poor State: Why Americans Vote the Way They Do*. Princeton, NJ: Princeton University Press.

Gerber, Elisabeth R., and Daniel Hopkins. 2011. "When Mayors Matter: Estimating the Impact of Mayoral Partisanship on City Policy." *American Journal of Political Science* 55 (2):326–39.

Gest, Justin. 2016. *The New Minority: White Working Class Politics in an Age of Immigration and Inequality*. New York, NY: Oxford University Press.

Giedo, Jansen, Geoffrey Evans, and Nan Dirk de Graaf. 2013. "Class Voting and Left-Right Party Positions: A Comparative Study of 15 Western Democracies." *Social Science Research* 42:376–400.

Gilens, Martin. 1999. *Why Americans Hate Welfare: Race, Media, and the Politics of Antipoverty Policy*. Chicago, IL: University of Chicago Press.

2012. *Affluence & Influence: Economic Inequality and Political Power in America*. Princeton, NJ: Princeton University Press.

Gilens, Martin, and Benjamin I. Page. 2014. "Testing Theories of American Politics: Elites, Interest Groups, and Average Citizens." *Perspectives on Politics* 12 (3):564–81.

Giles, Michael W., and Arthur Evans. 1986. "The Power Approach to Inter-group Hostility." *Journal of Conflict Resolution* 30:469–86.

Giles, Michael W., and Kaenan Hertz. 1994. "Racial Threat and Partisan Identification." *American Political Science Review* 88:317–26.

Gimpel, James G. 2017. "Immigration Policy Opinion and the 2016 Presidential Vote: Issue Relevance in the Trump–Clinton Election." Center for Immigration Studies, December 4. cis.org/Report/Immigration-Policy-Opinion-and-2016-Presidential-Vote. Accessed June 4, 2019.

Gimpel, James G., and Peter Skerry. 1999. "Immigration, Ethnic Competition, and Crime." Paper presented at the American Political Science Association Annual Meeting, Atlanta.

Glaser, James M. 1996. *Race, Campaign Politics, and Realignment in the South*. New Haven, CT: Yale University Press.

Glaser, James M., and Timothy J. Ryan. 2013. *Changing Minds, If Not Hearts: Political Remedies for Racial Conflict*. Philadelphia, PA: University of Pennsylvania Press.

Goren, Paul. 2005. "Party Identification and Core Political Values." *American Journal of Political Science* 49 (4):882–97.

Goren, Paul, and Christopher Chapp. 2017. "Moral Power: How Public Opinion on Culture War Issues Shapes Partisan Predisposition." *American Political Science Review* 111 (1):110–28.

Gottschalk, Marie. 2015. *Caught: The Prison State and the Lockdown of American Politics*. Princeton, NJ: Princeton University Press.

Green, Donald Philip, and Bradley Palmquist. 1990. "Of Artifacts and Partisan Instability." *American Journal of Political Science* 34 (3):872–902.

Green, Donald Philip, Bradley Palmquist, Eric Schickler, and Giordano Bruno. 2002. *Partisan Hearts and Minds: Political Parties and the Social Identity of Voters*. New Haven, CT: Yale University Press.

Greenberg, Michael. 2012. "What Future for Occupy Wall Street?" *New York Review of Books*, February 9.

Greenberg, Stanley. 2017. "The Democrats' 'Working Class Problem.'" *American Prospect*, June 1. prospect.org/article/democrats'-'working-class-problem'. Accessed May 28, 2019.

2018. "Macomb and America's New Political Moment." *Democracy Corps*, May 7, 2018. static1.squarespace.com/static/582e1a36e58c62cc076cdc81/t/5af05743f950b7ef0550767f/1525700420093/Macomb+%26+America%27s+New+Political+Moment_Democracy+Corps_May+2018.pdf. Accessed May 15, 2019.

Griffin, John D., and Brian Newman. 2007. "The Unequal Representation of Latinos and Whites." *The Journal of Politics* 69:1032–46.

2008. *Minority Report: Evaluating Political Equality in America.* Chicago, IL: University of Chicago Press.

Griffin, Robert, and Ruy Teixeira. 2017. "The Story of Trump's Appeal: A Portrait of Trump's Voters." Voter Study Group, June 2017. www.voterstudygroup .org/publication/story-of-trumps-appeal. Accessed May 14, 2019.

Grofman, Bernard, and Chandler Davidson, eds. 1992. *Controversies in Minority Voting: The Voting Rights Act in Perspective.* Washington, DC: The Brookings Institution.

Grofman, Bernard, and Chandler Davidson. 1994. "The Effect of Municipal Election Structure on Black Representation in Eight Southern States." In *Quiet Revolution in the South: The Impact of the Voting Rights Act, 1965–1990,* eds. Chandler Davidson and Bernard Grofman. Princeton, NJ: Princeton University Press. 302–28.

Gronke, Paul, Eva Galanes-Rosenbaum, and Peter A. Miller. 2007. "Early Voting and Turnout." *PS: Political Science & Politics* 40:639–45.

Grose, Christian R. 2011. *Congress in Black and White: Race and Representation in Washington and at Home.* New York, NY: Cambridge University Press.

Guinier, Lani. 1994. *The Tyranny of the Majority: Fundamental Fairness in Representative Democracy.* New York, NY: The Free Press.

Gulasekaram, Pratheepan, and S. Karthick Ramakrishnan. 2015. *The New Immigration Federalism.* New York, NY: Cambridge University Press.

Ha, Shang E., and J. Eric Oliver. 2010. "The Consequences of Multiracial Contexts on Public Attitudes Toward Immigration." *Political Research Quarterly* 63 (1):29–42.

Haberman, Maggie. 2014. "Ad Hits Shaheen on Immigration." Politico, July 28. www.politico.com/story/2014/07/new-hampshire-scott-brown-jeanne-shaheen-immigration-2014-elections-109428. Accessed May 28, 2019.

Hacker, Jacob S., and Paul Pierson. 2011. *Winner-Take-All Politics: How Washington Made the Rich Richer – and Turned Its Back on the Middle Class.* New York, NY: Simon and Schuster.

Haidt, Jonathan, and Marc Hetherington. 2012. "Look How Far We've Come Apart." *New York Times,* September 17.

Hainmueller, Jens and Michael J. Hiscox. 2010. "Attitudes Towards Highly Skilled and Low Skilled Immigration: Evidence from a Survey Experiment." *American Political Science Review* 101:61–84.

Hainmueller, Jens, and Daniel Hopkins. 2014. "Public Attitudes Toward Immigration." *Annual Review of Political Science* 17 (1):1–25.

Hajnal, Zoltan L. 2001. "White Residents, Black Incumbents, and a Declining Racial Divide." *American Political Science Review* 95 (3):603–17.

2003. "Black Candidates, White Voters: How Uncertainty and Information Shape the White Vote." In *Uncertainty in American Politics*, ed. Barry C. Burden. New York, NY: Cambridge University Press. 213–44.

2006. *Changing White Attitudes Toward Black Political Leadership*. New York, NY: Cambridge University Press.

2010. *America's Uneven Democracy: Turnout, Race, and Representation in City Politics*. Cambridge, UK: Cambridge University Press.

2018. "Why Does No One Vote in Local Elections? Timing Is Everything." *New York Times*, October 22.

Hajnal, Zoltan, and Taeku Lee. 2011. *Why Americans Don't Join the Party: Race, Immigration, and the Failure of Political Parties to Engage the Electorate*. Princeton, NJ: Princeton University Press.

Hajnal, Zoltan L. and Jessica L. Trounstine 2005. "Where Turnout Matters: The Consequences of Uneven Turnout in City Politics." *Journal of Politics* 67 (2):515–35.

2013. "What Underlies Urban Politics? Race, Class, Ideology, Partisanship, and the Urban Vote." *Urban Affairs Review* 49 (4):63–99.

Hajnal, Zoltan L., Elisabeth R. Gerber, and Hugh Louch. 2002. "Minorities and Direct Legislation: Evidence from California Ballot Proposition Elections." *The Journal of Politics* 64 (1):154–77.

Hajnal, Zoltan, Nazita Lajevardi, and Lindsay Nielson. 2017. "Voter Identification Laws and the Suppression of Minority Votes." *The Journal of Politics* 79:363–79.

Hamilton, Alexander, James Madison, and John Jay. 1961. *The Federalist Papers: A Collection of Essays Written in Support of the Constitution of the United States*, ed. Roy P. Fairfield. Garden City, NY: Anchor Books.

Handley, Lisa, and Bernard Grofman. 1994. "The Impact of the Voting Rights Act on Minority Representation: Black Officeholding in Southern State Legislatures and Congressional Delegations." In *Quiet Revolution in the South: The Impact of the Voting Rights Act, 1965–1990*, eds. Chandler Davidson and Bernard Grofman. Princeton, NJ: Princeton University Press. 335–50.

Hanson, Gordon H. 2005. *Why Does Immigration Divide America? Public Finance and Political Opposition to Open Border*. Institute for International Economics. gps.ucsd.edu/_files/faculty/hanson/hanson_publi cation_immigration_divide.pdf. Accessed June 4, 2019.

Harvard-Harris Poll. 2018 "CAPS – Harris Poll on Immigration and Foreign Policy." Center for American Political Studies. caps.gov.harvard.edu/news/ caps-harris-poll-immigration-and-foreign-policy. Accessed June 11, 2019.

Hawley, George. 2011. "Political Threat and Immigration: Party Identification, Demographic Context, and Immigration Policy Preference." *Social Science Quarterly* 92 (2):404–22.

2012. "Issue Voting and Immigration: Do Restrictionist Policies Cost Congressional Republican Votes?" *Social Science Quarterly* 94 (5):1185–1206.

Hayek, F. A., and Ronald Hamowy. 2011. *The Constitution of Liberty: The Definitive Edition (The Collected Works of F. A. Hayek)*. Chicago, IL: University of Chicago Press.

Haynes, Chris, Jennifer Merolla, and S. Karthick Ramakrishnan. 2016. *Framing Immigrants: News Coverage, Public Opinion and Policy*. New York, NY: Russell Sage Foundation.

Helderman, Rosalind. 2012. "As Republican Convention Emphasizes Diversity, Racial Incidents Intrude." *Washington Post*, August 29.

Hemmer, Nicole. 2017. "Republican Nativism Helped Turn California Blue. Trump Could Do the Same for the Whole Country." Vox, January 20. www.vox.com/the-big-idea/2017/1/20/14332296/reac tion-trump-democrats-organize-hispanic-turnout-prop187. Accessed May 28, 2019.

Hero, Rodney E. 1989. "Multiracial Coalitions in City Elections Involving Minority Candidates: Some Evidence from Denver." *Urban Affairs Quarterly* 25 (2):342–51.

1998. *Faces of Inequality: Social Diversity in American Politics*. New York, NY: Oxford University Press.

Hero, Rodney E., and Robert R. Preuhs. 2007. "Immigration and the Evolving American Welfare State: Examining Policies in U.S. States." *American Journal of Political Science* 51 (3):498–517.

Hero, Rodney E., and Caroline J. Tolbert. 1995. "Latinos and Substantive Representation in the U.S. House of Representatives: Direct, Indirect, or Non-Existent?" *American Journal of Political Science* 39:640–52.

Hibbs, Douglas A. 1987. *The American Political Economy: Macroeconomics and Electoral Politics*. Cambridge, MA: Harvard University Press.

Hibbs, Douglas A., and Christopher Dennis. 1988. "Income Distribution in the United States." *American Political Science Review* 82 (2):467–90.

Higham, John. 1985. *Strangers in the Land: Patterns of American Nativism: 1860–1925*. 2nd ed. New York, NY: Atheneum.

Highton, Benjamin. 2004. "White Voters and African American Candidates for Congress." *Political Behavior* 26 (1):1–25.

2011. "Prejudice Rivals Partisanship and Ideology When Explaining the 2008 Presidential Vote across the States." *PS: Political Science & Politics* 44:530–35.

Hochschild, Jennifer, Vesla Mae Weaver, and Traci R. Burch. 2012. *Creating a New Racial Order: How Immigration, Multiracialism, Genomics, and the Young Can Remake Race in America*. Princeton, NJ: Princeton University Press.

Holmberg, Soren, Bo Rothstein, and Naghmeh Nasiritous. 2009. "Quality of Government: What You Get." *Annual Review of Political Science* 12:135–61.

Holt, Thomas. 1979. *Black over White: Negro Political Leadership in South Carolina During Reconstruction.* Urbana, IL: University of Illinois.

Hood, M. V., and Irwin L. Morris. 1998. "Give Us Your Tired, Your Poor, . . . But Make Sure They Have a Green Card: The Effects of Documented and Undocumented Migrant Context on Anglo Opinion Toward Immigration." *Political Behavior* 20 (1):1–15.

2000. "Brother, Can You Spare a Dime? Racial/Ethnic Context and the Anglo Vote on Proposition 187." *Social Science Quarterly* 81:194–206.

Hood, M. V., Quentin Kidd, and Irwin L. Morris. 2012. *The Rational Southerner: Black Mobilization, Republican Growth, and the Partisan Transformation of the American South.* New York, NY: Oxford University Press.

Hooghe, Marc, and Ruth Dassonneville. 2018. "Explaining the Trump Vote: The Effect of Racist Resentment and Anti-Immigrant Sentiments." *PS: Political Science & Politics* 51 (3):528–34.

Hopkins, Daniel. 2009. "The Diversity Discount: When Increasing Ethnic and Racial Diversity Prevents Tax Increases." *The Journal of Politics* 71 (1):160–77.

2010. "Politicized Places: Explaining Where and When Immigrants Provoke Local Opposition." *American Political Science Review* 104 (1):40–60.

Hopkins, Daniel, and Jens Hainmueller. 2015. "The Hidden American Immigration Consensus: A Conjoint Analysis of Attitudes Toward Immigrants." *American Journal of Political Science* 59 (3):529–48.

Hopkins, Daniel, John Sides, and Jack Citrin. 2019. "The Muted Consequences of Correct Information About Immigration." *Journal of Politics* 81 (1):315–20.

Howell, William. 2003. *Power Without Persuasion: The Politics of Direct Presidential Action.* Princeton, NJ: Princeton University Press.

Huckfeldt, Robert, and Carol Weitzel Kohfeld. 1989. *Race and the Decline of Class in American Politics.* Urbana, IL: University of Illinois Press.

Hui, Iris, and David O. Sears. 2018. "Reexamining the Effect of Racial Propositions on Latinos' Partisanship in California." *Political Behavior* 1:149–74.

Huntington, Samuel. 2005. *Who We Are: The Challenges to America's National Identity.* New York, NY: Simon and Schuster.

Hutchings, Vincent L. 2009. "Change or More of the Same? Evaluating Racial Attitudes in the Obama Era." *Public Opinion Quarterly* 73:917–42.

Hutchings, Vincent L., and Nicholas A. Valentino. 2004. "The Centrality of Race in American Politics." *Annual Review of Political Science* 7:383–408.

ICMA (International City Management Association). 2011. "Municipal Form of Government Survey." icma.org/sites/default/files/303954_Municipal%

2oForm%2oof%2oGovernment%2oSurvey%2oSummary%202o11.pdf.
Accessed June 4, 2019.

Inglehart, Ron. 1990. *Culture Shift in Advanced Industrial Society*. Princeton, NJ: Princeton University Press.

Iyengar, Shanto, and Sean J. Westwood. 2015. "Fear and Loathing Across Party Lines: New Evidence on Group Polarization." *American Journal of Political Science* 59 (3):690–707.

Iyengar, Shanto, Gaurav Sood, and Yphtach Lelkes. 2012. "Affect, Not Ideology: A Social Identity Perspective on Polarization." *Public Opinion Quarterly* 76:405–31.

Jackman, Mary R., and Marie Crane. 1986. "'Some of My Best Friends Are Black …': Interracial Friendship and Whites' Racial Attitudes." *Public Opinion Quarterly* 50 (4):459–86.

Jackman, Simon, and Lynn Vavreck. 2010. "Primary Politics: Race, Gender, and Age in the 2008 Democratic Primary." *Journal of Elections, Public Opinion, and Policy* 20:153–86.

Jacobs, Lawrence R., and Benjamin I. Page. 2005. "Who Influences U.S. Foreign Policy?" *American Political Science Review* 99 (1):107–23.

Jacobs, Lawrence R., and Robert Y. Shapiro. 2000. *Politicians Don't Pander: Political Manipulation and the Loss of Democratic Responsiveness*. Chicago, IL: University of Chicago Press.

Jacoby, William. 2014. "Is There a Culture War? Conflicting Value Structures in American Public Opinion." *American Political Science Review* 108:754–71.

JCPES (Joint Center for Political and Economic Studies). 1974–2001. *The National Roster of Black Elected Officials*. Washington, DC: Joint Center for Political and Economic Studies.

Jeong, Gyung-Ho, Gary Miller, Camilla Schofield, and Itai Sened. 2011. "Cracks in the Opposition: Partisan Realignment in the U.S. Senate Negotiations over Immigration Policy." *American Journal of Political Science* 55 (3):511–525.

Johnson, J. H., and M. L. Oliver. 1989. "Inter-Ethnic Minority Conflict in Urban America: The Effects of Economic and Social Dislocations." *Urban Geography* 10:449–63.

Johnson, Martin. 2001. "The Impact of Social Diversity and Racial Attitudes on Social Welfare Policy." *State Politics and Policy Quarterly* 1:27–47.

Jones, Bradley. 2019. "Majority of Americans Continue to Say Immigrants Strengthen the U.S." Pew Research Center, January 31. www.pewresearch.org/fact-tank/2019/01/31/majority-of-americans-continue-to-say-immigrants-strengthen-the-u-s/. Accessed May 28, 2019.

Juenke, Eric Gonzalez, and Robert R. Preuhs. 2011. "Irreplaceable Legislators? Rethinking Minority Representatives in the New Century." *American Journal of Political Science* 56:705–15.

Kaiser Family Foundation. 2004. "Immigration in America." kff.org/other/poll-finding/immigration-in-america-toplines/. Accessed May 28, 2019.

Kalmoe, Nathan, and Spencer Piston. 2013."Is Implicit Prejudice against Blacks Politically Consequential? Evidence from the Amp." *Public Opinion Quarterly* 77 (1):305–22.

Kaplan, Jonathan S. 2010. "Race to the Bottom? California's Support for Schools Lags the Nation." California Budget Project.

Katznelson, Ira. 2005. *When Affirmative Action Was White: An Untold History of Racial Inequality in Twentieth-Century America*. New York, NY: W. W. Norton.

Keech, W. R. 1968. *The Impact of Negro Voting: The Role of the Vote in the Quest for Equality*. Chicago, IL: Rand McNally.

Keiser, Lael R., Peter R. Mueser, and Seung-Whan Choi. 2004. "Race, Bureaucratic Discretion, and the Implementation of Welfare Reform." *American Journal of Political Science* 48 (2):314–28.

Keiser, Richard A. 1997. *Subordination or Empowerment? African-American Leadership and the Struggle for Urban Political Power*. New York, NY: Oxford University Press.

Keister, Lisa A. 2014. "The One Percent."*Annual Review of Sociology* 40:347–67.

Keister, Lisa A., and Stephanie Moller. 2000. "Wealth Inequality in the United States." *Annual Review of Sociology* 26:63–81.

Keith, Bruce E., David B. Magleby, Candice J. Nelson, Elizabeth Orr, Mark C. Westley, and Raymond E. Wolfinger. 1992. *The Myth of the Independent Voter*. Berkeley, CA: University of California Press.

Kenworthy, Lane, Sondra Barringer, Daniel Duerr, and Garrett Schneider. 2007. "The Democrats and Working Class Whites." citeseerx.ist.psu.edu/viewdoc/download?doi=10.1.1.361.1778&rep=rep1&type=pdf. Accessed June 4, 2019.

Kernell, Sam. 1973. "A Re-Evaluation of Black Voting in Mississippi." *American Political Science Review* 67:1307–18.

1997. *Going Public: New Strategies of Presidential Leadership*. Washington, DC: CQ Press.

Kerr, Brinck, and Will Miller. 1997. "Latino Representation, It's Direct and Indirect." *American Journal of Political Science* 41:1066–71.

Kerr, Brinck, and Kenneth R. Mladenka. 1994. "Does Politics Matter? A Time-Series Analysis of Minority Employment Patters." *American Journal of Political Science* 38:918–43.

Kertscher, Tom. 2018. "Bernie Sanders: Bill Gates, Jeff Bezos, Warren Buffett Have More Wealth Than Bottom Half of U.S." Politifact.com, July 19. www.politifact.com/wisconsin/statements/2018/jul/19/bernie-sanders/bernie-sanders-bill-gates-jeff-bezos-warren-buffet/. Accessed June 1, 2019.

Key, V. O. 1949. *Southern Politics in State and Nation*. Knoxville, TN: University of Tennessee Press.

Keynes, John Maynard. 2007 [1936]. *The General Theory of Employment, Interest and Money*. Basingstoke, UK: Palgrave Macmillan.

Kiewiet, Roderick, and Mathew McCubbins. 1985. "Appropriations Decisions as a Bilateral Bargaining Game between President and Congress." *Legislative Studies Quarterly* 10:181–202.

Kim, Thomas. 2006. *The Racial Logic of Politics: Asian Americans and Party Competition*. Philadelphia, PA: Temple University Press.

Kinder, Donald R., and Allison Dale-Riddle. 2011. *The End of Race? Obama, 2008, and Racial Politics in America*. New Haven, CT: Yale University Press.

Kinder, Donald R., and Wendy Kam. 2012. *Us Against Them: Ethnocentric Foundations of American Opinion*. Chicago, IL: University of Chicago Press.

Kinder, Donald R., and Lynn Sanders. 1996. *Divided by Color: Racial Politics and Democratic Ideals*. Chicago, IL: University of Chicago Press.

King, Desmond S., and Rogers M. Smith. 2005. "Racial Orders in American Political Development." *American Political Science Review* 99:75–92.

2011. *Still a House Divided: Race and Politics in Obama's America*. Princeton, NJ: Princeton University Press.

Klinkner, Philip A. 2016. "The Easiest Way to Guess if Someone Supports Trump? Ask if Obama Is a Muslim." *Vox*, June 2. www.vox.com/2016/6/2/11833548/donald-trump-support-race-religion-economy. Accessed May 14, 2019.

Klinkner, Philip A., and Rogers M. Smith. 1999. *The Unsteady March: The Rise and Decline of Racial Equality in America*. Chicago, IL: University of Chicago Press.

Korte, Gregory, and Alan Gomez. 2018. "Trump Ramps up Rhetoric on Undocumented Migrants: 'These Aren't People. These Are Animals.'" *USA Today*, May 17. www.usatoday.com/story/news/politics/2018/05/16/trump-immigrants-animals-mexico-democrats-sanctuary-cities/617252002/. Accessed May 14, 2019.

Kousser, J. Morgan. 1974. *The Shaping of Southern Politics: Suffrage Restriction and the Establishment of the One-Party South, 1880–1910*. New Haven, CT: Yale University Press.

1992. "The Voting Rights Act and the Two Reconstructions." In *Controversies in Minority Voting: The Voting Rights Act in Perspective*, eds. Bernard Grofman and Chandler Davidson. Washington, DC: The Brookings Institution. 135–76.

1999. *Colorblind Injustice: Minority Voting Rights and the Undoing of the Second Reconstruction*. Chapel Hill, NC: The University of North Carolina Press.

Krantz, Matt. 2015. "Maximum Wage: How Much CEOs Earn an Hour." *USA Today*, April 6.

Krehbiel, Keith. 1998. *Pivotal Politics: A Theory of U.S. Lawmaking*. Chicago, IL: University of Chicago Press.

Kuk, John. 2019. "An Unequal and Polarized Democracy: Why Has Unequal Growth Caused Party Polarization in the American Public?" University of California San Diego Dissertation.

Kuo, Alexander, Neil Malhotra, and Cecilia Hyunjung Mo. 2017. "Social Exclusion and Political Identity: The Case of Asian American Partisanship." *The Journal of Politics* 79 (1):17–32.

Kurtzleben, Danielle. 2016. "Rural Voters Played a Big Part in Helping Trump Defeat Clinton." NPR, November 14.

Kuziemko, Ilyana, Michael I. Norton, Emmanuel Saez, and Stefanie Stantcheva. 2015. "How Elastic Are Preferences for Redistribution? Evidence from Randomized Survey Experiments." *American Economic Review* 105:1478–508.

Kuziemko, Ilyana, and Ebonya Washington. 2018. "Why Did the Democrats Lose the South? Bringing New Data to an Old Debate." *American Economic Review* 108 (10):2830–67.

Lajevardi, Nazita. 2017. "Political Discrimination against Muslim Americans." University of California, San Diego dissertation.

2018. "Access Denied: Exploring Muslim American Representation and Exclusion by State Legislators." *Politics, Groups, and Identities* 2018:1–29.

Lajevardi, Nazita, and Marisa Abrajano. 2019. "How Negative Sentiment toward Muslim Americans Predicts Support for Trump in the 2016 Presidential Election." *The Journal of Politics* 81 (1):296–302

Lamont, Michele, Bo Yun Park, and Elena Alaya-Hurtado. 2017. "Trump's Electoral Speeches and His Appeal to the American White Working Class." *The British Journal of Sociology* 68:153–78.

Latino Decisions. 2016. "2016 Latino Election Analysis." Latinodecisions.com. www.latinodecisions.com/files/5214/8106/0204/PostElection2016_-_Barreto_-_CAP.pdf. Accessed May 15, 2019.

Lau, Richard R., and David P. Redlawsk. 1997. "Voting Correctly." *American Political Science Review* 91:585–98.

Layman, Geoffrey C., and Ted Carmines. 1997. "Cultural Conflict in American Politics: Religious Traditionalism, Postmaterialism, and U.S. Political Behavior." *The Journal of Politics* 59 (3):751–77.

Layman, Geoffrey C., and Thomas M. Carsey. 2002. "Party Polarization and 'Conflict Extension' in the American Electorate." *Political Behavior* 24 (3):199-236.

Lax, Jeffrey R., and Justin H. Phillips. 2011. "The Democratic Deficit in the States." *American Journal of Political Science* 56(1):148–66.

Lee, Taeku. 2000. "Racial Attitudes and the Color Line(s) at the Close of the Twentieth Century." In *The State of Asian Pacific Americans: Race Relations*, ed. Paul Ong. Los Angeles, CA: LEAP.

  2002. *Mobilizing Public Opinion: Black Insurgency and Racial Attitudes in the Civil Rights Era*. Chicago, IL: University of Chicago Press.

  2016. "Analysis: How Exit Polling Missed the Mark on Asian Americans." NBC News, November 11. www.nbcnews.com/news/asian-america/analysis-how-exit-polling-missed-mark-asian-americans-n682491. Accessed May 14, 2019.

Leighley, Jan, and Jonathan Nagler. 2013. *Who Votes Now? Demographics, Issues, Inequality, and Turnout in the United States*. Princeton, NJ: Princeton University Press.

Lerman, Amy, and Vesla Mae Weaver. 2014. *Arresting Citizenship: The Democratic Consequences of American Crime Control*. New York, NY: Cambridge University Press.

Lewis, Kristen and Sarah Burd-Sharps. 2010. "A Century Apart: New Measures of Well-Being for U.S. Racial and Ethnic Groups." American Human Development Project.

Lewis-Beck, Michael S., Charles Tien, and Richard Nadeau. 2010. "Obama's Missed Landslide: A Racial Cost?" *PS: Political Science & Politics* 43 (1):69–76.

Lieberman, Robert. 1998. *Shifting the Color Line: Race and the American Welfare State*. Cambridge, MA: Harvard University Press.

Lien, Pei-te, M. Margaret Conway, and Janelle Wong. 2004. *The Politics of Asian Americans: Diversity and Community*. New York, NY: Routledge.

Lijphart, Arend. 1997. "Unequal Participation: Democracy's Unresolved Dilemma." *The American Political Science Review* 91 (1):1–14.

  1999. *Patterns of Democracy: Government Forms and Performance in Thirty-Six Countries*. New Haven, CT: Yale University Press.

Livingston, Gretchen, and Anna Brown. 2017. "Intermarriage in the U.S. 50 Years after Loving V. Virginia." Pew Research Center, May 18. assets.pewresearch.org/wp-content/uploads/sites/3/2017/05/19102233/Intermarriage-May-2017-Full-Report.pdf. Accessed June 10, 2019.

Lopez, German. 2016. "Most Ohio and Pennsylvania Counties That Flipped from Obama to Trump Are Wracked by Heroin." Vox, November 22. www.vox.com/policy-and-politics/2016/11/22/13698476/trump-opioid-heroin-epidemic. Accessed June 4, 2019.

Lublin, David. 1997. *The Paradox of Representation: Racial Gerrymandering and Minority Interests*. Princeton, NJ: Princeton University Press.

  2004. *The Republican South: Democratization and Partisan Change*. Princeton, NJ: Princeton University Press.

Lupia, Arthur. 1994. "Shortcuts Versus Encyclopedias: Information and Voting Behavior in California Insurance Reform Elections." *American Political Science Review* 88 (1):63–76.

MacKuen, Michael B., Robert S. Erikson, and James A. Stimson. 1989. "Macropartisanship." *American Political Science Review* 83 (4):1125–42.

MacManus, Susan A., and Charles S. Bullock. 1993. "Women and Racial/Ethnic Minorities in Mayoral and Council Positions." In *The Municipal Year Book*, ed. International City Management Association. Washington, DC: International City Management Association.

Malhotra, Neil, and Conor Raso. 2007. "Racial Representation and U.S. Senate Apportionment." *Social Science Quarterly* 88 (4): 1038–48.

Malhotra, Neil, Yotam Margalit, and Cecilia Hyunjung Mo. 2013. "Economic Explanations for Opposition to Immigration: Distinguishing Between Prevalence and Magnitude." *American Journal of Political Science* 57 (2):391–410.

Mansbridge, Jane. 1999. "Should Blacks Represent Blacks and Women Represent Women? A Contingent Yes." *The Journal of Politics* 61 (3):628–57.

Manza, Jeff. 2006. *Locked Out: Felon Disenfranchisement and American Democracy*. Oxford, UK: Oxford University Press.

Marschall, Melissa, and Paru R. Shah. 2007. "The Attitudinal Effects of Minority Incorporation Examining the Racial Dimensions of Trust in Urban America." *Urban Affairs Review* 42 (5):629–58.

Martin, Andrew, and Kevin Quinn. 2002. "Dynamic Ideal Point Estimation Via Markov Chain Monte Carlo for the U.S. Supreme Court, 1953–1999." *Political Analysis* 10 (2):134–53.

Mason, Lillian. 2018. *Uncivil Agreement: How Politics Became Our Identity*. Chicago, IL: Chicago University Press.

Massey, Douglas S. 2001. "Residential Segregation and Neigborhood Conditions in U.S. Metropolitan Areas." In *America Becoming: Racial Trends and Their Consequences*, eds. Neil Smelser, William Julius Wilson and Faith Mitchell. Washington, DC: National Academy Press.

Massey, Douglas S., and Nancy A. Denton. 1993. *American Apartheid: Segregation and the Making of the Underclass*. Cambridge, MA: Harvard University Press.

Masuoka, Natalie, and Jane Junn. 2013. *The Politics of Belonging: Race, Public Opinion, and Immigration*. Chicago, IL: University of Chicago Press.

Mayhew, David. 1991. *Divided We Govern: Party Control, Lawmaking, and Investigations, 1946–1990*. New Haven, CT: Yale University Press.

McCall, Leslie. 2013. *The Undeserving Rich: American Beliefs About Inequality, Opportunity, and Redistribution*. New York, NY: Cambridge University Press.

McCarty, Nolan, Keith T. Poole, and Howard Rosenthal. 2007. *Polarized America: The Dance of Ideology and Unequal Riches*. Boston, MA: MIT Press.

McConnaughy, Corrine, Ismail White, David Leal, and Jason Casellas. 2010. "A Latino on the Ballot: Explaining Coethnic Voting among Latinos and the Response of White Americans." *The Journal of Politics* 72 (4):1199–211.

McCrary, Peyton. 1990. "Racially Polarized Voting in the South: Quantitative Evidence from the Courtroom." *Social Science History* 14 (4):507–31.

McCurley, Carl, and Jeffery J. Mondak. 1995. "Inspected by #1184063113: The Influence of Incumbents' Competence and Integrity in U.S. House Elections." *American Political Science Review* 39 (4):864–85.

McGann, Anthony J., Charles Anthony Smith, Michael Latner, and Alex Keena. 2017. *Gerrymandering in America: The House of Representatives, the Supreme Court, and the Future of Popular Sovereignty*. New York, NY: Cambridge University Press.

McGillis, Alec. 2016. "Revenge of the Forgotten Class: Hillary Clinton and the Democrats Were Playing with Fire When They Effectively Wrote Off White Workers in the Small Towns and Cities of the Rust Belt." *ProPublica*, November 10.

McLaren, Lauren M. 2003. "Anti-Immigrant Prejudice in Europe: Contact, Threat Perception, and Preferences for the Exclusion of Migrants." *Social Forces* 81 (3):909–36.

McVeigh, Rory, David Cunningham, and Justin Farrell. 2014. "Political Polarization as a Social Movement Outcome: 1960s Klan Activism and Its Enduring Impact on Political Realignment in Southern Counties, 1960 to 2000." *American Sociological Review* 79 (6):1144–71.

McWhorter, John. 2008. "Racism in America Is Over." *Forbes*, December 30.

Meier, Kenneth J., and Robert E. England. 1984. "Black Representation and Educational Policy: Are They Related?" *American Political Science Review* 78 (2):392–403.

Meier, Kenneth J., and Joseph Stewart Jr. 1991. "Cooperation and Conflict in Multiracial School Districts." *The Journal of Politics* 53 (4):1123–33.

Menifield, Charles E., ed. 2001. *Representation of Minority Groups in the U.S.* Lanham, MA: Austin and Winfield Publishers.

Merrill, Laurie, Dianna Nanez, and Linnea Bennett. 2013. "Hundreds Protest Obama Outside Phoenix High School." *The Republic*, August 8.

Miller, Gary, and Norman Schofield. 2008. "The Transformation of the Republican and Democratic Party Coalitions in the US." *Perspectives on Politics* 6 (3):433–50.

Miller, Warren E., and J. Merrill Shanks. 1996. *The New American Voter*. Cambridge, MA: Harvard University Press.

Miller, Warren E., and Donald E. Stokes. 1963. "Constituency Influence in Congress." *American Political Science Review* 57 (1):45–57.

Minta, Michael. 2011. *Oversight: Representing the Interests of Blacks and Latinos in Congress*. Princeton, NJ: Princeton University Press.

Mladenka, Kenneth R. 1980. "The Urban Bureaucracy and the Chicago Political Machine: Who Gets What and the Limits of Political Control." *The American Political Science Review* 74 (4):991–98.

1981. "Citizen Demands and Urban Services: The Distribution of Bureaucratic Response in Chicago and Houston." *American Journal of Political Science* 25 (4):693–714.

Monogan, James. 2013. "The Politics of Immigrant Policy in the 50 U.S. States, 2005–2011." *Journal of Public Policy* 33(1):35–64.

Moyers, Bill. 2011. *Moyers on America: A Journalist and His Times* . New York, NY: New Press.

MPI (Migration Policy Institute). 2019. "Frequently Requested Statistics on Immigrants and Immigration in the United States." www.migrationpo licy.org/article/frequently-requested-statistics-immigrants-and-immigra tion-united-states. Accessed May 28, 2019.

Murakawa, Naomi. 2014. *The First Civil Right: How Liberals Built Prison America*. New York, NY: Oxford University Press.

Mutz, Diana. 2018. "Status Threat, Not Economic Hardship, Explains the 2016 Presidential Vote." *PNAS* 115 (19):E4330–E4339.

Myrdal, Gunnar. 1944. *An American Dilemma: The Negro Problem and Modern Democracy*. New York, NY: Harper and Brothers.

Nadeau, Richard, and André Blais. 1993. "Accepting the Election Outcome: The Effect of Participation on Loser's Consent." *British Journal of Political Science* 23 (4):553–63.

NAHJ (National Association of Hispanic Journalists). 2005. "The Portrayal of Latinos and Latino Issues on Network Television News."

NALEO (National Association of Latino Elected Officials). 1984–2018. *National Directory of Latino Elected Officials*. Los Angeles: National Association of Latino Elected Officials.

NCSL (National Conference of State Legislatures). 2019. "State Laws Related to Immigration and Immigrants." www.ncsl.org/research/immigration/state-laws-related-to-immigration-and-immigrants.aspx. Accessed June 6, 2019.

Nellis, Ashley. 2016. "The Color of Justice: Racial and Ethnic Disparity in State Prisons." The Sentencing Project. www.sentencingproject.org/wp-content /uploads/2016/06/The-Color-of-Justice-Racial-and-Ethnic-Disparity-in -State-Prisons.pdf. Accessed June 6, 2019.

Neustadt, Richard E. 1980. *Presidential Power: Politics of Leadership from F.D. R. to Carter*. New York, NY: Wiley and Sons.

Newkirk II, Vann R. 2017. "The Supreme Court Finds North Carolina's Gerrymandering Unconstitutional." *The Atlantic*, May 22. www .theatlantic.com/politics/archive/2017/05/north-carolina-gerrymandering /527592/. Accessed May 21, 2019.

Newman, Benjamin J. 2013. "Acculturating Contexts and Anglo Opposition to Immigration in the United States." *American Journal of Political Science* 57 (2):374–90.

Newton, Jim. 1998. "Ethnic Politics Shape Debate over Council Size." *Los Angeles Times*, August 24. A1.

Nicholson, Stephen P., and Gary M. Segura. 2005. "Issue Agendas and the Politics of Latino Partisan Identification." In *Diversity in Democracy: Minority Representation in the United States*, eds. Gary M. Segura and Shaun Bowler. Charlottesville, VA: University of Virginia Press.

Niemi, Richard G., and M. Kent Jennings. 1991. "Issues and Inheritance in the Formation of Party Identification." *American Journal of Political Science* 35 (4):9780–988.

Niskanen, William A. 2003. "A Case for Divided Government." Cato Institute, May 7. www.cato.org/publications/commentary/case-divided-govern ment. Accessed May 31, 2019.

Norris, Pippa. 2017. "Young and Old Are Voting Differently in the UK and the US. That's a Big Deal." *Washington Post*, June 14.

North, Hannah. 2017. "The Scope of Hate in 2017." *New York Times*, June 9.

Novak, Viveca. 2007. "Tough Guy on Immigration?" FactCheck.Org. www .factcheck.org/2007/11/tough-guy-on-immigration/. Accessed May 28, 2019.

NPR. 2016. "Rural Voters Helped Trump Win the Election: Here's How." NPR Politics, November 14. www.npr.org/2016/11/14/501737150/rural-voters -played-a-big-part-in-helping-trump-defeat-clinton. Accessed June 4, 2019.

Olzak, Susan. 1992. *The Dynamics of Ethnic Competition and Conflict*. Stanford, CT: Stanford University Press.

Otis, John. 2018. "A Mother's Determination Withstands Years of Tumult." *New York Times*, January 6.

Page, Benjamin I. 1983. *Who Gets What from Government*. Berkeley, CA: University of California Press.

Page, Benjamin I., and Lawrence Jacobs. 2005. "Who Influences U.S. Foreign Policy?" *American Political Science Review* 99 (1):107–23.

Page, Benjamin I., and Robert Y. Shapiro. 1983. "Effects of Public Opinion on Policy." *American Political Science Review* 77 (1):175–90.

1992. *The Rational Public: Fifty Years of Trends in Americans' Policy Preferences*. Chicago, IL: University of Chicago.

Page, Benjamin I., and James R. Simmons. 2000. *What Government Can Do: Dealing with Poverty and Inequality*. Chicago, IL: University of Chicago Press.

Parker, Ashley. 2015. "Donald Trump Gets Earful in Spanish." *New York Times*, August 26.

Parker, Christopher. 2016. "Race and Politics in the Age of Obama." *Annual Review of Sociology* 42 (1):217–30.

Parker, Christopher, and Matt Barreto. 2013. *Change They Can't Believe In: The Tea Party and Reactionary Politics in America*. Princeton, NJ: Princeton University Press.

Forthcoming. *The Great White Hope: Existential Threat and Demographic Anxiety in the Age of Trump*. Chicago, IL: University of Chicago Press.

Parker, Frank. 1990. *Black Votes Count: Political Empowerment in Mississippi after 1965*. Chapel Hill, NC: University of North Carolina.

Pasek, Josh, Tobias Stark, Jon Krosnick, Trevor Tompson, and Keith Payne. 2014. "Attitudes Toward Blacks in the Obama Era: Changing Distributions and Impacts on Job Approval and Electoral Choice." *Public Opinion Quarterly* 78 (S1):276–302.

Pasek, Josh, Alex Tahk, Yphtach Lelkes, Jon Krosnick, Keith Payne, and Trevor Tompson. 2009. "Determinants of Turnout and Candidate Choice in the 2008 US Presidential Election: Illuminating the Impact of Racial Prejudice and Other Considerations." *Public Opinion Quarterly* 73 (5):943–94.

Passel, Jeffrey S., and D'Vera Cohn. 2009. "A Portrait of Unauthorized Immigrants in the United States." Pew Research Center. www.pewhispanic.org/2009/04/14/a-portrait-of-unauthorized-immigrants-in-the-united-states/. Accessed May 29, 2019.

Passel, Jeffrey S., Wendy Wang, and Paul Taylor. 2010. "One-in-Seven New U.S. Marriages Is Interracial or Interethnic." Pew Research Center. www.pewsocialtrends.org/2010/06/04/marrying-out/. Accessed May 29, 2019.

Pérez, Efrén O. 2010. "Explicit Evidence on the Import of Implicit Attitudes: The IAT and Immigration Policy Judgments." *Political Behavior* 32 (4):517–45.

2016. *Unspoken: Implicit Attitudes and Political Thinking*. New York, NY: Cambridge University Press.

Pew. 2006. "America's Immigration Quandry." Pew Research Center, March 30. www.people-press.org/2006/03/30/americas-immigration-quandary/. Accessed June 4, 2019.

2009. "Health Care." Pew Research Center. www.pewresearch.org/topics/health-care/. Accessed June 6, 2019.

2013. "Faith on the Hill: The Religious Composition of the 113th Congress." Pew Research Center, November 16. www.pewforum.org/2012/11/16/faith-on-the-hill-the-religious-composition-of-the-113th-congress/. Accessed May 29, 2019.

2014. "One in Four Native Americans and Alaska Natives Are Living in Poverty." Pew Research Center, June 13. www.pewresearch.org/fact-tank/2014/06/13/1-in-4-native-americans-and-alaska-natives-are-living-in-poverty/. Accessed May 14, 2019.

2016. "On Views of Racial Inequality Blacks and Whites Are Worlds Apart." Pew Research Center, June 27. www.pewsocialtrends.org/2016/06/27/on-views-of-race-and-inequality-blacks-and-whites-are-worlds-apart/. Accessed May 14, 2019.

2017a. "Key Facts About Asian Americans, a Diverse and Growing Population." Pew Research Center, September 8. www.pewresearch.org/fact-tank/2017/09/08/key-facts-about-asian-americans/. Accessed May 14, 2019.

2017b. "Facts on US Latinos, 2015: Statistical Portrait of Hispanics in the United States." Pew Research Center, September 18. www.pewhispanic.org/2017/09/18/facts-on-u-s-latinos/. Accessed May 14, 2019.

2017c. "Most Americans Say Trump's Election Has Led to Worse Race Relations in the US." Pew Research Center, December 19. www.people-press.org/2017/12/19/most-americans-say-trumps-election-has-led-to-worse-race-relations-in-the-u-s/. Accessed June 10, 2019.

2018a. "Blacks and Hispanics Are Overrepresented in U.S. Prisons." Pew Research Center, January 12. www.pewresearch.org/fact-tank/2019/04/30/shrinking-gap-between-number-of-blacks-and-whites-in-prison/ft_18-01-10_prisonracegaps_2/. Accessed June 6, 2019.

2018b. "Unauthorized Immigrant Population Trends for States, Birth Countries and Regions." Pew Research Center, Hispanic Trends, November 27. www.pewhispanic.org/interactives/unauthorized-trends/. Accessed June 6, 2019.

Phillips, Amber. 2017. "'They're Rapists.' President Trump's Campaign Launch Speech Two Years Later, Annotated." *Washington Post*, June 16.

Phillips, Anne. 1998. "Democracy and Representation: Or, Why Should It Matter Who Our Representatives Are?" In *Feminism and Politics*. Oxford, UK: Oxford University Press. 224–40.

Piketty, Thomas. 2014. *Capital in the 21st Century*, translated by Arthur Goldhammer. Cambridge, MA: Harvard University Press.

2018. "Brahmin Left Vs. Merchant Right: Rising Inequality and the Changing Structure of Political Conflict (Evidence from France, Britain and the US,

1948–2017).” WID.world Working Paper 2018/7. piketty.pse.ens.fr/files/
Piketty2018.pdf. Accessed May 13, 2019.

Piston, Spencer. 2010. “How Explicit Racial Prejudice Hurt Obama in the 2008
Election.” *Political Behavior* 32 (4):431–51.

Piven, Frances Fox, and Richard A. Cloward. 1977. *Poor People's Movements:
Why They Succeed, How They Fail.* New York, NY: Pantheon Books.

Polling Report, The. Immigration. 2019. www.pollingreport.com/immigration
.htm. Accessed June 6, 2019.

Poole, Keith T., and Howard Rosenthal. 1997. *Congress: A Political-Economic
History of Roll Call Voting.* New York, NY: Oxford University Press.

Popkin, Samuel L. 1991. *The Reasoning Voter: Communication and Persuasion
in Presidential Campaigns.* Chicago, IL: University of Chicago Press.

Porter, Eduardo. 2016. “Where Were Trump's Voters? Where the Jobs Weren't.”
New York Times, December 13.

  2018. “Whites' Unease Shadows the Politics of a More Diverse America.”
New York Times, May 22.

Powell, G. Bingham. 1986. “American Voter Turnout in Comparative
Perspective.” *American Political Science Review* 80 (3):17–43.

Preston, Julia. 2012. “Republicans Reconsider Positions on Immigration.”
New York Times, November 9.

Prose, Francine. 2008. “Literature for a Post-Racial World.” *Washington Post,*
December 14.

Quillian, Lincoln. 1995. “Prejudice as a Response to Perceived Group Threat:
Population Composition and Anti-Immigrant and Racial Prejudice in
Europe.” *American Sociological Review* 60 (4):586–611.

Rahn, Wendy, and Thomas Rudolph. 2005. “A Tale of Political Trust in
American Cities.” *Public Opinion Quarterly* 69 (4):530–56.

Rakich, Nathaniel, and Dhrumil Mehta. 2018. “The Gender Gap among Midterm
Voters Looks Huge – Maybe Even Record Breaking.” fivethirtyeight.com,
August 3. fivethirtyeight.com/features/the-gender-gap-among-midterm-
voters-looks-huge-maybe-even-record-breaking/. Accessed June 10, 2019.

Ramakrishnan, S. Karthick. 2014. “Asian Americans and the Rainbow: The
Prospects and Limits of Coalitional Politics.” *Politics, Groups, and
Identities* 2 (3):522–29.

Ramakrishnan, S. Karthick, Janelle Wong, Taeku Lee, and Jane Junn. 2009.
“Race-Based Considerations and the Obama Vote.” *Du Bois Review* 6
(1):219–38.

Reagan, Ronald. 1981. “Remarks in Denver, Colorado, at the Annual
Convention of the National Association for the Advancement of Colored
People.” June 29. www.reaganlibrary.gov/research/speeches/62981a.
Accessed June 6, 2019.

Reeves, Keith. 1997. *Voting Hopes or Fears? White Voters, Black Candidates, and Racial Politics in America.* New York, NY: Oxford University Press.

Reich, Robert. 2012. *Beyond Outrage: What Has Gone Wrong with Our Economy and Our Democracy and How to Fix It.* New York, NY: Knopf.

Rhodes, Jesse, Brian Schaffner, and Sean McElwee. 2017. "Is America More Divided by Race or Class? Race, Income, and Attitudes among Whites, African Americans, and Latinos." *The Forum* 15 (1):71–91.

Rigby, Elizabeth, and Gerald Wright. 2013. "Political Parties and Representation of the Poor in American States." *American Journal of Political Science* 57 (3):552–65.

Rivera, Michael. 2015. "The Determinants of State Immigration Policy." University of California, San Diego PhD Thesis.

Rivlin, Gary. 1992. *Fire on the Prairie: Chicago's Harold Washington and the Politics of Race.* New York, NY: Henry Holt and Company.

Robertson, Campbell. 2011. "After Ruling, Hispanics Flee an Alabama Town." *New York Times*, October 3.

Rosenberg, Gerald N. 1991. *The Hollow Hope: Can Courts Bring About Social Change?* Chicago, IL: University of Chicago.

Rosenstone, Steven J., and John Mark Hansen. 1993. *Mobilization, Participation, and Democracy in America.* New York, NY: Macmillan Publishing Company.

Rumbaut, Ruben G. 2006. "Debunking the Myth of Immigrant Criminality: Imprisonment Among First- and Second-Generation Young Men." Migration Policy Institute, June 1. www.migrationpolicy.org/article/debunking-myth-immigrant-criminality-imprisonment-among-first-and-second-generation-young. Accessed June 4, 2019.

Saltzstein, Grace Hall. 1989. "Black Mayors and Police Policies." *The Journal of Politics* 51 (3):525–44.

Schaffner, Brian. 2011. "Racial Salience and the Obama Vote." *Political Psychology* 32:963–88.

Schaffner, Brian, Matthew MacWilliams, and Tatishe Nteta. 2018. "Understanding White Polarization in the 2016 Vote for President: The Sobering Role of Racism and Sexism." *Political Science Quarterly* 133 (1):9–34.

Schattschneider, E. E. 1970. *The Semi-sovereign People: A Realist's View of Democracy in America.* New York, NY: Harcourt Brace Jovanovich College Publishers.

Scheve, Kenneth F., and Matthew J. Slaughter. 2001. "Labor Market Competition and Individual Preferences over Immigration Policy." *Review of Economics and Statistics* 83 (1):133–45.

Schildkraut, Deborah. 2005. *Press One for English: Language Policy, Public Opinion, and American Identity.* Cambridge, UK: Cambridge University Press.

2011. *Americanism in the Twenty-First Century: Public Opinion in the Age of Immigration*. Cambridge, UK: Cambridge University Press.

Schrag, Peter. 2011. *Not Fit for Our Society: Immigration and Nativism in America*. Berkeley, CA: University of California Press.

Schuman, Howard, Charlotte Steeh, Lawrence Bobo, and Maria Krysan. 1997. *Racial Attitudes in America: Trends and Interpretations*. Revised edition. Cambridge, MA: Harvard University Press.

Scott, Dylan. 2018. "White Evangelicals Turned Out for the GOP in Big Numbers Again." Vox, November 7. www.vox.com/policy-and-politics/2018/10/29/18015400/2018-midterm-elections-results-white-evangelical-christians-trump. Accessed June 4, 2019.

Sears, David O., and Donald R. Kinder. 1985. "Whites' Opposition to Busing: On Conceptualizing and Operationalizing Group Conflict." *Journal of Personality and Social Psychology* 48 (5):1141–47.

Segura, Gary, and Matt Barreto. 2012. "Obama Wins 75% of Latino Vote, Marks Historic Latino Influence in Presidential Election." Latinodecisions.com, November 7. www.latinodecisions.com/blog/obama-wins-75-of-latino-vote-marks-historic-latino-influence-in-presidential-election/. Accessed June 4, 2019.

Sentencing Project, The. 2019. "Felony Disenfranchisement Laws in the United States." www.sentencingproject.org/the-facts/. Accessed May 29, 2019

Severson, Kim. 2011. "Southern Lawmakers Focus on Illegal Immigrants." *New York Times*, March 26.

Shafer, Byron E., and Richard Johnston. 2005. *The End of Southern Exceptionalism: Class, Race, and Partisan Change in the Postwar South*. Cambridge, MA: Harvard University Press.

Shear, Michael D. 2013. "Bipartisan Plan Faces Resistance in GOP." *New York Times*, Jan 28.

Shotts, Ken. 2003. "Does Racial Redistricting Cause Conservative Policy Outcomes? Policy Preferences of Southern Representatives in the 1980s and 1990s." *The Journal of Politics* 65 (1):216–26.

Sidanius, Jim, and Felicia Pratto. 1999. *Social Dominance: An Intergroup Theory of Social Hierarchy and Oppression*. New York, NY: Cambridge University Press.

Sides, John. 2017. "Race, Religion, and Immigration in 2016: How the Debate over American Identity Shaped the Election and What it Means for a Trump Presidency." Report, Democracy Voter Study Group, June. www.voterstudygroup.org/publication/race-religion-immigration-2016. Accessed May 14, 2019.

Sides, John, Michael Tesler, and Lynn Vavreck. 2017. "The 2016 U.S. Election: How Trump Lost and Won." *Journal of Democracy* 28 (2):34–44.

2018. *Identity Crisis: The 2016 Presidential Campaign and the Battle for the Meaning of America*. Princeton, NJ: Princeton University Press.

Sigelman, Carol K., Lee Sigelman, Barbara J. Walkosz, and Michael Nitz. 1995. "Black Candidates, White Voters: Understanding Racial Bias in Political Perceptions." *American Journal of Political Science* 39 (1):243–65.

Silver, Nate. 2016. "Education, Not Income, Predicted Who Would Vote for Trump." fivethirtyeight.com, November 22. fivethirtyeight.com/features/education-not-income-predicted-who-would-vote-for-trump/. Accessed May 14, 2019.

Skelley, Geoffrey. 2016. "The Suburbs – All Kinds of Suburbs Delivered the House to Democrats." Fivethirtyeight.com, November 8. fivethirtyeight.com/features/the-suburbs-all-kinds-of-suburbs-delivered-the-house-to-democrats/. Accessed June 10, 2019.

Skocpol, Theda, and Vanessa Williamson. 2013. *The Tea Party and the Remaking of Republican Conservatism*. New York, NY: Oxford University Press.

Smith, Rogers M. 1993. "Beyond Tocqueville, Myrdal, and Hartz: The Multiple Traditions in America." *American Political Science Review* 87 (3):549–66.

Sniderman, Paul M., and Edward G. Carmines. 1997. *Reaching Beyond Race*. Cambridge, MA: Harvard University Press.

Soroka, Stuart N., and Christopher Wlezien. 2008. "On the Limits to Inequality in Representation." *PS: Political Science & Politics* 41 (2):319–27.

Soss, Joe, Richard C. Fording, and Sanford F. Schram. 2008. "The Color of Devolution: Race, Federalism, and the Politics of Social Control." *American Journal of Political Science* 52 (3):536–53.

Soss, Joe, Laura Langbein, and Alan R. Metelko. 2006. "Why Do White Americans Support the Death Penalty?" *The Journal of Politics* 65 (2):397–421.

Soss, Joe, Sanford Schram, Thomas Vartanian, and Erin O'Brien. 2001. "Setting the Terms of Relief: Explaining State Policy Choices in the Devolution Revolution." *American Journal of Political Science* 45 (2):378–95.

Squire, Peverill. 2007. "Measuring State Legislative Professionalism: The Squire Index Revisited." *State Politics & Policy Quarterly* 7:211-27.

Stanley, Harold, William Bianco, and Richard Niemi. 1986. "Partisanship and Group Support over Time: A Multivariate Analysis." *American Political Science Review* 80 (3):969–76.

Stern, Ken. 2017. "Inside How Trump Won the White Working Class." *Vanity Fair*, January 5.

Stiglitz, Joseph. 2012. *The Price of Inequality: How Today's Divided Society Endangers Our Future*. New York, NY: Norton.

Stimson, James A., Michael A. Mackuen, and Robert S. Erikson. 1995. "Dynamic Representation." *American Political Science Review* 89 (3):543–65.

Stonecash, Jeffrey. 2000. *Class and Party in American Politics*. New York, NY: Westview.

2017. "The Puzzle of Class in Presidential Voting." *The Forum* 15 (1): 29–49.

Stout, Nicholas. 2009. "Impressive Crowd in City Used to Pomp." *New York Times*, January 21.

Stuart, Reginald. 1981. "Mayor of Birmingham Assailed for Runoff Role." *New York Times*, November 9. B15.

Sullivan, Sean. 2012. "Biden: Romney's Approach to Financial Regulations Will 'Put Y'all Back in Chains.'" *Washington Post*, August 14.

Sulzberger, A. 2010. "Growing Anti-Immigrant Sentiments in an Unlikely State." *New York Times*, October 3.

Swain, Carol M. 1995. *Black Face, Black Interests: The Representation of African Americans in Congress*. Cambridge, MA: Harvard University Press.

Taagepara, Rein, and Matthew Soberg Shugart. 1989. *Seats and Votes: The Effects and Determinants of Electoral Systems*. New Haven, CT: Yale University Press.

Tajfel, Henri. 1981. *Human Groups and Social Categories: Studies in Social Psychology*. Cambridge, UK: Cambridge University Press.

Takaki, Ronald. 1989. *Strangers from a Different Shore: A History of Asian Americans*. New York, NY: Penguin Books.

Tankersley, Jim. 2018. "Democrats' Next Big Thing: Government-Guaranteed Jobs." *New York Times*, May 22.

Tate, Katherine. 2003. *Black Faces in the Mirror: African Americans and Their Representatives in the U.S. Congress*. Princeton, NJ: Princeton University Press.

Tavernise, Sabrina, and Robert Gebeloff. 2018. "They Voted for Obama Then Went for Trump. Can Democrats Win Them Back?" *New York Times*, May 4.

Taylor, Marylee C. 1998. "How White Attitudes Vary with the Racial Composition of Local Populations: Numbers Count." *American Sociological Review* 63(4):512–35.

Taylor, Paul. 2014. *The Next America: Boomers, Millennials, and the Looming Generational Showdown*. New York, NY: Public Affairs.

Teixeira, Ruy. 2009. *The New Progressive America: The Millennial Generation*. Washington, DC: Center for American Progress.

Terkildsen, Nayda. 1993. "When White Voters Evaluate Black Candidates: The Processing Implications of Candidate Skin Color, Prejudice, and Self-Monitoring." *American Journal of Political Science* 37 (4):1032–53.

Tesler, Michael. 2012. "The Spillover of Racialization into Health Care: How President Obama Polarized Public Opinion by Race and Racial Attitudes." *American Journal of Political Science* 56 (3):690–704.

2016a. *Post-Racial or Most-Racial?: Race and Politics in the Obama Era (Chicago Studies in American Politics)*. Chicago, IL: University of Chicago Press.

2016b. "Trump Is the First Modern Republican to Win the Nomination Based on Racial Prejudice." *Washington Post*, August 1.

2016c. "A Racially Diverse America Could Make the Economy Less Important to Elections." *Washington Post*, August 12.

2016d. "Views About Race Mattered More in Electing Trump Than in Electing Obama." *Washington Post*, November 22.

Tesler, Michael, and David O. Sears. 2010. *Obama's Race: The 2008 Election and the Dream of a Post-Racial America*. Chicago, IL: Chicago University Press.

Thernstrom, Stephan, and Abigail Thernstrom. 1997. *America in Black and White: One Nation, Indivisible*. New York, NY: Simon and Schuster.

Tichenor, Daniel J. 2002. *Dividing Lines: The Politics of Immigration Control in America*. Princeton, NJ: Princeton University Press.

Tolbert, Caroline, and Rodney Hero. 1999. "Social Diversity and California Ballot Initiatives." Paper presented at the Midwest Political Science Association Annual Meeting, Chicago.

2001. "Dealing with Diversity: Racial/Ethnic Context and Social Policy Change". *Political Research Quarterly* 54 (3):571–604.

Tomz, Michael, Jason Wittenberg, and Gary King. 1999. "Clarify: Software for Interpreting and Presenting Statistical Results." gking.harvard.edu/files/clarify.pdf. Accessed June 5, 2019.

Umoh, Ruth. 2018. "CEOs Make $15.6 Million on Average – Here's How Much Their Pay Has Increased Compared to Yours Over the Year." CNBC, January 22. www.cnbc.com/2018/01/22/heres-how-much-ceo-pay-has-increased-compared-to-yours-over-the-years.html. Accessed June 1, 2019.

Ura, Joseph, and Chris Ellis. 2008. "Income, Preferences, and the Dynamics of Policy Responsiveness." *PS: Political Science & Politics* 41 (4):786–94.

US Census Bureau. 1966–2007. "U.S. Census of State and Local Governments." www.census.gov/data/datasets/2007/econ/local/public-use-datasets.html. Accessed June 10, 2019.

Valelly, Richard. 2004. *The Two Reconstructions: The Struggle for Black Enfranchisement*. Chicago, IL: University of Chicago Press.

Valentino, Nicholas A., and David O. Sears. 2005. "Old Times There Are Not Forgotten: Race and Partisan Realignment in the Contemporary South." *American Journal of Political Science* 49 (3):672–88.

Valentino, Nicholas A., Ted Brader, and Ashley E. Jardina. 2013. "The Antecedents of Immigration Opinion among U.S. Whites: General Ethnocentrism or Media Priming of Latino Attitudes?" *Political Psychology* 34 (2):149–66.

Vavreck, Lynn. 2014. "It's Not Too Late for Republicans to Win Latino Votes." *New York Times*, August 11.

Velencia, Janie. 2018. "The 2018 Gender Gap Was Huge." fivethirtyeight.com, November 9. fivethirtyeight.com/features/the-2018-gender-gap-was-huge/. Accessed May 28, 2019.

Verba, Sidney, Kay Lehman Schlozman, and Henry E. Brady. 1995. *Voice and Equality: Civic Voluntarism in American Politics.* Cambridge, MA: Harvard University Press.

Victor, Daniel. 2017. "'Access Hollywood' Reminds Trump: 'The Tape Is Very Real.'" *New York Times,* November 28.

Visalvanich, Neil. 2017. "When Does Race Matter? Exploring White Responses to Minority Congressional Candidates." *Politics, Groups, and Identities* 5:618–41.

Walsh, Deirdre, Phil Mattingley, Ashley Killough, Lauren Fox, and Kevin Liptak. 2017. "White House, GOP Celebrate Passing Sweeping Tax Bill." CNN Politics, December 20. www.cnn.com/2017/12/20/politics/house-Senate-trump-tax-bill/index.html. Accessed May 21, 2019.

Wasserman, David. 2017. "The One County in America That Voted in a Landslide for Both Trump and Obama." fivethirtyeight.com, November 9. fivethirtyeight.com/features/the-one-county-in-america-that-voted-in-a-landslide-for-both-trump-and-obama/. Accessed May 28, 2019.

Weaver, Vesla Mae. 2012. "The Electoral Consequences of Skin Color: The 'Hidden' Side of Race in Politics." *Political Behavior* 34:159–92.

Wetts, Rachel, and Robb Willer. 2018. "Privilege on the Precipice: Perceived Racial Status Threats Lead White Americans to Oppose Welfare Programs." *Social Forces* 97 (2):793–822.

Whitby, Kenny J. 1998. *The Color of Representation: Congressional Behavior and Black Constituents.* Ann Arbor, MI: University of Michigan Press.

Whitesides, John. 2017. "More Americans Say Race Relations Deteriorating: Reuters Poll." Reuters, April 28. www.reuters.com/article/us-usa-trump-poll-race/more-americans-say-race-relations-deteriorating-reuters-poll-idUSKBN17U1JU. Accessed June 10, 2019.

Wilkins, Brett. 2013. "Nobel Prize Winner Shiller: Inequality Biggest Problem Facing Us." Digital Journal, October 16. www.digitaljournal.com/article/360347#ixzz5q5g4ToTv. Accessed June 10, 2019.

Williams, Linda F. 1990. "White/Black Perceptions of the Electability of Black Political Candidates." *National Black Political Science Review* 2:45–64.

Winter, Nicholas J. G. 2006. "Beyond Welfare: Framing and the Racialization of White Opinion on Social Security." *American Journal of Political Science* 50 (2):400–20.

2008. *Dangerous Frames: How Ideas About Race and Gender Shape Public Opinion.* Chicago, IL: University of Chicago Press.

Wlezien, Christopher, and Stuart N. Soroka. 2009. *Degrees of Democracy: Politics, Public Opinion, and Policy.* New York: Cambridge University Press.

2011. "Inequality in Political Responsiveness?" In *Who Gets Represented?*, eds. Peter K. Enns and Christopher Wlezien. New York: Russell Sage. 1247–84.

Women Donors Network. 2015. "New WDN Study Documents the Paucity of Black Elected Prosecutors." womendonors.org/new-wdn-study-documents -the-paucity-of-black-elected-prosecutors/. Accessed May 29, 2019.

Wong, Cara. 2007. "'Little' and 'Big' Pictures in Our Heads: Race, Local Context and Innumeracy About Racial Groups in the U.S." *Public Opinion Quarterly* 71 (3):392–412.

Wong, Janelle S. 2018. *Immigrants, Evangelicals, and Politics in an Era of Demographic Change.* New York, NY: Russell Sage Foundation.

Wong, Janelle, S. Karthick Ramakrishnan, Taeku Lee, and Jane Junn. 2011. *Asian American Political Participation: Emerging Constituents and Their Political Identities.* New York, NY: Russell Sage.

Wong, Tom K. 2013. "The Political Determinants of U.S. Immigration Policy: A Theory and Test of Immigrant Political Agency." CCIS website.

Wright, Gerald. 2014. "CBS/New York Times National Polls, Ideology, Party Identification, 1976–2014." mypage.iu.edu/~wright1/. Accessed May 29, 2019

Wright, Matthew, and Jack Citrin. 2011. "Saved by the Stars and Stripes? Images of Protest, Salience of Threat, and Immigration Attitudes." *American Politics Research* 39 (2):323–43.

Wright, Sharon D. 1996. "The Deracialization Strategy and African American Mayoral Candidates in Memphis Mayoral Elections." In *Race, Politics, and Governance in the United States*, ed. Huey L. Perry. Gainesville, FL: University of Florida Press.

Yglesias, Matthew. 2018. "One Chart That Shows Racism Has Everything and Nothing to Do with Republican Election Wins." Vox, November 13. www .vox.com/policy-and-politics/2018/11/13/18080836/midterm-election -results-2018. Accessed May 28, 2019.

Zabludovsky, Karla. 2014. "The Americans Taking Immigration into Their Own Hands." *Newsweek*, July 23.

Zaller, John R. 1992. *The Nature and Origins of Mass Opinion.* Cambridge, UK: Cambridge University Press.

Zaller, John R., and Stanley Feldman. 1992. "A Simple Theory of the Survey Response: Answering Questions Versus Revealing Preferences." *American Journal of Political Science* 36 (3):579–616.

Zingher, Joshua. 2018. "Polarization, Demographic Change, and White Flight from the Democratic Party." *The Journal of Politics* 80 (3):860–72.

Zolberg, Aristide. 2009. *A Nation by Design: Immigration Policy in the Fashioning of America.* Cambridge, MA: Harvard University Press.

INDEX

363

Asian Americans (cont.)
  economy of, 223
  and governmental responsiveness,
    138–39
  as immigrants, 171
  inequality toward, 205
  partisan government control and eco-
    nomic well-being, 235–39
  in racial hierarchy, 35–36
Asian Americans and elections
  2014 election and, 276
  American National Election Survey
    trends, 67, 277
  lack of descriptive representation
    in, 90
  White opposition to candidacy,
    94–95, 281
Asian Americans and political parties
  Democrats and, 203, 213
  political party preference, 29, 53, 303
  Republican Party and, 173, 294
assimilation (immigrant), 153–54,
    271, 290
attitudes (racial). *see also* threat narrative
  contact hypothesis, 178–79, 294
  on immigration and voting trends, 289
  toward election results, 115–16
Ayers, J. C., 178

Bailey, M., 234, 301
balance (democratic), 32–33
Ball, K., 249
Barreto, M., 85, 149, 186, 224, 282
Bartels, L. M., 9, 21, 29, 70, 103, 110,
    119, 132, 208, 224, 232, 233,
    239–41, 285, 287, 298
Bean, F. D., 10, 153, 171, 290
Benedicts-Kessner, J., 300
Bertrand, M., 11, 225
Black, E., 74, 76, 178
Black, M., 74, 76, 178
Black Lives Matter movement, 201
Blais, A., 114, 115
Blalock, H. M., 14, 74, 178, 267
Blodget, H., 8

Bobo, L. D., 170, 182, 183, 293
Borjas, G., 148, 171, 184, 290
Borosage, R., 9
Bouie, J., 269
Bowler, E. G., 279
Bowler, S., 25, 36, 115, 116, 173
Brader, T., 25, 155, 170, 186
Bradley effect, 280
Broockman, D. E., 11, 140, 225, 286
Brown-Dean, K., 29
Browning, R. R., 282, 285, 286, 300
Bullock, C. S., 280, 281
Burns, P., 294
Butler, D. M., 11, 140, 225, 286

Cameron, C., 209, 263, 282, 284
Campbell, A., 53, 155, 166, 178, 267,
    278, 293
Carmines, E., 2, 10, 11, 15, 17, 24, 34,
    42, 75, 76, 154, 242, 253
Carnes, N., 9, 29, 70, 97, 111, 281
Carpini, M., 147
Carsey, T. M., 17, 34, 78, 252, 293
Carson, Ben, 99–100
Casellas, J. P., 282
Casselman, B., 2
Caughey, D., 8, 285, 298, 300
Center for American Women in
    Politics, 98
Chavez, L., 148
Chetty, R., 250
Chinese Exclusion Act, 171
Citrin, J., 25, 153, 178, 183, 281, 290
Civil Rights Movement, 206, 261, 294
class divisions (United States)
  and 2012 presidential election, 58
  and 2014 congressional election, 49–50
  and 2016 elections, 45, 171–72, 275
  American National Election Survey
    trends, 68–71, 278
  in elected office, 97–98
  and governmental responsiveness,
    118–20, 130–33, 207–8, 285
  immigration attitudes by, 171–72, 179
  inequality and, 8–9, 274